5100 Quotations for Speakers and Writers

5100 Quotations
for Speakers
and Writers

Herbert V. Prochnow
and
Herbert V. Prochnow, Jr.

BAKER BOOK HOUSE
Grand Rapids, Michigan 49516

ABOUT THE AUTHORS

Herbert V. Prochnow is the author or editor of over fifty books, among them *1000 tips and quips for Speakers and Toastmasters* and *A Treasury of Inspiration.* He is secretary of the Federal Advisory Council of the Federal Reserve System; he previously served as President and Director of The First National Bank of Chicago and Deputy Under Secretary of State.

Herbert V. Prochnow, Jr. has collaborated with his father on this revision and also on other books, including *The Toastmaster's Treasure Chest* and *A Treasure Chest of Quotations for All Occasions.*

CONTENTS

PREFACE

The first edition of this book and subsequent revised editions have met such a gratifying response over the years that the authors have been encouraged to bring out a newly revised and much enlarged edition.

This new edition not only shows how to give a good speech but also includes an entirely new section on improving daily conversation, studded with pertinent examples. This volume, with hundreds of new items, contains over 5,000 items in all to assist the speaker, toastmaster, or daily conversationalist.

The book has been written primarily for two groups of people: those who would like to improve their conversation and those who must occasionally give an address, introduce a speaker, or preside at a meeting. In addition, "armchair" speakers will find the humorous stories, epigrams, witticisms, quotations, definitions and illustrations entertaining and interesting.

The first four chapters of the book give practical suggestions to help you speak effectively in daily conversation.

Chapters 5–8 show you how to prepare a speech and how to make your speech sparkle. By studying these chapters, you should be able to grasp the essential steps in the preparation of any speech. Concrete illustrations will help both your conversation and your speeches.

Being able to speak well in daily conversation and committee meetings can be important in your life. It can even improve your writing. You will learn:

- To avoid using unnecessary words in expressing an idea
- To be well organized and logical as you seek to present your viewpoint
- To place emphasis on the major points and not on subjects of little significance
- To omit wholly irrelevant matters

To make the book a compendium of source material that may be used on many occasions, there are over 5,000 humorous stories, epigrams, similes, amusing definitions, quotations from literature and from modern sources, pertinent proverbs, interesting incidents from famous lives, humorous and witty verses, quotations for special days and events, and unusual phrases. These materials are the practical tools by which speeches and conversation are made interesting and colorful.

In this book, moreover, an effort has been made to show in a single volume not only how to converse well, but also how to prepare a good speech. Here you will find instantly available a treasure chest of all types of conversation and speech materials.

The most commonly used medium of making speeches and conversation more interesting is humor. There are times when a humorous story, well told, will strikingly illustrate a point or conveniently relieve a tense moment in discussion or argument. At other times a short, barbed epigram, subtly introduced, is helpful. Sometimes a witty definition is of assistance. But humor must never be dragged in or consist merely of a series of irrelevant jokes. It must be to the point, clearly told, and without any "that reminds me" introduction.

Quotations from the Bible and from literature are important speech materials because they frequently represent the most unusual, thoughtful, and classic expressions great men and women have made on significant subjects.

The simile is used by far too few people. Yet it is a simple, serviceable tool. An occasional simile can add a distinct character to your utterance and to your writing. Do consult Chapter 18.

There are also an infinite number of interesting incidents drawn from the stories of famous lives. In them we find illustrations of achievement, tragedy, patience, adversity, persistence, and all the experiences of human life. The broader your knowledge in this area, the richer your conversation. Finally, with careful reading you can add unusual phrases to your conversations or speeches, such as those in Chapter 19.

Eloquence is a product of the increased knowledge which comes from reading good books. Many of us don't have the time to invest in such a pleasurable activity nor the means to pursue such a breadth of information as is contained in this volume. To circumvent that, studying and using the source materials in this book will return rich rewards.

This book has grown in part out of the practical experience of addressing hundreds of business and banking conventions, associations of commerce, service clubs, high school and college commencements, professional societies, and other organizations. To the extent that it makes your speeches and conversations more effective and interesting, it will have served its purpose.

H.V.P.
H.V.P., Jr.

1

HOW TO GAIN BY TALKING WELL

Ideas are the most powerful things in the world.

With ideas, we make life better and richer. We are inventive. We make television sets, automobiles, airplanes, and modern homes. We discover new medicines to prevent disease and prolong life, new and interesting ways to improve our minds, new methods of getting the most out of each day. We sell goods and services more effectively, increase office efficiency, reduce waste, save time, and make ourselves valuable.

But have you ever stopped to think that if you have an idea, there are only two ways you can tell other people about it? You must write, or you must talk. And perhaps 90 percent or more of our ideas are expressed by talking.

We will consider, step by step, how you can learn to talk well and what you gain personally and in your day-to-day affairs by speaking convincingly and effectively.

You too can talk with greater assurance and greater confidence. You can speak better than you now do. Every one of us can with just a little extra effort. You know people you admire for their ability to speak effectively. You would like to talk as well as they do. They are not geniuses. Many of them have only average talent. However, they seem, somehow, to be able to convey their ideas to others with greater power and strength than the average person. There is a sincerity and a conviction in their manner of speaking that makes you wish to agree with them. They speak logically. They talk clearly. They make sense.

The truth is that your talk reflects your personality. It is you. It is in large measure what you say that makes people like or dislike you. It is what you say that reveals whether you are well informed or lack knowledge. It is what you say and how you say it that determines whether other people will act on your suggestions. Intelligent, lively, convincing, sincere talk is the foundation on which leadership is built.

ADVANTAGES IN SPEAKING WELL

What advantages are there in speaking well? There are at least seven. You may be able to think of even more.

When you talk well—

1. It helps you make your ideas plain to other people. They understand what you are talking about. Your comments are concise, clear, and sufficiently comprehensive to cover the subject.
2. It helps you influence others to accept your ideas. To speak well means, among other things, to speak logically and convincingly.
3. It compels you to use your mind. When you speak well, you must reason through the subject. That means organizing your thoughts. The result is that your ideas are in the right order and your talk is backed by sound reasoning.
4. It gives you a reputation as a thinker, someone who knows what he or she is talking about. It is worthwhile being known as that kind of person. Others will then come to you for counsel.
5. It leads others to choose you to present ideas to committees and conferences. They recognize that you express ideas better than others in the group.
6. It increases your confidence in yourself. If you know that you can state your ideas well, your self-reliance will increase.
7. It develops your personality. As you learn to appreciate the essentials of good talking, you will seek to improve your vocabulary, your grammar, your diction, and your general knowledge in order to become the best possible conversationalist. You will realize that good conversation flows from a well-stocked mind.

Who should speak well? The answer is that everyone gains by talking well. This includes the office receptionist, secretary, business executive, salesperson, stenographer, bank teller, lawyer, accountant, teacher, reporter, homemaker, airline agent, engineer, supervisor, and department head. It applies as well to the hotel clerk, conductor, doctor, truck driver, telephone operator, waitress, druggist, mechanic, and office worker. All benefit when they speak clearly, concisely, and convincingly.

Each of us can learn to talk well, and we can gain many significant advantages from effective conversation.

But what must we do to talk well? In this chapter, and in succeeding chapters, there are a number of practical suggestions and illustrations that will help you speak well. In later chapters we discuss some of the most valuable speech tools by which we express ideas clearly and forcefully. Now we consider some of the basic requirements of good talk and the steps necessary to master them.

Sincerity is the first indispensable element in all speech. You may have complete information about a subject. You may know the facts. But unless you speak with complete conviction and sincerity, your talk will be ineffective and anemic. There must be fire in your voice. You must be in earnest. You must seem alive. The listener must think, "Susan really means what she says. She knows what she is talking about. She has ideas and she believes in them."

COURTESY

Courtesy is closely related to sincerity as a factor in good conversation. Speech is a method of communicating your ideas to other human beings: sensitive, sincere people like yourself. Courtesy in speech—that is, respect for others in our conversation—sometimes may not seem worthwhile or profitable, but it always repays us well. Even when courtesy seems to be met with discourtesy, the thoughtful person has not lost. As Thomas Fuller said over two hundred years ago, "All doors are open to courtesy."

It is not only what you say, but how you say it. A woman telephoned an airline and asked if there were a plane for St. Louis around 3 or 4 o'clock in the afternoon. The airline agent said, "The plane for St. Louis leaves at 3:15 P.M." She replied, "I thought it was 3:50 P.M." The airline agent, his voice rising in anger, answered, "Madam, what are you asking me for if you know?" This woman was only thinking out loud. She may have wanted to be sure she had heard correctly. Someone else may have told her the airline had a plane at 3:50 P.M. Moreover, even airline agents may make errors! A passenger who is under the impression that the plane leaves at 3:50 P.M. wants to be certain that 3:15 P.M. is in fact correct.

NATURALNESS

Almost inseparable from sincerity is naturalness. Men and women like to talk with a person who is natural. No one likes a stuffed shirt. There is no warmth of personality about an artificial person. Anyone who is affected is trying to be something he or she isn't. You are actually a counterfeit when you try to make others believe you are what you aren't. You live in constant fear that you will be found out. No one can talk convincingly under those conditions.

Naturalness and simplicity are especially effective in speech. A person who is natural and simple in manner disarms others. They feel that you are sincere and not trying to promote something for your own advantage. They are willing to listen with receptive minds. You have won half your battle. You are yourself, and you talk from your heart. Walt Whitman said, "The glory of expression. . . is simplicity." Emerson observed, "To be simple is to be great."

Most people resent a conceited person. Conceit challenges the listener to doubt whether the person speaking is as able or as well informed as he wishes everyone to believe he is.

Sincerity, courtesy, naturalness, and simplicity all help to give you poise and to put you at ease—a necessary condition for effective speech. When you are at ease, you have confidence and assurance. You are in the best mental condition to talk convincingly and even meet unusual situations.

George Bernard Shaw was once about to make a speech. The audience applauded tremendously. As he stepped to the front of the platform with the audience cheering, a voice from the balcony cried, "Blah!" That would have been too much for many speakers, but Shaw merely turned to the balcony and said calmly: "Brother, I agree with you fully, but what can two of us do against so many?"

We may meet similar situations in business, and in social and civic affairs. Just as we are about to talk over an idea with several persons, one thoughtless individual makes a remark that is intended to upset us. If we are not stuffed shirts, without knowledge of what we are talking about, but have sincerity, courtesy, knowledge, and simplicity, we can take in stride, and with poise and assurance, attempts to distract us or to defeat our views. If our ideas are right and our facts are correct, we can proceed with confidence. We know that our ideas will prevail despite distractions, upsets, or even initial defeats.

BUILDING CONFIDENCE

Perhaps you lack confidence in yourself. You hesitate to take part in discussions or in committee meetings. You listen to others expressing themselves freely, and you even say to yourself, "I know more about that subject than he (she) does, and I could have explained it better." But still you say nothing, and you may even appear uninformed.

The best proof that you can learn to talk well is that others, with no more ability than you, have done it. They were not people of extraordinary ability. They merely had average ability with good sense. That's all.

How do you overcome your reluctance to speak, especially when you definitely feel you will be the loser by a lack of participation in discussions?

There are several steps you can take to increase your confidence in yourself and actually become a better conversationalist and active participant in group and committee discussions. If you are in a group or committee, a simple way to begin is to *ask a brief question.* Do not ask a question just to provoke an argument. Ask simply for information about some point made by the person talking. You will find this very easy, and you will have become a participant in the discussion. You may even get credit for being an intelligent listener who knows how to ask a good question.

The next time, *expand your question a little.* Give some reason for the question, perhaps indicating something about the subject that isn't clear to you. First, ask the question briefly; then explain the reason for your question, and finally, even repeat the question. Gradually you will find yourself actively participating in group and committee discussions. Your confidence in yourself will grow steadily.

Why should you have any fear of expressing your ideas if you express them only in the fields in which you have knowledge? It is not necessary that everyone agree with you. Perhaps they do not understand the subject. You can help them with your knowledge of it.

Knowledge itself is a very important builder of confidence and of enthusiasm, both of which are valuable if you wish to talk well. Salespeople who have little or no knowledge of their product or its services obviously cannot talk convincingly. The first simple question from a prospective buyer will reveal their ignorance of what they are selling. Usually it will upset them.

However, if salespeople know their product, they speak with confidence. They know exactly what the product will do. They won't be upset by a question from a customer. They know the answer.

Not all of us sell goods or services. But in much of the

talking we do each day, most of us are "selling" ideas. We try to change someone's views on a matter. We try to persuade others to do certain things. If we expect to talk with confidence about our ideas, we must have the knowledge and the facts that support those ideas. An ignorant person generally makes a poor conversationalist.

Knowledge of a subject not only enables you to speak with confidence, it also gives you enthusiasm. You know that you are informed. As a result of your knowledge, you can see all the good points about the subject you are discussing. Your information makes you enthusiastic and confident.

You may, for example, not be able to become wildly excited about a butterfly. But a scientist who knows butterflies—their unusual colorings, habits, and where they live—will run enthusiastically all over a 10-acre field with a net trying to catch a rare specimen. He can talk effectively about his unusual subject, and his joy can be contagious. He knows his butterflies.

A salesperson may show a customer two white shirts, both with the same neck size, sleeve length, and collar, one that sells for $14.50 and another that sells for $19.50. Why should the customer pay $19.50 for a white shirt when she can buy one for $14.50? The customer may ask the salesperson that question. If the salesperson can only reply that the $19.50 shirt is better because it costs more, the sales talk is completely unconvincing. The customer may then say: "But the shirts are both white and look the same to me." At that point, the salesperson must have the knowledge to give an intelligent answer, or he will fail to sell. Any salesperson must have knowledge to sell goods successfully, whether he is selling shirts, automobiles, or insurance. The higher priced the article, the more information salespeople may need to convince customers that they are getting qualities equal to the dollars they are asked to exchange for the article.

YOU HELP YOURSELF WHEN YOU HELP OTHERS

Perhaps the oldest rule of good conversation and good speech is that you must think always of the interests of the person or group to whom you are talking. Their thoughts are centered on the things that relate to their welfare. They give their attention readily to matters that involve them, their hopes, their families, their futures, their lives.

Notice how often a person who replies to your conversation speaks of the things that concern him. You say, "Monday seems to be the busiest day for work in the office." He replies, "I have my heaviest day on Tuesday." Like all of us, he usually thinks in terms of his affairs.

If you are an employee of a business, you gain if you can think of ideas that will help that business run more efficiently, serve its customers better, and earn profits. When you present ideas of that kind to your employer, you are thinking in terms of his or her interests. But actually what helps the business will help you.

Every good salesperson knows that customers buy a service or an article because they believe it will be of use to them. Consequently, the best salespeople not only know the article or service they are selling, but more important, they know the needs and desires of the customer and how their commodity will satisfy the customer. They must be "want-satisfying."

THE ESSENTIALS OF A GOOD SALES TALK

In the following outline of the essentials of a good sales talk, you will note that the two most important requirements are: (1) knowing the product and (2) showing how the product satisfies the customer's wants:

1. List all the advantages and any possible disadvantages of your product. Without this information, you are not prepared to do your best selling. Ignorance of a product generates no enthusiasm. In a sales talk, you may need to know just one more advantage or good quality about a product to clinch a sale. If you do not know all the advantages, you may lose the sale.

2. Prepare a written draft of your sales talk describing the advantages of your product. Generally you do not need to memorize this talk, except to keep the major points in mind.

3. Dramatize what your product will do for your customers—how it will satisfy their wants. Keep asking yourself how you can serve your customers.

4. If your customers wish to ask a question, permit them to do so. Answer it courteously and not with the attitude "How little you know" or "Surely you know better."

5. Do not exaggerate. If your customers believe you are exaggerating, they will discount your entire sales talk. They will assume the product is so unable to satisfy their wants that you must exaggerate in trying to sell it.

6. If your customers wish to make some comment, do not interrupt them in the middle of it. Let them speak. There may be some

reservation in their minds about your product. You may be able to satisfy them about it.

7.   After you close the sale, stop your sales talk.

HOW YOUR IDEAS WILL HELP OTHERS

Almost every advertisement ever written is an example of thinking in terms of what interests others—security in old age, money to pay hospital bills, building an estate, protection against body odors, pleasure in traveling, home ownership, a beautiful complexion, attractive clothes. Individuals also buy the ideas of others in conversation and speeches, because they believe those ideas will be of use and value to them.

Ideas that challenge a person's patriotism, charity, and interest in helping others also have a strong appeal. Most of us wish to be known as possessing such excellent attributes. We tend to respond to those who ask us to do things which indicate we are individuals possessing noble qualities. Therefore, an appeal for a person to render a service, an unselfish act, is quite likely to meet with a favorable response.

"I felt sure, Jill, you would want to do this," is a way of saying you know Jill has the fine qualities that are required. "I was confident, Mr. Jones, that you would want to give your child this protection," is a salesperson's method of telling Mr. Jones he knew he would have his child's interest constantly in mind. Mr. Jones, you are confident, is that kind of father.

2
ILLUSTRATIONS AND STORIES MAKE CONVERSATION INTERESTING

To speak convincingly and effectively, use vivid illustrations and striking examples. Recall how often Lincoln used illustrations, such as a house divided against itself, to make his point of view clear.

Perhaps the best-known instances of the use of illustrations are the biblical parables. For example, they liken the wise man to a man who built his house upon a rock: The house stood against rain and floods and winds. They liken the foolish man to the man who built his house upon the sand: The rain descended, the floods came, the winds blew, and the house fell.

That illustration was a very simple one. It is perfectly clear that the person who does not build his life upon the right principles is building a house upon sand—a foundation that can fall in time of trouble.

Illustrations, examples, and stories are extremely effective tools in conversation. If you are explaining some subject and say, "for example," and then give an illustration, you have made your talk doubly effective.

HUMOR

Your illustrations may take many different forms. One of the most frequently used, because of its appeal, is the humorous story. Don't become known simply as a teller of humorous stories. The humorous story should have a useful place in your conversation, or it will generally be a waste of time. If it is directly to the point, it can be exceptionally effective.

Here are a few rules you should observe in telling humorous stories:

1. Make the story as short as possible. A long story with only a little laugh falls flat. Do not add a great deal of needless detail to a story.

2. Tell the story in your own language.

3. Avoid dialects unless you are good at them.

4. Do not keep repeating the humorous part of the story to be certain everyone understands how good it is.

5. If a story produces no smiles or laughter, do not retell it in the hope that you will do better next time. You make few friends when you slap someone on the back and say, "Boy, wasn't that a good story I just told you."

6. A story making fun of yourself or of some mistake you made is usually well received.

7. The humorous punch line of a story should come exactly at the end and not in the middle of the story. If the punch line comes before the end, the rest of the story is an anticlimax.

8. Do not try to tell a story you do not know well. If you begin by saying, "I'm not certain. . . . let's see. . . . I think the story goes this way. . . . No, that's not it," frankly, you're better off forgetting the whole thing.

9. If you can use actual names with a story, it will be even more effective.

10. Generally, don't tell a humorous story dealing with a subject about which the listener is wholly uninformed. A story about cricket probably wouldn't be funny to most Americans. A humorous story about farming might bring little response from an accountant in a city office, but it might be greatly appreciated by a farmer or a salesman of farm implements or materials.

11. Do not use humorous stories that reflect poorly on the person to whom you are talking. Never use humor to injure others. You also gain nothing by telling off-color stories, except the wrong kind of reputation.

12. The point of the story must not be apparent before you finish, but must come as a complete surprise. The element of surprise helps create the humor.

Sometimes a humorous story or a brief humorous comment is of great help in avoiding a serious argument, or when the conversation becomes heated. A discussion in which tempers flare is ordinarily bad. People say things they do not mean and that sometimes are not easily forgotten. If you find yourself in that position, give the conversation a light or humorous touch if you possibly can. When the discussion is resumed, it will start on a less heated level.

Representatives of two groups may be discussing a subject on which there is a fundamental difference of opinion. Joe, a member of the group, finally says, "Well, I guess you have me up a tree on that point. Don't shoot, I'll come down." There is a ripple of laughter among all of them, in which Joe joins. Even those who disagree with Joe's general viewpoint will probably say to themselves, "Joe is fair. He admits it when he is wrong." After the laughter, Joe continues, "But on the second point, the following facts seem to me unanswerable." By his fairness and his touch of humor, Joe has strengthened his position.

While we are discussing humor, we ought to consider epigrams, or short, witty comments. Epigrams or witticisms are often easier to use and more helpful in your daily speech than humorous stories. They take less time than a humorous story, and they can slip into conversation unannounced. Thus they are doubly effective.

The following sentences are illustrations of epigrams or witticisms:

> Some people not only believe everything they hear, but they repeat it.
>
> If you want to live to see 90, don't look for it on the speedometer.
>
> Most of us have heard a good many decompositions sung on the radio.
>
> Give a young girl enough rope and she'll tie a knot.
>
> You don't have to be a magician to turn a conversation into an argument.
>
> The government seems to believe there is a taxpayer born every minute.
>
> Like most taxpayers, Uncle Sam has trouble keeping down his waste line.
>
> When you know nothing but good about a person, it's more fun to talk about someone else.
>
> Few things are as bad as enthusiastic ignorance.
>
> Freedom of speech is a great thing. It even permits some people to talk nonsense.
>
> Some persons think they aren't getting ahead unless they've cheated the other fellow.

Ignorance combined with silence is sometimes mistaken for wisdom.

A person who says "I'm not so dumb" is merely trying to quiet his own doubts.

Misfortune is a point of view. Your headache feels good to an aspirin salesman.

When you look at the federal debt, you're sure posterity will never be out of a job.

Most women have a skin they love to retouch.

If you can look in the mirror without laughing, you have no sense of humor.

You can get humorous stories and epigrams from many sources. Listen for them in discussions. Read about them in magazines, newspapers, and biographies. You may, with a little effort, occasionally create a good epigram yourself.

To speak clearly is the first test of good conversation and speech. The listener must be able to understand the idea you are trying to convey. Everything else must give way to your effort to obtain clearness of expression. Always speak directly to the point. Humorous stories and epigrams are never to be used to befuddle, confuse, or sidetrack the objective of your conversation. They are to emphasize and to make your conversation more interesting, convincing, and impressive.

SERIOUS ILLUSTRATIONS

Stories, however, need not always be humorous. Serious and inspiring stories of remarkable achievement and of overcoming handicaps may often be helpful and inspiring. Biographies of distinguished men and women are filled with them. They even appear in the advertisements of many companies.

In its national advertising, a telephone company featured the story of a telephone operator in a little Wisconsin town who stayed at her switchboard during a disastrous flood, warning people in its path and saving their lives. The advertisement was recognition of a heroic employee's service, but it also implied how great the service was that the company rendered in the community.

Millions of Americans work for companies that have long and notable records of accomplishment. Employees who talk with their neighbors and their friends, and salespeople who talk with their prospects, can find occasion to tell of the extraordinary services their companies render to their communities.

Such a conversation should not be long and boastful. It should simply reflect the pleasure of being associated with a business with a good record of public service. Enthusiasm is contagious. People like to deal with a business whose employees are proud of their association with it, and who do not hesitate to talk about it.

Your neighbors—or your customers, if you are a salesperson—may seem to relish criticism of your employer, but actually they will question your good judgment in talking in this manner. They may even think you are not doing well, or you would not criticize your employer to your neighbors and customers. "I guess Sally isn't doing so well or she wouldn't talk the way she does." In conversation with friends and customers, you always gain most when you talk constructively and enthusiastically about the business with which you are associated.

Our daily conversation paints, to a large degree, word pictures to clarify our ideas. You inform a customer of the service he can expect from a product you are selling. You explain a problem. You describe a situation. You tell an associate how something can be done better in a business.

You say, "This product gives a high gloss without any rubbing." The customer sees a mental picture of himself merely applying the product without having to rub it to obtain a high gloss. You add, "It shines instantly." He then has a mental picture of a glossy surface obtained immediately without any rubbing. The more vividly you paint the word picture, the easier it is to sell.

You may tell some friends about your vacation. If you paint a word picture of the cold, clear, blue water of the lake near your cabin; the snow-covered granite mountain peaks in the background; the deep green of the evergreen trees mixed with the white bark of the birches around the lake; and the sport of catching trout in the mountain stream, you are an interesting conversationalist because your speech is vivid and colorful. It is picturesque.

How do you make your everyday talk colorful? How can you paint interesting word pictures? We have already discussed humorous stories and epigrams and their use in making conversation interesting. But there are still other speech tools to examine.

SIMILES

A simile is a figure of speech by which something is compared, often with "as" or "like," to something of different kind or quality. That sounds technical and difficult, but it isn't.

For example, Fred Allen said on a radio program, "He

worked as hard as a man with one tooth trying to eat an olive." That was a humorous simile. It was descriptive. It was colorful. It painted an interesting picture. Here are some other similes:

> He is as happy as a cat in a birdcage.
> Her tongue wags like a bell clapper.
> He was as welcome as an income tax bill.
> That idea is as dead as a smoked herring.
> He had a laugh as hollow as his head.

You cannot use similes in every other sentence in conversation, but you can use them occasionally. And with a little practice and thought, you can make your own. Obviously, they will add vividness and life to your speech, and will help you to paint better, more easily understood, word pictures.

ALLITERATION

Alliteration means that two or more words in a phrase or line of speech have the same sound. Alliteration is a good speech tool to use occasionally, as it helps give color to conversation and speeches. It adds rhythm and harmony to your talk. But it must not be overdone.

Winston Churchill was well known for his use of alliteration. He said, "We cannot fail or falter," and once he spoke of "A man of light and learning."

Other examples of alliteration follow:

> He was a practical politician.
> He was long and lean
> The facts are that our farms and factories are the foundation of the nation.

SYNONYMS

A *synonym* is a word having the same or nearly the same essential meaning as another word. Synonyms help you to choose exactly the right words for what you wish to say. They help you to avoid boring and tiresome repetition. There are some people whose choice of words to describe what is good or bad is limited to "swell" or "lousy." To others, everything is "just darling," as in "The women's department of the store is just darling."

A practical way to improve your ability to speak, and to give your conversation vigor and vitality, is to list all the words you tend to repeat because you lack good synonyms. Then take a dictionary, or a book of synonyms, and find as many synonyms as possible for each word you are now abusing by using it too often. Try to use these new words from time to time in your conversation until they are a part of your vocabulary.

ANTONYMS

An *antonym* is a word whose meaning is opposite that of another word. For example, antonyms for "thrift" are "extravagance," "prodigality," "lavishness," and "wastefulness."

Antonyms are helpful in providing colorful speech because they enable you to give a picture of contrast. Contrast—or bringing out sharp and strong differences—is an exceedingly effective method for making speech interesting.

You say, "Sarah is thrifty, but Henry is extravagant," "Hiram is sluggish and listless, but Sam is alert and lively," "The lawn is well kept, but the street is dirty," or "This appliance is a little more expensive at the outset, but its low upkeep cost makes it cheaper in the long run." With a little thought and practice, you can use contrasting words and phrases to advantage in your conversation.

QUESTIONS

Questions also help to make conversation more stimulating. Undoubtedly, you have had the misfortune of listening to someone talk endlessly. It has been rather wisely observed that one reason many persons listen attentively to others is that they hope their turn to speak will come next.

In selling, it is often advisable to ask questions so that customers feel they are not being sold by the salesperson but are actually selling themselves on the merits and desirability of the product.

"Mrs. Jones, do you like the white or the pink border?" If Mrs. Jones says she likes the pink border, she is on the way to the conclusion of the sale.

"Would you prefer the border to run lengthwise or across the top?" Mrs. Jones explains that she wishes it to run lengthwise. Thus, we have Mrs. Jones' approval on color and the way the border is to run. She is participating in the sale rather than listening to a lecture.

You may be talking with a friend. You ask how her son likes college. She will like nothing better than to tell you about her son. You can ask countless questions that stimulate interest. "How do you get such a beautiful lawn?" "Your opinion is always so valuable. What do you think of this project?" People like to be asked for their opinions if your question is sincere.

To be certain that one person is not monopolizing the conversation—or boring others by unending talk—it is always advisable to stop and ask a question to bring others into the discussion.

VERBS, ADJECTIVES, ADVERBS

Verbs, adjectives, and adverbs are parts of speech that are especially helpful in making conversation colorful. A *verb* is a part of speech that expresses action. Verbs are often dynamic words that make conversation come to life and vibrate. A verb can give strength and power to a sentence. It can give vitality. It can make conversation march.

We say, "He procrastinates too much." In one sentence of only four words—one a powerful and dynamic verb—we have criticized someone severely. How strong and effective are such verbs as "dominate," "nag," "frustrate," "dawdle," "inflame," "abolish," "accuse," "conquer," "disparage," "destroy," "vacillate," and "annihilate."

One may say, "I *wish* to see the record" or "I *demand* to see the record!" The meaning is very different. A person may merely walk, or he may saunter, stroll, wander, ramble, or rove. Action is made more vivid by the use of different verbs.

An *adjective* is a word used to describe and to tell us some of the qualities of a person or thing. Adjectives help to give unusual and striking color to your ideas. Robert may have a vitriolic style of speech. He may be dogmatic in his views. He may be aristocratic, arbitrary, tyrannical, insolent, proud, and haughty. He may also be kind, pleasant, agreeable, civil, good-natured, amiable, affable, and gentle.

An *adverb* is a word that adds to, modifies or qualifies a verb, adjective, or another adverb and helps us to give clearer and more interesting word pictures. A person may act leisurely, deliberately, thoughtlessly, stupidly, foolishly, and gradually. One may also inadvertently, unintentionally, unnecessarily, and unwisely do something.

From these brief illustrations, it is readily apparent how great are the opportunities for using verbs, adjectives, and adverbs to enliven and brighten speech and to give it vigor, spirit, and action.

BUILDING YOUR VOCABULARY

A young couple was strolling in the June moonlight along a tree-shaded path that bordered a lovely lake. This conversation followed:

MARY: Do you think I have a sweet smile?

BILL: Yeah.

MARY: Do you think my eyes twinkle like the stars tonight?

BILL: Yeah.

MARY: Do you miss me terribly when I'm away?

BILL: Yeah.

MARY: Bill, you say the most wonderful things to me.

Bill seems to have made the grade with his one-word vocabulary. Under ordinary circumstances, he would have flunked.

Few assets you acquire will ever be more important to you than a good vocabulary. You cannot write, you cannot speak, you cannot convey a single idea without using words.

The number of words you have at your command and your ability to use them will, to a great extent, determine whether you can express an idea clearly and forcefully. Any time you spend enlarging your vocabulary is almost certain to increase the effectiveness of your speech.

Don't add to your vocabulary for the purpose of impressing friends, customers, or business associates with your learning, although a good vocabulary is often the mark of a person who is well educated. Don't look up long words in the dictionary for the purpose of using them to confuse people.

In building your vocabulary, first add those words which will help you to express yourself clearly and precisely in the particular activities in which you are primarily interested. For example, you may wish to have a good vocabulary of credit terms if you handle credit transactions, and of insurance terms if you sell insurance. It should be easy, because you should have a fairly good vocabulary in your business or profession. Next, you may want to increase your vocabulary in related areas. In the end you surely will seek to enlarge your vocabulary in all the fields in which you have a personal interest and about which you talk with your friends, customers, or clients.

You can make important additions to your vocabulary by increasing the areas in which you are interested. Read as many good books and as many good magazines as possible. As a child, you learned a vast number of words because you read countless books, and new words tumbled out of the pages in torrents. You must again read articles, books, and magazines in various fields to broaden your entire outlook and your ability to express your views intelligently on many important subjects.

Specifically, how can you improve your vocabulary? At the outset, you should have a good dictionary. As you read more material and see words you do not fully understand, add them to a list you keep in a notebook. Look up these words in your dictionary. Learn how to pronounce them and learn the actual meaning of each. Remember how to spell each word. See whether the word is a noun, adjective, adverb, verb, or some other part of speech. Use the word in a sentence.

Review your list of words frequently so these words become easy for you to use. You will be surprised to find how simple it is to build your vocabulary. You will be richly rewarded.

Learning new words is almost as interesting as a game, but it is far more worthwhile, because it gives you a decided advantage in the expression of your ideas. It has been said that the average person acquires 95 percent of his or her vocabulary before the age of twenty-five. After that, very few persons add more than twenty-four to thirty-six words in any one year. This is far from a commendable accomplishment. But these are the unfortunate facts.

Unless you make a little extra effort, there is danger that the growth in your vocabulary will come to a standstill early in life. For the great majority of men and women, it is a case of mental stagnation as far as their vocabularies are concerned. A good vocabulary does not assure achievement in life, but it is generally much more difficult to progress and to attain the satisfactions of life without an adequate vocabulary.

If you will learn only one new word each weekday—and surely that should not be too difficult—you can add over 1,500 words to your vocabulary in five years, and far surpass the growth in vocabulary most persons experience. By learning three or four new words a day, you would add a thousand new words to your speech in only a year. Would you like to attain this in only a year? Would you like to attain this proficiency in speech? Are you willing to put forth a little effort to achieve this competence?

Always remember that your ability to speak clearly, precisely, and effectively will be an asset of inestimable value to you throughout your entire business and social life. Acquiring a good vocabulary costs so little, and yet it yields such great returns.

How many new words will you learn in the next week, month, year?

To get you started, below is a list of useful words to add to your vocabulary. Replace each word you already know in the list with a new word. Then look up each word in the dictionary, learn its pronunciation and meaning, and use it in a sentence. See if you can change a word slightly and use the same word in some other form; for example, "lethargy" and "lethargic," "stoic" and "stoicism."

implications	effete	indefatigable	panacea
irreparable	ameliorate	lethargy	esthete
sardonic	specious	complacent	vicarious
scintillate	decorous	concomitantly	idiosyncrasy
maudlin	redundant	expiate	facet
paradox	precedence	introvert	deprecate
admonish	circumspectly	monopoly	nostalgia
debacle	asceticism	incongruous	perfunctory
ostracism	panegyric	insatiable	profligate
mulct	anomaly	omniscient	stoic
gregarious	persiflage	assiduously	diffidence
gullible			

CONFUSING WORDS

There are some words whose use may be confusing. Whenever you find such words—words about whose meanings you are not exactly certain—always look them up in the dictionary. Below are a few of these words about which it is easy to become confused:

formally	formerly	advice	advise
accept	except	conscience	conscious
prophecy	prophesy	consul	council, counsel
later	latter	besides	beside
lose	loose	effect	affect
respectably	respectfully	uninterested	disinterested
climactic	climatic	prescribe	proscribe
then	than	imply	infer
amazed	astonished	most	almost
cemetery	symmetry		

Other perplexing words will occur to you. Add them to your list, and learn how to use them correctly.

VERBOSITY AND OSTENTATION

Verbosity simply means using more words than are needed to express your thoughts.

Ostentation in speech is showing off by using big words and unnecessarily flowery language. If two words convey the same idea, it is better to use the more familiar word.

As you increase your vocabulary, you may be tempted to use large words or more words than you need to express your ideas. Don't acquire a good vocabulary just to puzzle your associates and friends with words of many syllables or vague, obscure meanings. Don't acquire a large vocabulary, either, just to add needless words to a sentence. Words are meant to convey ideas simply, clearly, and directly.

There is no good reason for saying, "There were five men who went by automobile" when you can say simply, "Five men went by automobile." "There is a complete lack of ablution facilities at the boys' camp" really means "There is no place to wash at the boys' camp." "The termination of the present controls cannot be effected" decoded means "The present controls cannot be ended."

We are guilty of wasting words by the thousands. We say in speech and in correspondence, "For your information, I should perhaps tell you about the use of this machine," when we can simply say, "Let me tell you about this machine."

We say, "In the initial stages, the machine needs to be oiled twice a month." "At first" is shorter and just as good a phrase as "in the initial stages."

How often do we unnecessarily add the phrase, "owing to the fact"? We say, "Owing to the fact that he did not write me, I did not arrange the trip." We could simply say, "He did not write me, so I did not arrange the trip."

Practice will help make your sentences sharp and crisp, instead of flabby with needless words.

IT'S UP TO YOU

You are the only one who can build your vocabulary. The time to start is today. As you add new words, you will increase in mental stature and in your ability to express your ideas with force and power. A good vocabulary is an asset you will use every day and will cherish your entire life.

3
WHAT TO AVOID IN SPEECHES AND CONVERSATION

To speak well, there are a few words, phrases, and conventions we must carefully avoid. For example, we all have some hackneyed expressions we use again and again.

OVERWORKED WORDS

1. *Swell.* Swell is a greatly abused word. Try not to use swell to mean excellent; that's slang. See your dictionary.

2. *Lousy.* To some people, everything they do not like is lousy. Repeated use of the word in conversation is evidence of sloppiness or of a poor vocabulary.

3. *Awful.* Be sure you remember the true meaning of this word: It means inspiring awe. So many persons use it to mean bad or very. Do not say "awfully difficult"; say "very difficult."

4. *Fascinate.* Fascinate means to charm, to bewitch, or to hold spellbound. Let's be honest, everything in life can't fascinate us.

5. *Uhh.* This is the sound some people make frequently during conversation and in more formal talks to groups of people. Try to eliminate it.

6. *Sweet.* Haven't you heard someone describe friends and objects as sweet? "It's a sweet house," "She's the sweetest girl." Watch out for this insulin shock to the brain.

7. *Ain't.* It ain't good to use it.

8. *Clever.* Clever does not mean educated, wise, or attractive. It means skillful and possessing quickness of intellect. "Jane is clever at making lace."

9.   *OK (okay).* This word probably came from the Choctaw Indians. It can be used in familiar conversation, but don't use it too often.

10.   *Cute, divine, darling, dumb, great, grand, keen, hectic.*

Any and all of these overworked words should usually be eliminated from your speech.

CLICHÉS

A *cliché* is a hackneyed, trite, wornout phrase. Each of us has some clichés that we have carefully nurtured over the years.

You will find below just a few of the hundreds of clichés that have crept into our vocabularies and that help to make our everyday speech dull and uninteresting.

fit for a king	all in all
you said it	a barrel of monkeys
as luck would have it	Grim Reaper
busy as a bee	better late than never
method in his madness	course of true love
fair sex	easier said than done
breakneck speed	green as grass
break the ice	black as night
feather one's nest	fly in the ointment
each and every one	face the music
sigh of relief	flash in the pan
few and far between	partake of refreshments
by and large	the acid test

One could go on almost endlessly listing stereotyped expressions like these which have become commonplace and tedious, and should be given a rest. List all the clichés you can, especially those you are using. With a little effort, you can be more original when you talk.

TACTLESS COMMENTS AND EMBARRASSING QUESTIONS

All of us have at some time resented tactless comments and disconcerting questions. "My, haven't you gained a lot of weight.

How much do you weigh?" Frankly, it's none of the questioner's business.

You buy a new car and your neighbor says, "I had a car of that make, and we had a great deal of trouble with it." You tell Betsy that you're going fishing at Silver Lake on your vacation. "I found last year that the mosquitoes there bite better than the fish." Some people just aren't happy unless they make someone else miserable.

When you sell goods or services, it is very important not to make tactless comments or to ask thoughtless questions. "I think this suit looks better than the one you are wearing." With that comment, you have told the customer he doesn't have good taste.

"With the impossible combination of colors you have in your living room, it's very difficult to suggest any covering for your sofa. You ought to do over the entire room." You may be right, but your lack of tact may cost you the sale. Ms. Jones may have planned the room herself! You could have said, "Would you be interested in having us suggest possible colors for the three chairs as well as the sofa? You could begin with the sofa in green."

A woman asks the clerk at the glove counter for a size 7 glove. The salesperson says, "Madam, your hand is much larger than a size 7." Why should the salesperson be so rude? She can show the customer a size 7. If it is too small, she can offer a larger size. Let the customer decide.

We needlessly lose friends and the goodwill of others by tactless remarks. If you are in doubt about a remark or a question, ask yourself how you would feel if someone directed the remark or question to you.

TRIVIALITIES

The best conversation has some importance. It should be informative and interesting, and it should build respect for the speaker. That means you must avoid boring and unnecessary trivialities. Time and life are priceless. To use someone's time merely to engage in random talk about nothing of importance or real interest, about endless and worthless details, is a serious offense.

One place where conversation may easily deteriorate into an exchange of comments on trifling, unimportant, and petty matters is in business offices. One person goes to another person's desk to discuss a matter of some consequence or to ask a question. After that discussion, the conversation turns to "What did you do last night?" "How's your golf score?" "Who's pitching for the Cubs?" "Did you see the bargains Smith's Department Store advertised today?" "I understand Joe's quitting," and so forth.

The only conversations comparable to these desk marathons are those over the telephone. Telephones in offices are necessarily used occasionally for personal matters, but everything worth saying on a subject in a telephone call can almost always be said in three minutes.

EXAGGERATION

If you wish people to have confidence in what you say to them, above all avoid exaggeration and overstatement, especially if you are selling goods or services of some kind. Everything isn't the best, the largest, the finest—or the worst, the most miserable, or the most rundown. If you always talk in superlatives, you'll soon find your remarks discounted.

SARCASM

Sarcasm—that is, a sharp, bitter, or cutting expression or remark —should be avoided in conversation. Respect the views of those with whom you engage in a discussion. That does not mean you must accept views you feel are wrong. You may properly disagree with these views, but you should do so without being sarcastic.

Presumably the people with whom you ordinarily talk sociably, or in your business or profession, are respectable people who have acquired their particular views sincerely. You make no friends nor do you arrive at the truth you seek in good conversation if you say, "That is the stupidest statement I ever heard," or "You certainly don't know anything about the subject."

If you want to express an opposite view, you can do so courteously. One way is to find some part of the discussion with which you can agree, and then proceed to the point on which you disagree. "Mr. Garcia, I think you are entirely right on your first point, which you expressed so clearly. On the second point, I had arrived at a different conclusion." Then go on courteously to explain your views, conveying the idea that you are sincerely seeking the truth.

CONCEIT CAN BE BORING

There is an old story about a young couple who had just been married. People said it would be a happy marriage because they both loved him. There are marriages like that, but they are not usually happy ones.

People who like only themselves, who talk constantly about what they did and what they think, are conversational pests. They say, "When I handled that job, it was done right," "I certainly told her how to do it," "If I were in Washington, I'd straighten out those problems," "Jim is a good fellow, but I could certainly tell him how to sell his product."

Most listeners are easily tired and irritated by conceited, pompous speakers.

QUIBBLERS AND ARGUERS

Quibblers and arguers never make the best talkers. They interrupt others with annoying questions that are often meant to show how wise they are or how the speaker is in error. They quibble about small matters and ignore the most important phases of a discussion. They love to argue.

Honest and intelligent differences of opinion may stimulate conversation when a group is trying to analyze some problem. But argument that indicates intolerance for the views of others, or simply a desire to argue, is the worst kind of conversation.

MUMBLERS

Have you ever listened to your own voice? Be candid: Do you mumble at times, your lips partly closed, so that your speech is low and confusing? Do you slur words, sliding or slipping over syllables or even over whole words in a sentence? Are you just slovenly in your speech? Should others have to strain and struggle to understand you? Of course not.

For example, do you make any errors similar to these:

DO YOU SAY	INSTEAD OF
hundurd	hundred
pertend	pretend
preform	perform
artic	arctic
distincly	distinctly
fith	fifth
pichur	picture
kichn	kitchen

dep	depth
attackt	attack
with	width
punkin	pumpkin
fak	fact
slep	slept
thinkin	thinking
thouzan	thousand
wrense	rinse
git	get
jist	just
lem me	let me

Watch your enunciation carefully for at least a few days to be certain you are uttering words clearly and pronouncing syllables distinctly. You don't have to assume an affected manner or deliver an oration when you say "Good morning." But whatever is worth saying is worth saying well.

4

IMPROVING YOUR SPEECH

Most of us have been taught the principal rules of grammar in school. But we tend to forget or become slovenly in the use of language. Before we are aware of it, we carelessly incorporate grammatical errors into our speech.

Let us consider some of the more common errors that creep into our daily talk:

DON'T SAY	SAY
I could of gone.	I could have gone.
I (must, might, would) of gone.	I (must, might, would) have gone.
He is that kind of a (sort of a) man.	He is that kind of (sort of) man.
It sure was cool today.	It surely was cool today.
I do not approve of him walking to work.	I do not approve of his walking to work.
You hadn't ought to go.	You ought not to go.
Give me the biggest one of the two.	Give me the bigger one of the two. (When you speak of three or more, use biggest.)
He don't play tennis. (Don't means do not).	He does not play tennis.
I feel very good. (If you feel good, you feel virtuous.)	I feel very well.
I feel badly. (Is something wrong with your sense of touch?)	I feel bad. (This means you are sick or in pain.)

He was angry at Mary.	He was angry with Mary. (You are angry at a situation or thing, not a person.)
That there suit is blue.	That suit is blue.
I had my leg broken below the knee. (This means you ordered your leg broken.)	My leg was broken below the knee.
Will you fix my watch?	Will you repair my watch?
I shall fix dinner.	I shall prepare dinner.
I'll fix him. (Fix is overworked. Moreover, fix generally means to fasten or to make firm.)	I'll attend to him.
We go every now and then.	We go now and then. (Or often, occasionally, frequently.)

Speech can also be improved by eliminating dangling phrases or modifiers, that is, phrases or modifiers which are attached to no word or to the wrong word. For example, you may say, "Having baited the hook, a fish nibbled immediately." The phrase "having baited the hook" must modify fish, so it means, "A fish, having baited the hook, nibbled immediately." It must have been a very stupid fish to nibble at the hook it had just baited. The sentence should have been: "After I baited the hook, a fish nibbled immediately."

If you say, "After mowing the lawn, a cool lemonade is refreshing," you mean a cool lemonade mowed the lawn. You may say, "After one mows (or you mow) the lawn, a cool lemonade is refreshing."

If you would like to improve your grammar, ask a local school teacher or the local librarian to recommend a modern grammar book. Ask also for books with lists of errors in English which you can study.

A BROAD RANGE OF INTERESTS

As we mentioned earlier, you can improve your vocabulary substantially if you read widely. It is also true that you are a better conversationalist and people will enjoy talking with you more if you have a broad range of interests, particularly if you have something more than a superficial knowledge on a number of subjects.

What do you know about music, fishing, baseball, literature, finance, painting, government, sewing, public health, education, astronomy, international affairs, and hundreds of other subjects? Obviously, you cannot know all fields well. But you can know something about many important activities, and you can know a great deal about some of them.

William Lyon Phelps once said that if a person knows baseball, he is alive on baseball; if he knows music, then he is alive on music. If he doesn't know anything about astronomy and fishing, he is dead on astronomy and fishing. How interesting your conversation is depends largely on the number of subjects on which you are alive.

It will reward you richly to broaden and deepen your interests. Your friends and associates will enjoy talking with you. They will seek your opinion and request your advice as they discover the great diversity of important subjects on which you can enlighten them and counsel them intelligently.

YOUR VOICE

You may study with great benefit entire books on the use of the voice. However, there are one or two simple fundamentals that embrace whole volumes of discussion on the voice.

First, *always speak so that your voice reflects the meaning you are trying to convey.* If your friend has had an unfortunate experience, the tone of your voice, as well as your words, can express your sorrow. If an associate has had good fortune, you can tell him or her how happy you are by the joy in your voice. If someone asks you to take over a new responsibility in your office, you can express appreciation and enthusiasm in your voice fully as well as in your words. If you are selling a product, you can express by your tone your confidence in the product and your pleasure in explaining its good qualities.

Sincerity, enthusiasm, happiness, regret, earnestness, dignity, consideration, concern—all can be shown not only by your words, but also by your voice.

Second, *adjust your voice to reach the person or persons to whom you are speaking.* No one likes to converse at any time (and certainly not in an elevator, restaurant, office, bus, or public place) with someone whose conversation can be heard the better part of a block. After all, we are not all engaged in auctioneering. Nor is it fun to participate in a group discussion with someone who speaks so low that many words are missed. The voice should have sufficient volume to meet the requirements of each different situation.

READING

We have emphasized the value of reading and of having a wide range of interests if you are to be a stimulating talker. Reading the best books is unquestionably one of the most dependable ways of becoming an intelligent, able conversationalist.

How many good books have you read in the last six months? the last year? the last five years? If you read even four books a year, you could acquire greater confidence in yourself because of your knowledge. You would speak with far more assurance. If you read six, eight, or ten books a year, you would vastly increase your knowledge, your perspective, and your understanding.

In addition to books, read good magazines containing short stories, articles on significant topics, and observations on current events. Become informed. You cannot contribute to a conversation with an empty mind.

LISTENING

Wilson Mizner once said, "A good listener is not only popular everywhere, but after a while he knows something." Having the courtesy to listen is a valuable asset in conversation. You learn by hearing other people's views and thereby earn the right to express your own. However, mere listening is not enough. You must listen intently and by your manner indicate your interest in the speaker's remarks.

The interrupter—the person who can't wait to give you some valuable ideas, even before he or she knows what you are going to say—is a conversational nuisance in any group, cutting off your comments with, "Pardon me, but the story is a little different," "Let me tell you what my Uncle Fred said," and "That isn't what I think." Interruption is especially bad when it deals only with details. If everyone interrupts repeatedly, the whole trend of a discussion may be lost.

Sympathetic and courteous listeners are highly prized by everyone. They listen to others' ideas and problems. Their advice is sought because it is known that they first listen carefully to hear the problem. To talk well, you must always listen well.

NOW—WHAT WILL YOU DO ABOUT IT?

You appreciate that the ability to speak convincingly and effectively is an asset of inestimable value. You realize that it is worthwhile to be known as a person who organizes thoughts intelligently, and expresses them clearly and logically. You want to have friends and business or professional associates respect you, because your speech is on important, instructive, and interesting matters, and is not lost in endless details, trifles, and gossip. You wish to have a good choice of words so you can say precisely what you have in mind. You have the commendable ambition to use the great gift of speech to your fullest advantage as well as to the advantage of those who listen to you.

For almost all of us, only one obstacle stands in the way of improving our ability to talk well: our unwillingness to make the slight additional effort required. Merely to profess that you would like to speak better is not enough. Cheerfully to hope and to dream that you may make the most of this wonderful asset will result in no real achievement.

However, if you courageously start today to take some of the steps outlined, you will begin to move toward your objective. Every day will show some gain. Gradually, you will speak with more self-assurance and more self-confidence in business and professional circles, in discussion groups, and in community affairs.

The rewards will be generous. The personal satisfaction will be large. You will be on the way to making the most of your speaking and thinking ability.

What will you do about it? Remember, if you really want to, *you can talk well.*

5

HOW TO PREPARE
YOUR SPEECH

Cicero, a great Roman orator and philosopher, once said, "Before beginning, prepare carefully." This is sound advice for anyone who is to make a speech or introduce a speaker.

Epictetus, the Stoic philosopher, once said, "No great thing is created suddenly, any more than a bunch of grapes or a fig. If you tell me that you desire a fig, I answer you that there must be time. Let it first blossom, then bear fruit, then ripen."

Someone once asked Senator Daniel Webster how long he had worked on his great "Reply to Hayne." Webster said, "Twenty years." He had had about five days for preparation, but he had formulated his ideas on the subject over many years. Few great speeches are created suddenly; the ideas they contain almost invariably grow out of years of experience. And the actual preparation of a speech generally requires many hours of concentrated thought and hard work if it is to be a significant contribution on any subject.

The unpardonable sin in public speaking is the sin of inadequate preparation. The experienced speaker understands how to organize and prepare an effective address. He or she uses a number of relatively simple tools of speech which anyone may readily learn and use.

Cicero said there were five essentials in public speaking: (1) determining exactly what one should say; (2) arranging the material in the proper order and with good judgment; (3) clothing the speech in well-chosen words and carefully phrased sentences; (4) fixing the speech in mind; (5) delivering it with dignity and grace. It will be helpful to keep in mind these five essential steps, which embrace the whole subject of public speaking.

When we proceed to the actual preparation of the speech itself, we find there are three simple divisions in almost every speech: the introduction, the body or discussion, and the conclusion or summary. The introduction should clearly state the subject to be discussed so the audience may thoroughly understand it. The body of the speech or discussion should be a carefully prepared, logically arranged statement of the ideas the speaker wishes to convey. It is advisable to divide the main body of the speech into several parts —generally, two, three, or four. Each of these parts should make a complete unit in itself so the audience will find it easier to keep the essential ideas of the speech clearly in mind. Finally, in the conclusion the speaker usually should summarize in a few brief sentences the two, three, or four ideas presented in the body of the speech. This plan of dividing a speech into an introduction, body, and conclusion is the most desirable form for most occasions, and for most speakers. Any deviation from it should come only after you have gained considerable experience in speaking.

Having taken what may be called a panoramic view of a speech, we are ready to present in considerably more detail the exact steps necessary for its preparation. Not everyone prepares speeches with the same thoroughness and attention. Consequently, not everyone gives equally good speeches.

The steps outlined here as necessary in preparing a speech are designed to be comprehensive and of assistance both to the beginner and to the more polished public speaker. With experience, some of the steps may be eliminated or modified—but finished public speaking is a high art, and it requires more than slipshod and careless preparation.

A distinguished former senator, Arthur H. Vandenberg, an able speaker, once advised us that in his opinion "scrupulous and painstaking preparation is indispensable. When brilliance and force are extemporaneous in a public address, they are the exception that proves the rule." Every conscientious speaker is acutely and sensitively aware of the serious nature of his or her responsibilities. Therefore, many speakers will spend from a half-hour to as much as one or two hours in preparation for each minute they expect to speak. A fifteen-minute speech would mean a minimum of seven and one-half hours of preparation.

When you address an audience of one hundred people for thirty minutes, it is the equivalent of taking 3,000 minutes of one person's time. That means fifty hours, or more than six days of eight hours each. It would be little short of criminal deliberately to waste another's time for six working days. Yet that is precisely what happens when an unprepared speaker takes the time of an audience of a hundred persons. If the audience is larger, the waste of time is proportionately greater. Should you receive an invitation to address a meeting and know that you will not have time to make proper preparation for the occasion, you should decline the invitation. To accept it would be unfair to the audience and harmful to yourself and the institution or business you represent. And yet everyone of us has had the painful experience of hearing speeches which were ill prepared and a waste of time.

An invitation to speak is a distinct honor. It may mean that a group of people believe the speaker has exceptional knowledge in a field, or command of some phase of a subject, superior to that of many others. It may mean that others believe the speaker has the ability to analyze and interpret a subject to the enlightenment of the audience. And in some instances, it may mean that the speaker has the extraordinary ability to inspire others to greater achievement in life. No speaker who seriously contemplates these possibilities and the responsibilities they carry will ever appear before any audience poorly prepared. Strive earnestly to fill each address with constructive ideas, logically arranged and eloquently presented. To paraphrase Ben Jonson, any fool may talk, but only a wise man, thoroughly prepared, can give a great speech.

The outline that follows presents in a rather definitive form the steps almost every speaker will find it helpful to take in preparing a speech:

STEPS IN PREPARING A SPEECH

I. Determine the exact subject of the speech so that it is clear in your mind. If you have only a hazy conception of the nature of your subject, if your mind is foggy or fuzzy, and if you do not see clearly the outline and limitations of your topic, how can you expect to leave your audience other than confused?

II. Think through the whole subject to be certain that you have formulated your own ideas and conclusions. In most cases, these ideas and conclusions will be predicated upon your own study, observation, and experience.

III. Read exhaustively speeches, pamphlets, and books on the subject of your speech. Take some notes. This is not as difficult as it may appear. No wise person will ordinarily agree to speak in a field about which he or she knows nothing. Nor will an intelligent chairperson of a program committee invite a speaker who is ignorant of the subject. Consequently, in preparing your address, you should already be intimately acquainted with much of the material available on the topic. But be certain that you have a comprehensive understanding of the entire subject and are familiar with the most recent studies in that field. A superficial or shallow understanding of the subject may lead to disaster before an intelligent audience.

IV.   Outline the speech into its three principal divisions and any minor subdivisions, as follows:
   A. Introduction.
   B. Main body of the speech or discussion, perhaps divided into two, three, or four subdivisions.
   C. The conclusion or summary.

V.   Write out the speech after it has been fully outlined.

Experienced speakers may find it possible simply to outline an address and speak from the outline. But the person who is striving for perfection should, in the beginning at least, write out each speech in its entirety. Otherwise, there is almost certain to be looseness in the structure of the speech. A mother who was criticizing an inadequately prepared speech of her own son said: "Jim, you may call that a speech, but I call it simply running off at the mouth." The failure of beginners to write out a speech results in sloppiness of expression. Writing a speech tends to give preciseness and exactness in wording. Most will find it easier to write a speech in longhand and then have it typed.

The late Senator Robert A. Taft once told us that he prepared his addresses by the following method:

I jot down a number of ideas. Then I arrange those ideas and work them out in greater detail, so that the notes may cover as much as two foolscap pages. Then I dictate the address. Then I correct the first draft and have it written. Sometimes there is a second correction.

I should judge that it may take me eight hours to prepare a thirty-minute address, assuming that I do not have any extensive reading or research.

Of course sometimes it is not possible to prepare an address fully, but it is much better to do so even if you intend to speak extemporaneously.

Dr. Harry Emerson Fosdick gave us the following instructive and interesting explanation of the procedure he used in preparing his sermons:

I always write out my sermons in full in advance. To the best of my recollection, after nearly forty years of preaching, I have never preached a sermon that was not written out fully. I do not see how any one can keep his substance serious, and his style flexible and varied unless he writes in full. At any rate, for myself there is no other method that is conceivable.

As for delivery, that I handle in varied ways; sometimes having the manuscript before me and reading freely; and sometimes drawing an outline from it and speaking from the notes.

With regard to the time spent on an average sermon it is very difficult to reckon that. How can one reckon the long period during which a sermon matures, oftentimes unconsciously germinating from some seed of an idea planted long before? All that I can do is to deal with the actual writing process, and not at all with the hours spent on the theme that contributed the substantial material to the sermon, and that there is no way of clocking. I would estimate that I spend a half hour in writing for each minute of the sermon.

No one can read the statements of these two eminent men without being impressed with the seriousness with which they assume the responsibility of speaking to an audience and the thoroughness with which they prepare their addresses.

WRITING THE INTRODUCTION

The two most difficult parts of an address to prepare are the introduction and the conclusion. Both must be relatively short. Both must be worked out with the greatest care.

In the introduction, the proposition to be discussed must be trimmed to its precise proportions. Sometimes, with experience, the introduction may be eliminated, particularly if the title clearly conveys the nature of the topic. However, it is almost always necessary to use an introduction. Seven possible methods of beginning an address are presented below, with illustrations:

I. Announce the Subject Directly in the First Sentence or Paragraph.

ILLUSTRATIONS

Former Secretary of State Dean Rusk used the following brief introductory statement:

I welcome this opportunity to talk with this distinguished group of American business leaders. I shall talk about the contribution of American business to furthering the key foreign policy objectives of the United States. I should like to see the business community focus its unique skills and resources on this great task.

John F. Kennedy accepted the presidential nomination with this concise opening paragraph:

With a deep sense of duty and high resolve, I accept your nomination. I accept it with a full and grateful heart—without reservation—and with only one obligation—the obligation to devote every effort of body, mind and spirit to lead our party back to victory and our nation back to greatness.

In one short paragraph, in fact, in only a few words, the speaker was into his subject.

II. Tell a Story of Human Interest, "Paint a Picture," or Give an Illustration.

Each of the examples that follow is different, but each introduces the subject with an interesting word picture.

ILLUSTRATIONS

Monroe E. Spaght, speaking on "International Education to Create a Better Understanding":

A century and a half ago, Charles Lamb, the famous English writer, was walking along a London street with a friend. And he stopped and pointed.

"Do you see that man over there?" he said, "I hate him."

"Hate him?" his friend said, "How can you hate him? You don't even know who he is."

And Lamb said: "Precisely."

We have all seen tragic examples of this very kind of hate born of ignorance—both within our country and without and beyond. In certain languages the word for "enemy" is "stranger." The problem comes down to "precisely" that alluded to by Charles Lamb. We don't know our fellow man! . . .

The future position of America in this changing world is dependent in part on how well we know other people, and how well they know us.

Jenkin Lloyd Jones:

I am very glad you got that plug in about my meteoric career from a reporter to an editor in eight short years. I have been asked on many occasions by journalism school students how that was done, and I am happy to tell them that I think I owe it all to superior diligence, considerable natural ability, and a father who owned the newspaper.

A couple of years ago I was passing through my old college town with my pretty daughter, and I stopped at my fraternity house to take her through the old card room.

This card room, I explained, was the house holy-of-holies. Each generation of the brothers carved their names in wooden table tops, and when the wood could hold no more the tops were hung along the wall to be regarded reverently by the undergraduates. I was anxious to show my daughter my name in the mouldering oak. It, undoubtedly, was the Kilroy in me. So, I took her into the fraternity house and led her up to the card room. But we couldn't get in. They had turned it into a kennel for the house dog.

As I turned away with burning cheeks it suddenly occurred to me that the boys had been pretty smart. Names are not to be worshipped. There is no particular inspiration in reading headstones in a graveyard or thumbing through the telephone directory. The comfort of the house dog is certainly of more legitimate concern than the collection of dusty initials.

... the only name that deserves reverence, whether famous or not, is attached to that person who in greater or lesser degree in accordance with his talents and opportunities changed things for the better.

Harry D. Gideonese:

Robert M. Hutchins, my former chief at the University of Chicago, used to say that it was a college president's principal duty in life to afflict the comfortable. This might well serve as my text for these remarks to an honors assembly.

Glenn E. Hoover:

Of all the ways in which man differs from other animals, his predilection for making and listening to speeches is perhaps the most significant. When our aboreal ancestors first began to gabble with each other, our species was cut off, irrevocably, from the rest of the animal kingdom. And so it is that both you and your speaker are again the common victims of a very ancient custom.

III. Use a Statement That Excites Attention, Arouses Curiosity, Surprises the Audience, or Is Particularly Informative.

ILLUSTRATIONS

Robert F. Goheen used this introduction at opening exercises for Princeton University:

Gentlemen of the Freshman Class, this service of worship is traditional for the beginning of the academic year at Princeton. It affirms the unity of the university and the high aspiration of mind and spirit which constitute its essential life and endeavor down through the years.

The custom of having the President speak at these Exercises calls to mind the story of the college president who, in a conversation with a young alumnus said: "By the way, did you ever hear me preach?" "Frankly, sir," the young man replied unflinchingly (and borrowing from Charles Lamb), "I never heard you do anything else."

I shall continue to try to avoid that reputation, but I am especially glad to have the opportunity to talk seriously to you as you begin your university careers.

John L. Burns:

No one who has just witnessed, as I have, the exhilarating aerial exploits of the Canadian International Air Show could possibly depart without the conviction, first, that space travel is not too many harvests away, and, second, that it might be fun to have a ticket on the first manned ship to explore the cosmos.

This urge for space travel seems to be spreading. I recently read that more than 300 people have volunteered. A man in San Francisco offered to send his wife! A man in London, who found a parking ticket on his car, wrote the judge that he had volunteered for space travel and wasn't certain he'd be available for a court hearing!

Dr. Louis M. Orr:

I was truly pleased when President Martin invited me, on behalf of the trustees and faculty of your university and mine, to deliver the commencement address. At the same time, I was somewhat awed by the responsibility of delivering such an address from the position of a returning alumnus.

A situation like this usually implies a kind of model for success who is going to tell you to go and do likewise. I am much better qualified, I can assure you, to discuss the mistakes I have made and to warn you against doing likewise.

However, I do want to talk about you and the mere fact of existence.

An engineer in one of America's largest companies has described a human being this way:

"Man is a complete, self-contained, totally enclosed power plant, available in a variety of sizes, and reproducible in quantity. He is relatively long-lived, has major components in duplicate, and science is rapidly making strides toward solving the spare parts problem. He is water-proof, amphibious, operates on a wide variety of fuels; enjoys thermostatically-controlled temperature, circulating fluid heat, evaporative cooling; has sealed, lubricated bearings, audio and optional direction and range finders, sound and sight recording, audio and visual communication, and is equipped with an automatic control called a brain." Thus ends his description.

IV. Tell a Humorous Story That Is Definitely Related to the Subject or to the Situation.

No story must be used simply to introduce humor. However, a good humorous story, well told and relevant, may provide an excellent introduction. If speakers can tell a humorous story on themselves, the audience especially enjoys it. Observe how frequently this device is used by actors on television or radio. Over 1,000 humorous stories of all kinds and suitable for many occasions are presented in this book.

ILLUSTRATIONS

General Laurence S. Kuter begins with this story:

I find that this club is full of former or reserve fighter pilots and aircraft artillery commanders. In this group of experts, I am to tell you of a subject which many of you know very well which leads me to the old story of the intoxicated man running through the park at night and seeing in a reflecting pool before him the moon and saying: "What's that?" And his friend said, "Well, that is the moon." He said, "Then what in the world am I doing up here?"

Herbert V. Prochnow, beginning a commencement address at the University of Wisconsin:

It is a heartwarming experience to be invited to speak in my home state, at my alma mater, and among friends, where one's faults are forgiven, one's eccentricities are looked upon as evidence of a sturdy individualism, and one's accomplishments are generously magnified. Mark Twain once said, "When I was fourteen years old my father was so ignorant I hated to have the old man around. But when I was twenty-one, I was surprised to see how much my father had learned in only seven years." The passing years bring wisdom, but they also bring humility. They bring less self-assurance, but they bring a larger sense of the abiding values of life.

The opening comments of former Secretary of Commerce Luther H. Hodges are preceded by the final observation of the chairman of the luncheon meeting at which Mr. Hodges spoke:

Gentlemen, I give you the all-round man, a man who started his business career as a secretary and who today is still a secretary, Luther H. Hodges.

The Hon. Luther H. Hodges: Thank you, Mr. President. I suppose you could say I didn't get very far, very fast. I started as a secretary and finished as a secretary. It reminds me of a story I heard about a fellow who had had some real warfare in World War II. He had been tired out, battle fatigue, and he had been drinking wine, too much of it in fact, in a French restaurant. He was looking out the window and he saw a wedding party come up, and he said to the Frenchman who couldn't speak English, "Who's that?"

And he said, "Je ne sais pas."

Well he kept drinking and about three hours later a funeral procession came up and he said, "Who's that?"

And the Frenchman said, "Je ne sais pas."

And he said, "He didn't last long, did he?"

In his closing comments a chairman presented the distinguished explorer Sir Edmund Hillary, who responded as indicated:

Gentlemen, our honored guest, keeper of the bees, conqueror of mountains, explorer of icy wastes, bearer of light to the dark corners of the world, Sir Edmund Hillary.

Sir Edmund: After that magnificent introduction by your president, I really feel almost bashful about speaking at all. I must tell you, Mr. President, I have never had a better and possibly a more inaccurate introduction.

V. Ask a Challenging Question.

A thought-provoking question, directly to the point of the address, focuses the attention of an audience immediately upon the subject.

ILLUSTRATIONS

A former Secretary of Commerce, Frederick H. Mueller, began an address:

Mr. President, Distinguished Guests, Gentlemen: "It was the best of times, it was the worst of times, it was the age of wisdom, it was the age of foolishness, it was the epoch of belief, it was the epoch of incredulity, it was the season of Light, it was the season of Darkness, it was the spring of hope, it was the winter of despair, we had everything before us, we had nothing before us."

Every student has read that introduction to *A Tale of Two Cities* by Charles Dickens.

He was describing other times. Yet, any reader of today's headlines and today's political speeches might conclude that history is repeating itself, for current talk also swings in sharp contrasts.

The important question about present conditions is simply this: What is the truth?

General Thomas S. Power, speaking before the Economic Club of New York City:

Soviet Russia, which ten years ago seemed as unlikely a challenger to our leadership as Communist China may seem today, almost overnight developed into a major threat, not only to our over-all supremacy but to our very survival. For the Soviets had achieved the capability to undertake what neither Lenin nor Stalin ever dreamed would be possible—a devastating attack on the United States.

It is, therefore, well to ask ourselves three pertinent questions. First, is our national policy of deterrence still feasible and desirable? Second, if we decide that it is, can our present and projected military posture support that policy adequately? And third, with continued advances in military technology, will we eventually reach a point where a policy of deterrence is no longer possible?

Dwight D. Eisenhower poses two questions:

Tonight I want to talk with you about two subjects: One is about a city that lies 4,000 miles away.

It is West Berlin. In a turbulent world it has been, for a decade, a symbol of freedom. But recently its name has come to symbolize, also, the efforts of imperialistic communism to divide the free world, to throw us off balance and to weaken our will for making certain of our collective security.

Next, I shall talk to you about the state of our Nation's posture of defense and the free world's capacity to meet the challenges that the Soviets incessantly pose to peace and to our own security.

VI. State Facts Which Show the Importance of the Subject to the Welfare of the Audience.

ILLUSTRATIONS

Reginald Maulding, Former President of the Board of Trade in the British cabinet, speaking before the Economic Club of New York City on "Trade Policies for a Free World":

The subject on which you ask me to speak is "trade policies for a free world." I take it that what you have in mind is the part that trade policies will play in securing the fundamental objectives of the free world, namely, the preservation of peace and the safeguarding of national and individual freedom. This is indeed a subject very close to my own heart because I believe that in facing these problems today trade policies are of quite overriding importance. . . .

We can expect lasting peace only if it is based on proper human understanding between nation and nation, between people and people throughout the world. This cannot be realized in a world divided by trade barriers. The free flow of goods and services, of travelers and work, people and capital between one country and another is, in my judgment, the greatest guarantee of the kind of international understanding upon which alone our hopes of peace can securely rest.

Congressman John W. Byrnes of Wisconsin, speaking before the American Farm Bureau Federation:

I'd like to point out this morning what I believe are some alarming developments in our national internal life and to suggest the role that you can play in helping our nation to meet these challenges.

As I do so, I hope I can avoid either the undue optimism of a Pollyanna or the unwarranted pessimism of a modern Cassandra. Rather, I hope to approach my theme with the attitude the modern farmer goes about his business, bringing to my task the same practical outlook, the same careful weighing of assets and liabilities and the same refusal to be governed by either false hope or fearful gloom.

At the start, I should make clear that I am basically an optimist. In the past few months, I have had the opportunity to travel the length and breadth of our land. Once again, I was reassured by what I saw. We live in a marvelous country. As one leaves the hothouse atmosphere of Washington and goes out among the people, one cannot help but be deeply impressed by the basic strength of our country. That strength is reflected in our abundant resources, in their dynamic development, and above all, in our energetic, freedom-loving, and God-fearing people.

I have no fear for the future of such a nation and such a people. I believe they can meet and conquer any problem once they understand the nature of the problem and its significance. . . .

As a prospering, highly developed nation, we face the same danger which has confronted every successful nation or civilization since history began. Our danger is that, as we enjoy our strength and prosperity, we neglect, and thus weaken, those very institutions and principles which made us strong and prosperous and free. Our danger lies in complacency, selfishness, ignorance, and irresponsibility.

VII. Begin with a Significant Quotation or Idea from Some Other Person.

ILLUSTRATIONS

H. Bruce Palmer, president of the Mutual Benefit Life Insurance Company, speaking on "Inflation Control":

America's No. 1 problem is what I would discuss with you today—the problem which Bernard Baruch, that preeminent financial advisor to American Presidents of both political parties, calls "the most important economic fact of our time—the single greatest peril to our economic health." This problem is the primary cause of our mountainous national debt. It is the reason for our high tax rates and record expenditures in what is called a time of peace. It is the force which has put our price structure on stilts and eroded the purchasing power of the dollar. I am talking about inflation.

On one occasion Newell Dwight Hillis states in an introduction to an address on "Conscience and Character":

Von Humboldt said that every man, however good, has a yet better man within him. When the outer man is unfaithful to his deeper convictions, the hidden man whispers a protest. The name of this whisper in the soul is conscience.

Devereux C. Josephs, former chairman of the board of New York Life Insurance Company, speaking before the New York State Bar Association:

I am delighted to be with you for dinner tonight for a number of reasons. I have a great respect for lawyers—their crisp minds and orderly process of thinking. I always hope that by association some of it will rub off on me. . . . This occasion also gives me a chance to share with you a concern I have about the rosy future that the prophets have pretty generally been projecting. Incidentally, I have tried to disassociate myself from them ever since I read in Samuel Butler's Notebook the dictum: "The lions would not eat Daniel, they would eat most anything but they drew the line at prophets." However, the future is where we will spend the rest of our lives and we had better be aware of it.

The question is often asked, "Should you ever apologize in opening a speech?" The answer is "No! never apologize in opening a speech." Do not say, "I did not have time to prepare." The audience is the best judge of that condition. Why should you tell them that this occasion did not mean enough to you to consider serious preparation? Do not say either, "I don't know how to talk," or "I have nothing to say." If not, why did you accept? Surely you would not willingly bore an audience. Moreover, these statements are a reflection upon the judgment of the program committee which invited you to speak. What the audience wants is not apologies. They want the best speech—and not even the second-best speech—you can possibly give with thorough preparation.

But some introductions that seem to be in the nature of apologies are not apologies of the kind we have described. They may be statements indicating that the speaker feels himself humble in the face of his responsibilities. They may even be sincere compliments to the audience. The listeners do not object to that kind of introduction. It is one thing actually to be unprepared and quite a different matter to be fully prepared, but humble when you contemplate the responsibilities of giving a good address. Introductions of this character follow:

A business executive addressing the Erie, Pennsylvania, Association of Commerce on "The Problems of Management":

I should be much less than frank if I did not tell you that I know there are men in this audience eminently better qualified to speak on this subject than I am, men who could bring to this discussion far richer experience, infinitely greater wisdom and more mature reflection.

The gray-headed business executives in that audience liked that statement. The speaker was not posing as a know-it-all. By his sincerity, they knew he proposed to give them the best thinking on the subject at his command.

The late Dr. Glenn Frank, as president of the University of Wisconsin, speaking on "The Statesmanship of Business and the Business of Statesmanship":

Of one thing I am sure, and that is that you did not invite me here under any delusion that I am a businessman, or that I know anything you do not know about the mystical secrets of office procedure, or high finance. It would, therefore, be a sterile presumption on my part to try to discuss with you any of the technical aspects of business organization or financial procedure. You do not, I am sure, expect me to do that. And I have no desire to assume the glib omniscience of the after-dinner speaker who can solve everybody's problem but his own within the limits of thirty minutes.

The classic example of a speaker who seemed to deprecate his ability was Mark Antony when he said:

> I am no orator, as Brutus is,
> But, as you know me all, a plain blunt man, . . .
> For I have neither wit, nor worth, nor words,
> Action, nor utterance, nor the power of speech
> To stir men's blood; I only speak right on.

WRITING THE BODY OF THE SPEECH

The body is the substance of the speech. Fill it with the necessary facts and figures. They speak in a singularly convincing fashion. In addition, the facts and figures presented consecutively throughout the body of the address must march directly to the conclusion the speaker hopes to establish. The listeners should never have to say, "What in the world did the remarks the speaker made on (this or that subject) have to do with his conclusion?"

Listeners must receive something definite that they can carry away with them. What a pitiful spectacle a speaker makes who is mired throughout an entire address in generalities and abstractions. Let us assume that the speaker has taken for a subject the hazards of operating a retail business. He says, "The retailer is engaged in a very hazardous business. His profits are small and his future is uncertain." Those are generalities. He might have said, "The retailer is engaged in a very hazardous business. The best studies available by the mercantile credit agencies indicate that the average retail store lives sixty-six months. In one middle western city, for example, there are 1,200 retail stores. Thirty of these stores go out of business every month—three hundred sixty stores die yearly. Thirty-two new stores are established monthly—many of them to lose their capital in a few months."

Every audience likes the speaker who digs out new facts, new figures, new material relating to their interests. No matter how skillful he or she may be with words, no speaker can satisfactorily paint and prop up a speech lacking substance. The speaker who will make a reasonable effort to build substance into the address is certain to be acclaimed by the audience. Out of every ten speakers, seven are almost certain to fail to make a serious effort to get worthwhile facts for an audience, two will do a fair job, and one will make a comprehensive and exhaustive study of the subject. Even a little effort will place a speaker among the first three out of ten. A little more effort will leave that speaker just one real competitor out of ten speakers in the average two-day convention program.

Specifically, what guiding principles can be set down for the preparation of the body of the speech? There are at least five:

I. Know the Subject Thoroughly.

Strange as it may seem, few of us have really mastered our fields. The author has made a number of studies in the field of selling. With the assistance of college students in business administration, he tested the knowledge which salespersons in various lines possess about the goods they sell. Certainly one would assume that hat salesmen, shirt salesmen, or hardware salesmen would have considerable knowledge about their particular field. However, these tests in a number of lines revealed that out of ten salespersons, six or seven knew practically nothing about the goods they sold, two or three knew a little and one person was well informed. And yet these people were supposed to make convincing sales speeches. Enthusiasm in selling and in speaking grows out of knowledge. If you don't know your subject, you have nothing about which to enthuse. Unfortunately, not a few speakers are compelled to play around in the suburbs of their subject because they are ignorant of it.

ILLUSTRATIONS

William Allen White, late editor of the *Emporia Gazette*, was probably the best-informed person in the United States on the functions and operations of a country town newspaper. Note how vividly he analyzed the foundation of the country town newspaper in this excerpt from an address.

The American country town paper rests entirely upon the theory of the dignity of the human spirit. It is democracy embodied. It emphasizes the individual. For instance, here is an item: "John Jones is in town today with the first load of hay from the third cutting of alfalfa." That item is the alpha and the omega of small town journalism. It dignifies John Jones. It dignifies labor. It dignifies small business. And now, Mrs. Jones has the first forsythia out in her Emporia garden—that's a news item. We're glorifying Mrs. Jones. We're glorifying the human spirit, making the Joneses proud to be Joneses, to buy themselves hay, to have a beautiful individual garden. Upon that glorification rests the American country newspaper, and incidentally, the American democracy.

   Roy G. Lucks, former president of California Packing Corporation:

Canned and packaged foods have been responsible in large part for a revolution in retailing. They also have played a role in a much broader revolution.

Two or three generations ago, the work of preparing three meals for the family occupied about five and a half hours every day. The same three meals today can be prepared in about ninety minutes' work. That is a net savings in time of four hours per day.

To put it another way, the food preparation which used to require about 2,000 hours a year now can be done in about 550 hours—a net savings of 1,450 hours, or about two solid months every year.

   A businessman describing a pair of pliers:

These pliers are hand-forged and hand-finished. They are made of high-carbon steel. If I could break one of those handles, I could show you a grain of steel as fine as the grain of a file. Ordinary pliers work loose at the pivot. The pivot wears, and after it's worn it jams. That's because the holes are punched. The holes in these pliers aren't punched; they're drilled. Take a good firm grip on the handles. Notice how they fit your hand—how they stick? See these little buttonlike things on the handles, with the little holes in the center? That's the suction grip idea. When you're working around your car with these pliers and the handles become greasy, they won't slip. Notice the finish. Ordinary pliers rust. The nickel plating chips off. The nickel on these pliers will stick; and that's because they are made perfectly smooth and clean, and then plated. These pliers will last a lifetime. They're guaranteed.

   Competitively, what chance has an ordinary salesman who does not know the product against this businessman who does? Simply no chance! In speaking, knowledge brings confidence and confidence brings enthusiasm.

II. Use Facts, Figures, and Illustrations.

It is worth repeating again and again that illustrative matter filled with illuminating facts and figures is persuasive and interesting material for the body of speeches. Figures frequently have an eloquence that cannot be captured in phrases.

ILLUSTRATIONS

President Tom E. Shearer of the College of Idaho, speaking on "The Road from Here to There":

Let us suppose that one of you wants to be a writer—a good writer, financially successful and critically approved. You may well find that the road from here to there, if you manage to negotiate it, is a long and tortuous one.

Take the case of the late Kenneth Roberts, author of that very successful novel—*Northwest Passage.* He tried to explain how he got "there" in his book *I Wanted to Write.*

He had been a very successful magazine writer commanding large amounts for articles from magazines of wide circulation. But he wanted to write fiction. So, acting upon the advice of his friends he severed his secure magazine connections, packed up his research materials, and with a $1,000 advance from a publisher, headed for Italy to write an historical novel.

Here is the road he took to get from "here" to "there." As he began his first novel, *Arundel,* he said:

"I hung a schedule on the wall beside my bed: It read 'Write a chapter every four days: Write one and one-third pages (1,500 words) every day for 120 days.' My heart," he says, "sank whenever I looked at it."

He began writing *Arundel,* after much research, in January and finished, under a grueling schedule, at the end of June. After a year of sales and with unusually good reviews—the book managed to sell only 9,266 copies. The financial return to the author was only a trifle more than he had been receiving for one magazine article. After continuing to pour out his energies on other novels, for eight more years, he finally hit the market with a critically acceptable and financially successful book—*Northwest Passage.*

Mr. Shearer used another interesting illustration in his address:

International politics is in the limelight today. You may dream of becoming a statesman of high position. Perhaps you would like to achieve such stature that, upon your passing, the President of the United States would be moved, in behalf of the whole nation, to say this about you:

"The lifetime of labor for world peace is ended. His countrymen and all who believe in justice and the rule of law grieve at the passing from the earthly scene of one of the truly great men of our time.

"All Americans have lost a champion of freedom."

I would remind you that the idea for the "there" which John Foster

Dulles achieved was born in the determination of a very young man to one day be the Secretary of State. I remind you also that he was a Phi Beta Kappa, a man scoring the highest marks in his professional law training; and that, as he moved on step by step, ultimately to arrive "there," he was never satisfied. He was a man who could say "Time is the most valuable thing in life, and I don't want to waste it."

It was a long road indeed from the Presbyterian minister's home to the place where it could be said of John Foster Dulles, "In all the lands of the globe where liberty and independence are prized, the free and the thoughtful mourn the tough old warrior who had fought their fight with rare purpose, skill and dedication."

These stories of real people say that you can get there from here—here, where you are now in education, in maturity, in work habits, in responsibilities. However, they emphasize the fact that you aren't there yet.

Educationally, you are not "there." Actually, we would hope that your drive to learn never stops.

Dr. Lionel Crocker, former professor of speech at Denison University, speaks to a high school graduating class:

Today you are a personality on its way to a full blossoming. We might call our schools personality laboratories. Your parents and friends may think they know who is sitting here tonight, but it will take another fifteen or twenty years to discover who you are really.

For example, a few years ago there graduated from Ironton, Ohio, a young man destined to be president of the University of Michigan, Harlan Hatcher; a few years ago at Spencerville, Ohio, there sat, as you are sitting here tonight at graduation, a young man by the name of Grayson Kirk who developed into the president of Columbia University. In the village of Fredericktown, Ohio, there grew up a young man who flowered into the great Methodist preacher, Ralph Sockman. Who could guess at their graduation their eventful unfolding? I repeat: Who knows who is sitting on this platform tonight? Really?

Did any of the teachers in Abilene or Denton single out Milton Eisenhower as the potential president of Manhattan State, Pennsylvania State, and Johns Hopkins University? Did one teacher whisper to another that she had the leader of the Crusade in Europe . . . the one to be chosen to be president of Columbia University, the one to be elected to two terms in the White House? So I say tonight, who knows the potential of this class?

Dr. Crocker gave another interesting illustration in the same address:

Straight from the shoulder, may I say that getting along with others is a problem you must solve. I hope you have learned in these twelve years to make yourself agreeable. I hope you have developed your manners so that people like to be with you. If your environment is not all you want it to be, start working on yourself. How about your relationships with those in your immediate family? The other day one of my students said he was not going home this summer because he and his father did not get along together. What a pity! Out of his home should come the love that will help him bear the slings and arrows of outrageous fortune. It has been said that greater than any other gift Henry Clay possessed was his talent for companionship. People liked to be with him.

Straight from the shoulder, have you found out who you are? Do you have any dreams? Do you have any ideals? One of my students told me it was the example of her grandmother that kept spurring her on. Has there been a person, a book, an event that has stirred you deeply? When you call on yourself, is there anybody home? I like the title of Althea Bigson's book, *I Wanted To Be Somebody.* That would make a fitting motto for every member of this class. We all need the pull of an ideal. As you study history, I am sure you have been impressed by the compassion of an Abraham Lincoln, the energy of a Theodore Roosevelt, the intelligence of a Woodrow Wilson, the integrity of a Robert Taft, and the devotion of a John Foster Dulles.

Ambition, determination, responsibility, follow through—these can not be measured and no one can give them to you.

No man has a greater battle than the conquest of himself: to liberate his God-given talents.

Dr. Richard C. Bates, a heart specialist, speaking on the subject, "How to Have a Heart Attack":

Now the usual medical speaker always begins by getting your instant attention with some grim and startling fact. For example, if we are going to talk about cancer, I would begin by saying, "One person in eight in this room is going to die of cancer"—which is true! On our subject today, I could be far more alarming by stating that half the people in this room are going to die of heart disease, which is also true, but then, these other speakers never go on and point out that the rest of you are going to die of something else, and this, of course, makes all the difference. As a matter of fact, if you escape dying of heart disease, you enormously increase your chances of dying of cancer. Everyone agrees that a heart attack is the best way to die. If you doubt that statement, recall how many times you have heard a conversation that goes like this:

Two people meet on the street and one says to the other, "Say, did you hear about poor old Bill?"

The other fellow says, "Yeah, the poor devil dropped dead of a heart attack last night."

Then you can just wait and one or the other, or both of them in unison, will say, "Still, if I have to die, that's the way I want to go." They never say, "When I die," they always say, "If I have to die."

III. If the Audience Is to Be Convinced of Some Proposition, Begin with Subject Matter with Which There Is Agreement.

This is the old principle of proceeding from the known, and agreed upon, to the unknown. There must be agreement between the speaker and the audience at the beginning. Read and reread the speech Shakespeare gave Mark Antony as his oration over the dead body of Caesar. Mark Antony began, "For Brutus is an honorable man. So are they all honorable men." Thus he called the conspirators honorable men. But gradually as he presented the facts, he turned the mob on Brutus and his conspirators. Before that address had been completed, those Roman citizens were crying, "We'll burn the house of Brutus. Away, then! Come, seek the conspirators." Antony began by agreement with the hostile listeners, but finally he led them to his viewpoint.

IV. Do Not Argue, But Do Explain.

No audience likes speakers who state at the outset that they are going to convince them of their viewpoint or change their ideas. The immediate reaction is "I don't believe it," or skeptically, "Well, let's hear what you have to say." Again, give the audience facts, information, and figures. Explain your story. Let the facts change the viewpoint of the audience. The proper attitude is one of "Come, let us reason together." A major objective of public speaking is to present truth convincingly.

ILLUSTRATIONS

A business executive who recently spoke on "Tests of Management" did not argue about the general merit of accurate cost accounting. He told a simple story to his audience, many of whom were retailers:

In a little middle western town, there is a very successful hardware retailer. Several years ago he determined to know more about the turnover of each class of goods in his store. He found over one hundred classes of goods—paint, stoves, cutlery, nails and many others. He discovered that some goods sold much less readily than other merchandise. In fact, some articles stayed in the store four, ten and sixteen times as long as other goods. Consequently, the capital invested and the space in the store were used four, ten, and sixteen times longer for these slower-moving items. Therefore, the interest cost and the rent were much higher on these items. Then he started to reduce his inventory on the slower-moving, less profitable items. An example of what this merchant accomplished after he knew the turnover and cost of each class of goods is enlightening. On one counter he reduced the space occupied by slow-moving goods 66 percent. In the vacant space he placed faster-moving items, with the result that in one year his sales on that one counter increased $7,000. He followed the same policy over his entire store, reducing the inventory of slow-moving items and increasing his sales and net profits.

No amount of argument could have been as influential as that one illustration of what another retailer had done with problems identical to those of the persons in the audience.

Frederick L. Schuman, noted author and educator, broadcasting an address, "And There Is No Peace," one year before World War II began, described the confusion in Europe and Asia. In pointing out the need, as he saw it, for action by the Western powers, he explained his viewpoint by a simple reference to Shakespeare's *Hamlet:*

I would suggest to you that the source of this confusion is quite simple. It is as simple and as bitter in its implications as Shakespeare's tragedy *Hamlet.* In that drama you will recall that the gloomy Prince of Denmark asks himself whether " 'tis nobler in the mind to suffer the slings and arrows of outrageous fortune or to take arms against a sea of troubles, and by opposing end them." He is hesitant and irresolute and confesses that his "native hue of resolution is sicklied o'er with the pale cast of thought." He shrinks from action and prefers empty words. He does nothing and thus plunges himself and his family and his people into disaster.

Hamlet's question is the question which for seven long years has faced those peoples and governments of the world which are committed to peace and are fearful of war.

V. State Briefly and Clearly Either at the Beginning of the Body of the Speech or Better, One by One, as the Main Part of the Address Unfolds, the Two, Three, or Four Points to Be Discussed.

ILLUSTRATIONS

Former Dean Ernest C. Arbuckle of the Graduate School of Business, Stanford University, stated concisely the subjects he wished to discuss:

I would like to ask, then try and answer four questions:

1.   What are the important trends that have been professionalizing the practice of business and are likely to become more important in terms of managerial qualifications in the next decade or two?

2.   What are the qualifications that make for managerial competence?

3.   How are these qualifications developed?

4.   How are they recognized—or how do you know a well-managed company when you see one?

WRITING THE CONCLUSION

The ability to prepare an address so that it gradually becomes more intensified in its thoughts from the beginning to the end is one of the highest achievements in public speaking. It enables speakers to hold an audience increasingly in suspense as they proceed. The audience is aware that the speech is becoming stronger and stronger in its argument and in its eloquence. Whenever a speech begins with a climax and then weakens in interest, it is certain to be a failure. After an introduction that obtains the attention of the audience, the first point in the body of the speech should be good. But each succeeding one should be better, until the speech reaches a grand climax.

Almost every American adult is familiar with the great climax of the address that won for William Jennings Bryan the nomination for the presidency of the United States when he said:

Having behind us the producing masses of this nation and the world, supported by the commercial interests, the laboring interests, and the toilers everywhere, we will answer their demand for a gold standard by saying to them: You shall not press down upon the brow of labor this crown of thorns; you shall not crucify mankind upon a cross of gold.

Abraham Lincoln's Second Inaugural Address had one of the most magnificent endings of any speech in history:

Fondly do we hope, fervently do we pray, that this mighty scourge of war may speedily pass away. Yet if God wills that it continue until all the wealth piled by the bondman's two hundred and fifty years of unrequited toil shall be sunk, and until every drop of blood drawn with the lash shall be paid by another drawn with the sword, as was said three thousand years ago, so still it must be said that "the judgments of the Lord are true and righteous altogether."

With malice toward none; with charity for all; with firmness in the right, as God gives us to see the right, let us strive on to finish the work we are in; to bind up the nation's wounds; to care for him who shall have borne the battle, and for his widow and his orphan—to do all which may achieve and cherish a just and lasting peace among ourselves, and with all nations.

The closing sentence of Daniel Webster's first Bunker Hill Monument Oration is also majestic in its sweep.

In a day of peace, let us advance the arts of peace and the works of peace. Let us develop the resources of our land, call forth its powers, build up its institutions, promote all its great interests, and see whether we also, in our day and generation, may not perform something worthy to be remembered. Let us cultivate a true spirit of union and harmony. In pursuing the great objects which our condition points out to us, let us act under a settled conviction, and an habitual feeling, that these twenty-four States are one country. Let our conceptions be enlarged to the circle of our duties. Let us extend our ideas over the whole of the vast field in which we are called to act. Let our object be our country, our whole country, and nothing but our country. And, by the blessing of God, may that country itself become a vast and splendid monument, not of oppression and terror, but of wisdom, of peace, and of liberty, upon which the world may gaze with admiration forever!

No speech should be left "hanging in the air" without a conclusion. The words at the end of the speech are generally remembered the longest by the audience. Therefore, the speaker must take the greatest possible advantage of the opportunity the conclusion affords to reemphasize the message. The following methods for closing a speech are practical and helpful to most speakers. Choose the method which is best suited for each of your speeches:

I. Outline Concisely the Major Points in the Body of the Speech.

This is the method which will be helpful on most occasions, as it serves to emphasize the points the speaker has tried to establish. It summarizes the entire speech in a few words.

A banker addressing a convocation at Allegheny College on the subject "The Banker's Stewardship" had discussed in the body of the address four essential requirements of that stewardship. In his conclusion, he summarized and repeated slowly and with emphasis the four points of that address, as follows:

These are but meager and insufficient outlines of the banker's stewardship, but they indicate four major requirements of his stewardship:

1. A knowledge of the development of the American banking system;
2. A knowledge of his bank;
3. A knowledge of the operation of the American economic order and of the importance of thrift in our economy; and finally
4. A knowledge of the world banking and financial problems.

Herbert V. Prochnow, former president of The First National Bank of Chicago, closed an address with a summary of the major points, historical material, and a question:

These then are three of the most far-reaching developments of our time:

First—The rise of communism with its threat to the foundations of our society;

Second—The rise of a vast world of one billion hungry men and women in the new nations who are struggling to create political stability out of chaos and economic growth out of poverty; and

Third—The rise of Western Europe to a position of potential power so great that it may with the United States now decisively influence the course of world events.

Sometimes it is good to look back over the years and bring the difficult problems of our time into perspective. As I prepared these remarks, my mind turned back one by one the pages of American history. I saw in retrospect again two world wars and a depression with all their hardships and heartaches. I saw the fabulous half-century from 1870 to 1920, when despite the crises of 1873 and 1893, our people were taking gigantic economic strides, spanning a continent with covered wagons and railroads, as they conquered the forests and rich prairies with their dreams. I saw Robert E. Lee struggling with those heartbreaking decisions in Virginia, and Lincoln at his second inaugural spreading the wings of his generous spirit over a great tragedy, urging malice toward none and charity for all.

Turning back the pages of history still further, I saw Washington in the bitter winter of 1778 at Valley Forge with only eleven thousand ragged men, one-fourth of them unfit for duty, and I heard him say, "We have no money, no powder, and no arms." I saw also a small group of dedicated men prepare a written Constitution and set up a new nation with Washington as president and Jefferson as secretary of state.

At last, I turned back over three hundred years to 1620 and saw a small group of courageous men and women, after five weary months on the Atlantic, bring a little boat to anchor in a driving snowstorm in Plymouth harbor. They cleared away snow and built log cabins. This was December.

By the end of the first winter, half of that immortal company had died. The first summer was one of relative plenty, but the second summer brought drought and an early frost. With starvation and winter confronting them, a day of fasting and prayer was set aside. Before the day arrived, through good fortune a ship from home came into the harbor bringing food, medicine and seed. Filled with gratitude at this manifestation of the goodness of Providence, they changed the day of fasting to one of Thanksgiving.

Thus was launched the conquest of a wilderness. Thus began a new venture in faith and ideals to determine whether any nation so conceived and so dedicated could long endure. The foundations of this nation were laid by men who were willing to endure hardship because of their convictions. They did not subscribe to the philosophy that power is the goal of government and pleasure the goal of the people. They never thought that the conditions of life ought to be anything but a challenge.

They did not believe that the rewards of life could be possessed except through valiant effort. They went their individual ways without dismay and with a definiteness of purpose and high aspiration. All the comforts of life had to be created. Work was honored as a virtue. With every man on his own, there grew up a feeling of equality and of the right to self-government. The march to empire was on its way, manned by people generally poor in the goods of this world, but rich in the qualities that make men and nations great.

The United States has now come to the pinnacle of world power largely because her people have had the opportunity to develop this nation with its vast resources under a government and a Constitution that encourage initiative, enterprise, industry, thrift and inventive genius. They have cherished and held secure the blessings of liberty, and they have recognized the dignity of man.

Two thousand years ago a question was asked which has challenged men down through the centuries. That question was, "For what will it profit a man if he shall gain the whole world and lose his own soul?" We may well ask today, "For what will it profit a nation to become the greatest economic power in history, if its people lose the qualities of their greatness—self-discipline, self-reliance, industry, thrift, courage, character, faith?" This is not a crisis of economic power. We have the potential power. This is not even a crisis of defense. We have the potential strength. This is a crisis of the inward spirit of man. The question is, "Have we as a people the spirit of greatness?"

II. Use a Quotation from the Bible or Literature.

An appropriate quotation is one of the most effective means of concluding a speech. It tends to lift the conclusion to a particularly high level because it adds style, dignity, and beauty. In later chapters, there are many quotations from the Bible, from the world's great literature, and from various other sources that will be helpful to you.

ILLUSTRATIONS

Herbert V. Prochnow, former president of The First National Bank of Chicago, concludes a commencement address at the University of Wisconsin:

This, then, is the decision, and the single and great objective in life: to take whatever occupation or profession one may be in—doctor, businessman, farmer, dentist, banker, attorney, school teacher, housewife—and to live life greatly, nobly—to live for those ideals that will outlast your own life.

As a good citizen earnestly trying to live a good life, you have certain responsibilities if you are to live your best.

For example, if you demand wise and honest government in your city, your state and your country, you must recognize that wise and honest government is the product of wise and honest citizens, and nothing else.

If you demand that crime is punished, you must support honest law enforcement in your community without any personal privileges or exceptions for yourself.

If you demand unfair advantages, government bonuses, and special privileges for your business, your union, your city, or your state, remember that the price of such selfishness is the destruction of a nation's character.

If you demand balanced budgets of your government, you must not advocate expenditures which, when demanded by all citizens, bring unbalanced budgets. Every dollar which a government spends comes from the toil and sweat of its citizens.

If you demand freedom of worship for yourself, you must respect the rights of other creeds.

If you demand free speech, you must not suppress it in others, or use it to destroy the government from which that privilege flows.

If you demand that the government give you complete economic security, you must not forget that a nation's strength comes from each person standing on his own feet.

If you would like to live in a community in which you may have pride, then dedicate yourself in a spirit of humility to your own responsibilities in that community. These are practical ways in which to live the good life as a citizen.

You may remember the play *Green Pastures*. In that play, Noah said to the Lord, "I ain't very much, but I'm all I got."

Well, you're all you've got. The question is, "What are you going to do with what you've got? Will you press for the goal of a great and good life? Will you use yourself to make life richer, better, nobler?"

Someone may say that this is the counsel of perfection. This is the good life. And so it is. The person who lives it will be able to say with joy, "I have fought the good fight, I have finished my course, I have kept the faith."

Dr. Edgar DeWitt Jones, talking about great Americans of the past—Washington, Jefferson, Webster, Clay, Lincoln, Cleveland, and Bryan:

And as for these great characters that I have presented tonight, and the still larger company of which there is a glorious galaxy, let me say in the noble words of Tennyson:

"They are gone who seem'd so great.—
Gone; but nothing can bereave them
Of the force they made their own
Being here, and we believe them
Something far advanced in State,
And that they wear a truer crown
Than any wreath that man can weave them.

"Speak no more of their renown,
Lay your earthly fancies down,
And in the vast cathedral leave them,
God accept them, Christ receive them."

Newton N. Minow, attorney and former chairman of the Federal Communications Commission:

Let us recall what Henry David Thoreau wrote more than 100 years ago. Thoreau said:

"We are in great haste to construct a magnetic telegraph from Maine to Texas; but Maine and Texas, it may be, have nothing important to communicate. Either is in such a predicament as the man who was anxious to be introduced to a distinguished deaf woman, but when he was presented, and one end of her trumpet was put into his hand, had nothing to say. As if the main object were to tunnel under the Atlantic and bring the Old World some weeks nearer to the new; but perchance the first news that will leak through into the broad, flapping American ear will be that the Princess Adelaide has the whooping cough."

We live in an hour of testing the nerves of man and of his suicidal weapons. It is a complex time, not a simple time. It is a time of trouble, not a time of ease. Yesterday's slogans and yesterday's answers have little meaning. . . .

What can save us? It has been wisely observed that mankind's saving grace may be just this—our technical capacity for mass communication has kept pace with our mastery of the means of mass destruction.

To survive, we can and we must talk to each other. And we must talk not only of Princess Adelaide's whooping cough.

III. Bring the Speech to a Grand Climax.

The difficulty of bringing a speech to a grand climax has already been discussed. However, after experience and practice, a speaker may use this form of conclusion.

ILLUSTRATIONS

Franklin D. Roosevelt, speaking on "International Affairs":

We seek to dominate no other nation. We ask no territorial expansion. We oppose imperialism. We desire reduction in world armaments.

We believe in democracy; we believe in freedom; we believe in peace. We offer to every nation of the world the handclasp of the good neighbor. Let those who wish our friendship look us in the eye and take our hand.

John David Lodge, former United States Ambassador to Spain, closes a Lincoln Day address:

And so, my Spanish and American friends of the American Club of Madrid, it is in a spirit of reverence and love for Lincoln, a hero, and, like most heroes, a martyr, that we gather here today. We Americans are happy to share this precious commemoration with our Spanish friends, for we truly believe that the real meaning of Lincoln is not simply American, but that it is universal. We believe that, while for us Americans Lincoln is still a beacon light of hope and faith in a dark and distracted world, he symbolizes to all men everywhere the higher aspirations of man. His life and works remind us that our constant objective must be the brotherhood of man under the fatherhood of God. Abraham Lincoln does indeed belong to the ages and he belongs to all mankind.

IV. Compliment the Audience or Leave a Note
of Encouragement or Optimism.

A sincere compliment or expression of hope for the future pleases
an audience.

ILLUSTRATIONS

Henry J. Kaiser, Jr., closed with a note of encouragement:

In closing I would like to leave you with these few lines which have
become a favorite of us Kaisers:

> "What do we plant, when we plant a tree
> We plant a ship, that will cross the sea
> We plant the mast to carry the sails,
> We plant the planks to withstand the gales,
> The keel and keelson, beam and knee,
> We plant a ship, when we plant a tree."

We have it in our power, friends, to plant such a tree, which, instead of a
single ship, may provide an endless fleet of vessels, bringing a flourishing
trade and with it, the possibility of an enduring peace to all of humanity.
With God's help, and with work and faith, I know we will do these things.
Thank you, friends, for this opportunity. May God bless each and everyone
of you.

Arthur J. Goldberg closed with a message of encouragement:

This ambition—to create a world without fear, without hunger, a world
where justice rules supreme and where a man can stand erect—can be
realized if we are firm in our support of peace in freedom. This aspiration
can be achieved if we maintain the faith of the founders of this nation, if we
believe, as the President does, that liberty is winning and will win because
mankind, enriched by the divine spirit, was not made for slavery. That is
the message we are bringing and must continue to bring to the world.

V. Describe a Dramatic Scene, a Great Moment in History,
Science, or Business, or Give a Brief Biographical Story.

ILLUSTRATIONS

Lieutenant General Ira C. Eaker concluded an address on
"Leadership":

One of my favorite quotations in this vein comes from a message General Foch sent to General Joffre during the first battle of the Marne—"My right has been rolled up, my left has been driven back, my center has been crushed. I shall attack."

There have been great leaders who were blind, more who were deaf, but there have been none who were dumb. All have had the wit, the timing and the courage to influence their followers to action at the critical time by a few well-chosen words or by example, or both.

Herbert V. Prochnow, former president of The First National Bank of Chicago, closed an address on "A Time for Critical Decisions" with an illustration:

Perhaps I may close with a brief story of the first time I met John Foster Dulles. It was an experience I shall never forget.

The Secretary and I had discussed travel over the world. I commented that my major interest in visits abroad was in the economic and financial problems of foreign nations. As the discussion turned to other nations, the Secretary became deeply reflective. When he spoke, his words came with great feeling. "When I travel in various parts of the world," he said, "I seem to see different things than many other persons. For example," he explained, "many persons who visit Egypt marvel at the pyramids as great monuments of earlier civilizations. But the pyramids do not appeal to me primarily as great monuments of earlier civilizations. When I see the pyramids, I see tens of thousands of poor, undernourished Egyptians carrying heavy physical burdens as they painfully struggle to build the pyramids. I see these poverty-stricken people carrying for years the oppressive burden of the great costs of the pyramids. Thousands toiled, suffered and died to build them. That is what I see when I look at the pyramids."

After a moment the Secretary continued, "And when I look at the world today, I see hundreds of millions of men and women carrying on their backs the crushing burden of the costs of government and the costs of war. We must remove from the backs of the common people some of the great burdens of the mounting costs of government and armament so that men and women over the world may enjoy the fruits of their labor. We must find the way to lasting peace for all mankind. This is what I see when I look at the world."

The Secretary was speaking with a profound conviction. He was pouring out thoughts that were deep in his heart. This was his great challenge and his great goal.

Later, as we walked to the door, the Secretary said, "Every person needs to make the decision to dedicate at least a part of his life to his country and to the attainment of these objectives."

We may also say that today our people need to make great decisions. We are heirs to a priceless and costly legacy. In our hearts you and I know that there are no easy devices by which men or nations attain distinction and greatness. We know that sound economic and fiscal policies require principles to which men hold fast. We know that hard work and thrift require character and self-denial. We know that balanced budgets rest on financial integrity.

If we have the courage to make the right decisions in these times, and if we have an abiding faith that only the right will ultimately survive, we shall meet the difficult problems of our time with a deep inner serenity and a calm confidence. We shall know that we are helping to build a nation and a world in which the finer values of man's spirit may flower.

Dr. Charles H. Malik, former president of the General Assembly of the United Nations, made a call to a heroic mission:

The basic truth today is that there is an inescapable confrontation between Communism and the rest of the world calling for historic decision, and I am not sure the effective forces of freedom are sufficiently aware of what is at stake, nor whether they are adequately prepared, on every level of human existence, to meet the challenge. Perhaps the Berlin crisis or the Middle East crisis or the Tibet crisis will awaken them; but I am not sure. A vision of something great and tremendous, a call to an heroic mission, the challenge of a truly universal message—this is what is required today and this is, alas, what is lacking. The immediate situation then presents the aspect of a final and total judgment: everything is being weighed—one's life, one's values, one's culture, the vitality of the whole civilization to which one belongs.

It is very much then like the last day. And those who believe will tell you that God is there and that most certainly He watches over His own, even if He should sorely chasten them still.

T. Keith Glennan of the Aeronautics and Space Administration spoke of the great challenge of space:

Speaking more prosaically—as I wrote these words I was reminded of a story told about Mark Twain. In a discussion with the pilot of a river boat at the time in our history when steam was beginning to replace sail, Twain answered the protests of the pilot against the newfangled invention by saying to him—"When it's steamboat time, you steam."

This is the time for space research and space travel. It is a time of challenge and change. Let us remind ourselves of the words of Brutus spoken in Shakespeare's *Julius Caesar:*

> "There is a tide in the affairs of men
> Which, taken at the flood, leads on to fortune;
> Omitted, all the voyage of their life
> Is bound in shallows and in miseries.
> On such a full sea are we now afloat;
> And we must take the current when it serves
> Or lose our venture."

Bob Trout, CBS news commentator, broadcasting a speech on "Cardinal of Charity" at the time of the death of Patrick Cardinal Hayes, Archbishop of New York:

In the dim soft light, George Cardinal Mundelein stood high above the body of the seventy-one-year-old Cardinal and sang the solemn Mass. With holy water and incense, the final blessing was given, while outside in the sunshine, listening through loudspeakers, men knelt in the streets, and women wept and forgot to dry their tears.

Sabers flashed, and white gloves snapped to salute when a bugle sounded taps, and the flags were dipped one last time. And the words of the prayer were all around, louder than the muffled drums, louder than the tolling bells:

> "Eternal rest grant unto him, Oh Lord,
> And let perpetual light shine upon him."

Thus, in shadowy cathedral and in city streets, did New York say farewell to a dear and great friend, His Eminence, Patrick Cardinal Hayes, Prince of the Church, Cardinal of Charity.

VI. Ask the Audience to Take Some Action or Adopt a Certain Viewpoint.

ILLUSTRATIONS

Dr. Preston Bradley closed an address with a challenge to the audience to adopt the viewpoint of sacrifice, and not greed, if America is to stand as a great example to the world:

Let us, ladies and gentlemen, settle down to the task of making this thing called democracy work, and when we make it work in America, and in our hearts, God will see to it that it finally works in all the world. And this world will become the kingdom of our God and the brotherhood of man, a reality, because of the Fatherhood of God.

And the challenge to you, and the challenge to me, is that before we are Democrats, or Republicans, before we are any of the things that separate us, let us, above all, and in all, and through all, let us upon the altar of our country place a sacrifice and stop treating that altar as a crib out of which to feed.

Herbert V. Prochnow closed an address before the Oregon Bankers Association with the following appeal:

If we could read the human story back of every savings and commercial passbook; if we could see the home, the work, the business trials, and the hopes each passbook represents; if we could clearly visualize the problems of each depositor, the education of his children, the care of dependents, the hope, after years of work, for a competence in old age; if we could really evaluate the significant role the banker plays in the economic advancement of a nation; I believe we would approach our daily work tomorrow with a new sense of its great importance. No other responsibility in our business life transcends it. Let us bring to it thorough knowledge, broad experience, and outstanding management ability.

VII. Tell a Humorous Story or Give a Suitably Witty Comment.

Humor that definitely relates itself to the speech makes a splendid conclusion. This book provides an almost inexhaustible source of materials for this purpose.

ILLUSTRATIONS

Professor C. Northcote Parkinson, author, concluded an address as follows:

And at this point I end my talk in order to leave time for any questions, if there are any questions, from any members who should happen by any chance to be awake.

Professor Parkinson then answered questions and closed his questions with a comment on socialized medicine and the general practitioner in medicine:

Another result, and I think this is one common to Britain and the United States and perhaps not directly the result of socialized medicine, is the disappearance of that creature known as the G.P. or general practitioner, a rare form now on the zoological landscape and his place is being taken by the medical clerk, the new character of lower-level medicine who simply sorts out the patients by a quick glance as they say, "I have got a cough," and the medi-clerk says, "Down that corridor, the first door on the left for coughs."

Another patient says, "I have got a tummy ache," and he says, "Down that corridor, third door to the left," and that goes for tummy pains and so forth.

In other words, the basic function of the general practitioner is to sort people out and put them in an appropriate medical slot. As it happens, I live in one of the few places of the world where the general practitioner still flourishes. That is, in the Channel Islands between England and France, and there is a sort of preserve of wild life and the general practitioner is still to be observed in his natural habitat. He is to be detected by his drab plumage, his plaintive cry and his long bill.

6

HOW TO MAKE YOUR SPEECH SPARKLE

After the first written draft or outline of a speech is prepared, it should be painstakingly revised and refined. Each sentence must be written and rewritten until every unnecessary word is eliminated. However, great care must be exercised that the revisions and polishing do not remove the freshness, naturalness, and vigor that may have been in the first draft.

In seeking to give style and effectiveness to the wording and phrasing of a speech, clearness of expression is the first imperative. Everything in style must yield to clarity.

The effort eloquent speakers make to show style and effectiveness of expression is well illustrated by the comment of Phyllis Moir, writing on Winston Churchill in *I Was Winston Churchill's Private Secretary.*

I can see him now, pacing slowly up and down the room, his hands clasped behind his back, his shoulders hunched, his head sunk forward in deep thought, slowly and haltingly dictating the beginning of a speech or an article. I wait, my pencil poised in midair, as he whispers phrases to himself, carefully weighing each word and striving to make his thoughts balance. Nothing may be put down until it has been tested aloud and found satisfactory. A happy choice brings a glint of triumph to his eye; a poor one is instantly discarded. He will continue the search until every detail—of sound, rhythm and harmony—is to his liking. Sometimes there are long halts, during which he patiently sounds out a phrase a dozen times, this way and that, making the cigar in his hand serve as a baton to punctuate the rhythm of his words.*

* Phyllis Moir, *I Was Winston Churchill's Private Secretary* (New York: Wilfred Funk, 1941), pp. 154–155.

From this statement it is evident that Winston Churchill's eloquence did not just happen. It was not accidental. It was the most carefully studied effort of a great mind that had struggled word by word and phrase by phrase for the brilliant expression of ideas that would move nations.

A number of tools of effective speech enable us to refine and perfect expression. They enable even the most inexperienced speaker to give a speech a sparkling quality. The order in which they are presented is not one of their relative importance, because these speech tools may be used on different occasions and for different purposes. Keep these effective speech tools in mind as you revise your speeches to make them sparkle.

I. Insert Suitable Humorous Stories, Epigrams, and Amusing Definitions.

Study the written draft or outline of your speech thoughtfully to determine exactly where a humorous comment would be appropriate, if the speech permits humor. Chapter 9 contains over 1,000 humorous stories suitable for introducing a speaker, beginning an address, making statistical or other dry material interesting, lightening a speech that has necessarily been long or has dwelt on many subjects, expressing appreciation for attention, and generally assisting a speaker to give just the right touch of humor to make a speech successful. Speeches on particularly serious occasions may not permit the use of humor. However, for the great majority of addresses, and also in daily conversation, no tool of speech is more generally helpful than good humor. Abraham Lincoln's political speeches and conversation, with their generous use of humor, are excellent illustrations.

The humorous stories of Chapter 9 have been chosen from many thousands. Each story may be successfully adapted to a large number of different types of situations. For example, consider the following story:

A professor in a western university taught mathematics and statistics. One day he was standing, dressed in his bathing suit, at the edge of a swimming pool on the university campus when a beautiful coed accidentally dropped her camera into the deep end of the pool. She called to the elderly professor for help. He said he would be glad to dive for the camera, but first wanted to know why she happened to choose him when there were so many young men within easy reach to do the job. She answered, "Professor, you have apparently forgotten me, but I am in your large statistics class. I have found that you can go down deeper, stay down longer, and come up drier than anyone I know."

The speaker can use this story in almost any address containing statistics or facts which may be essential to the address, but a bit dry. She may add that in explaining her statistics she does not propose to go down too deep, stay down too long, or come up too dry. The story may also be used in connection with the relationships of professors and students, and with topics dealing with education.

The speaker should select those humorous stories which are definitely appropriate to the subject matter and illustrate points he or she wishes to emphasize. The humor should not all come at one point, but should be spaced at intervals through the speech. However, never use a humorous story which is entirely irrelevant and inserted merely to wake up a drowsy audience in the hope that its members will listen to a dull speech. The way to wake up a drowsy audience is to wake up the speaker. The humor must always relate itself directly to the discussion.

Sometimes another tool—an epigram or witty comment—is more effective than a humorous story. Subtly introduced, the epigram may serve fully as well as a comparatively long humorous story. Moreover, it conserves time. A speaker talking about the shortage of labor in some fields might say, "A woman doesn't hire domestic help now; she marries it." The change from a serious statement to a witty comment is so rapid it surprises listeners, and as they catch the full significance of the humor, they enjoy it. It takes but a moment to give a witty comment, and the speaker goes on immediately. The humor provides "the pause that refreshes" for the audience.

Dr. Will Durant, the distinguished philosopher, was giving an address before the Rotary Club of Chicago in which he was discussing for a few minutes the philosophy of Friedrich Nietzsche. Remember that Dr. Durant had for many years been a university professor. Commenting on Nietzsche, Dr. Durant said:

In 1870 ... Friedrich Nietzsche walked out of a hospital. He had been rejected from military service. He had weak ribs. He had poor eyes. He was flat-footed. He was a professor.

The last sentence caught the audience by surprise, but in a moment the laughter spread over that large audience. It was a terse, unexpected, humorous comment, and it was on the speaker, which made it twice as good.

A businessman was speaking of the necessity for work and thrift in any economic order, whether it be capitalistic or socialistic. "Of course," he added, "I know there are some persons who would say that my philosophy is one of 'Work hard and save your money, and when you are old, you can have the things that only the young can enjoy.' " The audience liked the bit of humor, which the speaker credited to his critics. Then he went on to prove his case.

A speaker on international problems might say, "You may ask why the nations of the world cannot live as one big family. The answer is they do." A brief, humorous comment of this kind often provides a stimulating pause in an address.

Over 500 epigrammatic comments from many sources and on many subjects are included in Chapter 10. These short and pointed statements will be of great assistance in creating effective speeches. They also assist in making ordinary conversation sparkle. Almost every address has a place for one or two pertinent epigrams.

Occasionally a speaker may find an opportunity to use an amusing definition. Many definitions will be found in Chapter 11. With a little practice, anyone can create such definitions out of humorous stories and jokes. They provide a different type of humor, combining some of the qualities of jokes and epigrams. Dr. Joseph Jastrow, famous professor of psychology at the University of Wisconsin, began one of his addresses with this amusing definition: "The psychologist has been slanderously defined as a man who tells you what everybody knows in language nobody can understand." That definition made an attention-winning introduction.

Fred Allen's definition of a conference as "a gathering of important people who singly can do nothing, but together can decide that nothing can be done" is a typical amusing definition which tells a good story in one sentence.

II. Use Illustrations from Biography, from Plays, or from Literature.

If the speech is one of inspiration, perhaps to a body of students, a college graduating class, a church congregation, or an after-dinner audience, stories of achievement, persistence, courage, tact, and patience from the lives of statesmen, scientists, industrialists, writers, musicians, artists, and others will help to illustrate the speech and make it entertaining and instructive. Few things in the world are more inspiring to an audience than stories of lives lived significantly. Chapter 12 includes a number of such short stories.

ILLUSTRATIONS

Herbert V. Prochnow closed an address with illustrations and a quotation from a book:

With a massive political, economic and social revolution over the world, we need to be certain our own house is in order. It is a time to be strong. One evening at the height of a Presidential campaign some of us visited on a university campus with one of the most respected and experienced members of the Senate of the United States. He said regretfully that it was no longer possible to be elected and to ask anything of the American people. One could only promise them benefits without sacrifices. This was not the comment of a cynic. It was the thoughtful judgment of a public servant who had served his country for many years with distinction. If a nation ultimately is only as strong, and only as great, as the character, integrity, ideals, and vision of its people, then this statement constitutes a tragic indictment. But is it true? Is there a widespread intellectual and social disintegration of our people, or is it a failure to understand clearly that continued sacrifices are essential if a nation is to remain free? Have we offered this alternative, or have we offered the people merely the deceptive lure of benefits without sacrifices? We may well be at a critical turning point in our history when a courageous decision to put our affairs in order would meet the overwhelming approval of the American people.

Several years ago a few of us were at luncheon with a leading statesman of West Germany. One American asked this question, "How do you explain the remarkable economic growth, or so-called economic miracle, of West Germany since the end of World War II?" The German statesman replied, "This was not a miracle. When a people lack bread, four walls for a room, and a bed in which to sleep, they will work hard for long hours and save. The economic rewards have been great for our people. But some of us are fearful that wealth and comforts are beginning now to bring ease and complacency."

We may ask ourselves, "Is it necessary for the people of any nation continually to face hardships in order to live greatly?"

In a recent book, *The Agony and the Ecstasy,* the teacher of Michelangelo, the great artist, says, "Sculpture is hard, brutal labor. . . . Talent is cheap; dedication is expensive. It will cost you your life." Michelangelo replies, "What else is life for?"

May I ask, What else is life for in a nation if it is not for a dedication by the people to freedom and to greatness? But a dedication to freedom and to greatness carries with it responsibilities and strict disciplines. It carries with it the challenge to individual men to strive to make the most of their abilities and talents. It carries with it the responsibility of hard work, so that the economic well-being of all our people may be improved. It carries with it the responsibility of living within the nation's income. It demands self-reliance and self-discipline. To paraphrase John Adams, freedom requires that each individual conduct himself so that his life demonstrates the dignity of man and the noble rank man holds among the works of Providence. This is the meaning of freedom and these are its responsibilities in our time.

Dr. Glenn Frank, speaking on "If the Young Can But See," used a dramatic illustration from a play:

I was a guest at the Chicago opening of Shaw's *Saint Joan* as her triumphant spirit sang through the lips of Katharine Cornell. . . . For me the high moment of the play came in the much abused Epilogue.

Here was the scene.

It was twenty-five years after the burning of the maid. The curtain rose on the bed-chamber of King Charles the Seventh of France, who, at the opening of the play, was the none-too-bright Dauphin. The spirits of those who played a part in the trial and burning at the stake of Joan were entering the King's chamber. Among them was an old rector, formerly a chaplain to the Cardinal of Winchester, a little deaf and a little daft. He had gone somewhat crazy from brooding over the burning of Joan, but insisted that the sight of that burning had saved him.

"Well you see," he said, "I did a very cruel thing once because I did not know what cruelty was like. I had not seen it, you know. That is the great thing: You must see it. And then you are redeemed and saved."

"Were not the sufferings of our Lord Christ enough for you?" asked the Bishop of Beauvais.

"No," said the old rector. "Oh no, not at all. I had seen them in pictures, and read of them in books, and been greatly moved by them, as I thought. But it was no use. It was not our Lord that redeemed me, but a young woman whom I saw actually burnt to death. It was dreadful. But it saved me. I have been a different man ever since."

Poor old priest, driven astray in his wits by the haunting memory of his youthful inability to see what cruelty is like without watching a maid burn slowly to death at the hands of her executioners, a man who had to wait for events to educate his judgments!

The Bishop of Beauvais looked at him pityingly and, with infinite pathos in his voice, cried out, "Must then a Christ perish in torment in every age to save those that have no imagination?"

I covet for you who are about to be graduated . . . the godlike gifts of insight and understanding. You will need them in the days ahead.

There are many stories in literature. Wide reading in the field of biography is strongly recommended. Interesting facts and interesting incidents from interesting lives may make the difference between a dull and a worthwhile and colorful speech. Searching until you find this material pays rich rewards.

An official of the American Bankers Association addressed a convention of the American Institute of Banking, which has as its members many thousands of young people in the banking business. Note the use of biography at the end of the discussion.

Hard work—sheer application, resolute, persevering and tough-fibered —is imperative to attain success.

There has never been an army in which the rank and file did not picture the leaders as enjoying ease and luxury. But the great military leaders— Caesar, Napoleon, Grant, Pershing, Eisenhower—were indefatigable workers. They had almost unbreakable health. They had bulldog tenaciousness. Early and late they were at their problems. They outdid other men in leadership, just as an engine that runs longer and faster will outdo the motor that slows down, that runs intermittently, that never produces in any twenty-four hours all the power that maximum operation would derive from it.

Business is full of the romance of youngsters whose chief characteristic was working hard and keeping at it.

There was a green farmer boy who decided he would rather stand behind a counter than follow a plow. He seemed so obviously lacking in sales ability that for a time no merchant would hire him. He failed in his first position, and in his second his salary was reduced. He even agreed that he was a misfit—but he stuck. Out of his first five stores, I believe, three failed. But he persisted and worked hard. And that boy, Frank W. Woolworth, became one of the greatest retail merchants in the world with a store in every city of 8,000 or more population in this country.

There was a young man named Cyrus McCormick who worked and waited eight harvest times for a chance to sell a queer new contraption.

Finally he sold a reaper—and the revolution of the agricultural industry began.

Leadership is not play. Leadership in the banking of the future, as I have tried to visualize it, offers countless positions of varying opportunity, of which the highest pinnacles will carry almost unbearable responsibility in the new era that may lie just over the next hill. There will be men and women with the fire and iron to qualify even for these places. Such men and women must have had the very finest preparation and the most grueling tests which the banking profession knows. Their reward will be the attainment of these highest pinnacles of achievement, and the rendering of an immeasurable service to their times.

III. Repeat Some Words or Phrases to Stamp Them Indelibly upon the Minds of the Listeners.

ILLUSTRATIONS

A classic example of reiteration is found in one of the greatest addresses of all time, the Sermon on the Mount. In that address, as it is recorded in Chapter 7 of St. Matthew, verses 24 to 27, the Master says, "Therefore whosoever heareth these sayings of mine, and doeth them, I will liken him unto a wise man, which built his house upon a rock: And the rain descended, and the floods came, and the winds blew, and beat upon that house; and it fell not: for it was founded upon a rock. And everyone that heareth these sayings of mine, and doeth them not, shall be likened unto a foolish man, which built his house upon the sand: And the rain descended, and the floods came, and the winds blew, and beat upon that house; and it fell: and great was the fall of it."

Again in St. Matthew, Chapter 5, verses 29 and 30, we find the Master saying, "And if thy right eye offend thee, pluck it out, and cast it from thee: for it is profitable for thee that one of thy members should perish, and not that thy whole body should be cast into hell. And if thy right hand offend thee, cut it off, and cast it from thee: for it is profitable for thee that one of thy members should perish, and not that thy whole body should be cast into hell."

The late Dr. Glenn Frank, speaking on "The Statesmanship of Business and the Business of Statesmanship," used repetition at the beginning only of three sentences to reemphasize the fact that the nation had changed.

So I suggest that sooner or later, as a nation, we shall have to face the political implications of the following obvious facts:

We are no longer a small nation; we are a large nation.

We are no longer a simple civilization; we are an increasingly complex and technical civilization.

We are no longer an agricultural nation alone; we are an industrial nation as well.

In an address before the Mortgage Bankers Association of America, Herbert V. Prochnow used repetition to emphasize the seriousness of our international problems:

Thoughtful men are today asking whether all that mankind has painstakingly built over the long centuries is to come to a decisive and disastrous end as nations engage in the grim enterprise of nuclear destruction. Where once we were certain that human genius could wisely guide our society, there is now a cynical distrust of the course of world events. Where once there was a buoyant confidence that mankind was equal to the challenge of peace, there now is a disturbing fear which haunts the minds of free men as they face crisis after crisis in a mounting cold war. Where once such phrases as democracy and dictatorship, freedom and regimentation, individualism and collectivism, were only abstract ideas for college debate, they now are the center of a vast and bitter world struggle for the minds of men.

We are in a period of grave confusion. We seem sometimes to be in the grip of a paralyzing fatalism. We thrust great satellites far into the skies as if to defy the very heavens, while we talk of shelters on earth where each man will run like a frightened animal for his little cave to save himself, if he can, from the terrible fury of the last wrath. But must the outlook for humanity be so dismal? Must it be one of despair? Are the cards of destiny stacked against us? Are the skies of freedom darkening hopelessly across the earth? Is mankind prepared to accept complete subserviency to the state as its way of life, sheer materialism as its goal and self-destruction as its inevitable end? Can this nation ride through the storms of these years without political liberty and private enterprise being ultimately brought to their ruin? To gain some insight into the answers to these questions, let us consider what may be the major world developments of our time, their challenges to American foreign policy and their possible impact upon the future of our people.

One of the best known and most striking illustrations of repetition is to be found in the following quotation from an address by Robert Ingersoll:

A little while ago, I stood by the grave of the old Napoleon—a magnificent tomb of gilt and gold, almost fit for a dead deity—and gazed upon the sarcophagus of black Egyptian marble, where rest the ashes of that restless man. I leaned over the balustrade and thought about the career of the greatest soldier of the modern world.

I saw him walking upon the banks of the Seine contemplating suicide. I saw him at Toulon; I saw him putting down the mob in the streets of Paris; I saw him at the head of the army in Italy; I saw him crossing the bridge of Lodi with the tricolor in his hand; I saw him in Egypt in the shadow of the pyramids; I saw him conquer the Alps and mingle the eagles of France with the eagles of the crags; I saw him at Marengo, at Ulm, and Austerlitz; I saw him in Russia where the infantry of the snow and the cavalry of the wild blast scattered his legions like winter's withered leaves; I saw him at Leipzig in defeat and disaster—driven by a million bayonets back upon Paris—clutched like a wild beast—banished to Elba. I saw him escape and retake an empire by the force of his genius. I saw him upon the frightful field of Waterloo, where Chance and Fortune combined to wreck the fortunes of their former king, and I saw him at St. Helena, with his hands crossed behind him, gazing out upon the sad and solemn sea.

I thought of the orphans and widows he had made, of the tears that had been shed for his glory, and of the only woman he ever loved, pushed from his heart by the cold hand of ambition; and I said I would rather have been a French peasant and worn wooden shoes; I would rather have lived in a hut with a vine growing over the door and the grapes growing purple in the rays of the autumn sun; I would rather have been that poor peasant with my loving wife by my side, knitting as the day died out of the sky, with my children about my knee and their arms about me, I would rather have been that man and gone down to the tongueless silence of the dreamless dust than have been that imperial personification of force and murder.

Note also in the following short passage fròm Edmund Burke's address, "The Age of Chivalry Is Gone," how repetition aids the emphasis:

But the age of chivalry is gone. That of sophisters, economists, and calculators, has succeeded; and the glory of Europe is extinguished forever. Never, never more, shall we behold that generous loyalty to rank and sex, that proud submission, that dignified obedience, that subordination of the heart, which kept alive, even in servitude itself, the spirit of an exalted freedom. The unbought grace of life, the cheap defence of nations, the nurse of manly sentiment and heroic enterprise, is gone. It is gone, that sensibility of principle, that chastity of honour, which felt a stain like a wound, which inspired courage . . . which ennobled whatever it touched.

A simple but slightly different use of repetition in which a question is first asked, and then followed by variations in the question, is illustrated in the following quotation from an address on the subject of a liberal education by Thomas Henry Huxley:

Let us ask ourselves, what is education? Above all things, what is our ideal of a thoroughly liberal education?—of that education which, if we could begin life again, we would give ourselves—of that education which, if we could mould the fates to our own will, we would give our children.

In a speech on "The Romance of Life," Dr. Preston Bradley, well-known Chicago minister, lecturer, and author, said:

First, there must be within our democracy a revival, a renaissance, a new birth—call it what you will—there must be a new realization of the value of human personality. We must have a new birth of value as to human personality.

Note in this quotation also the mastery of the art of repetition.

IV. Intersperse Short Sentences with Long Ones

In baseball this is called changing the pace. It makes it easier for listeners to understand the speech, because they do not continually have to follow tedious, long sentences. Monotony can result if you use nothing but long sentences or staccato-like short sentences.

ILLUSTRATIONS

The late Dr. Glenn Frank, giving a baccalaureate address at The University of Wisconsin:

I am not so old as to have lost my memory of what must be surging through the minds of you who are about to step from the sheltered life of the student into active participation in the life of your time. And unless I have forgotten the emotions that swept my mind, some twenty-five years ago, when I completed my university training and stood poised, as you are poised, for a plunge into the outer world, I know that all sorts of anxieties haunt your minds, anxieties about the first and further steps in your careers. And these normal anxieties that you would feel even if all skies were cloudless, have, I know, been trebled by the political and economic distraction through which your nation has been passing as you have pursued your training.

What shall you do with these anxieties?

I want to be honest with you. I do not want to minimize one whit the uncertainties that infest the economic affairs of your time. I do not want to raise in your minds a single hope that will be doomed to die unfulfilled. But I do want to stir in you, if I can, every hope that can be fulfilled.

What, then, shall I say?

With a full sense of my responsibility to be realistic with you, I beg you not to let anxiety rest too heavily upon your minds.

Life is still conquerable for your generation both in the field of public policy and in the field of personal achievement.

Herbert V. Prochnow used this technique in a commencement address:

You will remember the story of the two sons. The younger son said to his father, "Give me the share of goods now that I am to inherit later." The father gave it to him and the young man left for a far country, where he wasted his entire estate. A depression came in that country, and the young man was in great need. He was hungry. He had no friends. He was destitute. As this young man meditated, he might have thought: "Well, my father was too indulgent. He was mature. I was a boy. He should not have been so foolish as to give me my estate." But this young man learned a hard lesson from this sobering and bitter experience. He said to himself, "Many servants in my father's house have bread enough and to spare, and I perish with hunger!" And then came his great decision. He said, "I will go to my father, and will say to him, 'Father I was wrong . . . and am no more worthy to be called your son; make me one of your hired servants.' " Of course, his father accepted him, and with that courageous decision, the young man found the life that he had lost.

Dr. Will Durant, speaking on "What Are the Lessons of History?":

Now we come to another lesson of history, which is a little more dangerous: That the concentration of wealth in the hands of a minority of the population is inevitable in any society. Why? Because men are naturally unequal. Some are clever; some are virtuous; some are strong; some are weak; some are healthy; some are sickly; some are brave; some are timid; and out of small natural differences that give you a head start come the tremendous differences in the development of society such as you see in America.

V. Use a Series of Short, Crisp Sentences.

The experienced speaker may not only intersperse occasional short sentences with longer ones, but he may also insert in his address one or two paragraphs of short, sharp, and clean-cut sentences that introduce a certain briskness.

ILLUSTRATIONS

In one of his addresses, Arthur M. Hyde said:

Justice is not social, economic, or political. It is all of them. Justice is Justice, plain and unqualified. It cannot be qualified. If limited to a class, it is no longer justice. Every citizen, not merely a class, is entitled to justice.

Herbert V. Prochnow used this idea in an address to university students:

As Walt Whitman said, "I was simmering, simmering, simmering: Emerson brought me to a boil." Many of us in life succeed to where we almost reach the boiling point. Nearly, you see, almost, but not quite.

It takes struggles in life to make strength. It takes fight for principles to make fortitude. It takes crises to give courage. Suffering to make sympathy. Pain to make patience. It takes singleness of purpose to reach an objective.

The late Knute Rockne, famous football coach of Notre Dame, in talking on "Athletics and Leadership," gave an excellent example of the use of a series of terse comments.

Some of you may say, this will to win is a bad thing. In what way is it a bad thing? Education is supposed to prepare a young man for life. Life is competition. Success in life goes only to the man who competes successfully. A successful lawyer is the man who goes out and wins—wins law cases. A successful physician is a man who goes out and wins—saves lives and restores men to health. A successful sales manager is a man who goes out and wins—sells the goods. The successful executive is the man who can make money and stay out of the bankruptcy court. There is no reward for the loser. There is nothing wrong with the will to win. The only penalty should be that the man who wins unfairly should be set down.

All these illustrations indicate how the short, crisp sentence may be used to give a speech punch.

VI. Use Similes Occasionally.

A simile compares two things that are not alike and often uses the introductory words "like" or "as." The simile is one of the oldest forms of speech. Three hundred are included in Chapter 18. These similes do not exhaust the field, for there are thousands of illustrations in speeches, literature, and newspaper and magazine articles. New similes are being created daily. Similes given don't need to be memorized. With a little patience and practice, you can create similes for your own use—similes fully as fresh and fascinating as those in this book. How much more interesting it is to say "The man went through things like a customs inspector," instead of "He examined everything." How much more colorful to state "The village was as desolate as a cemetery," instead of "The village was desolate." Make it a practice to use similes in speeches and in conversation.

VII. Avoid Boring Repetition by the Use of Appropriate Synonyms.

The dictionary and a book of synonyms are necessary additions to your library if you wish to speak, write, or converse well. They will enable you to find the right word for a particular use.

A *synonym* is a word having the same or nearly the same meaning as another word. Synonyms enable you to have some variation in your language when otherwise you might use the same word repeatedly. A well-known American executive repeats the word "tremendous" twenty-five or more times in one speech. In fact, he uses the word a tremendous number of times.

There are few perfect synonyms—that is, words with exactly the same meaning as other words—so choose your synonym carefully. The word "weak," for example, may suggest: feeble, infirm, faint, sickly, exhausted, groggy, spent, wasted, powerless, helpless, impotent, spineless, frail, fragile, flimsy, enervated, languishing, and debilitated. Examine a speech carefully, sentence by sentence, to see whether suitable synonyms may be chosen for words that have been used so often they have become monotonous.

VIII. Use Appropriate Antonyms to Create Contrasts.

As noted in an earlier chapter, an *antonym* is a word whose meaning is opposite to that of another word. The choice of good antonyms is necessary to create strong contrasts. A possible choice, for example, of antonyms for "weak" or "weakness" might be strength, power, potency, energy, vigor, force, stamina, virility, vitality, or puissance. Examine a speech critically to see whether words that are used to bring out contrasts do so with the greatest effectiveness; if not, replace them with words that do.

IX. Use Questions.

A question often serves to challenge an audience and to give emphasis to a point. We have called attention to the possibility of using questions in the introduction. However, questions are equally valuable in the body of the address.

ILLUSTRATIONS

John Sergeant, speaking on "Militarism and Progress":

I would ask: What did Cromwell, with all his military genius, do for England? He overthrew the monarchy, and he established dictatorial power in his own person. And what happened next? Another soldier overthrew the dictatorship, and restored the monarchy. The sword effected both. Cromwell made one revolution, and Monk another. And what did the people of England gain by it? Nothing. Absolutely nothing.

Chief Justice Marshall, speaking on the "Federal Constitution":

What are the favorite maxims of democracy? A strict observance of justice and public faith and a steady adherence to virtue. These, sir, are the principles of a good government. No mischief, no misfortune, ought to deter us from a strict observance of justice and public faith. Would to heaven that these principles had been observed under the present government! Had this been the case the friends of liberty would not be so willing now to part with it. Can we boast that our government is founded on these maxims? Can we pretend to the enjoyment of political freedom or security when we are told that a man has been, by an act of Assembly, struck out of existence without a trial by jury, without examination, without being confronted with his accusers and witnesses, without the benefits of the law of the land? Where is our safety when we are told that this act was justifiable because the person was not a Socrates? What has become of the worthy member's maxims? Is this one of them? Shall it be a maxim that a man shall be deprived of his life without the benefit of law? Shall such a deprivation of life be justified by answering that a man's life was not taken *secundum artem*, because he was a bad man? Shall it be a maxim that government ought not to be empowered to protect virtue?

These questions are vital ones. They go directly to the heart of Justice Marshall's discussion.

X. Place Ideas in Contrast to Each Other.

Placing ideas in contrast to each other is sometimes called *antithesis*. Occasionally one even finds antithesis within single sentences, as in Burke's speech on "The Age of Chivalry" when he speaks of "All the pleasing allusions which made power gentle and obedience liberal." Note the contrast between "power" and "gentle," "obedience" and "liberal." In another place, he says: "Never, never more shall we behold ... that proud submission, that dignified obedience...." Again note the contrast, particularly of "proud" and "submission."

ILLUSTRATIONS

Demosthenes often used contrasts in his addresses, as illustrated in his speech "On the Crown."

Contrast now the circumstances of your life and mine, gently and with temper, Aeschines; and then ask these people whose fortune they would each of them prefer. You taught reading, I went to school: you performed initiations, I received them: you danced in the chorus, I furnished it: you were assembly-clerk, I was a speaker: you acted third parts, I heard you: you broke down, and I hissed: you have worked as a statesman for the enemy, I for my country. I pass by the rest; but this very day I am on my probation for a crown, and am acknowledged to be innocent of all offense; while you are already judged to be a pettifogger, and the question is, whether you shall continue that trade, or at once be silenced by not getting a fifth part of the votes. A happy fortune, do you see, you have enjoyed, that you should denounce mine as miserable!

Herbert V. Prochnow used contrast in repeated paragraphs of the commencement address quoted earlier:

As a good citizen earnestly trying to live a good life, you have certain responsibilities if you are to live your best.

For example, if you demand wise and honest government in your city, your state and your country, you must recognize that wise and honest government is the product of wise and honest citizens, and nothing else.

If you demand that crime be punished, you must support honest law enforcement in your community without any personal privileges or exceptions for yourself.

If you demand unfair advantages, government bonuses, and special privileges for your business, your union, your city or your state, remember that the price of such selfishness is the destruction of a nation's character.

If you demand balanced budgets of your government, you must not advocate expenditures, which, when demanded by all citizens, bring unbalanced budgets. Every dollar which a government spends comes from the toil and sweat of its citizens.

If you demand freedom of worship for yourself, you must respect the rights of other creeds.

If you demand free speech, you must not suppress it in others, or use it to destroy the government from which that privilege flows.

If you demand that the government give you complete economic security, you must not forget that a nation's strength comes from each person standing on his own feet.

If you would like to live in a community in which you may have pride, then dedicate yourself in a spirit of humility to your own responsibilities in that community. These are practical ways in which to live the good life as a citizen.

The element of contrast is present also in these sentences of Dr. Glenn Frank's: (1) "A stage-coach citizenship may prove the undoing of an express-train world." (2) "And whether it be noble or ignoble, religious or irreligious, the able young man of today is not interested in the exclusive task of 'labeling men and women for transportation to a realm unknown' and sedulously avoiding straightforward consideration of that reconstruction of human society which Jesus of Nazareth had in mind when he talked of the Kingdom of God coming on earth."

XI. Use Colorful Phrases and Figures of Speech.

Chapter 19 contains many phrases and figures of speech that can give an address character and style. "Barkis is willin'," "Greeks bearing gifts," "a Jason's quest" are typical expressions which assist the speaker and writer to give more color to ideas. A speaker who was describing the slow evolution of great ideas in industry, and in all fields of life, mentioned the gradual development of the automobile from the earliest models three decades ago to the streamlined cars of the present day. "It is apparent," he said, "that this great industry did not develop overnight. It did not spring Minerva-like from the head of Jove."

Dr. Will Durant, speaking on "What Are the Lessons of History?" said: "So I should say that civilizations begin with religion and stoicism; they end with skepticism and unbelief, and the undisciplined pursuit of individual pleasure. A civilization is born stoic and dies epicurean." In that one last short sentence of only eight words, using two colorful words, "stoic" and "epicurean," Dr. Durant made a splendid summary of his viewpoint.

Comprehensive reading will be helpful in adding many figures of speech to your vocabulary. Those chosen for Chapter 19 will make an excellent start.

XII. Use Suitable Biblical Quotations.

Biblical quotations may be used not only in the introduction and the conclusion of many speeches, but also to express ideas in the body of the speech. It is not possible to use a biblical quotation in every speech, but where it can be done to emphasize a point, it makes a distinctly worthwhile addition. The Bible is the richest sourcebook of quotations in the world. Presidents of the United States have often quoted from the Old and New Testaments to convey their messages to the people. Study of the biblical quotations in Chapter 13 will bring gratifying returns in the ability to express your ideas well.

ILLUSTRATIONS

Dr. Glenn Frank, delivering a baccalaureate address on the subject, "If the Young Can But See":

Down the ages the capacity to anticipate and to discount bad ideas and the capacity to sense in advance and to appropriate good ideas, without waiting for events to indicate their badness or goodness, has been considered the supreme achievement of man as a thinking animal.

When the Lord of Ancient Israel was searching for the most withering rebuke and the most devastating penalty he could lay upon a recreant people, he asked that they be robbed of the capacity to see and to understand.

"Make the heart of this people fat," he cried, "and make their ears heavy, and shut their eyes; lest they see with their eyes, and hear with their ears and understand with their heart, and be healed."

And from Isaiah to Bernard Shaw this belief that insight and understanding are the godlike gifts has held.

President John F. Kennedy used a biblical quotation as follows in an address:

But neither can two great and powerful groups of nations take comfort from our present course—both sides overburdened by the cost of modern weapons, both rightly alarmed by the steady spread of the deadly atom, yet both racing to alter that uncertain balance of terror that stays the hand of mankind's final war.

So let us begin anew—remembering on both sides that civility is not a sign of weakness, and sincerity is always subject to proof. Let us never negotiate out of fear. But let us never fear to negotiate.

Let both sides explore what problems unite us instead of belaboring those problems which divide us.

Let both sides, for the first time, formulate serious and precise proposals for the inspection and control of arms—and bring the absolute power to destroy other nations under the absolute control of all nations.

Let both sides seek to invoke the wonders of science instead of its terrors. Together let us explore the stars, conquer the deserts, eradicate disease, tap the ocean depths and encourage the arts and commerce.

Let both sides unite to heed in all corners of the earth the command of Isaiah—to "undo the heavy burdens . . . (and) let the oppressed go free."

XIII. Use Appropriate Quotations from Literature.

Other than the Bible, perhaps the most frequently quoted sources are the writings of Shakespeare. Among the more than 1,100 quotations in Chapter 14, there are many from Shakespeare. The 1,100 quotations have been carefully selected from the world's great literature, from addresses, and from other sources. In almost every speech you will be able to use one or more quotations. Choose them carefully, and they are certain to give style to your address.

ILLUSTRATIONS

An educator addressing a Wisconsin high school commencement class on the great significance of decision in life said:

On the importance of decision we may say with James Russell Lowell: ... Once to every man and nation comes the moment to decide, In the strife of Truth and Falsehood, for the good or evil side.

John Haynes Holmes, speaking at Lehigh University on "Are We in the Hands of Fate?":

There is no such thing as security any more. There is as little permanency in values as stability in institutions. For years, the preachers of religion have proclaimed "the deceitfulness of riches," and the emptiness of all merely material possessions. Well, here they are—the prophecies come true! Now we know that the things of the spirit alone endure. In our time, as in times before, there has come the moment described by Prospero, in Shakespeare's play *The Tempest,* when

> "... all which (we) inherit shall dissolve,
> And, like this insubstantial pageant faded,
> Leave not a rack behind."

XIV. Use Words, Phrases, Clauses, and Sentences in Groups of Two or Three Occasionally.

The use of words, phrases, and sentences in groups of two or three gives rhythm and force to a speech. No attempt should be made to arrange these groups in every sentence or paragraph, as it would lead to monotony. But most of us will not be guilty of the excessive use of this tool of speech.

ILLUSTRATIONS

In just three famous words, "Veni, vidi, vici," or "I came, I saw, I conquered," Julius Caesar described his triumph over King Pharnaces of the Bosporus in 47 B.C. Those words, "having all the same cadence," said Plutarch, "carry with them a very suitable air of brevity," which brevity conforms to the swiftness and completeness of Caesar's victory. Cadence runs thought a close second in evoking the applause of an audience.

"Give me liberty, or give me death" was the expression of a great conviction. But it was even more. It was the brilliant expression of that conviction. Consider the sentence carefully. Two ideas are balanced on each side of the word "or." The ideas of liberty or death also are in contrast. Both clauses begin with the same words "give me," so that there is alliteration.

The eulogy delivered by General (Light Horse Harry) Henry Lee on the death of George Washington contains a famous phrase illustrating the grouping of three phrases. Lee said upon that historic occasion: "To the memory of the man, first in war, first in peace, and first in the hearts of his countrymen."

Franklin D. Roosevelt concluded an address with this climactic sentence:

And with that inner strength that comes to a free people conscious of their duty, conscious of the righteousness of what they do, they will—with divine help and guidance—stand their ground against this latest assault upon their democracy, their sovereignty and their freedom.

Observe the rhythm and the power in the last eight words.

Herbert V. Prochnow used two or three words of phrases several times in the following remarks. Note particularly the quotation from Winston Churchill, with the three ideas in Churchill's second sentence.

One night in August 1914, the members of the British Cabinet waited, hour after hour, as the deadline approached for the German reply to the British ultimatum. At last there fell upon their ears the deep boom of Big Ben, the great clock above the Parliament buildings, as it sounded the midnight hour. Then Lloyd George, his voice heavy with emotion, uttered the fateful words, "It's war."

Lloyd George said in his autobiography that the heavy boom of Big Ben sounded like doom to him through the stillness of that August night. Lloyd George was right. It was the doom of the world as we then knew it. By the end of the First World War, great empires began to totter. Communist revolutions erupted. Dictatorships sprang up. Currencies collapsed. Economic depression overtook the world. Then, unbelievably, came the Second World War with its disastrous consequences, engulfing almost all of mankind. War recruits emotional energies as it seeks to justify its motives with subtle hypocrisies and flaming phrases promising a brave new world in the future. Then it proceeds ruthlessly to destroy what mankind has achieved in a slow and painful struggle upward through the centuries. Winston Churchill could say at the end of World War II, "What is Europe now? It is a rubbleheap, a charnel house, a breeding ground of pestilence and hate."

Those were dark and disillusioning days as men awakened from their wartime dreams and surveyed the dismal wreckage. There were few grounds for courage. And yet, as we now know, the raw materials of economic and social renewal were present in Western Europe, waiting only to be given the leadership which was in less than two decades to make this one of the great areas of strength in the world.

At the outset of World War II in 1939, Soviet Russia was the only country in the world controlled by communists. Then a relentless drift to socialism and communism began. Ten years later communism had swept over one-third of the world's population, one-fourth of the earth's surface and a number of nations.

Herbert V. Prochnow speaking before a state bankers' association said:

It would be gratifying if it were possible to suggest here a program of the banker's responsibility, so comprehensive in its plan, so complete in its parts, and so convincing in its presentation that it would challenge the thinking of this intelligent audience.

This sentence not only illustrates the grouping of three phrases, but also the use of alliteration, which follows in point XV.

XV. Use Alliteration.

Alliteration means simply repeating the same sound or sounds in words near each other as in "penny wise, pound foolish" or Gilbert Chesterton's "fashionable fallacies."

Alliteration gives a speech sparkle because it adds harmony and rhythm. It would become tiresome if used in every sentence, but employed occasionally in a speech it thrills an audience. The speaker who may hope that at least parts of his speeches will be quoted, or will live, will find (1) the arrangement of words, phrases, clauses, and sentences in groups of two or three, and (2) the use of alliteration to be two of the most effective speech tools.

Winston Churchill knew that alliteration fascinates an audience and makes speeches moving and forceful. In a great emergency, he declared: "Let us to the task, to the battle and the toil."

Claude G. Bowers, distinguished American diplomat, talking to the Phi Beta Kappa chapter at Yale, said:

The American democracy is mobilized today to wage a war of extermination against privilege and pillage. We prime our guns against bureaucracy and plutocracy.

"Privilege and pillage," "bureaucracy and plutocracy" are ringing phrases because of the alliteration.

The late Dr. Glenn Frank was one of the greatest masters of alliteration America has ever known, as indicated by the following examples from his speeches and writings:

They say that when the acid test was applied, the prophet turned politician, and the realist was lost in the rhetorician.

We are convicted of plain bankruptcy of political intelligence.

It is better that we frankly take our latitude and longitude in relation to our wartime ideals than that we attempt the perilous practice of self-delusion.

The mind and the mood of the masses is the soil of the policy.

We place our foreign affairs in the hands . . . of men who bring to the politics of a planet the vision of a parish.

The most perilous disease in the world is not leprosy, but lopsidedness.

The West may face ruin instead of renaissance.

Shall we give our loyalty to leaders who will clarify our needs or to leaders who will cater to our desires?

Facts are not concerned with flattery.

He became the partisan and pamphleteer of Christianity.

It is not the analyses of the classroom, but the actualities of the marketplace.

A nation's army is only the clenched fist of its factories and farms.

Alliteration enables one to give to a speech what Lynn Harold Hough called "the gracious loveliness of finely wrought phrases."

7
THE REQUIREMENTS
OF PUBLIC SPEAKING

To help you plan your speech, here is a quick summary of the points we covered earlier.

HOW TO PREPARE YOUR SPEECH

I. Determine the exact subject so that it is entirely clear in your mind. If you have a hazy conception of the precise limitations of your topic, the audience naturally will be confused.

II. Think through the whole subject and formulate your own ideas and conclusions.

III. Read exhaustively important speeches, pamphlets, and books on the subject with which you are not familiar. Take notes on significant points.

IV. Outline the subject as follows:
   A. Introduction.
   B. Body of the speech, subdivided generally into two, three, or four parts.
   C. Conclusion.

V. Write out the speech fully. Experienced speakers may find it possible simply to outline an address and speak from the outline, but writing a speech eliminates wordiness and gives exactness to expression.
   A. The introduction must be short. It may be developed in one of the following seven ways:
      1. Announce the subject directly in the first sentence or paragraph.

 2. Tell a story of human interest, "paint a picture," or give an illustration.

 3. Use a statement that excites attention, arouses curiosity, surprises the audience, or is particularly informative.

 4. Tell a humorous story that is definitely related to the subject or to the situation under which you are addressing the audience.

 5. Ask a challenging question.

 6. State facts which show the importance of the subject to the welfare of the audience.

 7. Begin with a significant quotation or idea from some other person.

B. The body is the substance of the speech. Fill it with facts and concrete illustrations, and not simply with generalities. The following ideas will be of assistance in writing this part of your speech.

 1. Know the subject thoroughly.

 2. Use facts, figures, and illustrations.

 3. If the audience is to be convinced of some proposition, begin with subject matter with which there is agreement.

 4. Do not argue, but do explain.

 5. State briefly and clearly either at the beginning of the body of the speech or one by one, as the main part of the address unfolds, the two, three, or four points to be discussed. To provide suspense, it is generally better to give the points one by one, as the speech progresses.

C. The conclusion must ordinarily be short, and it is generally advisable to use it to reemphasize the points developed in the body of a speech. The following seven methods may be used to conclude a speech:

 1. Outline concisely the major points you have made in the body of the speech.

 2. Use a quotation from the Bible or literature.

 3. Bring the speech to a grand climax.

 4. Compliment the audience or leave a note of encouragement or optimism.

 5. Describe a dramatic scene, a great moment in history, science, or business, or give a brief biographical story.

6. Ask the audience to take some action or adopt a certain viewpoint.

7. Tell a humorous story or give a suitable witty comment.

HOW TO MAKE YOUR SPEECH SPARKLE

Rewrite and refine the speech until every unnecessary word is eliminated. The following fifteen effective speech tools will greatly assist you in the revision of your speech and will help to make it sparkle:

I. Insert suitable humorous stories, epigrams, and amusing definitions.

II. Use illustrations from biography, from plays, or from literature.

III. Repeat some words or phrases to stamp them indelibly upon the minds of the listeners.

IV. Intersperse short sentences with long ones.

V. Use a series of short, crisp sentences.

VI. Use similes occasionally.

VII. Avoid tiresome repetition by the use of appropriate synonyms.

VIII. Use appropriate antonyms to create contrasts.

IX. Use questions.

X. Place ideas in contrast to each other.

XI. Use colorful phrases and figures of speech.

XII. Use suitable biblical quotations.

XIII. Use appropriate quotations from literature.

XIV. Use words, phrases, clauses, and sentences in groups of two or three occasionally.

XV. Use alliteration.

WHEN YOU ARE STANDING BEFORE THE AUDIENCE

I. Open your mouth and speak distinctly and loudly enough to be heard by every person in the audience.

II. Don't worry about being nervous as you start speaking. It's a good sign. Almost every able speaker is nervous at the outset. It indicates he or she is on edge and ready. The time to worry is when you are not keyed up with nervous energy. If you have prepared thoroughly, you will master the situation.

III. Give your speech in one of the following ways:

    1. Read it if you must, but read it so well it sounds as if you were speaking without a manuscript.

    2. You may have your manuscript before you, but refer to it only occasionally. This requires reading the manuscript over and over until you are thoroughly familiar with it.

    3. Write out the address or outline it in detail. Then go over it repeatedly until you are completely familiar with it. Speak without notes.

    5. Write out the speech and memorize it. Be sure you speak naturally. Follow whichever method is best for you. Try gradually to eliminate reading as much as you can. Whatever you do read must be read well, or you will lose your audience at once. All important state addresses necessarily must be read to avoid even the slightest misstatement.

IV. Should you gesture? You may, but your gestures must come naturally. You never learn gestures from a book of rules. The following simple suggestions may help you:

    1. Merely permit your hands to fall loosely to your sides. You may place your hands behind your back and even occasionally in your pockets if you wish.

    2. If you must twiddle your fingers, do it behind your back.

    3. Stand in one place, and do not pace up and down the platform like a caged lion. These nervous movements distract an audience.

    4. Do not point your forefinger at the audience as if you were scolding your children.

    5. Generally avoid: repeated wide swings of the arms; numerous lightninglike movements of the forearms; and constant pounding on the table. Any frequently repeated gesture is tiresome.

    6. It is better to err on the side of too few gestures than too many.

    7. Above all, be natural.

V. Keep your speech within the limits of the time allotted to you.

WHAT PUBLIC SPEAKING REQUIRES

I. Sincere convictions earnestly expressed. You cannot convince others of what you do not believe.

II.   Unquestioned knowledge of your subject. You cannot explain to others what you do not understand.

III.   Painstaking preparation. You are deeply indebted to the audience for the privilege they have given you. A good speech is the best expression of your gratitude.

IV.   Practice at home, but never before an audience.

SINCERITY, KNOWLEDGE, PREPARATION, and PRACTICE—these are the four great requirements of public speaking.

8
TEN COMMANDMENTS FOR SPEAKERS

1. Never accept an invitation to speak on a subject on which you are not competent.

2. Never speak without the preparation necessary to give a speech that will reward the audience for its presence and attention. You have no right to plead unpreparedness, as this simply means wasting the time of an audience. The audience deserves the best address you can give—nothing less.

3. Your thoughts must be organized and presented in logical order. You can then talk straight to the point.

4. Use illustrations, stories, examples, epigrams, and other tools of speech to help you make an effective speech.

5. Stick closely to the speech you have prepared. Otherwise, you may ramble and take time that was meant to be given to your carefully prepared remarks.

6. Find out how long you are to speak, and stay within the time limit.

7. Do not underestimate the intelligence of an audience. The audience may be wiser than you think, and will resent any idea that you are talking down to them.

8. Never tell a questionable story. You may offend one or perhaps many in your audience.

9. Speak clearly, and make certain you are heard easily in all parts of the room.

10. The only way you can bring enthusiasm to a speech is to know your subject thoroughly. You cannot enthuse about something of which you know little.

9
HUMOROUS STORIES*

---

1   *A Great View*
At his wife's insistence, a man purchased a home on a hilltop in a very exclusive section of the community.

"I'll bet there is quite a view from way up there," said his friend enviously.

"Yes," replied the homeowner, "on a clear day you can see the bank that holds the mortgage."

2   *Practice*
A lady was entertaining the small son of a friend.

"Are you sure you can cut your own meat, Tommy?" she inquired.

"Oh, yes, thank you," answered the child politely. "I've often had it as tough as this at home."

3   *And Then?*
The retiring usher was instructing his youthful successor in the details of his office. "And remember, my boy, that we have nothing but good, kind Christians in this church—until you try to put someone else in their pew."

4   *Progress*
"Good news, Jackson, starting next month your take-home pay will exceed your deductions!"

* The numbers which appear in consecutive order at the left-hand margin beginning with Chapter 9 refer to the index. The use of the index will make it possible to refer instantly to related ideas and source material throughout the book.

5   *There Are Times*

It's nice to see people with plenty of get-up-and-go, especially if some of them are visiting you.

6   *Cramped in His Style*

A speaker said that as he surveyed the breadth of his subject, he could not help but think of Bishop Jones who was invited to speak before a great convention. A telegram he received from the program committee read as follows: "We should like to have you address our convention on the subject, 'THE WORLD, THE WAR, AND THE CHURCH.' " He gave the matter some consideration and felt he would like to address the convention, but the magnitude of the subject bothered him considerably. So he wired them as follows: "Gentlemen, I should like to address your great convention. However, I should not like to be cramped in my style or restricted in my remarks by any such narrow subject as 'THE WORLD, THE WAR, AND THE CHURCH.' I should be glad to come if you will add to it, 'THE SUN, THE MOON, AND THE STARS.' " (A story to use when one is given a very broad subject to discuss.)

7   *Out the Window He Must Go*

There are audiences and audiences. Some rank high in the scale of intelligence (like this one), and have a peculiar ability to disconcert a speaker. Even those low in the scale of intelligence provide their embarrassing moments. Henry Brown had a great desire to become a public speaker and accepted every invitation that came his way. One day the superintendent of the state insane asylum asked him to speak to an assembly of the inmates. The day came for the speech. Brown had hardly begun when a fellow in the back of the room said, "Rotten." Brown was nervous, but continued. The inmate yelled "Rotten" still louder. Brown considered the nature of his audience and decided to give his speech one more whirl. He began all over, but the fellow yelled "Rotten" again so loudly that the whole audience was disturbed. Brown finally turned to the superintendent and said, "Steve, shall I go on, or shall I stop?" The superintendent said, "Henry, you go right ahead. We've had that fellow in here ten years, and this is the first time he ever showed any intelligence."

8   *Worth Remembering*

We knew a man who thought he was overloaded in the "trouble department" until he found this memo on his desk: "Be thankful for the problems, for if they were less difficult, someone with less ability would have your job."

9   *Seldom Dines Well*

HUSBAND: I have no bad habits.

FRIEND: Don't you even smoke?

HUSBAND: Only in moderation. I like a cigar after a good dinner, but I don't suppose I smoke two cigars a month.

10   *Start Over*

CUSTOMER: I haven't come to any ham in this sandwich yet.

WAITER: Try another bite.

CUSTOMER (taking huge mouthful): Nope, not yet.

WAITER: Too bad! You must have gone right past it.

11   *This Is Discipline*

MRS. SHOPALOT: Can you alter this dress to fit me?

SALESMAN: Certainly not. That isn't done any more. You will have to be altered to fit the dress.

12   *A Wee Bit Too Pious*
A Scottish lady invited a gentleman to dinner on a particular day, and he accepted with the reservation, "If I am spared."
"Weel, weel," replied she, "if ye're deid I'll no' expect ye."

13   *Sometimes We All Do*
Said a frustrated young mother as she heard her children crying and looked over her dirty house: "I sometimes wish I'd loved and lost."

14   *It Made a Difference*

VISITOR: If your mother gave you two apples and told you to give one to your brother, would you give him the little one or the big one?

JOHNNY: Do you mean my little brother or my big one?

15   *You Put Him to Sleep*
A man fell asleep in an audience. The speaker stopped and asked a young boy sitting beside the man to wake him. The boy said, "Wake him up yourself—you put him to sleep." (Suitable if a speech is long.)

16   *Seems Fair*

The phone rang and the young mother answered. Came her mother's voice saying: "I phoned, dear, to find out if Dad and I could leave your children with Tom and you tonight. We are invited out for the evening."

17   *Concise*

A waitress came to the tired traveler who had just seated himself in a small-town restaurant. The menu was a very short one. The waitress said, "Will you have roast beef for dinner?" He said, "No." She said, "In that case dinner's over." (A good illustration of conciseness.)

18   *Proud Father*

Two parsons were having lunch at a farm during the progress of certain anniversary celebrations. The farmer's wife cooked a couple of chickens, saying that the family could dine on the remains after the visitors had gone. But the hungry parsons wolfed the chickens bare.

Later the farmer was conducting his guests round the farm, when an old rooster commenced to crow ad lib. "Seems mighty proud of himself," said one of the guests.

"No wonder," groused the farmer, "he's got two sons in the ministry."

19   *Visiting Card*

Sandy joined a golf club and was told by the professional that if his name was on his golf balls and they were lost, they would be returned to him when found.

"Good," said the Scot. "Put my name on this ball."

The pro did so.

"Would you also put M.D. after it?" said the new member. "I'm a doctor." The pro obeyed.

"There's just one more thing," went on the Scot. "Can ye squeeze 'Hours 10 to 3' on it as well?"

20   *Spelling*

"How is Hennery gettin' along with school, Eph?"

"Not so well, Garge. They're learnin' him to spell taters with a 'p'."

21   *Fair Enough*

An exasperated candidate was being heckled.

"There seem to be a great many fools here tonight," he exclaimed. "I wonder if it would be advisable to hear one at a time."

"That's fair enough," shouted a man in the audience. "Finish your speech."

22   *Who Wouldn't!*

A candidate for the police force was being verbally examined. "If you were by yourself in a police car and were pursued by a desperate gang of criminals in another car doing sixty miles an hour along a lonely road, what would you do?" The candidate looked puzzled for a moment. Then he replied: "Seventy."

23   *From Missouri*

"Aren't people funny?"

"Yes. If you tell a man that there are 270,678,934,341 stars in the universe, he'll believe you—but if a sign says 'Fresh Paint,' that same man has to make a personal investigation."

24   *Stumbling Block*

PRISONER: Judge, I don't know what to do.

JUDGE: Why, how's that?

PRISONER: I swore to tell the truth, but every time I try some lawyer objects.

25   *Good Aim*

The big game hunter took his wife on his newest safari. After several weeks, they returned. The sportsman had bagged a few minor trophies, but the great prize was the head of a huge lion, killed by his wife.

"What did she hit it with?" asked a friend admiringly. "That fine rifle you gave her?"

"No," answered her husband, dryly. "With the station wagon we hired!"

26   *He Learned*

A Chicago teacher received the following from one of her pupils: "Dear Miss Gorman: I've ingoid having you for a teacher. Insted of forsing lerning, you inspiare it. You do not yell, you have pachines, and thats the way a teacher shood be. I think you are the best teacher in the hole school. I've lerned more in your room than in the hole school. Your pupal, Robert."

27   *Not Over-Demanding*

REXFORD: I suppose you think I'm a perfect idiot?

ROBERTS: Oh, none of us is perfect.

28 *Too Busy for Current Events*

A traveler was marooned in a town because of a landslide caused by heavy rain, which was still falling in torrents after three days. Looking out of the window of the restaurant, he remarked to the waitress: "This is like the flood."

"The what?"

"The flood. Surely you have heard about the great flood and Noah and the Ark."

"Mister," she replied, "I haven't seen a paper for four days."

29 *Success*

"How is your doctor son getting on in his practice?"

"Excellently—he has made enough money so he can occasionally tell a patient that there is nothing wrong with him."

30 *Plenty*

"What would I get," inquired the man who had just insured his property against fire, "if this building should burn down tonight?" "I would say," replied the insurance agent, "about ten years."

31 *No Regrets*

"I'm sorry—I quite forgot your party the other evening!"

"Oh, weren't you there?"

32 *Chit-Chat*

OFFICER (to driver who has been whipping his horse which is pulling a tourist surrey): Don't whip him, man—talk to him.

DRIVER (to horse, by way of opening conversation): Ah comes from N'Awleans. Where does you-all come from?

33 *Diagnosis*

The middle-aged man shuffled along, bent over at the waist, as his wife helped him into the doctor's waiting room. The doctor's nurse viewed the scene in sympathy. "Arthritis with complications?" she asked.

The wife shook her head. "Do-it-yourself," she explained, "with concrete blocks."

34   *With a Speedy Recovery*

HEWITT: You don't seem to think much of him.

JEWELL: If he had his conscience taken out, it would be a minor operation.

35   *On the Spot*

OFFICE BOY (nervously):   Please, sir, I think you're wanted on the phone.

EMPLOYER: You think! What's the good of thinking?

OFFICE BOY: Well, sir, the voice at the other end said, "Hello, is that you, you old idiot?"

36   *He Made Sure*

Many stories are told about the care General Smedley D. Butler always took in looking after the welfare of the men in his command—especially in regard to their food. Once when he was in command of Camp Pontenazen, France, he met two soldiers carrying a large soup kettle from the kitchen.

"Here you," he ordered, "let me taste that."

"But, Gen——"

"Don't give me any buts—get a spoon!"

"Yes sir!" the soldier replied, and running back in the kitchen, brought a spoon.

The general took the desired taste, and gingerly spat it out. "You don't call that stuff soup, do you?" he shouted. "No, sir!" replied the soldier. "That's what I was trying to tell you—it's dishwater, sir!"

37   *Be Careful*

MIKHAIL: You look positively beautiful tonight.

ELSIE: You, you flatterer!

MIKHAIL: No, it's true. I had to look twice before I recognized you.

38   *Educational*

A young mother was looking at a toy for her small child. "Isn't this awfully complicated for him?" she asked the salesman.

"That, madam," replied the salesman, "is an educational toy, designed to prepare the child for life in today's world. Any way he puts it together is wrong."

39   *Enthusiastic*

HUSBAND (after the theater):   But, dear, what did you object to?

WIFE: Why, the idea of your bellowing 'Author! Author!' at a Shakespearean drama.

40   *He Will Fix It*

"Waiter, I find that I have just enough money to pay for the dinner, but I have nothing in the way of a tip for yourself."

"Let me add up that bill again, sir."

41   *Advantages of a Small Town*

A traveling salesman visited a small town, and sold the proprietor of its general store an order of jewelry.

When the jewelry arrived it was not as represented, and the merchant returned it. But the wholesale house, nevertheless, attempted to collect the bill, and drew a sight draft on the merchant through the local bank, which returned the draft unhonored.

The wholesaler then wrote to the postmaster inquiring about the financial standing of the merchant, and the postmaster replied laconically that it was "O.K."

By return mail the wholesaler requested him to "hand the enclosed account to the leading lawyer of the place for collection."

This is the reply they received.

"The undersigned is the merchant on whom you attempted to palm off your worthless goods.

"The undersigned is the president and owner of the bank to which you sent your sight draft.

"The undersigned is the postmaster to whom you wrote, and the undersigned is the lawyer whose service you sought to obtain for your nefarious business.

"If the undersigned were not also pastor of the church at this place, he would tell you to go jump in the lake."

42   *Heard at the Zoo*

A huge elephant and a tiny mouse were in the same cage at the zoo. The elephant was in a particularly ugly and truculent mood. Looking down at the mouse with disgust, he trumpeted: "You're the puniest, the weakest, the most insignificant thing I've ever seen!" "Well," piped the mouse in a plaintive squeak, "don't forget, I've been sick."

43   *Exclusive*

"Yes," said the boastful young man, "my family can trace its ancestry back to William the Conqueror."

"I suppose," remarked his friend, "you'll be telling us that your ancestors were in the Ark with Noah?"

"Certainly not," said the other. "My people had a boat of their own."

44 *He Should Know*

Professor (much annoyed by his students' interruptions): "The minute I get up to speak some fool begins to talk."

45 *Staying Safe*

In a small hotel in Kingston, Ontario, so a returning traveler reports, there is a yellowing sign tacked to the dingy wall behind the desk on which the proprietor proclaims his fixed and inbred skepticism of all humanity. It reads: "No checks cashed. Not even good ones."

46 *Music*

DAUGHTER: Did you ever hear anything so wonderful? (as the radio grinds out the latest music).

FATHER: Can't say I have, although I once heard a collision between a truckload of milk cans and a car filled with ducks.

47 *Insulted*

"What do you mean," roared the politician, "by publicly insulting me in your old rag of a paper? I will not stand for it, and I demand an immediate apology."

"Just a moment," answered the editor. "Didn't the news item appear exactly as you gave it to us, namely, that you had resigned as city treasurer?"

"It did, but where did you put it?—in the column headed 'Public Improvements.'"

48 *Still Advertising*

A salesman seeking advertisements for a local paper called at the village grocer's. Upon presenting his card, he was surprised when the gray-haired proprietor said: "Nothing doing. Been established eighty years, and never advertised."

"Excuse me, sir, but what is that building on the hill?" asked the traveler.

"The village church," said the grocer.

"Been there long?" asked the other.

"About three hundred years."

"Well," was the reply, "they still ring the bell."

49 *Statistics*

CHIEF INSTRUCTOR: Now remember, men, statistics don't lie. Now, for an example, if twelve men could build a house in one day, one man could build the same house in twelve days. Do you understand what I mean? Jeep, give me an example.

JEEP: If one boat could cross the ocean in six days, six boats could cross the ocean in one day.

50 *It Is, Dear*

"You know, dear, John doesn't seem to be as well dressed as he was when you married him."

"That's funny. I'm sure it's the same suit."

51 *Believe in Signs*

TEACHER (to tardy student):   Why are you late?

BOBBY: Well, a sign down there—

TEACHER: Well, what has a sign got to do with it?

BOBBY: The sign said: "School ahead; go slow."

52 *Was That Nice?*

An author, in referring to his books, said: "They will be read long after Milton and Homer have been forgotten—" "And not till then," replied a listener.

53 *A Dry Speaker*

Everything that could be done to make the meeting a success had been accomplished. A large hall and a good speaker had been engaged. When the latter arrived, he was in a crabby frame of mind. Looking around, he beckoned the chairman.

"I would like to have a glass of water on my table, if you please," he said.

"To drink?" was the chairman's idiotic question.

"Oh, no," was the sarcastic retort, "when I've been speaking a half-hour, I do a high dive."

54 *From the Inside*

"Look at that one—the one staring at us through the bars. Doesn't he look intelligent?"

"Yes. There is something uncanny about it."

"He looks as if he understood every word we're saying."

"Walks on his hind legs, too, and swings his arms."

"There! He's got a peanut. Let's see what he does with it."

"Well, what do you think about that! He knows enough to take the shell off before he eats it just like we do."

"That's a female alongside of him. Listen to her chatter at him. He doesn't seem to be paying much attention to her, though."

"She must be his mate."

"They look kind of sad, don't they?"

"Yes. I guess they wish they were in here with us monkeys."

55   *Finished His Speech But Hasn't Stopped Talking*

A man walked out of a hall where a speaker was addressing a meeting. Someone in the corridor asked him if the speaker had finished his speech. He said, "Yes, he finished his speech shortly after he started, but he hasn't stopped talking." (Suitable if a speech is long.)

56   *Over the Line*

WIFE: Don't you think, dear, that a man has more sense after he is married?

HUBBY: Yes, but it's too late then.

57   *Subtle, Indeed*

Little Georgie received a new drum for Christmas, and shortly thereafter, when Father came home from work one evening, the following conversation took place:

MOTHER: I don't think that man upstairs likes to hear Georgie play his drum, but he's certainly subtle about it.

FATHER: Why?

MOTHER: Well, this afternoon he gave Georgie a knife, and asked him if he knew what was inside the drum.

58   *Good Hunting*

1ST HUNTER: Hey, Bill.

2ND HUNTER: Yeah.

1ST HUNTER: Are you all right?

2ND HUNTER: Yeah.

1ST HUNTER: Then I've shot a bear.

59   *The Good Old Way*

JUDGE: Couldn't this case have been settled out of court?

DEFENDANT: Yer honor, shure an' that is exactly what we wuz thryin' to do whin a couple av police butted in.

60   *When Uncertain*

The kind of alertness that makes wit possible is shown in Lincoln's case, who, as a captain in the Mexican War, led his company to a fence but did not know what order to give to get them over.

"Halt," said he, "the company will disband and meet on the other side of the fence."

61   *Full Information*

HE: If you'll give me your telephone number, I'll call you up some time.

SHE: It's in the book.

HE: Fine! And what's your name?

SHE: That's in the book, too!

62   *Putting on the Ritz*

The newly rich woman was trying to make an impression: "I clean my diamonds with ammonia, my rubies with wine, my emeralds with brandy, and my sapphires with fresh milk."

"I don't clean mine," said the quiet woman sitting next to her. "When mine get dirty, I just throw them away."

63   *Daddy*

OFFICER (to man pacing sidewalk at three o'clock in the morning):   What are you doing here?

GENTLEMAN: I forgot my key, officer, and I'm waiting for my children to come home and let me in.

64   *Likely*

MOTHER (to son wandering around the room):   What are you looking for?

SON: Nothing.

MOTHER: You'll find it in the box where the candy was.

65   *Queer Names*

ENGLISHMAN: Odd names your towns have. Hoboken, Weehawken, Oshkosh, Poughkeepsie.

AMERICAN: I suppose they do sound queer to English ears. Do you live in London all of the time?

ENGLISHMAN: No indeed. I spend part of my time at Chipping Norton, and divide the rest between Bigglewade and Leighton Buzzard.

66   *Full Stop*

The genius of a local man had carried him to big success in business without much aid of education.

He was asked to distribute the prizes at a school, and made the usual speech of good counsel.

"Now, boys," he said, "Always remember that education is a great thing. There's nothing like education. Take arithmetic. Through education we learn that twice two makes four, that twice six makes twelve, that seven sevens make—and then there's geography."

67   *A Letter to Teacher*

Dear Teacher: Kindly excuse Joe's absence yesterday, as he fell into the mud on his way to school. By doing the same you will oblige   *Mrs. Henry Jones*

68   *His Example*

TEACHER: Can you give me a good example of how heat expands things and cold contracts them?

PUPIL: Well the days are much longer in the summer.

69   *Difficulties*

JOE: What's become of the Hikers' Club?

JIM: Oh, it disbanded. It was getting too hard to persuade passing motorists to pick us up and give us a lift.

70   *Repartee*

Edward Everett and Judge Story were at a public dinner, during which Story proposed this sentiment: "Genius is sure to be recognized where Everett goes."

Everett promptly responded with the sentiment: "Equity and jurisprudence—no efforts can raise them beyond one Story."

71   *Point Scored*

Waiters, of course, are not in a position to snap back at ill-bred guests; but one English headwaiter once made the perfect retort to an uncouth customer:

"My position, sir," he said, "does not allow me to argue with you; but if it ever came to a choice of weapons, I would choose grammar."

72   *Appeal to Reason*

Answer received by the credit department of a Chicago firm: "I don't expect to beat you out of any money. But I am going to say one thing. I am not working so I don't make anything and until I go to work I can't pay you anything so keep your shirt on and as soon as I start to work I will send some money. But if you don't keep it on, well just take it off and hold it until after Christmas."

73   *Understandable*

"What is your kitty's name, Jimmy?" asked the woman.

"Ben Hur," answered Jimmy.

"That's a funny name for a cat. Why did you name it that?"

"Well, we just called him Ben until he had kittens."

74   *Problem*

FATHER: Isn't it wonderful how little chicks get out of their shells?

SON: What gets me is how they get in.

75   *Where Else?*

The teacher was working with her first-grade children and their writing skills. She looked over the shoulder of a little girl and said, "That looks nice, but where is the dot over the 'i'?"

"Oh," said the little girl, "it's still in my ballpoint pen."

76   *Hmm*

"Weak eyes have you? Well how many lines can you read on that chart?"

"What chart?"

77   *Naturally*

USHER: How far down do you wish to sit, sir?

PATRON: All the way, of course.

78   *No Mystery*

JONES: How do you spend your income?

SMITH: About 30 percent for shelter, 30 percent for clothing, 40 percent
           for food, and 20 percent for amusement.

JONES: But that adds up to 120 percent.

SMITH: That's right.

79   *Futile*

TEACHER TOURIST: This seems to be a very dangerous precipice. It's a
                     wonder they don't put up a warning sign.

NATIVE: Yes, it is dangerous, but they kept a warning sign
                     up for two years and no one fell over, so it was
                     taken down.

80   *Match*

MIKE: That's a strange pair of stockings you have on, Pat—one red and
          the other green.

PAT: Yes, and I've got another pair like it at home.

81   *Called*

The teacher was testing the knowledge of the kindergarten class. Slapping a half-dollar on the desk, she asked sharply, "What is that?" Instantly a voice from the back row said, "Tails."

82   *A Good Reason*

A youngster was being chided for his low grades. As an alibi, he said: "Well, all the boys at school got Cs and Ds too."

"All of them?" he was cross-questioned. "How about little Johnny Jones, who lives down the street?"

"Oh, he got high grades," the youngster admitted. "But you see, he's different. He has two bright parents."

83   *Alibi*

This repartee took place between two rabid Californians during a heavy rainstorm in Los Angeles. Both watched the downpour with embarrassed expressions. . . . Finally, after a deep silence, one said to the other: "Boy, some terrible weather certainly blows in from Nevada, doesn't it?"

84   *Whiskers*

ERNIE: My uncle can play the piano by ear.

GURNEY: That's nothing. My uncle fiddles with his whiskers.

85   *Polite*

A New York traffic expert says that the London drivers and chauffeurs enliven many occasions by their wit and sarcasm. One London driver drew up when he saw a pedestrian directly in his way, leaned over, and very politely inquired: "I say, sir, may I ask what are your plans?"

86   *Strategy*

OFFICER: Now tell me, what is your idea of strategy?

ROOKIE: It's when you're out of ammunition, but keep right on firing.

87   *Rest in Peace*

A party of sailors were being shown over the cathedral by a guide. "Behind the altar," he told them, "lies Richard the Second. In the churchyard outside lies Mary Queen of Scots; also Henry the Eighth. And who," he demanded, halting above an unmarked flagstone, "who do you think is a-lying 'ere?"

"Well," answered a salt, "I don't know for sure, but I have my suspicions."

88   *Sunday*

Of all the days that's in the week,
I dearly love but one day,
And that's the day that comes betwixt
A Saturday and Monday.

—*Henry Carey*

89   *Acid Tongue*

CHEMISTRY PROFESSOR: Jones, what does HNO_3 signify?

CADET JONES: Well, ah, er—I've got it right on the tip of my tongue, sir.

CHEMISTRY PROFESSOR: Well, you'd better spit it out. It's nitric acid.

90   *Too Restless*

ANGLER: You've been watching me for three hours. Why don't you try fishing yourself?

ONLOOKER: I ain't got the patience.

91   *That's Different*

"You didn't take a vacation this year, did you?"

"No, I thought I needed a rest."

92   *Doctor's Prescription*

"Your doctor's out here with a flat tire."

"Diagnose the case as flatulency of the perimeter and charge him accordingly," ordered the garage man. "That's the way he does."

93   *Salesmanship*

A fruit dealer in Georgia has a sign above his wares that reads:

Watermelons

Our choice	$1.00
Your choice	1.50

94   *Ambition*

> I want to be an author,
> My hand up to my face;
> A thought upon my forehead,
> An air of studied grace!
> I want to be an author,
> With genius on my brow;
> I want to be an author,
> And I want to be it now!
>
> —*Ella Hutchison Ellwanger*

95   *Hard Question*

VISITOR: How old are you, sonny?

BOSTON BOY: That's hard to say, sir. According to my latest school tests, I have a psychological age of 11. Anatomically, I'm 7; mentally I'm 9. But I suppose you refer to my chronological age. That's 8—but nobody pays any attention to that nowadays.

96   *Not Wholly Dumb*

"Don't they teach you to salute in your company?" roared the major to Patrick Malone, who had passed him without raising his hand.

"Yes, sir," replied Pat.

"Then why didn't you salute?"

"Well, sir," was the candid reply, "I didn't want to attract more attention than I had to, 'cause I ain't supposed to be out here without a pass."

97   *Lucky*

"Mr. Chairman," complained the speaker, "I have been on my feet for nearly ten minutes, but there is so much interruption I can hardly hear myself speak."

"Cheer up, my friend," came a voice from the rear, "you are not missin' much."

98   *Experienced Partygoer*

"Your friend Joe seemed to be the life of the party."

"Yes, he was the only one who could talk louder than the TV."

99   *Silencer*

BETTY: Your new coat is pretty loud, isn't it?

BILLY: Yeah, but I'm gonna buy a muffler to go with it.

100   *Preachers*

Everyone has at least one sermon in him.

101   *Stretching the Point*

A railroad agent in Africa had been bawled out for doing things without orders from headquarters. One day his boss received the following startling telegram:

"Tiger on platform eating conductor. Wire instructions."

102   *Efficiency*

A retailer, on receiving the first delivery of a large order, was annoyed to find the goods not up to sample. "Cancel my order immediately," he wired the manufacturer.

The manufacturer replied: "Regret cannot cancel immediately. You must take your turn."

103   *One That Was Too Fast for Him*

A Frenchman was relating his experience in studying the English language. He said: "When I first discovered that if I was quick, I was fast;

that if I was tied, I was fast; if I spent too freely, I was fast; and that not to eat was to fast, I was discouraged. But when I came across the sentence, 'The first one won one dollar prize,' I gave up trying."

104   *Variety*

"What are you raising in your garden this year?"

"Johnson's Plymouth Rocks, Brown's Leghorns, and Smith's Wyandottes."

105   *Only When Necessary*

PREACHER: Do you say your prayers at night, little boy?

JIMMY: Yes, sir.

PREACHER: And do you always say them in the morning, too?

JIMMY: No, sir. I ain't scared in the daytime.

106   *Smart Youngster*

A young schoolteacher was telling a small boy about a lamb that had strayed from the flock and had been eaten by a wolf.

"You see, Billy," she said, "had the lamb been obedient and stayed in the flock, it would not have been eaten by the wolf, would it?"

"No," the youngster answered quickly. "It would have been eaten by us."

107   *Welcome Relief*

LITTLE MARY: Mother, they are going to teach us domestic silence at school now."

MOTHER: Don't you mean domestic science?

FATHER: There is a bare hope our little girl means what she is saying.

108   *Nature Story*

A tourist traveling through the Texas Panhandle got into conversation with an old settler and his son at a filling station.

"Looks as though we might have rain," said the tourist.

"Well, I hope so," replied the native, "not so much for myself as for my boy here. I've seen it rain."

109   *Was He?*

"Father," said a little boy, "did Solomon have seven hundred wives?"

"I believe so, my son," said the father.

"Well, Father, was he the man who said, 'Give me liberty or give me death'?"

110   *Legitimate Objection*

The teacher was trying to impress upon her class the advantages of peace and disarmament. "How many of you boys object to war?" she asked. Up went several hands.

"Jimmy, will you tell the class why you object to war?"

" 'Cause wars make history," replied Jimmy soberly.

111   *The Egotist*

HIM: I dreamed I was married to the most beautiful girl in the world.

HER: Were we happy?

112   *Appropriate*

John D. Rockefeller, Jr., once asked a clergyman to give him an appropriate Bible verse on which to base an address he was to make at the latter's church.

"I was thinking," said Rockefeller, "that I would take the verse from the Twenty-third Psalm: 'The Lord is my shepherd.' Would that seem appropriate?"

"Quite," said the clergyman. "But do you really want an appropriate verse?"

"I certainly do," was the reply.

"Well, then," said the clergyman, with a twinkle in his eye, "I would select the verse in the same Psalm: 'Thou anointest my head with oil; my cup runneth over.' "

113   *Correct*

TEACHER: Johnny, can you tell me the name of an animal that travels great distances?

JOHNNY: Yes, a goldfish. It travels around the globe.

114   *In Reverse*

Little Dickie, aged six, seized with hiccups, ran to his mother and said: "Oh, Mother, I'm coughing backwards."

115   *A Vote of Thanks*

An elderly maiden aunt received this note from her ten-year-old niece: "Dear Aunt: Thank you for your nice present. I have always wanted a pincushion, but not very much."

116   *Harder Than a Diamond*

DOROTHY (admiring
   her engagement
      ring):   There's nothing in the world harder than a dia-
               mond, is there?

   HOWARD: Yes, sweetheart—keeping up the installment
             payments on it.

117   *Success*

CUSTOMER: To what do you owe your extraordinary success as a
            house-to-house salesman?

SALESMAN: To the first five words I utter when a woman opens the
            door—"Miss, is your mother in?"

118   *Man's Wants*

> "Man wants but little here below
> Nor wants that little long,"
> 'Tis not with me exactly so;
> But 'tis so in the song.
> My wants are many, and, if told,
> Would muster many a score;
> And were each wish a mint of gold,
> I still should long for more.
>
> —*John Quincy Adams*

119   *A Warning*

TEACHER: Yes, Johnny, what is it?

JOHNNY: I don't want to scare you, but Papa said if I didn't get better
          grades someone is due for a licking.

120   *Love Letters*
An advertisement appeared in the student newspaper of a state university: "Sweet little old lady wishes to correspond with university student
—six-footer with brown eyes answering to initials J.A.D. Signed, His
Mother."

121   *A Martyr to Her Faith*
"Marie," observed Muriel, "has suffered much for her belief."
   "Indeed?" asked Millicent, lifting her eyebrows in polite curiosity.
"What is her belief?"
   "That she can wear a size four shoe on a size six foot."

122   *Don't Worry*

MR. NEWLYWED: Darling, did you sew the button on my coat?

MRS. NEWLYWED: No, sweetheart, I couldn't find a button, but it's all right now. I sewed up the buttonhole.

123   *Silence*

BALL: What is silence?

HALL: The college yell of the school of experience.

124   *One Year Later*

"Oh, George, do you realize it's almost a year since our honeymoon, and that glorious day we spent on the sands? I wonder how we'll spend this one?"

"On the rocks."

125   *Not Yet Out of Danger*

"How's your son coming along with his driving?"

"He took a turn for the worse last week."

126   *A Shining Face*

"The new patient in Ward B is very good looking," said the nurse.

"Yes," agreed the matron, "but don't wash his face. He's had that done by four nurses this morning."

127   *Reason for Being Present*

TEACHER: How is it you cannot answer any of my questions?

PUPIL: Well, if I could, what would be the use of my coming here?

128   *He Should Know*

PROSPECTIVE BRIDEGROOM (gaily):   Will it take much to feather a nest?

FURNITURE DEALER: Oh, no; only a little down.

129   *Is This Routine?*

FIRST DOCTOR: I operated on him for appendicitis.

SECOND DOCTOR: What was the matter with him?

130   *Dry Country*

The mayor of a tough border town was about to engage a preacher for the new church.

"Parson, you aren't by any chance a Baptist, are you?"

"No. Why?"

"Well, I was just going to say that we have to haul our water five miles."

131   *Wasted Effort*

PROFESSOR (finishing long algebra problem):	And so we find X equals zero.
SOPHOMORE:	All that work for nothing.

132   *Blended Coffee*

"What kind of coffee do you serve here?" asked the diner. "It's terrible."

"That's good blended coffee," defended the waiter, "last week's and this week's."

133   *'Tain't Fair*

Life isn't fair to us men. When we are born, our mothers get the compliments and the flowers. When we are married, our brides get the presents and the publicity. When we die, our widows get the life insurance and the winters in Florida.

134   *Jujitsu*

"Did I ever tell you how I tried my jujitsu on a burglar?"

"No."

"Well, I got hold of his leg and twisted it over his shoulder. Then I got hold of his arm and twisted it round his neck, and before he knew where he was I was flat on my back."

135   *Wrong Number*

IRATE SUBSCRIBER TO OPERATOR:	Am I crazy or are you?
OPERATOR:	I am sorry, but we do not have that information.

136   *Independence*

WIFEY:	Oh, Bill, baby can walk.
HUBBY:	That's fine. Now he can walk up and down at night by himself.

137   *Squall or Squeal*

YOUNG FATHER:	In your sermon this morning you spoke about a baby being a new wave on the ocean of life.

MINISTER: That's right. Do you think a fresh squall would have been nearer the truth?

138   *Make It Snappy*

A man rushed into a barbershop.

"Cut everything short," he said. "Hair, whiskers, and conversation."

139   *Etiquette*

The district engineer and his wife were entertaining at dinner. Suddenly a child's voice was heard from the floor above. "Mother." "What is it Archie?" she asked. "There's only clean towels in the bathroom. Shall I start one?"

140   *Spendthrift*

TRAMP: Lady, I'm almost famished.

HOUSEWIFE: Here's a nickel. But how did you fall so low?

TRAMP: I had your fault. I was too extravagant.

141   *Commence*

A coach was teaching some cowboys how to play football. He explained the rules and ended as follows:

"Remember, fellows, if you can't kick the ball, kick a man on the other side. Now let's get busy. Where's the ball?"

One of the cowboys shouted: "Forget the ball! Let's start the game!"

142   *Matrimonially Inclined*

DORIS: When is your sister thinking of getting married?

TOM: Constantly.

143   *Cramped*

"That fellow must live in a very small flat."

"How can you tell?"

"Why, haven't you noticed that his dog wags his tail up and down, instead of sideways?"

144   *Epitaph*

"Here Lies an Atheist; All Dressed Up and No Place to Go."

145   *Coincidence*

"So he is a reckless driver?"

"Say, when the road turns the same way as he does, it's just a coincidence."

146 *Thoughtful*

FRESHMAN: Say, what's the idea of wearing my raincoat?

ROOMMATE: Well you wouldn't want your new suit to get wet, would you?

147 *Substitute*

"Tommy, what is a synonym?" the teacher asked.

"A synonym," said Tommy, wisely, "is a word you use when you can't spell the other one."

148 *Tsk! Tsk!*

MRS. KNICKER: We are told one-third of the nation is ill-housed, ill-nourished, and ill-clad.

MR. KNICKER: I didn't realize so many go away for the summer.

149 *Slightly Scrambled*

Another audition in the family of Mr. and Mrs. Jed Draper occurred Friday night, this time a bouncing boy. *Martinex (Cal.) Citizen*

The bride is a member of Coulton's social set, a member of the Junior League, and a skillet musician. *Coulton (Ore.) Advocate*

150 *In Hunting Season*

"Sorry, sir, but I'm all out of wild ducks. I could let you have a fine end of ham."

"Don't kid me. How could I go home and say I shot an end of ham?"

151 *Correct*

Here's to the man who is wisest and best.
Here's to the man who with judgment is blest.
Here's to the man who's as smart as can be—
I mean the man who agrees with me.

152 *Not Necessary*

MOTHER: Did you give the goldfish some fresh water this morning?

JOHNNIE: No. They haven't finished the water I gave them yesterday.

153 *Transport Has Changed*

"If witches came back they'd flourish in some parts of the country as much as they ever did," says a writer. "But they'd find it a little awkward getting about on a vacuum cleaner, wouldn't they?"

154   *Trees*

I think that I shall never see along the road an unscraped tree, with bark intact, and painted white, that no car ever hit at night. For every tree that's near the road has caused some auto to be towed.

Sideswiping trees is done a lot by drivers who are plumb half shot. God gave them eyes so they might see, yet any fool can hit a tree.

155   *Considerate*

SOPHMORE: But I don't think I deserve a zero.

PROFESSOR: Neither do I, but it's the lowest mark I'm allowed to give.

156   *Try a Sextant*

GOLFER (far off in the rough):   Say, caddy, why do you keep looking at your watch?

CADDY: It isn't a watch, sir; it's a compass.

157   *Permanent Guest*

A little Logan Heights girl said there was a new baby at her home.

"Has the baby come to stay?" she was asked.

"I think so," she said, "he's taken all his things off."

158   *Both Ends against the Middle*

Two men who had been bachelor cronies met for the first time in five years.

"Tell me, Tom," said one, "did you marry that girl, or do you still darn your own socks and do your cooking?"

"Yes," was Tom's reply.

159   *One on the Button*

MR. GROUCH: Woman is nothing but a rag, a bone, and a hank of hair.

MRS. GROUCH: Man is nothing but a brag, a groan, and a tank of air.

160   *This Modern Age*

"Why, what are you crying so for, sonny?" asked Dad of his four-year-old heir.

"I heard you say you were going to get a new baby and I suppose that means you'll trade me in on it," he sobbed.

161   *Like a Cricket in a Cabbage*

"When a man is asleep, he's a mere vegetable," says a scientific writer. "He is, however, not edible—only audible."

162 *Cashing in on a Correspondence Course*

My friend laughed when I spoke to the waiter in French, but the laugh was on him. I told the waiter to give him the check.

163 *That Silver Lining*

JEAN: So you mortgaged our little home.

JOE: Just temporarily, honey, until the mortgage is foreclosed.

164 *Costly Delusion*

"My wife had a dream last night and thought she was married to a millionaire."

"You're lucky! My wife thinks that in the daytime."

165 *Safety First*

DINER: Waiter, this soup is cold. Bring me some that's hot.

WAITER: What do you want me to do? Burn my thumb?

166 *Alger Heroes Are Extinct*

GRUFF FATHER TO SON: Why don't you get out and find a job? When I was your age I was working for $3 a week in a store, and at the end of five years I owned the store.

SON: You can't do that nowadays. They have cash registers.

167 *Minus a Mind*

WIFE: I can't decide whether to go to a palmist or to a mind-reader.

HUSBAND: Go to a palmist. It's obvious that you have a palm.

168 *Couldn't Miss Him*

"Waiter, have you forgotten me?"

"Oh, no, sir, you are the ham."

169 *Call a Plumber*

CITY BOY: Say, Dad, how many kinds of milk are there?

FATHER: Well, there is evaporated milk, buttermilk, malted milk, and —but why do you want to know?

CITY BOY: Oh, I'm drawing a picture of a cow and I want to know how many spigots to put on her.

170   *Or Try Head Cheese*
"Yes, I know fish is brain food, but I don't care so much for fish. H'ain't there some other brain food?"
"Well, there's noodle soup."

171   *Hometown Custom*

BOY: Do you know, Dad, that in some parts of Africa a man doesn't know his wife until he marries her?
DAD: Why single out Africa?

172   *Boom in Agriculture*
"How's your farm work coming?"
"Oh fine! Got the billboard and hotdog stand painted and the filling station full of gas."

173   *Ready for the Worst*

DOROTHY: How long is it to my birthday?
MOTHER: Not very long dear.
DOROTHY: Well, is it time for me to begin to be a good girl?

174   *Game to the Last*
"So you are undertaking to keep bees?"
"Yes," answered Farmer Corntossel. "I don't want to miss anything, and I've been stung every other way there is."

175   *Immobilizing Bossy*
The little city boy stood and watched the farmer milk the only cow he had. The next morning the farmer was much excited, as the cow had been stolen during the night.

FARMER: Drat the thief that stole that cow. He's miles away from here by now.
LITTLE BOY: I wouldn't worry 'bout it, mister; they can't get so far away with it, 'cause you drained her crankcase last night.

176   *Strange*
Margery had been watching a fashionable wedding from outside the church. Returning home, she reported: "Well, I can't make out who she married. She went in with quite an old man and when she came out she was with a different one altogether."

177   *Sold!*
"Do you guarantee this hair restorer?"
"Better than that, sir. We give a comb with every bottle."

178   *Well, It Helps*

"Murphy got rich quick, didn't he?"

"He got rich so quick that he can't swing a golf club without spitting on his hands."

179   *He'll Catch Up*

NEIGHBOR: Where is your brother, Freddie?
FREDDIE: He's in the house playing a duet. I finished first.

180   *Good Description*

Johnny, who had been to the circus, was telling his teacher about the wonderful things he had seen.

"An' teacher," he cried, "they had one big animal they called the hip—hip—

"Hippopotamus, dear," prompted the teacher.

"I just can't say its name," exclaimed Johnny, "but it looks just like 9,000 pounds of liver."

181   *A Little Less of Something*

HE: You are always wishing for what you haven't got.
SHE: Well, what else can one wish for?

182   *He'll Get Along*

Small Bobby had been to a birthday party and, knowing his weakness, his mother looked him straight in the eye and said: "I hope you didn't ask for a second piece of cake?"

"No," replied Bobby. "I only asked Mrs. Smith for the recipe so you could make some like it and she gave me two more pieces just of her own accord."

183   *And Like It*

"I never clash with my boss."

"No?"

"No; he goes his way and I go his."

184   *Independent*

ARTHUR: So your new job makes you independent?
ALBERT: Absolutely. I get here any time I want before eight, and leave just when I please after five.

185   *Two Seasons*

It happened on New York's Lower East Side.

"How many seasons are there?" asked the teacher.

"Just two," answered Rachel.

"What are they?" inquired the puzzled instructor.

"Slack and busy," replied Rachel.

186   *That's Prevarication*

EMPLOYER (to newly
hired typist):   Now I hope you thoroughly understand the importance of punctuation?

STENOGRAPHER: Oh, yes, indeed. I always get to work on time.

187   *It's an Expensive Way*

"Has your son's college education been of any value?"

"Oh, yes; it cured his mother of bragging about him."

188   *Take That*

"It's going to be a real battle of wits, I tell you," said the sophomore member of the debating team.

"How brave of you," said his roommate, "to go unarmed."

189   *Not At All Exclusive*

DINER: Do you serve crabs here?

WAITER: We serve anyone; sit down.

190   *Methuselah*

Methuselah ate what he found on his plate, and never, as people do now, did he note the amount of the calorie count; he ate because it was chow.

He wasn't disturbed as at dinner he sat, devouring a roast or a pie, to think it was lacking in granular fat, or a couple of vitamins shy. He cheerfully chewed each species of food, unmindful of troubles or fears lest his health might be hurt by some fancy dessert—and he lived over nine hundred years!

191   *Forgive and Forget*

A man was arrested and brought before a commissioner for having a still on his premises. He was asked by the commissioner, "How do you plead?"

The man said: "I plead guilty and waive the hearing."

"What do you mean, 'Waive the hearing'?" asked the commissioner.

"I mean I don't want to hear no more about it."

192   *Milquetoast in Africa*

ANGRY GUIDE: Why didn't you shoot that tiger?

TIMID HUNTER: He didn't have the right kind of expression on his face for a rug.

193   *Pity the Moth*

"A moth leads an awful life."

"How come?"

"He spends the summer in a fur coat and the winter in a bathing suit."

194   *Surprise*

He was at the fountain pen counter making a purchase. "You see," he said, "I'm buying this for my wife."

"A surprise, eh?"

"I'll say so. You see, she's expecting a mink coat."

195   *Takes Experience*

A boyish-looking minister, serving his first church, noticed that one of his flock had been absent from services several Sundays in a row, so he decided to see her and ask the reason.

The woman shook her head and looked at him pityingly. "Son," she said, "you're not old enough to have sinned enough to have repented enough to be able to preach about it."

196   *Nerve*

"I envy the man who sang the tenor solo."

"Really? I thought he had a very poor voice."

"So did I, but just think of his nerve."

197   *Bankruptcy*

FIRST BUSINESSMAN:	Old Sharklee is going to retire from business.
SECOND BUSINESSMAN:	I heard him say that before.
FIRST BUSINESSMAN:	I know, but the judge said it this time.

198   *Conceit*

"I hope you don't think I'm conceited," he said, after he had finished telling her all about himself.

"Oh, no," she replied, "but I'm just wondering how you keep from giving three hearty cheers whenever you look at yourself in the mirror."

199   *That's Different*

STRANGER IN TOWN:	Did you see a pedestrian go by here awhile ago?
VILLAGER:	No, sir. I've been here for an hour, and there hasn't been a thing go by except one man, and he was walking.

200   *Are They Strict?*

FROSH: Are they very strict at Cornell?

SOPH: Are they? Why, when a man dies during a lecture, they prop him up in the seat until the end of the hour.

201   *Honestly?*

A candidate came home in the small hours and gave his wife the glorious news:

"Darling, I have been elected."

She was delighted. "Honestly?" she said.

He laughed in an embarrassed way. "Oh, why bring that up?"

202   *How Many Learn It?*

YOUNG MOTHER: Nurse, what is the most difficult thing for a young mother to learn?

NURSE: That other people have perfect children too.

203   *Suitability*

"Aren't some of the hats women wear absurd?"

"Yes," replied Miss Cayenne, "and yet when some people put them on they do look so appropriate."

204   *Opportunity Knocks*

A new pulpit having been erected, the minister and the verger tested the acoustics.

"Stand well to the back and see how this sounds," said the minister, repeating the text.

"Fine, Minister, fine!"

"Now you go up into the pulpit and say anything you like."

The verger went up. "I have not had a raise in pay for three years. How does that sound?"

205   *Take the Bad with the Good*

WIFE (heatedly):   You're lazy, you're worthless, you're bad-tempered, you're shiftless, you're a liar.

HUSBAND (reasonably):   Well, my dear, no man is perfect.

206   *Last Stand*

The father was reading the school report which had just been handed to him by his hopeful son. His brow was wrathful as he read: "English, poor; French, weak; mathematics, fair." He gave a glance of disgust at the quaking lad. "Well, Dad," said the son, "it isn't as good as it might be, but have you seen that?" And he pointed to the next line, which read: "Health, excellent."

207   *Letters From Home*
A college student wrote a letter home, and it said in its entirety: "Dear Mom and Dad, Please write soon, even if it's only a few dollars."

208   *Sign Reading*
A denizen of the hills, who was appearing as a witness in a lawsuit, was being questioned as to his educational qualifications by the plaintiff's lawyer.

"Can you write?" asked the lawyer.

"Nope."

"Can you read?"

"Wa'al, I kin read figgers pretty well, but I don't do so good with writin'."

"How is that?"

"Wa'al take these here signs along the road when I want to go sommers; I kin read how fur, but not whurto."

209   *Salesmanship*

CUSTOMER:	Are those eggs strictly fresh?
GROCER (to his clerk):	Feel of those eggs, George, and see if they're cool enough to sell yet.

210   *Why Not?*
At a meeting of senior citizens, the speaker reached the climax of his talk and declared: "The time has come when we must get rid of socialism and communism and anarchism, and . . ."

At that point, a little old lady at the rear of the room arose feebly but with enthusiasm and shouted: "Let's throw out rheumatism, too!"

211   *Eternity Case*
The doctor's five-year-old answered the call at the door. "Is the doctor in?" inquired the caller.

"No, sir."

"Have you any idea when he will be back?"

"I don't know, sir—he went out on an eternity case."

212   *Slow Service*
A kindergarten tot described the painting "Whistler's Mother" as: "It shows a nice old lady waiting for the repairman to bring back her TV set."

213   *Romeo Miz'n*

> Sam held her hand and she held his'n
> And then they hugged and went to kiz'n.
> They did not know her dad had riz'n.
> Madder than hops and simply siz'n;
> And really 'tiz'n right to liz'n.
> But Sam got hiz'n and went out whiz'n.

214   *Young Webster*

TEACHER: Johnny, can you tell me the difference between perseverance
           and obstinacy?

JOHNNY: One is a strong will, and the other is a strong won't.

215   *Yes!*

"Mr. Brown, these are very small oysters you are selling me."

"Yes, ma'am."

"They don't appear to be very fresh, either."

"Then it's lucky they're small."

216   *Ho, Hum*

An English tourist was on his first visit to Niagara Falls, and the guide
was trying to impress him with its magnificence.

"Grand," suggested the guide.

The visitor did not seem much impressed.

"Millions of gallons a minute," explained the guide.

"How many in a day?" asked the tourist.

"Oh, billions and billions," answered the guide.

The visitor looked across, and down and up, as if gauging the flow.
Then he turned away with a shrug, apparently unaffected.

"Runs all night, too, I suppose," he remarked.

217   *A Riddle to End All Riddles*

A train operated by a Norwegian engineer starts to New York from
Albany just as a train with a drunken engineer leaves New York for
Albany. There's only one track, no switches or sidings, yet the trains do
not collide. Why? Because Norse is Norse and Souse is Souse and never
the twain shall meet.

218   *Economics*

"It's tough to pay two dollars a pound for meat."

"Mmm. But it's tougher when you pay only one dollar."

219   *It's Perfect*

"Is that hair tonic any good?"

"Say, I spilled some of it on my comb last week and now it's a brush."

220   *In a Big Way*

A tourist was enjoying the wonders of California as pointed out by a native.

"What beautiful grapefruit," he said as they passed through a grove of citrus trees.

"Oh, those lemons are a bit small owing to a comparatively bad season," explained the Californian.

"What are those enormous blossoms?" questioned the tourist a little bit farther on.

"Just a patch of dandelions," answered the guide.

Presently they reached the Sacramento River.

"Ah," said the tourist, "someone's radiator is leaking."

221   *Farsighted*

A father was taking his blonde toddler on a tour of the zoo and they had stopped outside the lion's cage.

"Daddy," the little tyke asked, "if the lion gets out and eats you up, what bus do I take to get home?"

222   *Librarians*

A newspaper in the county seat printed the following announcement: "The Public Library will close for two weeks, beginning August 3, for the annual cleaning and vacation of the librarians."

223   *An Old Saying at Dinner in India*

More was prepared than was served.
More was served than was eaten.
More was eaten than was necessary.

224   *Simpler*

"Give me a glass of milk and a muttered buffin."

"You mean a buffered muttin."

"No, I mean a muffered buttin."

"Why not take doughnuts and milk?"

225   *Viewpoint*

SHE: Doesn't the bride look stunning?

HE: Yeah, and doesn't the groom look stunned?

226   *Happy Ending*

Three Britons, each hard of hearing:

FIRST LIMEY:	Is this Wembley?
SECOND PELTER:	No, it's Thursday.
THIRD LIMEY:	So am I. Let's have a Scotch and soda.

227   *Current Case*

A man was arraigned for assault and brought before the judge.

JUDGE:	What is your name, occupation, and what are you charged with?
PRISONER:	My name is Sparks; I am an electrician, and I'm charged with battery.
JUDGE (after recovering his equilibrium):	Officer, put this guy in a dry cell.

228   *Grammar*

"Are your father and mother in?" asked the visitor of the small boy who opened the door.

"They was in," said the child, "but they is out."

"They was in. They is out. Where's your grammar?"

"She's gone upstairs," said the boy, "for a nap."

229   *Right Answer*

An old man had the habit of always prophesying great calamities to his friends. One day he was predicting to a disgusted listener that a great famine was coming soon, and dolefully asked: "And what would you say, my friend, if in a short time the rivers in our country would all dry up?"

"I'd say," was the tired answer, "go thou and do likewise."

230   *Addition*

RICH MAN:	There's no sense in teaching the boy to count over 100. He can hire accountants to do his bookkeeping.
TUTOR:	Yes, sir, but he'll want to play his own game of golf, won't he?

231   *Cautious*

Father was standing at the edge of a cliff admiring the sea below, the sandwiches clutched in his hand. His son approached him and tugged at his coat.

"Mother says it isn't safe here," said the boy, "and you're either to come away or else give me the sandwiches."

232 *Open-Handed*

FIRST CADDIE: What's your man like, Skeeter?

SECOND CADDIE: Left-handed, and keeps his change in his right-hand pocket.

233 *Efficient Nagging*

"My husband is an efficiency expert in a large office."

"What does an efficiency expert do?"

"Well, if we women did it, they'd call it nagging."

234 *Practically Bald*

CUSTOMER: Does a man with as little hair as I've got have to pay full price to have it cut?

BARBER: Yes, and sometimes more. We usually charge double when we have to hunt for the hair.

235 *Of Course*

PROFESSOR: I forgot my umbrella this morning.

STUDENT: How did you remember you forgot it?

PROFESSOR: Well, I missed it when I raised my hand to close it, after it had stopped raining.

236 *Correct Spelling*

A teacher was taking her first golf lesson. "Is the word spelled 'put' or 'putt'?" she asked the instructor.

" 'Putt' is correct," he replied. " 'Put' means to place a thing where you want it. 'Putt' means a vain attempt to do the same thing."

237 *Of Course Not*

ARTIST: That, sir, is a cow grazing.

VISITOR: Where is the grass?

ARTIST: The cow has eaten it.

VISITOR: But where is the cow?

ARTIST: You don't suppose she'd be fool enough to stay there after she'd eaten all the grass, do you?

238 *She Knows*

A man who had been keeping company with a girl for a number of years took her out one night to a Chinese restaurant. They began studying the menu and he asked, "How would you like your rice—fried or boiled?"

She looked at him and said: "Thrown."

239 *He Almost Got Angry*

A bricklayer working on top of a high building carelessly dropped a brick, which landed on the head of his helper below.

"You better be careful up there, boss," said the helper, dusting his helmet off. "You made me bite my tongue!"

240 *A Burned Offering*

SHE (on the telephone): I'm afraid your dinner will be burned a little tonight, darling.

HE: What's the matter? Did they have a fire at the delicatessen?

241 *What Mother Calls Father*

TEACHER (pointing to a deer at the zoo): Johnny, what is that?

JOHNNY: I don't know.

TEACHER: What does your mother call your father?

JOHNNY: Don't tell me that's a louse!

242 *Cure for Nervousness*

PHYLLIS: Were you nervous when George proposed?

MABEL: No, dear, that's when I stopped being nervous.

243 *Speaking from Experience*

WALLY: Gee Pop, there's a man in the circus who jumps on a horse's back, slips underneath, catches hold of its tail, and finishes up on the horse's neck.

FATHER: That's nothing. I did all that, and more, the first time I ever rode a horse.

244   *Why Worry about It?*

TEACHER: Take 13½ from 29¼ and what's the difference?
CLASS DUNCE: Yeah, that's what I say, who cares anyhow?

245   *Thoughtful Reply*

A high school freshman just couldn't seem to behave. Nearly every day he was sent to the principal's office for one misdemeanor or another. The principal finally said to him: "This is the fifth time that you have been sent to my office this week for misbehaving. Now what do you have to say for yourself?"

I'm glad it's Friday," he said.

246   *Modest*

GOODSBY: Did anyone in your family ever make a brilliant marriage?
HAREFOOT: Only my wife.

247   *The Inevitable End*

> Man wants but little here below,
> He's ready to admit it,
> And if Uncle Sam keeps taxing him
> He's pretty sure to get it.

248   *Remiss*

VICAR (benevolently):   And what is your name, my little man?
SMALL BOY: Well, that's the limit. Why, it was you that christened me.

249   *Having Wonderful Time*

Says a postcard from a truth-telling vacationist at an expensive mountain resort: "Having a wonderful time; wish I could afford it."

250   *Modern Youth*

"Is your daughter home from school for the holidays?"
"I think so. One of her sisters said she saw her day before yesterday."

251   *Unpredictable*

"I turned the way I signaled," said the driver indignantly, after the crash.
"I know it," retorted the man. "That's what fooled me."

252   *Live on His Income*
"Do you love me?"
    "Yes, handsome."
"Can you live on my income?"
    "Yes, but what will you live on?"

253   *Knew It All the Time*

JIM: When you proposed to her, I suppose she said "This is so sudden"?

GEORGE: No, she was honest about it and said: "The suspense has been terrible."

254   *Doubtful Character*

CUSTOMER: Remember that cheese you sold me yesterday?

GROCER: Yes, madam.

CUSTOMER: Did you say it was imported or deported from Switzerland?

255   *Too Coarse*

MR. NEWLYWED: What's wrong with this cake, dear? It tastes kind of gritty.

MRS. NEWLYWED: Don't be silly, darling. The recipe calls for three whole eggs and I guess I didn't get the shells beaten up fine enough.

256   *Sponged Cake*

HUBBY: What are we having for dessert tonight, dear?

WIFE: Sponge cake. I sponged the eggs from Mrs. Brown, the flour from Mrs. Smith, and the milk from Mrs. Jones.

257   *Too Long to Wait*
"What inspired the old-time pioneers to set forth in their covered wagons?"
    "Well, maybe they didn't want to wait about thirty years for a train."

258   *Tough On Everybody*
"I feel so sorry for the Joneses."
    "Why?"
    "With all this inflation, they can hardly keep up with themselves."

259   *Commercial*

BRITISH GUIDE
(showing places of
historical interest):   And it was in this room that Lord Wellington
received his first commission.

INSURANCE MAN: How many renewals?

260   *He Must Be an Economist*

"I'm glad you're so impressed, dear, by all these explanations I have been giving you about banking and economics," remarked the young husband.

"Yes, darling. It seems wonderful that anybody could know as much as you do about money without having any."

261   *Criticism*

A woman who had been in modest circumstances before she came into a large inheritance attended a baseball game. She was wearing a smart tweed outfit with a diamond brooch.

"My dear," said a woman friend, "you shouldn't wear such a large piece of jewelry with tweeds."

"I know," snapped the wealthy woman. "That's what I always said . . . before I owned one!"

262   *Or Minnie the Moocher*

"Now boys," said the teacher, "tell me the signs of the zodiac. You first, Thomas."

"Taurus, the Bull."

"Right! Now, you, Harold, another one."

"Cancer, the Crab."

"Right again. And now it's your turn, Albert."

The boy looked puzzled, hesitated a moment, and then blurted out, "Mickey, the Mouse."

263   *Hard Problem*

A father had taken his small son to church. The boy listened attentively without saying a word until the clergyman announced: "We will now sing hymn two hundred and twenty-two: 'Ten Thousand Times Ten Thousand,' two hundred and twenty-two."

The puzzled boy nudged his father. "Daddy, we don't have to work this out, do we?"

264   *Injustice*

TENANT: This roof is so bad that it rains on our heads. How long is this going to continue?

OWNER: What do you think I am, a weather prophet?

265   *Cure*

VOICE OVER TELEPHONE: I can't sleep, Doctor. Can you do anything for me?

DOCTOR: Hold the 'phone and I'll sing you a lullaby.

266   *Witness*

The men were swapping stories.

"When I was logging up in Oregon," said one of them, "I saw a wildcat come right up to the skidder one day. It was a fierce beast, but with great presence of mind, I threw a bucket of water in its face and it slunk away."

"Boys," said a man sitting in the corner, "I can vouch for the truth of that story. A few minutes after that happened, I was coming down the side of the hill. I met this wildcat and, as is my habit, stopped to stroke its whiskers. Boys, those whiskers were wet!"

267   *Worried*

A visitor at the Capitol was accompanied by his small son. The little boy watched from the gallery when the House came to order.

"Why did the minister pray for all those men, Pop?"

"He didn't. He looked them over and prayed for the country."

268   *Truth*

TEACHER (brightly):   As we walk out-of-doors on a cold winter's morning, and look about us, what do we see on every hand?

CLASS: Gloves!

269   *We Wonder Too*

HUSBAND: Have you ever wondered what you would do if you had Rockefeller's income?

WIFE: No, but I have often wondered what he would do if he had mine!

270   *Darn!*

"Does your husband talk in his sleep?"

"No, and it's terribly exasperating. He just grins."

271   *Epithet*

"Yes, the smallest things seem to upset my wife. The other day she was doing a crossword puzzle and she asked me, 'What is a female sheep?' I said, 'Ewe,' and she burst into tears."

272   *Toasts*

To woman: the only loved autocrat who governs without law; and decides without appeal.

Here's to the light that lies in women's eyes,
And lies and lies and lies.

273   *Generous*

The young bride was extolling the virtues of her husband to a friend. "George is just the most generous man in the world," she declared. "He gives me everything credit can buy."

274   *Eye for Eye*

A small boy leading a donkey passed by an army camp. A couple of soldiers wanted to have some fun with the lad.

"What are you holding onto your brother so tight for, sonny?" said one of them.

"So he won't join the army," the youngster replied without blinking an eye.

275   *Too Easy*

During a review one Sunday, the teacher asked if the class knew who the twin boys were in the Bible.

"That's easy," said Charles. "First and Second Samuel."

276   *Good Formula*

When the late Mr. and Mrs. Henry Ford celebrated their golden wedding anniversary, a reporter asked them: "To what do you attribute your fifty years of successful married life?"

"The formula," said Ford, "is the same formula I have always used in making cars—just stick to one model."

277   *Still Circulating*

An old gentleman approached a nattily attired man at an elaborate wedding.

"Pardon me," said the old man, "are you the bridegroom?"

The young man shook his head dolefully. "No, sir," he replied, "I was eliminated in the semi-finals!"

278   *Two Years Should Do It*

HER SUITOR: Sir, I came to—er ask you whether you would object—er —to my marrying your daughter.

HER FATHER: My boy, you're only twenty-one and my daughter is twenty-seven. Why not wait a few years till you're both about the same age?

279   *Highly Competent*

A man of six feet eight inches applied for a job as a lifeguard.

"Can you swim?" said the official.

"No, but I can wade pretty far out."

280   *Slow Motion*

PATIENT: What do you charge for extracting a tooth?

DENTIST: Fifty dollars.

PATIENT: Fifty dollars for only two seconds' work?

DENTIST: Well, if you wish, I can extract it very slowly.

281   *Working Late at the Office*

"I don't see Charlie half as much as I used to."

"You should have married him when you had the chance."

"I did."

282   *Not That Bold*

MA: That new couple next door seem to be very devoted. He kisses her every time they meet. Why don't you do that?

PA: I don't know her well enough.

283   *Credit*

A man mortgaged his home to buy an automobile. Then he tried to mortgage the car to get money to build a garage.

"How are you going to buy gas?" inquired the man of whom the loan was asked.

"Well," replied the other slowly, "if I own a house, a car, and a garage, I should think any dealer would be willing to trust me for gas."

284   *Correct*

NEW TEACHER: Where is the elephant found?

JANE: It's so big, it's hardly ever lost.

285   *Too Inquisitive*

PROFESSOR: And whatever on earth made you write a paragraph like that?

STUDENT: I quoted it, sir, from Dickens.

PROFESSOR: Beautiful lines, aren't they?

286   *Power*

"What is the greatest water power known to man?"
  "Woman's tears."

287   *Wrong Number*

"I called on Mabel last night, and I was hardly inside the door before her mother asked me about my intentions."
  "That must have been embarrassing."
  "Yes. But the worst of it was Mabel called from upstairs and said: 'That isn't the one, mother!' "

288   *Sad Mistake*

MR. BROWN: So your son had to leave college on account of poor eyesight?

MR. WHITE: Yes, he mistook the dean of women for a coed.

289   *O Wonderful Horse!*

O horse, you are a wonderful thing;
No buttons to push, no horn to honk;
You start yourself, no clutch to slip;
No spark to miss, no gears to strip;
No license buying every year,
With plates to screw on front and rear;
No gas bills climbing up each day,
Stealing the joy of life away;
No speed cops chugging in your rear,
Yelling summons in your ear.
Your innertubes are all O.K.
And thank the Lord, they stay that way;
Your spark plugs never miss and fuss;

Your motor never makes us cuss.
Your frame is good for many a mile;
Your body never changes style.
Your wants are few and easy met;
You've something on the auto yet.

—*Northwestern Banker*

290   *Following Orders*

BILL: You look all out of sorts. What's the matter?

JACK: Plenty. On account of my rheumatism the doctor told me to avoid all dampness—and you've no idea how silly I feel sitting in an empty bathtub and going over myself with a vacuum cleaner.

291   *Schemer*

BILLY (who has eaten his apple):   Let's play Adam and Eve.

SMALL SISTER: How do you play that, Billy?

BILLY: Well, you tempt me to eat your apple and I'll give in.

292   *Knowledge*

A junior high school student wrote about the "writ of hideous corpus" in an examination.

Another junior high student quoted thus from the Declaration of Independence: "Every man should be divided equal."—*NEA Journal*

293   *Taking No Chances*

PASSERBY: Kinda cold sitting on your front porch this weather, isn't it, Mr. Davis?

MR. DAVIS: Well, yes, a little, but you see my wife is taking her singing lesson, and I don't want the neighbors to think I'm arguing with her.

294   *The Way It Sounded*

WAITER: May I help you with that soup, sir?

DINER: What do you mean, help me? I don't need any help.

WAITER: Sorry, sir. From the sound, I thought you might want to be dragged ashore.

295   *Reason Enough*

"Just tell me one good reason why you can't buy a new car now," said the persistent automobile salesman.

"Well, I'll tell you, man," replied the farmer. "I'm still paying installments on the car I swapped for the car I traded in as part payment on the car I own now."

296   *Slight Transposition*

The visitor paid his bill at the fashionable hotel, and as he went out, he noticed a sign near the door: "Have you left anything?"

So he went back and spoke to the manager. "That sign's wrong," he said. "It should read 'Have you anything left?' "

297   *Spoiled His Wish*

SONNY: Kin I have the wishbone, mother?

MOTHER: Not until you've eaten your spinach.

SONNY: Yes, but I wanted to wish I didn't have to eat it.

298   *His Oversight*

WAITER: How did you order your steak, sir?

DINER (impatiently):   Orally, but I realize now I should have ordered it by mail in advance.

299   *Candid Answer*

BOYFRIEND: You're dancing with me tonight, and I suppose tomorrow you'll be making a date with some other man.

GIRLFRIEND: Yes, with my chiropodist.

300   *Spelling*

TEACHER: Why did you spell "pneumatic" n-e-u-m-a-t-i-c?

PUPIL: The "k" on my typewriter isn't working.

301   *Quite Important*

A Chinese was worried by a vicious-looking dog.

"Don't be afraid of him," the owner reassured. "You know the old proverb, 'A barking dog never bites.' "

"Yes," replied the Chinese, "you know ploverb, me know ploverb, but do dog know ploverb?"

302   *The Parrot*

Orville Wright was reproached by a friend for not taking up the challenge of some that it was Professor Langley, and not the Wright brothers, who flew first.

"Your trouble," said the friend, "is that you're too taciturn. You don't assert yourself enough. You should talk more."

"My friend," replied Mr. Wright, "the best talker and the worst flier among the birds is the parrot!"

303   *Evolution of a Man's Ambition*

Two oldtimers were discussing the evolution of their ambitions.

"When I was twenty I made up my mind to get rich," one of them said.

"But you never got rich."

"No. By the time I was twenty-five I decided it was easier to change my mind than to make a million dollars. Once I wanted to be a circus clown, then a football star and then I wanted fame. Now I want to make ends meet and get an old age pension."

304   *So Unselfish*

TEACHER: Unselfishness means going without something you need, voluntarily. Can you give me an example of that Bobby?

BOBBY: Yessum. Sometimes I go without a bath when I need one.

305   *Logical Request*

Three-year-old Bobby didn't like the routine of being scrubbed, especially when soap was applied.

"Bobby, don't you want to be nice and clean?" his mother asked.

"Sure," replied Bobby, "but can't you just dust me?"

306   *Secondhand*

DAUGHTER OF FIRST FILM STAR: How do you like your new father?

DAUGHTER OF SECOND FILM STAR: Oh, he's very nice.

DAUGHTER OF FIRST FILM STAR: Yes, isn't he? We had him last year.

307   *Genesis*

A surgeon, an architect, and a politician were arguing as to whose profession was the oldest.

Said the surgeon: "Eve was made from Adam's rib, and that surely was a surgical operation."

"Maybe," said the architect, "but prior to that, order was created out of chaos, and that was an architectural job."

"But," interrupted the politician, "somebody created the chaos first!"

308   *Sorry, Wrong Number*

A young woman meant to call a record shop, but dialed the wrong number and got a private home instead.

"Do you have 'Eyes of Blue,' and 'Love That's Real'?" she asked.

"Well, no," answered the perplexed homeowner. "But I have a wife and eleven children."

"Is that a record?" the surprised woman inquired.

"I don't think so," replied the man, "But it's as close as I want to get."

309   *A Little Slow*

New typist (following rapid-fire dictation): "Now, Mr. Jones, what did you say between 'Dear Sir' and 'Sincerely yours'?"

310   *Peace*

Grandmother decided to send a playpen to her daughter on the arrival of her fourth child.

"Thank you so much for the pen," she wrote. "It is wonderful—I sit in it every afternoon and read. The children can't get near me."

311   *Not Even on Cable TV*

TEACHER: Where is the English Channel?

HERBIE: I don't know, ma'am. We don't get that station on our television set at home.

312   *Makes a Difference*

PASSENGER: Have I time to say goodby to my wife?

STEWARDESS: I don't know, sir; how long have you been married?

313   *Gradual Progress*

VICTIM: Hey, that wasn't the tooth I wanted pulled.

DENTIST: Calm yourself, I'm coming to it!

314   *Tactful*

FIRST CLERK: Have you and your boss ever had any differences of opinion?

SECOND CLERK: Yes, but he doesn't know it!

315   *Definition*

An instructor was conducting a science course at a high school. One of the requirements in the written quiz was: "Define a bolt and nut and explain the difference, if any."

A student wrote: "A bolt is a thing like a stick of hard metal such as iron with a bunch on one end and a lot of scratching wound around the other end. A nut is similar to the bolt only just the opposite being a hole in a little chunk of iron sawed off short with wrinkles around the inside of the hole."

The startled professor marked that one with a large A.

316   *Obliging*

FAT MAN (in a movie to a little boy sitting behind him):   Can't you see, little fellow?

LITTLE FELLOW: Not a thing.

FAT MAN: Then keep your eye on me and laugh when I do.

317   *A Long Way*

The fine symphony orchestra from the big city had played in a small New England town, the first experience of the kind for many of the inhabitants. Next day some of the oldtimers gathered in the general store and expressed their opinions. The comment of one of the oldest inhabitants was: "All I got to say is—it was an awful long way to bring that big bass drum only to bang it twice."

318   *Difference*

"That means fight where I come from!"

"Well, why don't you fight then?"

" 'Cause I ain't where I come from."

319   *Enough*

The telephone rang in the clergyman's office of the Washington church which President Franklin Roosevelt attended. An eager voice inquired, "Do you expect the President to be in church Sunday?"

"That," answered the clergyman, "I cannot promise. But we expect

God to be there and we fancy that should be incentive enough for a reasonably large attendance."—*Together*

320 *Ameliorating Circumstances*

An old farmer was moodily regarding the ravages of the flood.

"Hiram," yelled a neighbor, "your pigs were all washed down the creek."

"How about Flaherty's pigs?" asked the farmer.

"They're gone, too."

"And Larsen's?"

"Yes."

"Humph!" ejaculated the farmer, cheering up. " 'Tain't as bad as I thought."

321 *Moving Right Along*

"A telegram from George, dear."

"Well, did he pass the examination this time?"

"No, but he is almost at the top of the list of those who failed."

322 *What a Life!*

HUSBAND (reading): The tusks of 4,700 elephants were used last year to make billiard balls.

WIFE: Isn't it wonderful that such big beasts can be taught to do such delicate work!

323 *Following Orders*

MR. WIMPUS: You sure made a poor job of painting the door.

MRS. WIMPUS: Well, you declared this morning that it needed painting badly.

324 *It's a Clean Life!*

MOTHER: Junior, go wash your hands and face.

JUNIOR: Aw, I just took a bath this morning.

MOTHER: Then go wash the bathtub.

325 *Food Jargon*

She balanced herself daintily on a stool at the hamburger counter, looked over the pastries and, after a few minutes of indecision, addressed the counter man: "I would like to have two hamburgers well done; no pickle, but you may put a little mustard on them, if you don't mind."

Without turning his head, the counter man shouted to the short-order cook: "Elmers, on two; hobnailed; hold the pucker and make 'em dirty."

326   *Wrong Impression*

JUNIOR: That man wasn't a painless dentist like he advertised.

SENIOR: Why? Did he hurt you?

JUNIOR: No, but he yelled when I bit his thumb, just like any other dentist.

327   *Correct*

TEACHER: Now, which boy can name five things that contain milk?

JIMMIE: Butter, cheese, ice cream, and two cows.

328   *Payment*

An editor once received a letter accompanying a number of would-be jokes in which the writer asked: "What will you give me for these?"

"Ten yards' start," was the editor's offer.

329   *His Error*

The owner of a cheap watch brought the timepiece into the jeweler's shop to see what could be done for it. "The mistake I made, of course," he admitted, "was in dropping this watch."

"Well, I don't suppose you could help that," the jeweler remarked. "The mistake you made was picking it up."

330   *Good Question*

The optimist said, "A year from now we will all be begging."

The pessimist asked, "From whom?"

331   *His Good Deed!*

A naval officer fell overboard. He was rescued by a deck hand. The officer asked how he could reward him.

"The best way, sir," said the gob, "is to say nothing about it. If the other fellows knew I'd pulled you out, they'd throw me in."

332   *Hopes Realized*

BILL: Have you ever realized any of your childhood hopes?

PETE: Yes; when mother used to comb my hair, I often wished I didn't have any.

333   A "Tense" Situation

A schoolteacher was correcting a boy who said, "I ain't gwine."

TEACHER: You have not studied your lesson. Listen: "We are not going. You are not going. They are not going." Now do you understand?

BOY: Yes, teacher. Nobody ain't gwine.

334   Identified

SENTRY: Halt; who's there?

VOICE: American.

SENTRY: Advance and recite the second verse of "The Star Spangled Banner."

VOICE: I don't know it.

SENTRY: Proceed, American.

335   Possibly

"What a boy you are for asking questions," said the father. "I'd like to know what would have happened if I'd asked as many questions when I was a boy."

"Perhaps," suggested the young hopeful, "you'd have been able to answer some of mine."

336   Question

"Did youse git anyt'ing?" whispered the burglar on guard as his pal emerged from the window.

"Naw, de bloke wot lives here is a lawyer," replied the other in disgust.

"Dat's hard luck," said the first. "Did youse lose anyt'ing?"

337   Head of the Firm

"Is this Peabody, Finchley, Longworth, and Fitzgerald?"

"Yes, this is Peabody, Finchley, Longworth, and Fitzgerald."

"I want to speak to Mr. Smith."

338   People Are Too Suspicious

JUDGE: How could you swindle people who trusted in you?

PRISONER: But, Judge, people who don't trust you cannot be swindled.

339   Sunk

Two old settlers, confirmed bachelors, sat in the backwoods. The conversation drifted from politics and finally got around to cooking.

I got one o' them cookery books once, but couldn't do nothing with it."

"Too much fancy work in it, eh?"

"You've said it! Every one o' them recipes began the same way: 'Take a clean dish'—and that settled me."

340   *New Twist*

HOUSEHOLDER: Well, I see you brought your tools with you.

PLUMBER: Yeah, I'm getting more absent-minded every day.

341   *Rapid*

A golf professional, hired by a big department store to give golf lessons, was approached by two women.

"Do you wish to learn to play golf, madam?" he asked one.

"Oh, no," she said, "it's my friend who wants to learn. I learned yesterday."

342   *How're You Betting?*

"The people in our part of town are watching the result of a very interesting conflict."

"What is it?"

"An irresistible blonde just met an immovable bachelor."

343   *Poser*

"Why does a woman say she's been shopping when she hasn't bought a thing?"

"Why does a man say he's been fishing when he hasn't caught anything?"

344   *More Next Week*

Dora had returned from Sunday school, where she had been for the first time.

"What did my little daughter learn this morning?" asked her father.

"That I am a child of Satan," was the beaming reply.

345   *Public Speaking*

Someone has said that the writer of Psalm 91 must have been speaking at a luncheon club when he wrote about "The Destruction that wasteth at noon day." Perhaps he referred to banquets when he spoke of "The Pestilence that walketh in darkness."—Charles F. Banning, in *Church Management*

346   *Nothing to Worry About*

Overheard on the beach: "Mummy, may I go in for a swim?"

"Certainly not, my dear, it's far too deep."

"But Daddy is swimming."

"Yes, dear, but he's insured."

347   *On the Fairways*

GOLFER: Listen, kid, I'll swat you with a club if you don't stop making cracks about my game!

CADDIE: Yeah, but you wouldn't know which club to use!

348   *Here We Go*

LADY: So you are on a submarine. What do you do?

SAILOR: Oh, I run forward, ma'am, and hold her nose when we want to take a dive.

349   *Big Game Hunters*

Two nimrods flew deep into remote Canada for elk hunting. Their pilot, seeing that they had bagged six elk, told them the plane could carry only four out.

"But the plane that carried us out last year was exactly like this one." the hunters protested. "The horsepower was the same, the weather was similar, and we had six elk then."

Hearing this, the pilot reluctantly agreed to try. They loaded up and took off, but sure enough there was insufficient power to climb out of the valley with all that weight, and they crashed. As they stumbled from the wreckage, one hunter asked the other if he knew where they were.

"Well, I'm not sure." replied the second, "but I think we are about two miles from where we crashed last year." *Walter Johnson, Rotarian, Amarillo, Texas*

350   *Smart Pills*

A sick man went to the pharmacist with some prescriptions from his doctor. The chemist explained to him: "You have three kinds of pills here: one to soothe your nerves, another to take away your headache, and the third to calm your stomach."

The man was amazed. "Tell me," he said, "how on earth can three little pills know just where to go?"

351   *Justified*

Johnnie was gazing at his one-day-old brother, who lay squealing and wailing in his crib.

"Has he come from Heaven?" inquired Johnnie.

"Yes, dear."

"No wonder they put him out."

352   *Call the Manager*

"Look here, waiter, is this peach or apple pie?"

"Can't you tell from the taste?"

"No, I can't."

"Well, then, what difference does it make?"

353   *And Collect Your Commission*

"Doctor, I want you to look after my office while I'm on my vacation."

"But I've just graduated, Doctor. I've had no experience."

"That's all right, my boy. My practice is strictly fashionable. Tell the men to play golf and send the lady patients abroad."

354   *Let's Go!*

SONNY: Mother, we're going to play elephants at the zoo and we want you to help us.

MOTHER: What on earth can I do?

SONNY: You can be the lady who gives them peanuts and candy.

355   *There's a Time*

There's a time to part and a time to meet,
There's a time to sleep and a time to eat,
There's a time to work and a time to play,
There's a time to sing and a time to pray,
There's a time that's glad and a time that's blue,
There's a time to plan and a time to do,
There's a time to grin and to show your grit,
But there never was a time to quit.

356   *Budget*

"What is a budget?"

"Well, it is a method of worrying before you spend instead of afterward."

357   *Gentlemen of the Jury*

The prosecuting counsel was having a little trouble with a rather difficult witness. Exasperated by the man's evasive answers, he asked him if he was acquainted with any of the jury.

"Yes, sir, more than half of them," replied the man in the box.

"Are you willing to swear that you know more than half of them?" asked the counsel.

"If it comes to that, I'm willing to swear that I know more than all of 'em put together," said the witness.

358   *The Good Old Joke*

Here's to the joke, the good old joke,
The joke that our fathers told;
It is ready tonight and is jolly and bright
As it was in the days of old.

When Adam was young it was on his tongue,
And Noah got in the swim
By telling the jest as the brightest and best
That ever happened to him.

So here's to the joke, the good old joke—
We'll hear it again tonight.
It's health we will quaff; that will help us to laugh,
And to treat it in manner polite.

—*Lew Dockstader*

359   *Who's Driving This Car?*

Timid wife (to husband who was dozing at the wheel): "I don't mean to dictate to you, George, but isn't that billboard coming at us awfully fast?"

360   *And a Dollar*

TEACHER: Tommy, if your father could save a dollar a week for three weeks, what would he have?

TOMMY: A radio, a new suit, and a lot of furniture.

361   *Where It Belonged*

JUDGE (to amateur burglar):   So they caught you with this bundle of silverware. Whom did you plunder?

YEGG: Two fraternity houses, your honor.

JUDGE (to sergeant):   Call up the downtown hotels and distribute the stuff.

362 *Reverse English*

TEACHER: Correct the sentence, "Before any damage could be done the fire was put out by the volunteer fire brigade."

BOY: The fire was put out before any damage could be done by the volunteer fire brigade.

363 *Too Many Committee Meetings*

An Englishman watched his first American football game. He looked intently as the team gathered into a huddle after each play. His American host asked what he thought of the proceedings.

"Not a bad sport," remarked the visitor, "but they do seem to engage in an excessive number of committee meetings."

364 *Too Good*

A newspaper man named Fling
Could make "copy" from any old thing.
But the copy he wrote
Of a five dollar note
Was so good he is now in Sing Sing.

—*Columbia Jester*

365 *Acquainted*

JUDGE: Have you ever seen the prisoner at the bar?

WITNESS: Yes, that's where I met him.

366 *City and Country*

AMOS: Did you find much difference between the city and the country, Hiram?

HIRAM: They h'ain't much difference. In the country you go to bed feeling all in, and you get up feeling fine. In the city you go to bed feeling fine, and you get up feeling all in.

367 *No Objection*

SUITOR: I am seeking your daughter's hand, sir. Have you any objection?

FATHER: None at all. Take the one that's always in my pocket.

368   *Not So Dumb*

JACK: Why is your car painted blue on one side and red on the other?

MAC: It's a great scheme. You should hear the witnesses contradicting each other.

369   *Foolin' Himself*

A boy was taking a stroll through a cemetery and reading the inscriptions on tombstones. He came to one which declared: "Not dead, but sleeping."

After contemplating the phrase for a moment, and scratching his head, he exclaimed: "He sure ain't foolin' nobody but himself."

370   *Repartee*

The audience in the college auditorium was impatiently awaiting the appearance of the out-of-town entertainer, who was already an hour late. The chairman of the evening, fearing the people would leave, scribbled a frantic appeal for help and had it passed down the aisle to Professor B, who was a ready and witty speaker. To break up the stony atmosphere, Professor B began: "I've just received a message asking me to come up here and say something funny."

A young student at the back of the room called loudly: "You'll tell us when you say it, won't you?"

To which the professor made instant reply: "I'll tell you; the rest will know!"

371   *Wrong Diagnosis*

DOCTOR: Did you tell that young man I think he is no good?

DAUGHTER: Yes, I did, Dad, but he did not seem at all upset. He said it wasn't the first wrong diagnosis you have made.

372   *Puzzling*

Henry James once reviewed a new novel by Gertrude Atherton. After reading the review, Mrs. Atherton wrote to Mr. James as follows:

"Dear Mr. James: I have read with much pleasure your review of my novel. Will you kindly let me know whether you liked it or not? Sincerely, Gertrude Atherton"

373   *Lost Cause*

"They say your daughter has made up her mind to marry a struggling young doctor."

"Well, if she's made up her mind, he might as well stop struggling."

374   *X Marks the Spot*

Gus and Ole, at a northern fishing resort, rented a hotel boat and found great fishing at a certain spot in a nearby lake, so great that they decided to mark the place and come back for more the next day. At the dock, Gus said: "Ole, did you mark the spot?"

"Yah," replied Ole, "Ay put a chalk mark on this side of the boat."

"Boy, are you dumb!" exclaimed Gus. "Maybe ve von't get the same boat."

375   *Her Responsibility*

There was a terrible crash as the train struck the car. A few seconds later, Mr. and Mrs. crawled out of the wreckage. Mrs. opened her mouth to speak, but her husband stopped her. "Don't say a word," he snapped. "I got my end of the car across. You were driving in the back seat, and if you let it get hit it's no fault of mine."

376   *The Cad at Eve*

HUSBAND:	If a man steals, no matter what, he will live to regret it.
WIFE (coyly):	You used to steal kisses from me before we were married.
HUSBAND:	Well, you heard what I said.

377   *Why Worry?*

FATHER:	Ned, why are you always at the bottom of your class?
NED:	It doesn't really matter, Dad. We get the same instruction at both ends of the class.

378   *Throw Out Antiques?*

HUSBAND:	One more payment and the furniture's ours.
WIFE:	Good! Then we can throw it out and get some new stuff.

379   *Taking No Chances*

OLD LADY TO OLD TAR:	Excuse me. Do those tattoo marks wash off?
OLD TAR:	I can't say, lady.

380   *Looking Backward*

"George comes from a very poor family."

"Why, they sent him through medical school, didn't they?"

"Yes, that's how they got so poor."

381   *Let's Forget the Whole Thing*

EMPLOYER: There's $10 gone from my cash drawer, Johnny; you and I were the only people who had keys to that drawer.

OFFICE BOY: Well, s'pose we each pay $5 and say no more about it.

382   *The Whole Story*

Johnny had been the guest of honor at a party the day before, and his friend was regarding him enviously.

"How was it? Have a good time?" he asked.

"Did I?" was the emphatic reply. "I ain't hungry yet!"

383   *Tact*

That a certain young man is wise beyond his years was proved when he paused before answering a widow who had asked him to guess her age.

"You must have some idea," she said.

"I have several ideas," said the young man, with a smile. "The only trouble is that I hesitate whether to make you ten years younger on account of your looks, or ten years older on account of your intelligence."

384   *Did He Get the Job?*

EMPLOYER: Personal appearance is a helpful factor in business success.

APPLICANT: Yes, and business success is a helpful factor in personal appearance.

385   *Add Golf Woe*

"When I put the ball where I can reach it," said the stout golfer, on being asked how he liked the game, "I can't see it, and when I put it where I can see it I can't reach it."

386   *Can't Complain, Sir*

"Are you the waiter who took my order?"

"Yes, sir."

"H'm, still looking well, I see. How are your grandchildren?"

387   *Presto!*

Teacher was giving a lesson on the weather idiosyncrasies of March. "What is it," she asked, "that comes in like a lion and goes out like a lamb?"

And little Julia, in the back row, replied: "Father."

388 *Day of Doom*

FLO: I don't intend to be married until I'm thirty.

REA: I don't intend to be thirty until I'm married!

389 *She Had No Mechanical Taste*

Betty (who has been served with a wing of chicken): "Mother, can't I have another piece? This is nothing but hinges."

390 *Modern Model*

WIFE (reading):   It says here they have found sheep in the Himalaya mountains that can run forty miles an hour.

HUSBAND: Well, it would take a lamb like that to follow Mary nowadays.

391 *Mistakes*

A certain fraternal society sent out announcements that the annual "instillation" would be held. It caused a great deal of amusement. They meant, of course, "Installation." One letter makes a big difference, as, for example, when a man wrote a letter addressed, "Dear Fiends," having omitted the "r," and the newspaper that spoke of the "bottle-scarred veterans" who marched in the parade. This was almost as bad as the other paper which spoke of the "battle-scared veterans."

392 *Sh-h!*

A Union Pacific shopman had been drawn on a federal grand jury and didn't want to serve. When his name was called he asked Judge Pollock to excuse him. "We are very busy at the shops," said he, "and I ought to be there."

"So you are one of those men who think the Union Pacific couldn't get along without you," remarked the judge.

"No, your honor," said the shopman. "I know it could get along without me, but I don't want it to find out."

"Excused," said the judge.

393 *Sit Down*

TEACHER: Johnny, can you define "nonsense"?

JOHNNY: Yes, teacher—an elephant hanging over a cliff with his tail tied to a daisy.

394   *The Restless Age*

TEACHER: Willie, give the definition of "home."

WILLIE: Home is where part of the family waits until the others are through with the car.

395   *Smart Boy*

A schoolteacher from the city was questioning her small farm nephew to see how his country school education was progressing. "If a farmer had 5,000 bushels of corn," she asked, "and corn is worth 40 cents a bushel, what will he get?"

"A government loan!" promptly replied the nephew.

396   *One Kind*

TEACHER: What is capital punishment?

PUPIL (whose father was a big businessman):   It's when the government sets up business in competition with you, and then takes all your profits with taxes in order to make up its loss.

397   *Bossy's Epitaph*

A farmer was trying hard to fill out a railway company claim sheet for a cow that had been killed on the track. He came down to the last item: "Disposition of the carcass." After puzzling over the question for some time, he wrote: "Kind and gentle."

398   *Special Alarm Clock*

"Have you any alarm clocks?" inquired the customer. "What I want is one that will rouse father without waking the whole family."

"I don't know of any such alarm clock as that, madam," said the shopkeeper. "We keep just the ordinary kind that will wake the whole family without disturbing father."

399   *Tit for Tat*

SHE: You certainly do keep your car nice and clean.

HE: It's an even deal—my car keeps me clean, too.

400   *Solomon Said It First*

"Anything new in the paper today, George?"

"No, my dear—just the same old things, only happening to different people."

401 *Correct Analysis*

A suburbanite put on a last-minute spurt of speed to catch his train—but missed it. A bystander remarked, "If you had just run a little faster, you would have made it."

"No," the suburbanite replied, "it wasn't a case of running faster, but of starting sooner."

402 *Growls of Recognition*

While on the bench one day, Judge Daniel called a case for trial, and two lawyers appeared as attorneys for the litigants.

"You're a dirty shyster," snarled one of the lawyers to the other, "and before this case is through I'll show you up for the crooked ape that you are."

"Sez you," snapped the other. "You are a cheat and a liar."

"Come, come," broke in the judge. "let the case proceed now that the learned counsel have identified each other."

403 *Typographical Error*

Describing a young bride, the editor wrote: "Her dainty feet were encased in shoes that might be taken for fairy boots." It appeared in print, "Her dirty feet were encased in shoes that might have been taken for ferry boats."

404 *Finally*

Diogenes met a World War I veteran.

"What were you in the war?" he asked.

"A private," the soldier answered.

And Diogenes blew out his lamp and went home.

405 *Fashions*

A man who had been waiting patiently in the Post Office could not attract the attention of either of the women behind the counter.

"The evening cloak," explained one of the women to her companion, "was a redingote design in gorgeous lamé brocade with fox fur and wide pagoda sleeves."

At this point the long-suffering customer broke in with, "I wonder if you could provide me with a neat purple stamp with a kinky perforated hem. The *tout ensemble* deliberately treated on the reverse side with mucilage. Something at about twenty cents."

406 *School*

"Were you copying his paper?"

"No, sir, I was only looking to see if he had mine right."

407   *Skating*

1ST FROSH: My, what a skating rink!

2ND FROSH: Yes. It has a seating capacity of 5,000.

408   *Amazing*

PROFESSOR: What happens when the human body is immersed in water?

STUDENT: The telephone rings.

409   *Lesser of Two Evils*

During a recent flood in the Kentucky lowlands, one family sent its little boy to stay with an uncle in another part of the state, accompanied by a letter explaining the reason for the nephew's sudden and unexpected visit. Two days later, the parents received a message: "Am returning boy. Send the flood."

410   *Another Version*

PROF: Mr. Smith, will you tell me why you look at your timepiece so often?

SMITH (suavely):   Yes, sir! I was afraid that you wouldn't have time to finish your interesting lecture, sir.

411   *Quickly Explained*

In speaking of the song "The Bonnie Banks o' Loch Lomond," a country teacher asked his pupils for an explanation of the line, "Yu'll tak' the high road and I'll tak' the low road."

"One was going by air and the other by bus," answered a boy.

412   *Prepared*

Little Tommy had been forbidden to swim in the river, owing to the danger. One day he came home with signs of having been in the water. His mother scolded him.

"But I was tempted, Mother," said Tommy.

"That's all very well. But how did you come to have your bathing suit with you?" Tommy paused and said: "Well, Mother, I took my bathing suit with me, thinking I might be tempted."

413   *Debtor or Creditor*

"What is a debtor, Pa?"

"A man who owes money."

"And what is a creditor?"

"The man who thinks he's going to get it."

414   *All Set for Thrift Week*

An insurance man walked into a lunchroom, and taking his place on one of the vacant stools, ordered bread and milk. The fellow sitting on the next stool asked:

"On a diet?"

"No. Commission."

415   *Ancestry*

A modest gentleman, in speaking of his family, said: "The Hardson family is a very, very old family. The line runs away back into antiquity. We do not know how far back it runs, but it's a long, long way back, and the history of the Hardson family is recorded in five volumes. In about the middle of the third volume, in a marginal note, we read, 'About this time the world was created.'"

416   *Of Course*

BOB: Did you see what happened to the Boston fern plant in the math room?

ROB: No, what?

BOB: It grew square roots.

417   *Modern*

GRANDMA: Would you like to go to the fair and ride in the merry-go-round, dear?

MODERN CHILD: I don't really mind, if it will amuse you.

418   *Naturally Fitted*

"What profession is your boy going to select?"

"I'm going to educate him to be a lawyer," replied Jones. "He's naturally argumentative and bent on mixing into other people's troubles, and he might just as well get paid for his time."

419   *Suspense*

OLD LADY (to parachutist):   I really don't know how you can hang from that silk thing. The suspense must be terrible.

PARACHUTIST: No, mum; it's when the suspense ain't there that it's terrible.

420   *Touched*

A college boy's definition of a parent is, "The kin you love to touch."

421   *Strategy*

"Talk about Napoleon! That fellow Johnson is something of a strategist himself."

"As to how?"

"Got his salary raised six months ago, and his wife hasn't found it out yet."

422   *Dual Purposes*

A husband and wife came to a bank to open a joint account. Being in a hurry, the man made out his signature card and left.

"Let me see," an official of the bank said to the wife. "This is to be a joint account, is it not?"

"That's right," smiled the wife. "Deposit for him—checking for me."

423   *Such Gallantry*

"Dearest Annabelle," wrote a lovesick swain, "I could swim the mighty ocean for one glance from your lovely eyes. I could walk through a wall of flame for one touch of your little hand. I would leap the widest stream for a word from your warm lips.—As always, your own Oscar."

"P.S.—I'll be over to see you Sunday night, if it doesn't rain."

424   *Salesmanship*

She was a new salesclerk. She had a slow mind and a quick tongue and thought herself awfully smart.

A timid-looking man entered the store. "Do you keep fountain pens?" he asked.

"No, we sell them," snapped she.

"Well," said he, "You'll keep the ones you might have sold me. Good morning."

425   *His Political Opponent*

English political speeches, at their best, have long been noted for their pungent humor. A rejoinder of John Morley, given in the heat of battle, is a typical example.

Morley had just finished a campaign address by requesting his listeners to vote for him, when a man jumped angrily to his feet and shouted, "I'd rather vote for the devil!"

"Quite so," rejoined Morley with a smile, "but in case your friend declines to run, may I count on your support?"

426   *Memories*

"Dear Clara," wrote the young man, "pardon me, but I'm getting so forgetful. I proposed to you last night, but really forgot whether you said yes or no."

"Dear Will," she replied by note, "so glad to hear from you. I knew that I had said no to somebody last night, but had forgotten who it was."

427 *Just a Difference*

"Oh, what a strange looking cow," exclaimed the sweet young thing from Chicago. "But why hasn't she any horns?"

"Well, you see," exclaimed the farmer, "some cows are born without horns and never had any, and others shed theirs, and some we dehorn, and some breeds aren't supposed to have horns at all. There are a lot of reasons why some cows haven't got horns, but the reason why that cow hasn't got horns is because she isn't a cow—she's a horse."

428 *Likewise*

CONDUCTOR: Next station is Long Wait Junction. Change cars for Mauch Chunk, Squeedunk, Quakake, and Podunk, Hokendaqua, Catasaqua, Mecanaqua, and Tamaqua.

GREEN BRAKEMAN
(at other end of car):   Same at this end.

429 *Mistake*

They were twins. It was bathing time and from the twins' bedroom came sounds of hearty laughter and loud crying. Their father went up to find the cause.

"What's the matter up here?" he inquired.

The laughing twin pointed to his weeping brother.

"Nothing," he giggled, "only Mother has given Alexander two baths and hasn't given me any at all."

430 *Raw Recruit*

RIFLE INSTRUCTOR: Do you know where you are aiming?

NEW RECRUIT: No, sir. I'm a stranger in this district.

431 *Corpse*

MATHEMATICS TEACHER: Robert, can you tell me what is meant by a polygon?

ROBERT (a freshman):   I guess it means a parrot that's died, doesn't it?

432   *Easily Pleased*

FATHER: Remember, son, beauty is only skin deep.

SON: That's deep enough for me. I'm no cannibal.

433   *Do As I Say, etc.*

STUDENT (to Prof):   What's that you wrote on my paper?

PROF: I told you to write plainer.

434   *Statistics*

OFFICE BOY: I et six pancakes for breakfast this morning.

BOOKKEEPER: You mean ate, don't you?

OFFICE BOY: Well maybe it was eight I et.

435   *Biting*

GAME WARDEN: Are the fish biting today?

WEARY ANGLER: I don't know. If they are, they're biting each other.

436   *Seeking a Pastor*

When a church seeks a pastor,
They often want
The strength of an eagle,
The grace of a swan,
The gentleness of a dove,
The friendliness of a sparrow,
And the night hours of an owl;
And when they catch that bird
They expect him to live
On the food of a canary.

437   *Information, Please*

An example of youthful pessimism was provided by a little boy who was about to start on a railway journey. It was the first time he had ever traveled alone, and his mother told him to write his name and address on a card and keep it in his pocket. He wrote: "In case of accident, this was Johnny Jones."

438   *Dumb Trees*

Sonny sat on the lower steps, his face resting in his two chubby hands.
"What's the matter, Sonny?"

"Nothin'—just thinkin'."

"What about?"

"Thinkin' how dumb trees are to take off their clothes in winter and put 'em on in summer."

439   *Two to One*

Some few years ago, just after Jimmy Foxx had broken into the regular lineup with the Philadelphia Athletics, the Boston Red Sox came to Philly to play a series. George Moriarty was umpiring behind the plate.

Foxx took two terrific cuts at the first two pitches, and let the third one float by.

"Strike three, you're out," said Moriarty.

Foxx turned indignantly, "You missed that one, George."

"Well, you missed the other two," Moriarty replied. "You're still one up on me."

440   *Earning His Bit*

The plumber was working and his new assistant was looking on. The latter was learning the trade, and this was his first day.

"Say," he inquired, "do you charge for my time?"

"Certainly," was the reply.

"But I haven't done anything."

The plumber had been inspecting the finished job with a lighted candle, which he handed to his helper. "Here," he said, "if you've got to be so conscientious, blow that out!"

441   *Too Bad*

Mary had a little lamb
'Twas awful dumb and so
It couldn't tell the red from green
Nor which was stop or go.
It followed her to school one day
A silly thing to do
Was caught between the red and green
And now it's mutton stew.

442   *Sometimes It Sounds That Way*

As the soprano began to sing, little Johnnie became greatly excited over the gesticulations of the orchestra conductor.

"What's that man shaking his stick at her for?" he demanded.

"Shh! He's not shaking his stick at her."

But Johnnie was not convinced.

"Then what is she hollering for?"

443   *Sinister Connotation*

"I wish you boys wouldn't call me Big Bill."

"Why not?"

"Those college names stick—and I'm going to be a doctor."

444   *Two-thirty Plenty*

CHINESE PATIENT (on telephone):	Doctor what time you fixee teeth for me?
DOCTOR:	Two-thirty—all right?
CHINESE:	Yes, tooth hurty, all right, but what time you fixee?

445   *One Drawback*

TOM:	How do you like your new job selling on the road?
HARRY:	Oh, it's dandy. You meet some fine fellows at the hotels and have lots of fun in the evenings, but what I don't like is calling on those jobbers every day.

446   *Revenge*

A wholesaler wrote a threatening letter. This is the reply he received:

"Dear Sir: What do you mean by sending me a letter like that?

"Every month I place all my bills in a basket and then figure out how much money I have to pay them. Next, I draw as many bills out of the basket as I have money to pay.

"If you don't like my way of doing business, I won't even put your bill in the basket next month."

447   *Observant*

"Mother, I'm the best-looking boy in Sunday school."

"Why, Tommy! Who told you that?"

"Nobody, Mother. Nobody told me. I saw all the rest of them."

448   *Left in Doubt*

POLICEMAN (after the collision):	You saw this person driving toward you. Why didn't you give him the road?
MOTORIST:	I was going to, as soon as I could discover which half he wanted.

449   *What Goes Up*

It seems that one of the boys on army maneuvers in Texas came floating into camp near the Davis Mountains. When he was brought to the officer's tent, slightly bruised, he was told:

"You've got real nerve to come down in a parachute with this 100-mile wind blowing. That's dangerous!"

"I didn't come down in a parachute," said the private. "I went up in a tent."

450   *Calvin Coolidge*

A reporter attempted an interview with Calvin Coolidge. "Do you wish to say anything about the strike?" was the first question.

"No."

"About the farm bloc?"

"No."

"About the World Court?"

"No."

The reporter turned to go. "By the way," added Coolidge, unexpectedly calling him back, "don't quote me."

451   *Wise*

STUDENT: To whom was Minerva married?

PROFESSOR: My boy, when will you learn that Minerva was the Goddess of Wisdom? She wasn't married.

452   *Nutshell*

STUDENT: Yes, sir, I always carry my notes in my hat.

PROFESSOR: I see—knowledge in a nutshell.

453   *He's Safe*

"You know the old saying, what you don't know won't hurt you."

"So what?"

"You lucky dog, you're invulnerable."

454   *Gulf Club Lunch Menu*

Scotch Broth

Club Sandwich   Sliced Tomatoes

Dandelion Greens   Link Sausage   Puttatoes

Parsnips

Cup Custard

Rolls   Nuts

Tea

455   *Sometimes Too Long Also*

The American public dinner has been described by a popular after dinner speaker as "an affair where a speaker first eats a lot of food he doesn't want and then proceeds to talk about something he doesn't understand to a lot of people who don't want to hear him."

456   *Considerable Difference*

"Give me a chicken salad," said the man in a suburban restaurant.

"Do you want the $1 one or the $1.50 one?" asked the waitress.

"What's the difference?"

"The $1 ones are made of veal and pork and the $1.50 ones are made of tuna."

457   *Mountain Guide*

Be careful not to fall here. It's dangerous. But if you do fall, remember to look to the left. You get a wonderful view on that side.

458   *It Helps*

"I drink about twenty cups of coffee a day."

"Doesn't that keep you awake?"

"It helps."

459   *Not a Total Loss*

> There was a young man of Devises,
> Whose ears were of different sizes;
> The one that was small
> Was of no use at all
> But the other won several prizes.

460   *Number, Please*

A gentleman visiting in Washington wanted to phone someone in Baltimore. It proved annoying when the operator said: "Deposit one dollar, please."

"What!" he cried. "One dollar to call Baltimore? Why, at home we can phone to Hades and back for a quarter."

"Oh, yes," she replied, "but that's a local call."

461   *College Exams*

Professor (gazing over the room during an examination): "Will some gentleman who isn't using his textbook be so kind as to permit me to have it for a few minutes?"

462   *Capital and Labor*

WILLIS: What is the difference between capital and labor, Dad?

DAD: Well, son, the money you lend represents capital—and getting it back represents labor.

463   *Cross-examination*

STATE'S ATTORNEY:	Are you sure this is the man who stole your car last Thursday?
MUCH-BEFUDDLED PLAINTIFF:	Well, I was. Now after the cross-examination, I'm not sure I ever owned a car.

464   *Modest Fellow*

HER: I suppose all geniuses are conceited.
HIM: Some of them—but I'm not.

465   *Never Mind the Details*
A somewhat inebriated gentleman was walking down State Street and did not know his location. He turned to a passerby and said: "Mister, where am I?" The passerby answered: "You're at the corner of State and Madison streets." The inebriated gentleman said: "Never mind the details, what city?"

466   *Conspicuous*
An American advertising man told an Englishman that an electric sign being constructed had 30,000 white lights, 40,000 green lights, 60,000 pink lights, and in addition, would have a great sunburst of 10,000 orange lights. The Englishman looked at it a moment and said: "Yes, that's a marvelous sign, but don't you think it is going to be a little bit conspicuous?"

467   *A Difficult Golf Course*
A guest on a golf course placed the ball in position, missed three times, hit it the fourth time, and then turned to his host and said: "This is a difficult course, isn't it?"

468   *Fast Driving*
Two fraternity brothers headed toward Philadelphia. They were zipping along the highway at some eighty or ninety miles an hour, when a policeman appeared from nowhere and forced them over to the side of the road.
    "What's the matter, officer?" they asked. "Were we driving too fast?"
    "No," he answered. "You were flying too low."

469   *The Way to Do It*
"What's the best way to appeal to audiences?"
    "First find out what they think about something," answered the orator, "and then tell 'em they're perfectly right."

470 *Tin You?*

> I bought a wooden whistle,
> But it wooden whistle,
> So I bought a steel whistle,
> But steel it wooden whistle,
> So I bought a lead whistle,
> Still they wooden lead me whistle,
> So I bought a tin whistle,
> And now I tin whistle.

471 *The Old Gent Should Know*

"Now," said the lad to his father, at the college football game, "you'll see more excitement for five dollars than you ever saw before."

"I don't know," replied the old gent. "That's what my marriage license cost me."

472 *That's All*

"Say, pal, how much money does your wife demand every payday?"

"Don't ask foolish questions. You know my salary is three hundred dollars a week."

473 *Expensive*

"Can you tell if the defendant was expensively garbed?"

"Indeed she was. I know expensive garbage when I see it."

474 *A Good Question*

When the family returned from Sunday morning service, father criticized the sermon, daughter thought the choir's singing was atrocious, and mother found fault with the organist's playing. The small boy of the family piped up, "But it was a good show for a dollar, don't you think, Dad?"

475 *Invoice*

HUBBY: You never tell me what you buy! Don't I get any voice in the buying?

WIFEY: Certainly, darling! You get the invoice.

476 *Clever, These Chinese*

A sailor, after placing some flowers on a grave in a cemetary, noticed an old Chinese man placing a bowl of rice on a nearby grave, and asked: "What time do you expect your friend to come up and eat the rice?"

The old Chinese man replied with a smile: "Same time your friend come up to smell flowers."

477 *Back in the Good Old Days*

"Crop failures?" asked the oldtimer. "Yep, I've seen a few of 'em in my days. Now in 1940 the corn crop was purt' nigh nothing. We cooked some for dinner one day, and Dad ate fourteen acres of corn at one meal!"

478 *Nearby*

HE: Meet me at the Waldorf-Astoria at eight.

SHE: The Waldorf? . . . Say, that's a nice place.

HE: Yeah, and it's close to where we're going, too.

479 *Behind His Ears*

In a church, at the font, her small brother was being christened.

Little girl: "Behind his ears too, Reverend Smyth!"

480 *In Demand*

An epicure, dining at Crewe,
Found quite a large mouse in his stew.
Said the waiter, "Don't shout,
And wave it about,
Or the rest will be wanting one, too!"

481 *Play Ball*

In a small town in Louisiana on a hot, dusty day, two baseball teams, surrounded by their devotees, were engaged in a very important game.

The preacher of the community had been approved by both teams for the position of umpire in this contest—because, as the home team pointed out, a parson couldn't do wrong.

The visiting team's cleanup man stood in the batter's box. The bases were loaded.

"Ball one, high!" the voice of authority boomed.

"Ball two, low!"

"Ball three, inside!"

"Ball four, low and wide—you are out!"

"I get a base for that!" screamed the mutinous hitter.

"Brother, you are right—but the bases are loaded, and there is no place to put you. You are out!"

482 *Not Ashamed of Dad!*

"My boy," said the millionaire, "when I was your age, I carried water for a gang of bricklayers."

"I'm mighty proud of you, Father. If it hadn't been for your pluck and perseverance, I might have had to do something like that myself."

483   *Not So Big*

"He's not as big a fool as he used to be."

"Getting wiser?"

"No, thinner."

484   *Architectural Triumph*

Two ladies were attending a concert at the Civic Auditorium.

"Nice building," said one lady. "What style of architecture is it?"

"I'm not quite sure," said the other lady, "but I think it's Reminiscence."

485   *And Lady Uncles Are OK*

A teacher asked the pupils to write a short essay and to choose their own subjects.

A little girl sent in the following paper:

"My subjek is 'Ants.' Ants is of two kinds, insects and lady uncles.

"Sometimes they live in holes and sometimes they crawl into the sugar bole, and sometimes they live with their married sisters.

"That is all I know about ants."

486   *Grandpappy Knew*

A Yankee motorist, driving through Georgia, lost his way. Coming to a stop alongside an elderly native, he asked: "Which way's Atlanta?"

The old man surveyed the car's license plate, then said, "Your grandpappy didn't have any trouble finding it!"

487   *Looking Ahead*

They had just become engaged.

"I shall love," she cooed, "to share all your troubles."

"But darling," he murmured, "I have none."

"No," she agreed, "but I mean when we are married."

488   *Stolen Sweets*

The rector had invited the village boys to the rectory for strawberries. After they had finished, he, seeking to point the moral, said: "Now, boys, wasn't that nicer than breaking into my garden and helping yourselves?"

"Oh, yes," chorused the boys.

"And why was it nicer?" he asked a chubby-faced boy.

"Because, sir," was the reply, "we wouldn't have had any sugar and cream with them."

489   *Bird of Paradise*

CUSTOMER: That chicken I bought yesterday had no wishbone.

BUTCHER (smoothly):   It was a happy and contented chicken, madam, and had nothing to wish for.

490   *He Will Start Now*

The colonel got a case of cold feet before the battle. Calling his command together, he said: "Boys, we're going to get licked, but you must fight as you never fought before. If worse comes to worst, run for it; as for me, I'm a little lame, so I'll start now."

491   *Not Near Enough*

"Mr. Jones," asked the instructor, "how far were you from the correct answer?"

"Only three seats, sir."

492   *Experienced*

HENRY: My dear, I really don't believe you can ever teach that dog to obey you.

MRS. PECK: Nonsense, darling. Just remember how obstinate you were when we were first married.

493   *Heard on the Links*

At the club golf tournament the club secretary caught one of the entrants driving off about a foot in front of the teeing mark.

"Here!" he cried indignantly. "You can't do that. You're disqualified!"

"What for?" demanded the golfer.

"Why, you're driving off in front of the mark."

The player looked at the secretary with pity. "G'wan back to the clubhouse," he said tersely. "I'm playing my second stroke!"

494   *Wins Her Diploma*

An inspector, examining a class in religious knowledge, asked the following question of a little girl, intending it for a catch:

"What was the difference between Noah's Ark and Joan of Arc?"

He was not a little surprised when the child, answering, said: "Noah's Ark was made of wood and Joan of Arc was maid of Orleans."

495   *The Best Reason*

The average citizen works 70 days a year to earn enough money to pay his taxes, and he does it because he loves his country, is patriotic, and can't figure out any way of getting out of them.

496   *Not to Pitch*

Vernon "Lefty" Gomez, famed pitcher of the New York Yankees during the thirties, was separated for a time from his actress wife, but effected a reconciliation just before the World Series started. In the lobby of the Yankees' hotel, Gomez was accosted for an interview by a woman reporter.

Gomez greeted her and then introduced Mrs. Gomez. "Oh, dear," blurted the reporter. "Am I to construe this as a reconciliation?"

Without batting an eye, Gomez retorted: "Well, I didn't bring her along to pitch."—Donald McGraw, in *True*

497   *Double Jointed*

FIFER: What sort of fellow is Groot?

ZIMPIR: Oh, he's one of those people who will pat you on the back before your face and hit you in the face behind your back.

498   *Blackout*

A mother noticed the other night that her high school son, who was getting ready to go to a dance, got dressed in record time.

"Did you take a bath?" she asked him accusingly.

"No," came the reply.

"Now listen, son," she remonstrated, "you wouldn't go to a dance without taking a bath, would you?"

"Sure I would, Mom," came the reply. "It's not formal."

499   *You're Fired*

The foreman, a tough, conceited individual, was boasting of his strength.

"I can lick any man working for me!" he declared.

"You can't lick me," said a new employee.

The foreman looked over the young man's muscular frame very carefully, then spoke.

"You're fired," he said.

500   *Knows His Neptune*

A young naval student was being put through the paces by an old sea captain. "What would you do if a storm sprang up on the starboard?" "Throw out an anchor, sir." "What would you do if another storm sprang up aft?" "Throw out another anchor, sir." "And if another terrific storm sprang up forward, what would you do?" "Throw out another anchor." "Hold on," said the captain, "Where are you getting all your anchors from?" "From the same place you're getting your storms, sir."

501   *Domestic Business College*

MOMMA (singing):   By low, my baby.

POPPA: That's right; you tell him to buy low and I'll teach him to sell high.

502   *Triumph of Comfort*

"I'm not sure I quite understand those flexible-action wheels."

"Why, it's like this—the wheels give. So if you run over a pedestrian, you hardly feel it."

503   *Shouldn't Be Tight*

HE: What part of the car causes the most accidents?

SHE: The nut that holds the wheel.

504   *A Happy Family*

P. T. Barnum, the great showman, used to exhibit a happy family. This family consisted of a lion, a tiger, a wolf, a bear, and a lamb, all in one cage.

"Remarkable," a visitor said one day to Mr. Barnum. "Remarkable, impressive. How long have these animals dwelt together in this way?"

"Eight months," Barnum replied. "But the lamb has to be replaced occasionally."

505   *Stop, Thief!*

NIECE (in the picture gallery): Aunt Sarah, this is the famous "Angelus" by Millet.

AUNT SARAH: Well, I never! That man had the nerve to copy the calendar that has hung in our kitchen for a dozen years or more.

506   *Rattling the Skeleton*

PUPIL (after lesson on creation): But, teacher, Daddy says we are descended from monkeys.

TEACHER: We can't discuss your private family affairs in class.

507   *Give It Time*

NEIGHBOR: How is that incubator doing that you bought?

MRS. NEWBRIDE: I suppose it's all right, but I'm a little worried about it. It hasn't laid a single egg yet.

508   *Gets 'Em Going and Coming*

SCHULTZ: Your opening sale has closed. What now?

SCHWARTZ: Our closing sale opens.

509   *Right*

TEACHER: William, construct a sentence using the word "archaic."

WILLIAM: We can't have archaic and eat it too.

510   *Politically Inclined*

A farmer had a razorback hog that was a great runner. One day he set out to find her, and after hours following the tracks, over the creek and back, he came home and said: "I can't find that hog, but after studying her tracks, I believe she's on both sides of the creek."

511   *Cover Charge*

WAITER: Would you mind settling your bill, sir? We're closing now.

IRATE PATRON: But, hang it all, I haven't been served yet.

WAITER: Well, in that case, there'll only be the cover charge.

512   *Travel Note*

"What is the difference between valor and discretion?"

"Well, to eat at a restaurant without tipping would be valor."

"I see."

"And later to eat at a different restaurant would be discretion."

513   *He Knew His Neck*

The barber had used his electric clippers in cutting small Bobby's hair. "I guess my neck wasn't clean," he told his mother on coming home, " 'cause that man used his vacuum cleaner on it."

514   *It Certainly Helped*

SUNDAY SCHOOL TEACHER: Why was Solomon the wisest man in the world?

SARKIS: Because he had so many wives to advise him.

515   *And Was His Face Red!*

In the congregation of an Oak Park church during Sunday morning service was a young bride whose husband was an usher. Becoming terribly worried about having left the roast in the oven, she wrote a note to her husband, sending it to him by another usher.

The latter, thinking it was a note for the pastor, hurried down the aisle and laid it on the pulpit. Stopping abruptly in the middle of his sermon to read the note, the astonished pastor was met with the written injunction:

"Please go home and turn off the gas."

516   *But Did She Fall for It?*

WIFE: Mrs. Jones has another new hat.

HUBBY: Well, if she were as attractive as you are, my dear, she wouldn't have to depend so much upon the milliner.

517   *Just a Smart Dreamer*

A woman was stopped on the street by a ragged man.

"Could you spare a dollar for something to eat, ma'am?"

"Why are you begging—a big, strong man like you? I should think you'd be ashamed."

"Mademoiselle," he said, removing his hat and bowing courteously. "I am a disappointed romanticist. I have woven dreams of cobweb stuff and the wind has swept them away. And so I have turned to this profession—the only one I know in which a gentleman can address a beautiful girl without the formality of an introduction."

Yes, he got five dollars.

518   *"Atchoo!"*

"Who invented the hole in the doughnut?"

"Oh, some fresh air fiend, I suppose."

519   *Noblesse Oblige*

Professor: "This exam will be conducted on the honor system. Please take seats three seats apart and in alternate rows."

520   *Cure for Extravagance*

"Are you saving any money?"

"Sure. We have a budget. By the time we balance it every evening, all the places we could spend money are closed."

521   *Just Lucky*

"I've got an idea," said the freshman.

"Beginner's luck," said the sophomore.

522   *In Time*

"Have you forgotten that you owe me $50?"

"Not yet, but give me time."

523   *Perfect Alibi*

HUBBY: What became of that unpaid bill Dunn and Company sent to us?

WIFE: Oh, that? I sent it back marked insufficient funds.

524   *Slightly Different*

MAUD: So Jack said that I had a skin one loves to touch.

MARIE: Not exactly, dear; he said you had a skin you love to retouch.

525   *Long-winded Toastmaster*

"What is the hardest part of your work as a lecturer?" asked the toastmaster.

"As a rule," replied the speaker, "the hardest part of my work is waking the audience up after the man who introduces me has concluded his remarks."

526   *Rock of Ages*

"What is a mortarboard?" asked the little girl.

"I'll try to explain," said Miss Cayenne, "although it is a slightly complicated matter. A mortarboard carried by a builder often has cement on top and worn by a college professor often has concrete under it."

527   *All Sewed Up*

"John, I found this letter in your coat pocket this morning. I gave it to you a month ago to mail."

"Yes, dear, I remember. I took that coat off for you to sew a button on and I'm still waiting."

528   *Dead Letter Baritone*

"I've learned to sing."

"Where did you learn to sing?"

"I graduated from a correspondence school."

"Boy, you sure lost lots of your mail."

529   *What Is So Funny?*

"Did you ever hear that joke about the museum in Philadelphia that had a skull of Benjamin Franklin when he was twelve in one room, and a skull when he was fifty in another?"

"No," said the Englishman. "What was it?"

530   *When Words Fail*

The golfer stepped up to the tee and drove off. The ball sailed straight down the fairway, leaped onto the green, and rolled into the hole. The golfer threw his club in the air with excitement.

"What have you suddenly gone crazy about?" asked his wife, who was trying to learn something about the game.

"Why, I just got a hole-in-one," yelled the golfer, a wild gleam of delight in his eyes.

"Did you?" asked his wife placidly. "Do it again, dear, I didn't see you."

531   *Executive Ability*

"What is executive ability, Father?" asked a serious lad.

"Executive ability, my son, is the art of getting the credit for all the hard work that somebody else does."

532   *Out of Tune*

Two elderly men at a club were discussing the table manners of a new member.

"Well, what do you think of him?" asked one.

"Very remarkable," replied the other, thoughtfully; "I've heard soup gargled and siphoned, but that's the first time I've ever heard it yodeled."

533   *Chronic Knocker*

"Anything the matter with the car?"

'Well, there's only one part of it that doesn't make a noise and that's the horn."

534   *He Done Fine*

"Well, Albert, how did you get along in the examination in English grammar today?"

"Oh, I done fine, Pop. I only made one mistake and I seen that as soon as I done it."

535   *Irresistible*

CUSTOMER: I've come back to buy that car you showed me yesterday.

SALESMAN: That's fine, I thought you'd be back. Now tell me, what was the dominant feature that made you decide to buy this car?

CUSTOMER: My wife, sir.

536   *Unanimous*

WARDEN: Boys, I've had charge of this prison for ten years and we ought to celebrate the occasion. What kind of party would you suggest?

PRISONERS (in unison):   Open house.

537   *Attributed Sometimes to Lincoln*

A business firm considering the employment of a young attorney wrote to Lincoln about him.

Lincoln wrote: "He's a bright young fellow, hasn't had much practice yet, but is ambitious. He has an office in the Blackstone block, small library, worth $50, a table and two chairs, $5 will cover them, and in the southeast corner of the room is a rat hole that will bear looking into."

538   *What They Think*

What they think when little Oswald starts to school for the first time:

His mother: "Just think, my litle darling is almost grown up."

His father: "I hope he becomes a fullback."

His older sister: "That means I've got to walk to school with him and can't go to school with the kids."

His teacher: "I hope he's smarter than he looks."

His neighbors: "Thank heaven! Now we can have peace for a few hours a day."

His dog: "Yo-o-ow-l-l-l."

539   *He Knows*

TEACHER: Johnny! Can you tell me what a waffle is?

JOHNNY: Yes'm; it's a pancake with a non-skid tread.

540   *"Socialized" Medicine*

JANICE: So Lillie threw over that young doctor she was going with!

CLARICE: Yes, and what do you think? He not only requested she return his presents, but sent her a bill for forty-seven visits.

541   *Couldn't Fool Him*

John Smith happened to witness a minor holdup. In due time the police arrived, and one officer asked the witness his name.

"John Smith," said Smith.

"Cut the comedy," snapped the cop. "What's your real name?"

"All right," said Smith, "put me down as Winston Churchill."

"That's more like it," said the officer. "You can't fool me with that John Smith stuff."

542   *Quiz*

"Are you a good student?"
"Yes and no."
"What do you mean?"
"Yes, I am no good."

543   *Vacancy*

"Now," said the teacher, "give me a definition of space."
Junior stood up, flustered and red. "Space," he began, "is where there is nothing. I can't explain it exactly, but I have it in my head."

544   *A Nag, a Bone, and a Hunk of Hay*

HE: How do you feel after your ride on that horse?
SHE: Gosh! I never thought anything filled with hay could be so hard!

545   *Boston*

A motorist driving through Boston drew up to the curb and asked one of the highly sophisticated natives:
"My good man, could you tell me where I might stop at?"
"I would advise," said the native coldly, "stopping just before the 'at.'"

546   *Diplomacy*

CUSTOMER: Have you anything for gray hair?
CONSCIENTIOUS DRUGGIST: Nothing, madam, but the greatest respect.

547   *In Real Trouble*

A patient told a psychiatrist that he could not remember anything for more than a few minutes at a time.
"How long has this been going on?" asked the psychiatrist.
"How long has what been going on?" replied the man.

548   *Careful*

The Shelby (Alabama) *Democrat* reports the case of a man who was defeated ignominiously when he ran for the office of sheriff.
He got 55 votes out of a total of 3,500, and the next day he walked down Main Street with two guns hanging from his belt.

"You were not elected, and you have no right to carry guns," fellow citizens told him.

"Listen, folks," he replied, "A man with no more friends than I've got in this county needs to carry guns."

549 *One Stubborn*

The jury foreman was asked by the sheriff if he should send in twelve dinners as usual. "No," said the foreman, "make it eleven dinners and a bale of hay."

550 *Results Dubious*

"Did Mr. Borer sing a popular song at the concert?"

"Well, it had been popular before he sang it."

551 *With One Exception*

"Why, he's the loudest-mouthed man I ever heard."

"Shush, dear, you forget yourself."

552 *It's Easy*

HUNTER: How do you detect an elephant?

GUIDE: You smell a faint odor of peanuts on his breath.

553 *The Old Thief*

"The laundry has kept two of our towels."

"Which ones, dear?"

"The ones we got from the hotel in Miami."

554 *Modern Art*

CRITIC: Ah! And what is this? It is superb! What soul! What expression!

ARTIST: That's where I clean the paint off my brushes.

555 *Clipped Wings*

At a costume party for children, a police officer stationed at the door was instructed not to admit any adults.

An excited woman came running up to the door and demanded admission.

"I'm sorry, ma'am," replied the officer, "but I can't let anyone in but children."

"But my child is in there as a butterfly," exclaimed the woman, "and has forgotten her wings!"

"Can't help it," replied the officer, "orders is orders. You'll have to let her represent a caterpillar!"

556   *Wrong*

PROFESSOR: What is a taxidermist?
STUDENT: The skin of a cab driver?

557   *A Gracious Rival*

Modern political campaigners might take a lesson in graciousness and kindness from Edward Campbell, the great British statesman.

Once when Campbell was opposing Thackeray for a seat in Parliament, the two contenders, in the course of their campaigning, met and engaged in friendly conversation.

On taking leave of his rival, Thackeray remarked: "May the best man win!"

"Oh, no," replied Campbell, "I hope not, I want to win!"

558   *Really Remarkable*

"If Shakespeare were here today, he would be looked on as a remarkable man."

"Yes, he'd be more than 400 years old."

559   *Highland Playboys*

MacGregor and MacPherson decided to become teetotalers, but Mac-Gregor thought it would be best if they had one bottle of whiskey to put in the cupboard in case of illness.

After three days, MacPherson could bear it no longer and said: "MacGregor, Ah'm not verra weel."

"Too late, MacPherson, Ah was verra sick m'sel' all day yesterday."

560   *Correct Answer*

"When Lot's wife looked back," said the Sunday School teacher, "what happened to her?"

"She was transmuted into chloride of sodium," answered the boy with the high IQ.

561   *No Driver*

An inebriate boarded a double-decker bus and sat near the driver. He talked so much that the driver suggested he go to the top deck and enjoy the fresh air. In a few minutes he was back.

"Didn't you like it upstairs?" said the driver.

"Yes, nice view," answered the drunk, "but it ain't safe—no driver!"

562   *Good Swimmer*

SALLY ANNE (aged six):   Granddad, were you in the Ark?

GRANDDAD: Why no, honey.

SALLY ANNE: Then why weren't you drowned?

563   *Short Cut*

"Officer, what's the quickest way to the hospital?"

"Close your eyes, cross this street, and you'll be there in fifteen minutes."

564   *Another Hardship*

The Pilgrim mothers stood all the trials the Pilgrim fathers stood, but in addition, stood the Pilgrim fathers.

565   *Safety First*

SINGER: Now that you've heard my voice, what would you suggest to accompany me?

IMPRESARIO: A bodyguard.

566   *The Average Motorist*

SERVICE STATION ATTENDANT: How much gasoline does the tank in your car hold?

MOTORIST: I don't know. I've never had enough money to get it filled yet.

567   *Did His Best*

SERGEANT: Did you sleep well on your cot? I'm afraid it was a little hard and uneven, but—

PRIVATE: It was all right, sir. I got up now and then during the night and rested a little, you know.

568   *Flattered*

The new traffic cop had been told by his inspector to overtake and stop a speeding car. Ten minutes later, he called to report: "Car was being driven by an actress. I stops her, pulls out my notebook. She snatches it, writes her autograph, and drives on."

569 *Arctic Style Hints*

TEACHER: Now, Freddy, why does a polar bear wear a fur coat?

FREDDY: Oh—er, well, I suppose he would look funny in a tweed one.

570 *Same Bread*

The officer received a complaint about the issue of bread. "Soldiers should not make a fuss about trivialities, my man," he said. "If Napoleon had had that bread when he was crossing the Alps, he'd have eaten it with delight."

"Yes, sir," said the corporal, "but it was fresh then."

571 *Sphere of Influence*

Frederick S. Isham, the novelist, has offered this story to refute the belief that the Chinese are not a humorous people.

Two Chinese many years ago were discussing a visit William Howard Taft had just made to Shanghai.

"Taft is a big man," one of them exclaimed, making a gesture to outline a big circle.

"Big man," the other repeated. "We have certainly had large sphere of American influence in our midst recently."

572 *Perfect Fit*

SALESMAN: See there, mister, that hat fits perfectly. How does it feel?

BUYER: Okay, unless my ears get tired.

573 *Unexpected*

EDITOR: Did you write this poem yourself?

CONTRIBUTOR: Yes, every line of it.

EDITOR: Then I'm glad to meet you, Edgar Allan Poe, I thought you were dead long ago.

574 *Standing Room*

PATIENT: Doctor, is my mouth opened wide enough?

DOCTOR: Yes. You see, I always stand on the outside while pulling a tooth.

575 *Safety Zone*

COP: Hey, what are you doing there?

DRIVER: Parking my car. It seemed such a good place. The sign said "Safety Zone."

576   *Of Course Not*

INTERVIEWER: What have you to say about anonymous letters?

PROFESSOR: They're stupid; I read them, but I never answer them.

577   *Just a Pawn*

"He is the secretary of a chess club."

"But what does he do?"

"He reads the hours of the last meeting."

578   *Correct*

"What is the chief end of man?" said the teacher to the class.

"The end with the head on," said the small boy.

579   *Always Faithful*

"Is he the sort of fellow who forgets you when you have no money?"

"No, he's an installment collector."

580   *Generous*

SUE: My husband is the most generous man in the world.

LOU: How's that?

SUE: Well, I gave him a dozen of the loveliest neckties for Christmas, and he took them right down and gave them to the Salvation Army.

581   *A Very Good Preacher*

The new minister in a Georgia church was delivering his first sermon. The janitor was a critical listener from a back corner of the church. The minister's sermon was eloquent, and his prayers seemed to cover the whole category of human wants.

After the service, one of the deacons asked the old janitor what he thought of the new minister. "Don't you think he offers up a good prayer, Joe?"

"I most certainly do. Why, that man asked the good Lord for things the other preacher didn't even know He had!"

582   *Fame*

A hundred autograph collectors after one man who will soon be forgotten.

583   *Just Curious*

BOSS: Now what do you want? I thought I fired you two weeks ago.

EX-OFFICE BOY: Oh, I just came back to see if you were still in business.

584   *A Happy Home*
Where a wife asks her husband's opinion and accepts it.

585   *Broad-minded Traveler*

MR. NEWRICH (touring in his new car): Where are we now?

CHAUFFEUR: Halfway between Paris and Marseilles, sir.

MR. NEWRICH: Don't bother me with little details. What country are we in?

586   *Mug Drill*

SERGEANT: Did you shave this morning, Jones?

RECRUIT: Yes, sergeant.

SERGEANT: Well, next time stand a bit closer to the razor.

587   *Streamlined*
"Say," said the woman customer over the phone, "the next time I order chicken don't send me any more airplane fowls."

"What do you mean—airplane fowls?" asked the butcher.

"You know what I mean: all wings and machinery and no body."

588   *Cheerful Deadhead*

GAS-STATION ATTENDANT: Here comes another I.W.W. customer.

PATRON: What's that?

ATTENDANT: A motorist who wants only Information, Wind, and Water.

589   *Fresh Eggs*
A bachelor was breakfasting in a restaurant when he saw an inscription on an egg: "Should this meet the eye of some young man who desires to marry a farmer's daughter, age 20, write . . ."

The bachelor wrote, and in a few days received the following note: "Your letter came too late. I am now married and have a son."

590   *Never Wrong*

A gentleman, quite backward about proposing to the lady of his choice, finally popped the question by saying:

"I was chatting with Mr. Smith the other day and I asked him if he thought you would say yes if I asked you to marry me. He thought you would."

"Mr. Smith is never wrong," was her tactful answer.

591   *Another Scotch Story*

"How much are your peaches?"

"Forty cents each, lady."

"I'll have one, please."

"Givin' a party?"

592   *Alpine Journey*

"Does the giraffe get a sore throat if he gets wet feet?"

"Yes, but not until the next week."

593   *Canine Erudition*

"Lay down, pup; lay down," ordered the man. "Good doggie—lay down, I say."

"You'll have to say, 'Lie down,' mister," declared a small bystander. "That's a Boston terrier."

594   *Sign on Back of Truck*

Crime doesn't pay. Neither does trucking.

595   *Nowadays One Specifies*

"Get my broker, Miss Jones."

"Yes, sir, stock or pawn?"

596   *Chicago or New York*

A bookseller wrote to a publisher in Chicago asking that a dozen copies of *Seekers after God* be shipped to him at once.

Within two days, he received this reply by wire:

"No seekers after God in Chicago or New York. Try Philadelphia."

597   *Up the Other Alley*

The congressman's wife sat up in bed, a startled look on her face. "Jim," she whispered. "There's a robber in the house."

"Impossible," was her husband's sleepy reply. "In the Senate, yes, but in the House, never."

598   *Modern Child*

PHOTOGRAPHER: Watch and see the birdie.

CHILD: Just pay attention to your exposure so that you do not ruin the plate.

599   *On the Safe Side*

Sam was in trouble again, and the judge asked him if he was guilty or not guilty.

"Guilty, sir, I think, but I'd rather be tried and make sure of it."

600   *Frank Prospect*

LIFE INSURANCE AGENT: Do you want a straight life?

PROSPECT: Well, I like to step out once in a while.

601   *Grammar*

The question before the class was whether "trousers" was singular or plural.

The point was settled by declaring them singular at the top and plural at the other extremity.

602   *Not a Bad Wish*

Mother was telling stories of the time she was a little girl. Little Harold listened thoughtfully as she told of riding a pony, sliding down a haystack, and wading in the brook on the farm.

Finally he said with a sigh, "I wish I had met you earlier, Mother."

603   *One at a Time*

A very stout man was walking on the promenade of a seaside town when he noticed a weighing machine with the notice: "I speak your weight."

He put a coin in the slot and stood on the platform. A voice answered: "One at a time, please!"

604   *Grrr*

Noticing that little Joan was struggling with an ear of corn, her mother offered to cut off the kernels. However, she was quickly rebuffed when Joan replied: "No, I like it on the bone!"

605 *Comparisons*

SHE: The Brownes must be awfully rich, judging from the clothes they wear.

HE: Oh, one can never tell. Some of the most gorgeous flowers haven't got a scent.

606 *Back on the Payroll*

"Did that star football player graduate last year?"

"No, he renewed his contract for another year."

607 *Bragging*

"I started in life without a penny in my pocket," said Smith.

"And I," put in Jones, "started in life without a pocket."

608 *Couldn't Fool Him*

A sheriff was taking a prisoner to jail. A gust of wind came around the corner and blew off the prisoner's hat. The prisoner made a sudden lunge forward to get it.

"No, you don't, wise guy," said the sheriff. "You stand where you are. I'll run and get it."

609 *Surely Feminine*

VISITOR: And what will you do, little girl, when you get as big as your mother?

LITTLE GIRL: Diet!

610 *A Problem over the World*

A fellow was walking along the street one day with two small boys, each wailing loudly. A neighbor yelled to him, asking what was the matter. "The problem that's wrong with the whole world," replied the man. "I've got three pieces of candy and each boy wants two."

611 *Well Charged*

Two women were discussing a mutual acquaintance.

"She has a very magnetic personality," said one woman.

"She ought to have," replied the other woman, "every stitch she has on is charged."

612 *High-Hat Pooch*

CUSTOMER: Has this dog a good pedigree?

SALESMAN: Has he? Say, if that dog could talk, he wouldn't speak to either of us.

613   *Tried Them All*

"Do we have to wait very much longer for Mommy, Daddy?"

"No, not now. They've just taken the last pair of shoes from the shelf."

614   *Courteous Retort*

OPERATOR: Pardon me, madam, but your girl seems more than twelve.

HER MOTHER: Operator, would you take me to be the mother of a girl that age?

OPERATOR: Lady, don't tell me you're her grandmother!

615   *Common Failing*

MOTHER: Do you know what happens to little girls who tell lies?

SMALL BETTY: Yes, they grow up and tell their little girls they'll get curly hair if they eat their spinach.

616   *Pretty Smart*

After a speech, a famous lecturer and wit was approached by a little white-haired woman who told him how much she had enjoyed his talk. "I take the liberty to speak to you," she admitted, "because you said you loved old ladies."

"I do, I do," was the gallant reply, "and I also like them your age, my dear."

617   *Compliment*

STOUT LADY (at a street crossing): Officer, could you see me across the street?

OFFICER (inclined to flattery): Why, Ma'm, I could see you a mile off.

618   *Government Spending*

An exasperated woman, being questioned by an Internal Revenue Service agent about her deductions, was heard to say: "I wish the government were half as fussy about how it spends money as it is about how I spend it!"

619   *Hmm*

It was during the impaneling of a jury that the following colloquy occurred:

"You are a property holder?"

"Yes, your honor."

"Married or single?"

"I have been married five years, your honor."

"Have you formed or expressed an opinion?"

"Not in five years, your honor."

620   *Right*

"So you want to try that proofreader job, eh?"

"Yes, sir."

"And do you understand all the responsibility attached to it?"

"Yes, sir, when you make a mistake, I take all the blame."

621   *Psychiatrists*

Two psychiatrists passed each other. One said: "You're feeling fine, how am I doing?"

622   *Unnatural History*

TEACHER: Can anyone tell me what causes trees to become petrified?

BRIGHT STUDENT: The wind makes them rock.

623   *Not Taking a Chance*

Two caterpillars were crawling across the grass when a butterfly flew over them. They looked up, and one nudged the other and said: "You couldn't get me up in one of those things for a million dollars!"

624   *House Detective*

"Mummy, I want to whisper something."

"Darling, big girls who are nearly five never whisper before company."

"All right then, but that gentleman over there took another cake when you weren't looking."

625   *New Crop*

"What do you think is the trouble with farming?"

"Well," replied Farmer Bentover, "in my day when we talked about what we could raise on 60 acres, we meant corn—not government loans."

626   *Soviet Russia*

In contrast to the United States, the position of woman in Soviet Russia is only equal to that of man.

627   *Evolution*

TEACHER: Yes, go on, Tommy. After the horse comes the
                  motor car, and (prompting) after the motor car
                  comes the . . .

TOMMY (whose
father has a car):   Installment man, teacher.

628   *More Than Was Expected*

Johnny, ten years old, applied for a job as grocery boy for the summer.
The grocer wanted a serious-minded youth, so he put Johnny to a little
test. "Well, my boy, what would you do with a million dollars?" he
asked.

"Oh, I don't know—I wasn't expecting so much at the start," said
Johnny.

629   *Pressing*

"I must pay my tailor's bill first."
"Why so?"
"Well, it's the most pressing one."

630   *To Have Lived*

'Tis better to have lived and loved
Than never to have lived at all.

—*Judge*

631   *All Explained*

JOHNNIE: Why does the whistle blow for a fire?"
BILLY: It doesn't blow for the fire, it blows for water. They've got the
             fire.

632   *Theological Mainspring*

Two ministers were driving in a cab to the station, and were in some
anxiety lest they should miss their train. One of them pulled out his
watch and discovered it had stopped.

"How annoying!" he exclaimed. "And I always put such faith in that
watch!"

"In a case like this," answered the other, "good works would evi-
dently have answered the purpose better."

633 *Still Cackling*

CUSTOMER: Are these eggs fresh?

GROCER: Fresh! Why, the hens haven't missed them yet.

634 *Lucid Intervals*

An American film actress was applying for a passport.

"Unmarried?" asked the clerk.

"Occasionally," answered the actress.

635 *Proof*

ORATOR: I thought your paper was friendly to me?

EDITOR: So it is. What's the matter?

ORATOR: I made a speech at the dinner last night, and you didn't print a line of it.

EDITOR: Well, what further proof do you want?

636 *Long, Long Trail*

The chief objection to the school of experience is that you never finish the postgraduate courses.

When you graduate from that school, brother, your diploma is a tombstone.

637 *Fleas and Elephants*

TEACHER (to bring out the idea of size): Mention a difference between an elephant and a flea.

TOMMY: Well, an elephant can have fleas, but a flea can't have elephants.

638 *Strictly Original Blundering*

TEACHER: Did your father help you with the problem?

WILLIE: No, I got it wrong myself.

639 *Prosperity*

May bad fortune follow you all your days
And never catch up with you.

640   *Down and Out*

The aviation instructor, having delivered a lecture on parachute work concluded:

"And if it doesn't open—well, gentlemen, that's what is known as 'jumping to a conclusion.' "

641   *Bossie's Little Weakness*

A city girl visiting her uncle on the farm was watching a cow chewing her cud.

"Pretty fine cow, that," said her uncle as he came by.

"Yes," said the girl, "But doesn't it cost a lot to keep her in chewing gum?"

642   *When Maude Gets Left*

"Doesn't that mule ever kick you?"

"No, sir, not yet, but he frequently kicks the place where I recently was."

643   *Chapter and Verse*

"My wife has the worst memory I ever heard of."

"Forgets everything, eh?"

"No, remembers everything."

644   *Out for the Long Shots*

"Where's the cashier?"

"Gone to the races."

"Gone to the races in business hours?"

"Yes, sir, it's his last chance of making the books balance."

645   *Only When New*

Betty, on a visit to her aunt, being offered some leftovers, politely declined them.

"Why, dear, don't you like turkey?" inquired her aunt.

"Only when it's new," said Betty.

646   *Out of the Frying Pan*

TEACHER: Really, Johnny, your handwriting is terrible. You must learn to write better.

JOHNNY: Well, if I did, you'd be finding fault with my spelling.

647 *Patient Research*

A party of tourists was enjoying the wonders of the Grand Canyon. A native passing by was asked by the driver of the car:

"I say, neighbor, can you tell us what caused this terrible gorge?"

"Well, they say a Scotchman once owned a range near here, and one day he lost a golf ball down a gopher hole."

648 *Emulating a Master*

"You say your son plays the piano like Paderewski?"

"Yes. He uses both hands."

649 *Educational Limitations*

"How soon will I know anything after I come out of the anesthetic?"

"Well, that's expecting a lot from an anesthetic."

650 *Blessed Are the Humble*

EDITOR: Do you know how to run a newspaper?

APPLICANT: No, sir.

EDITOR: Well, I'll try you. You talk like you've had experience.

651 *Shocking Politeness*

POLICEMAN: How did you knock him down?

MOTORIST: I didn't! I pulled up to let him go across—and he fainted.

652 *Salvation*

JIM: Some rich people seem to think they can buy their way into heaven by leaving a million dollars to a church when they die.

JOHN: I don't know but that they stand as much chance as some of the people who are trying to get in on the installment plan of one dollar a Sunday while they're living.

653 *Too Much Competition*

Not long ago a jury went out early in the day on a simple case, and when it came near the time for court to adjourn, the judge sent for the jury, and asked the foreman if they required any further instruction. "We need no instruction, your honor," replied the foreman, "but here are eleven prejudiced and unreasonable persons who won't agree to anything."

654   *In a Conference*

A little boy was saying his go-to-bed prayers in a very low voice.

"I can't hear you, dear," his mother whispered.

"Wasn't talking to you," said the small one firmly.

655   *Pedagogy*

At a recent "panel discussion" at one of our great universities, several speakers aired their views on "creative education," solemnly or otherwise. One speaker got up to remark: "I have discovered that if you have pupils of greater ability, you will get better results" and the wall of that university (it is averred) rocked with this momentous announcement. Someone suggested that the speaker would have been much better advised had he said something like this: "If the correlation of intrinsic competency to actual numerical representation is definitely high, then the thoroughly objective conclusion may inexpugnably be reached that the scholastic derivations and outgrowths will attain a pattern of unified superiority." No one would have known what he was talking about, and he would thereafter have been regarded with awe as a pedagogical pundit.—*Henry Grattan Doyle*

656   *Cheers for Willie!*

"Who gave the bride away?"

"Her little brother, Willie. He stood right up in the middle of the ceremony and yelled, 'Hurray, Louise, you've got him at last!'"

657   *No Reference*

WOULD-BE EMPLOYER: Young man, do you have references from your last place of employment?

APPLICANT: Yes, sir. Here's their letter. It reads: "To whom it may concern. We had Sam Jones working for us for three weeks and we can say we are satisfied!"

658   *Frigid Air*

An electrician was examining a refrigerator that was using too much electricity and could not find the reason.

He idly asked the cook, "How do you like the refrigerator?"

"I like it fine," she said. "I open the door and it cools off the whole kitchen."

659   *Call an Ambulance*

"Waiter, are you sure this ham was cured?"

"Yes, sir."

"Well, it's had a relapse."

660   *A Challenge*

A certain young pastor in his first charge announced nervously:

"I will take for my text the words, 'And they fed five men with five thousand loaves of bread and two thousand fishes.' "

At this misquotation, an old parishioner said audibly:

"That's no miracle—I could do it myself."

The young preacher said nothing, but the next Sunday he announced the same text again. This time he got it right:

"And they fed five thousand men on five loaves of bread and two fishes."

He waited a moment and then, leaning over the pulpit and looking at the parishioner, he said:

"And could you do that, too, Mr. Smith?"

"Of course I could," Mr. Smith replied.

"And how would you do it?" said the preacher.

"With what was left over from last Sunday," said Mr. Smith.

661   *Inn Luck or Inn Dutch*

"Why don't you give your new bungalow a name? Something appropriate. Other people do. There's 'Seldom Inn,' 'Walk Inn,' 'Cosy Inn,' and a lot of others."

"That's an idea. As I've just finished paying for it, I'll name it 'All Inn.' "

662   *Mom Was No Prophet*

When supper was served, Helen refused a second helping of ice cream with a polite but wistful, "No, thank you!"

"Do have some more, dear!" her hostess urged.

"Mother told me to say, 'No, thank you,' " Helen explained naively, "but I don't think she could have known how small that first helping was going to be!"

663   *Super Service*

A customer opened his first checking account. At the end of the month he got a statement which meant absolutely nothing to him, but he was delighted to receive his checks.

"It's a smart bank I'm dealing with," he told a pal.

"Is it?" was the rejoinder.

"It sure is. Those fellows were smart enough to get every one of my checks back for me."

664   *Southpaw*

"Does it make any difference on which side of you I sit?" she asked.

"Not a bit," he replied. "I'm ambidextrous."

665   *Alive and Fresh*

FISH DEALER: Lobsters, madam; nice lobsters? Look, they're all alive.

LADY: Yes, but are they fresh?

666   *Short Circuit*

An electrician returned home from work one night to find his small son waiting for him with his right hand swathed in a bandage.

"Hello, sonny!" he exclaimed. "Cut your hand?"

"No, Dad," was the reply. "I picked up a pretty little fly and one end wasn't insulated."

667   *Annual Stew*

"Do you summer in the country?"

"No, I simmer in the city."

668   *A Common Experience*

"The first day out was perfectly lovely," said the young lady just back from abroad. "The water was as smooth as glass, and it was simply gorgeous. But the second day was rough and—er—decidedly dis-gorgeous."

669   *Thumbs Down Slightly*

Children have their own peculiar way of expressing themselves.

"Well, Peggy," said the neighbor, "and how do you like your new teacher?"

Peggy thought a moment and then said: "I half like her and I half don't like her, but I think I half don't like her the most."

670   *The Worst Boom*

When the president of the Los Angeles Chamber of Commerce was asked recently how the recession had hit Los Angeles, he replied: "Recession? We have no recession in Los Angeles, but I will admit that we are having the worst boom in many, many years."

671   *Cheering Innovation*

REAL ESTATE AGENT: Well, what do you think of our little city?

PROSPECT: I'll tell you, brother. This is the first cemetery I ever saw with lights.

672   *When Dads Disappoint*

TOMMY: That problem you helped me with last night was all wrong, Daddy.

FATHER: All wrong, was it? Well, I'm sorry.

TOMMY: Well, you needn't exactly worry about it, because none of the other daddies got it right, either.

673   *Call for Progress*

LITTLE JOAN: What do the angels do in Heaven, Mummy?

MOTHER: They sing and play harps.

LITTLE JOAN: Haven't they any radios?

674   *Ducking Destiny*
"Pop, will I look like you when I grow up?"
    "Everybody seems to think so, son."
    "Well, I won't have to grow up for a long time, will I, Pop?"

675   *Accredited Delegate*
"Who will help a man to correct personality defects if not his wife?" asks a heart-throb editor.
    Well, sister, there is his wife's mother.

676   *Full Explanation*
A man who was invited to a house party he didn't wish to attend telegraphed to the hostess: "Regret I can't come. Complete lie follows by letter."

677   *Let Him Do His Stuff*
"What! Another new dress? How ever do you think I can find the money to pay for it?"
    "Darling, you know I'm not inquisitive."

678   *Financial Genius*

"Father," said Junior, "what is a financial genius?"

"A financial genius, my son," answered his harassed pater, "is a man who can earn money faster than his family can spend it."

679   *When Nerves Are Raw*

HIS WIFE: It's about time to think about where we shall spend the summer.

HUSBAND: I wish you'd say "pass" the summer, Helen; "spend" is so confoundedly suggestive.

680   *Human Nature*

"Bill," groaned the managing editor of the tabloid, "nothing scandalous has happened in twenty-four hours. What'll we do for the front page?"

"Aw, don't get discouraged, Steve," the city editor comforted. "Something'll happen. I've still got faith in human nature."

681   *Housebroken*

We congratulated a lady on her silver wedding anniversary for living twenty-five years with the same man.

"But he is not the same man he was when I first got hold of him," she replied.

682   *Figs of Thistles*

"Your methods of cultivation are hopelessly out of date," said the youthful agricultural college graduate to the old farmer. "Why, I'd be astonished if you even got ten pounds of apples from that tree."

"So would I," replied the farmer. "It's a pear tree."

683   *Balancing the Budget*

TEACHER: We borrowed our numerals from the Arabs, our calendar from the Romans, and our banking from the Italians. Can any one think of other examples?

CHARLIE: Our lawnmower from the Smiths, and our ladder from the Browns.

684   *Pawnshop*

"What do the three balls in front of a pawnshop mean?"

"Two to one you don't get it back."

685   *Wanted to Help on the Treasure Hunt*

A burglar, who had entered a poor minister's house at midnight, was disturbed by the occupant of the room he was in. Drawing his weapon, he said:

"If you stir, you are a dead man. I'm hunting for your money."

"Let me get up and turn on a light," said the minister, "and I'll hunt with you."

686   *Conclusions*

The young bachelor was asked which he thought were happier, people who were married or people who were not.

"Well, I don't know," he replied, "sometimes I think there is as many as is that aren't, as aren't that is."

687   *He Won't Win That Way*

As the politician said, "This occasion gives me an opportunity to shake hands with many old faces."

688   *Read the Directions That Come with Each One*

The city girl watching the farmer milk a cow: "That looks easy, but how do you turn it off?"

689   *Boys Who Tell Lies*

MOTHER: Do you know what happens to little boys who tell lies?

JOHNNY: Yes, Mother; they travel for half-fare.

690   *Philosophy*

Philosophy is finding out how many things there are in the world which you can't have if you want them, and don't want if you can have them.
—*Puck*

691   *Center Aisle*

A woman who had approached the office of a Broadway theater was making a great fuss over the seat they gave her.

"Are you quite positive," she asked for the third time, "that this seat is near enough to the stage?"

"Madam," said the box office man, "if it was much nearer, you'd have to act in the play."

692   *English*

A Frenchman learning English said to his British tutor: "English is a queer language. What does this sentence mean: 'Should Mr. Noble, who sits for this constituency, consent to stand again, he will in all probability have a walkover'?"

693   *Page the Government Weather Bureau*

A Swedish farmer who wanted to make his permanent home in this country appeared for his naturalization papers.

"Are you satisfied with the general conditions of this country?" he was asked.

"Yah, sure," answered the hopeful one.

"And does this government of ours suit you?"

"Well, yah, mostly," stammered the man, "only I lak see more rain."

694   *The Rewards of Authorship*

The critic started to leave in the middle of the second act of the play.

"Don't go now," said the manager. "I promise there's a terrific kick in the next act."

"Fine," was the retort. "Give it to the author."

695   *Indecisive*

Politician to aide: "About their charge that I'm indecisive—do you think I should answer it, or let it go, or answer it in part, or what?"

696   *Good Reason*

"But this officer says that while you were in a drunken state you tried to climb a lamp post."

"Yes, I did, your worship, but three crocodiles had been following me about all night, and they were getting on my nerves."

697   *It's All Clear Now*

A Cockney telephoned to inquire about the rate to Ealing, a suburb of London. The man at the other end of the line couldn't catch the name of the station, so in desperation he asked the Cockney to spell it. Quickly came the reply: "E—for 'Erbert, A—wot the 'orses heat, L—w'ere yer goes w'en yer dies, I—wot yer sees wiv, N—wot lays a hegg, G—Gowd bless me. Get me?"—*Wall Street Journal*

698   *Not Sure*

"You've been out with worse-looking fellows than I am, haven't you?"

She did not reply.

"I said, you've been out with worse-looking fellows than I am, haven't you?"

"I heard you the first time. I was trying to think."

699   *How to Paraphrase*

The pupil was asked to paraphrase the sentence: "He was bent on seeing her."

He wrote: "The sight of her doubled him up."

700   *Silence*

Sir Lewis Morris was complaining to Oscar Wilde about the neglect of his poems by the press. "It is a complete conspiracy of silence against me, a conspiracy of silence. What ought I to do, Oscar?" "Join in," replied Wilde.

701   *Not Brave But Generous*

"Did he take his misfortunes like a man?"
     "Precisely. He laid the blame on his wife."

702   *Stew Bad*

DINER:	Waiter! This stew is terrible. What kind is it?
WAITER:	The chef calls this his enthusiastic stew.
DINER:	Why?
WAITER:	He puts everything he has into it.

703   *Slightly Sarcastic*

"How is it that you are late this morning?" the clerk was asked by his manager.
     "I overslept," was the reply.
     "What? Do you sleep at home as well?" inquired the manager.

704   *So That's Where They Go after Graduation*

TOURIST (in Yellowstone Park):	Those Indians have a bloodcurdling yell.
GUIDE:	Yes, ma'am; every one of 'em was a college cheerleader.

705   *The Enemy*

"Sir, the enemy are before us as thick as peas!"
     "All right, shell them!"

706   *Why Stay Longer*

MOTHER (to small son who is going to a party):	Now, dear, what are you going to do when you've had enough to eat?
LITTLE TOMMY:	Come home.

707   *Three Beans*

A teacher called for sentences using the word "beans."

"My father grows beans," said the bright boy of the class.

"My mother cooks beans," said another pupil.

Then a third popped up: "We are all human beans."

708   *No Thanks*

MOTHER: Marilyn, were you a good little girl at church today?

MARILYN: Yes, mother. A man offered me a big plate of money, and I said, "No, thank you."

709   *Using His Head*

SERGEANT: Why is it important not to lose your head in an attack?

RECRUIT: Because that would leave no place to put the helmet.

710   *The Frog Are a Wonderful Bird*

This short essay on frogs, by a young immigrant, was reported by the Chicago Board of Education: "What a wonderful bird the frog are. When he stand, he sit almost. When he hop, he fly almost. He ain't got no sense hardly. He ain't got no tail hardly, either, when he sit on what he ain't got almost."—*Houston Chronicle*

711   *Hash*

"Bring me a plate of hash," said the diner.

The waiter walked over to the kitchen elevator. "Gent wants to take a chance," he called down the speaking tube.

"I'll have some hash too," said a second customer.

The waiter picked up the tube again. "Another sport," he yelled.

712   *Her Address*

Jane was always glad to say her prayers, but she wanted to be sure she was heard in heaven.

One night after the usual "Amen," she dropped her head upon her pillow and closed her eyes. After a moment she said, "Lord! this prayer comes from 203 Selden Avenue."

713   *I Didn't Do It*

"John," the teacher said in class one day, "correct this sentence, 'It was me who broke the window.'"

"That's easy," John said. "It wasn't me who broke the window."

714   *Smart Worms*

Earth flew in all directions as the crimson-faced would-be golfer attempted to strike the ball. "My word," he blurted out to his caddie, "the worms will think there's been an earthquake."

"I don't know," replied the caddie, "the worms 'round here are smart. I'll bet most of them are hiding underneath the ball for safety."

715   *The Last Word*

WIFE: Must I persuade you to have some more alphabet soup?

HUBBY: No, thanks, not another word.

716   *Definitely*

"My wife doesn't know what she wants."

"Hah, you're lucky. Mine does!"

717   *It Southernly Was*

HE: Honey, will yo'all marry me?

SHE: Oh, this is so southern!

718   *Aquatic Engineer*

"My brother's an aquatic engineer."

"What's that?"

"He's in charge of the dishwashing!"

719   *Make Mine Well*

An old cowpuncher entered a restaurant and ordered a steak. The waiter brought it to him, and it was rare, very rare. The cowpuncher demanded that it be taken back and cooked.

"It's already cooked," the waiter snapped.

"Cooked," roared the cowpuncher. "I've seen cows hurt worse than that and they got well."

720   *Weighty Evidence*

The portly man was trying to get to his seat at the circus. "Pardon me," he said to a woman, "did I step on your foot?"

"Possibly so," she said, after glancing at the circus ring. "All the elephants are still out there. You must have."

721   *How Many Rabbits Make a Mink Coat?*

GLAD: Wonder why the magician wanted to borrow my mink coat.

PUSS: He probably wanted to pull rabbits out of it.

722   *A Sound Sleeper*

"I slept like a log."

"Yes, I heard the sawmill."

723   *One Is Enough*

"There are ten reasons why I won't marry Joe."

"What are they?"

"Well, the first is he hasn't any money and the other nine are things I want."

724   *Sweet Young Thing*

Virginia Military Institute, the pride of the South, is sometimes referred to as "The West Point of the South." A sweet young thing from Lexington, Virginia, had been invited to one of the dances at West Point, and after a busy day of sightseeing over the grounds, she was asked by her escort how it had impressed her.

"Oh, it's wonderful," she answered admiringly. "Why, this must be the VMI of the North."

725   *Soon or Late*

There swims no goose so gray, but soon or late
She finds some honest gander for her mate.

—Pope

726   *Poor Memory*

SCIENTIST (to pharmacist):   Give me some prepared monaceticacid-ester of salicylic acid.

PHARMACIST: Do you mean aspirin?

SCIENTIST: That's right! I can never think of that name.

727   *Something to Remember*

"Spaghetti can be eaten most successfully," film star Sophia Loren once advised, "if you inhale it like a vacuum cleaner."

728   *Disillusioned*

Every year college deans pop the routine question to their undergraduates: "Why did you come to college?" Traditionally the answers match the question in triteness. But last year one University of Arizona coed unexpectedly confided: "I came to be went with—but I ain't yet!"

729   *How To Reduce in One Lesson*

"What's the best exercise for reducing?"

"Just move the head slowly from right to left when asked to have a second helping."

730   *Too Personal*

JUDGE: Are you guilty or not guilty?

PRISONER: It seems to me that is a mighty personal question.

731   *Well Laid Out*

"Isn't this town laid out prettily?"

"It's laid out all right. How long has it been dead?"

732   *Two Sides to Every Question*

"There are two sides to every question," proclaimed the wise man.

"Yes," said the fool, "and there are two sides to a sheet of flypaper, but it makes a difference to the fly which side he chooses."

733   *One Stranger Present*

The preacher was at ease after service Sunday night.

"Many folks in church?" asked his wife.

"Yes, good attendance—and a stranger was present, but I did not see him."

"But how do you know?"

"There was a twenty dollar bill in the contribution box."

734   *The American Tourist*

"Yes, there is something smaller still than an atom," said the patriotic citizen to his friend.

"What is it?"

"The American tourist in Europe who curries favor by knocking his own country."

735   *Holding Out*

MR. MEEK: Darling, haven't I always given you my salary check the first of every month?

MRS. MEEK: Yes, but you never told me you got paid twice a month.

736   *Are You Ill?*

Consider the member of the Chamber of Deputies who had been a veterinarian before he became a politician. One day, during a bitter debate, an aristocratic opponent who was being worsted in the argument descended to personal remarks.

"Is it true, my good man," he inquired sneeringly, "that you are actually a veterinarian?"

"It is, sir. Are you ill?"

737   *Too Fresh*

MRS. NEWLYWED: Aren't these eggs rather small today?

GROCER: Yes'm but the farmer who sells me my eggs had to start to town early this morning and took them out of the nest too soon.

738   *Ghost Stories*

"I'm a great lover of ghost stories."

"So'm I, pal. Let's shake."

739   *There Is a Difference*

TEACHER: What is the difference between results and consequences?

BRIGHT PUPIL: Results are what you expect; consequences are what you get.

740   *Courtesy*

"What would be the proper thing to say if, in carving the duck, it should skid off the platter and into your neighbor's lap?"

"Be very courteous. Say, 'May I trouble you for that duck?' "

741   *In the Dumps*

"Whenever I'm in the dumps I just get myself another hat."

"I wondered where you get them."

742   *Try Eatie Wheaties*

THE MAN: I want a loaf of Mumsie's Bread, a package of Krunchies, some Goody Sanny Spread, Ole Mammy's Lasses, Orange Pulley, a pound of Aunt Annie's sugar candy, Bitsey-bite size.

THE CLERK: Sorry. No Krunchies. How about Krinkly Krips, Oatsie-Toasties, Malty - Wheaties, Riceltes, or Eatum-Wheatums?

THE MAN: The Wheatums, then.

THE CLERK: Anything else? Tootsies, Tatery Chips, Cheesie Weesies, Gingile Bits, Itsey Cakes, Sweetzie Toofums, or Dramma's Doughnies?

743   *Weighed and Found Wanting*

"So you met Marian today?"

"Yes. I hadn't seen her for ten years."

"Has she kept her girlish figure?"

"Kept it? She's doubled it."

744   *Definite Proof*

COUNSEL (to police witness):   But if a man is on his hands and knees in the middle of the road, that does not prove he is drunk.

POLICEMAN: No, sir, it does not. But this one was trying to roll up the white line!

745   *Special Service*

OWNER OF MIDGET CAR: I want a pint of gasoline and a cup of oil, please.

GARAGE HAND: And shall I cough into the tires, sir?

746   *A Raise Was Necessary*

BOOKKEEPER: I'll have to have a raise, sir; there are three other companies after me.

EMPLOYER: Is that so? What companies?

BOOKKEEPER: Light, phone, and gas.

747   *Colorful Writing*

The native student, writing a letter to the superintendent of the mission, desired to end with the words: "May Heaven preserve you."

Not being quite confident of the meaning of "preserve," he looked it up in a dictionary. When the letter reached the superintendent, it ended with the words: "And may Heaven pickle you."

748   *The Wrong Time*

One night, as a messenger from the office of an evening paper was passing along the way on the banks of the river, he heard the sound of someone struggling in the water.

"Are you drowning?" he shouted.

"I am," replied a feeble voice from the water.

"What a pity!" said the lad consolingly. "You are just too late for the last edition tonight. But cheer up; you'll have a nice little paragraph all to yourself in the morning."

749 *Obstinate*

The clergyman was walking through the village when he met one of his parishioners.

"How's your cold, Donald?" he asked.

"Verra obstinate," replied the parishioner.

"And how is your wife?"

"About the same."

750 *Wild Oats and Rye*

MOTHER: After all, he's only a boy, and boys will sow their wild oats.

FATHER: Yes, but I wouldn't mind if he didn't mix so much rye with it.

751 *He May Be Right*

"How many students are there in the university?"

"About one in every five."

752 *Hypnotism and Marriage*

"I was hypnotized last week."

"What's 'hypnotized' mean?"

"Why, to hypnotize is to get a man in your power, and make him do whatever you want."

"That's not hypnotism, that's marriage."

753 *No Mind Reader*

FIRST NEW YEAR'S EVE CELEBRATOR: What are you doing?

SECOND CELEBRATOR: Writing a letter to myself.

FIRST: What does it say?

SECOND: I don't know. I won't get it until tomorrow.

754 *Spelling*

SCHOOL VISITOR: What's the matter my boy?

PUPIL: Palpitation and insomnia.

SCHOOL VISITOR: But you can't be suffering from these things.

PUPIL: It isn't suffering, sir. It's spelling.

755 *He Looked Familiar*

An enthusiastic golfer came home to dinner. During the meal his wife said: "Willie tells me he caddied for you this afternoon."

"Well, do you know," said Willie's father, "I thought I'd seen that boy before."

756   *Teaching by Illustration*

PROFESSOR: How much does a twelve-pound shot weigh?

FRESHMAN: Don't know, sir.

PROFESSOR: Well, then, what time does the ten o'clock train leave?

FRESHMAN: Ten o'clock.

PROFESSOR: Then what is the weight of the twelve-pound shot?

FRESHMAN: Ten pounds, sir.

757   *Giving the Password*

The young recruit was the victim of so many practical jokes that he doubted all men and their motives. One night while he was on guard, the figure of one of the officers loomed up in the darkness.

"Who goes there?" he challenged.

"Major Moses," replied the officer.

The young recruit scented a joke.

"Glad to meet you, Moses," he said cheerfully. "Advance and give the Ten Commandments."

758   *Punctual*

"Well, son," wrote the fond mother to her soldier son, "I hope you have been punctual in rising every morning so that you haven't kept the regiment waiting breakfast for you."

759   *False Arrest*

"What were you arrested for?" asked the friend.

"I found an automobile."

"Found? Nonsense! They wouldn't arrest you for finding an automobile."

"Well, you see I found it before the owner lost it."

760   *The Tied and the Untied*

INQUIRING
SCHOOLBOY: Dad, what effect does the moon have on the tide?

DAD (from the
depths of his
newspaper):   Not any, son. Only on the untied.

761   *Five Men on a Horse*

BETA (at riding academy):   I wish to rent a horse.

GROOM: How long?

BETA: The longest you've got, there will be five of us going."

762 *Without Asking Questions*

A doctor was called in to see a very testy aristocrat. "Well, sir, what's the matter?" he asked cheerfully.

"That, sir," snapped the patient, "is for you to find out."

"I see," said the doctor thoughtfully. "Well, if you'll excuse me for an hour or so, I'll go along and fetch a friend of mine—a veterinarian. He's the only chap I know who can make a diagnosis without asking questions."

763 *Trees to a Golfer Poet*

"I think that I shall never see a hazard rougher than a tree—a tree o'er which my ball must fly if on the green it is to lie; a tree which stands that green to guard, and makes the shots extremely hard; a tree whose leafy arms extend, to kill the mashie shot I send; a tree that stands in silence there, while angry golfers rave and swear. Niblicks were made for fools like me, who cannot ever miss a tree."

764 *He Knew the Answers*

A member of a psych class on tour asked an inmate his name.

"George Washington," was the reply.

"But," said the perplexed lad, "last time we were here you were Abraham Lincoln."

"That," said the inmate sadly, "was by my first wife."

765 *Keep on Going*

Keep on going and the chances are you will stumble on something, perhaps when you are least expecting it. I have never heard of anyone stumbling on something sitting down.—*C. F. Kettering*

766 *The Sergeant and the Rookie*

"Com-pa-nee atten-shun," bawled the drill sergeant to the awkward squad. "Com-pa-nee, lift your left leg and hold it straight in front of you."

By mistake one member held up his right leg, which brought it out side by side with his neighbor's left leg.

"And who is the galoot over there holding up both legs?" shouted the hardboiled sergeant.

767 *Counsel for the Defense Rests*

A case was being heard in court in which a farmer was claiming indemnity for a cow killed by a railway train. Counsel for the defense put many tedious and superfluous questions.

"Was the cow on the track?" he asked the engineer.

The engineer had had about enough. He replied: "No, of course not. She was in a field half a mile away. But when it saw her, the engine left the rails, jumped the fence, and chased her across the field and up a tree. There it strangled her to death."

768   *Hopeless*

"You've read my last book, haven't you?" asked the author.

"I hope so," groaned the critic.

769   *Straight to the Point*

During the progress of a lawsuit a witness was on the stand for cross-examination regarding the character and habits of the defendant. "I believe you testified a little while ago," began the counsel for the plaintiff, "that Mr. Smith, defendant in this case, has a reputation for being very lazy and personally incompetent."

"No, sir; no, sir," protested the witness. "I didn't say that. What I said was he changed jobs pretty often; that he seemed to get tired of work very quickly."

"Has he or has he not a reputation in the community for being lazy?" persisted the lawyer.

"Well, sir, I don't want to do the gentleman any injustice, and I don't go so far as to say he is lazy; but it's the general impression around the community that if it required any voluntary and sustained exertion on his part to digest his food, he would have died years ago from lack of nourishment."

770   *Worried about His Future*

JOE: You look downhearted, old man. What are you worried about?

BILL: My future.

JOE: What makes your future seem so hopeless?

BILL: My past.

771   *The Poor Animal*

When Mrs. Berg's expensive new fur coat was delivered to her home, she fondled it ecstatically for a time, and then looked sad for a moment.

"What's the matter, aren't you satisfied with it?" inquired her husband.

"Yes," she answered, "but I feel so sorry for the poor thing that was skinned."

"Thanks," said Mr. Berg.

772 *Information, Please*

MOTHER: Stop asking so many questions. Don't you know that curiosity killed the cat?

SMALL DAUGHTER: Is that so? What did the cat want to know?

773 *The Strategy of Handling People*

A woman was driving in her new car when something went wrong with the engine. The traffic light changed from green to red and back to green and still she could not get the car to budge. The traffic cop came up.

"What's the matter, miss?" he inquired. "Ain't we got colors you like?"

774 *Curious*

"These rock formations," explained the guide, "were piled up here by the glaciers."

"But where are the glaciers?" asked a curious old lady.

"They've gone back, madam, to get more rocks," said the guide.

775 *Politeness*

FATHER: Well, Willie, what did you learn at school today?"

WILLIE (proudly): I learned to say "Yes, sir" and "No, sir" and "Yes, ma'am" and "No, ma'am."

FATHER: You did?

WILLIE: Yeah.

776 *Showers for the Groom*

"Daddy," said Bobby, "don't they ever give any showers for the groom?"

"No, son," replied his dad, "there will be plenty of storms for him after the bride begins to reign."

777 *Middle Class*

WILLIAM: Dad, what is the middle class?

DAD: The middle class consists of people who are not poor enough to accept charity and not rich enough to donate anything.

778 *All Prepared*

"I want to grow some trees in my garden. Can you sell me a few seeds?" inquired Mrs. Newlywed.

"Certainly, madam," replied the clerk. He fetched her a packet.

"Can you guarantee these?" she asked.

"Yes, madam, we can."

"Will the trees be tall and thick in the trunk?"

"They should be, madam."

"And quite strong at the roots, I suppose?"

"Oh yes, madam."

"Very well, I'll take a hammock at the same time."

779   *A Poor Substitute*

There is a church that holds annual strawberry festivals. Each year they put out the same large sign in front of the church. A stranger was driving through the town. He saw the big sign in front of the church reading: "Everybody come to the annual strawberry festival. All the delicious strawberry shortcake you can eat for $2. Everybody welcome at the strawberry festival." Then at the bottom, they had tacked on this small notice: "P.S. This year, because of the drought, we are serving prunes." (This story can be used when one is called upon to substitute for another speaker. To illustrate, the substitute speaker might say after telling the story, "I rather fear that tonight what you will get will be prunes compared to the strawberry shortcake you would have received if the distinguished speaker who is absent could have addressed you.")

780   *All of One Mind*

It is sometimes dangerous to have only one idea. In this case, there were three men who had taken a few too many drinks. They had one idea in mind, which was to catch the 11:05 P.M. train. A moment before train time, they rushed into the depot and got to the train just as it was pulling out. One of them managed to get aboard; the second one caught hold of the handrail on the coach and finally pulled himself up; the third fellow missed the train altogether. As he sat on the platform, he began laughing, and one of the spectators said: "I don't see what you have to laugh about, when you missed the train." He said, "Well, the joke is on the other fellows who caught the train, because they just came down to see me off."

781   *Credit Only*

Mr. Smith, a southern merchant, had sold to a cotton grower on credit during the period before the cotton was ready to be picked and sold. When the grower sold his cotton, he went to Smith's competitor across the street and bought for cash. The next time Smith met the grower he said: "I sold to you on credit for months and now the first time you get cash you go across the street and buy, instead of coming to me. What's the idea?" The grower said: "I'm sorry, but I didn't even know you-all sold for cash."

782   *Professor*

> I once had a classmate named Guesser
> Whose knowledge got lesser and lesser.
> It at last grew so small
> He knew nothing at all—
> And now he's a college professor.

> *—Arizona Kitty Kat*

783   *A Good Simile*

As successful as a traffic cop selling tickets for the policemen's ball.

784   *The Golfer*

> "Who's the stranger, mother dear—
> Look, he knows us, ain't he queer?"
> "Hush, my own, don't talk so wild;
> That's your father, dearest child."
> "That's my father? No such thing!
> Father died away last spring."
> "Father didn't die, you dub;
> Father joined a golfing club.
> Now the club is closed, so he
> Has no place to go, you see.
> No place left for him to roam,
> This is why he's coming home.
> Kiss him, he won't bite you, child;
> All them golfing guys look wild."

> *—Boardwalk Illustrated News*

785   *Same Fellow*

The guide was showing the tourist the sights of Italy. He said, "Now here is the Leaning Tower of Pisa." The tourist said, "I didn't get the name." The guide repeated, "This is the Leaning Tower of Pisa." The tourist answered, "I still don't recognize the name, but it looks like the work of the contractor who built my garage."

786   *It Has to Be Heard*

A musical critic wrote: "Here is Tchaikovsky at his best. Music so beautiful it has to be heard to be appreciated."

A lot of music is like that.

787 *Help, Your Honor*

To swear to tell the truth in a courtroom and then have some lawyer constantly object.

788 *Up on His Hybrids*

Little Jimmy, age four, was looking at a picture book. When he came to a picture of a zebra, mother asked him what animal that was.

Jimmy thought a moment, then replied, "That's a horse that ate hybrid corn."

789 *Troubled Him Just Once*

DOCTOR: Have you ever had trouble with dyspepsia?

PATIENT: Only once.

DOCTOR: And when was that?

PATIENT: When I tried to spell it.

790 *Paid in Full*

A country doctor called upon a widow, soon after the death of her husband, and announced his intentions of cutting his bill, for services rendered, in half. With tears in her eyes, the old lady reached out and clasped the doctor's hand and in a trembling voice said, "God bless you, my good friend. I'll be as good as you and knock off the other half."

791 *Comedian's Lament*

> I cannot repeat the good old gags,
> Which always stop the show,
> Because you hear them nightly
> On TV and radio.

792 *Give 'em More Time*

"Have you any children, Mr. Smith?"

"Yes—three."

"Do they live at home with you?"

"Not one of them—they are not married, yet."

793 *Magic*

A little girl went into a large business establishment, and had her first ride in an elevator. "How did you like it?" asked her father.

"Why, it was so funny," answered the child. "We went into a little house, and the upstairs came down."

794   *Completely Outfitted*

VISITOR (speaking of
      little boy):   He has his mother's eyes.
      MOTHER: And his father's mouth.
      CHILD: And his brother's trousers.

795   *Just a Small Error*

Three piano movers knocked on the door of a house. A meek-looking man with an inferiority complex opened the door.

"Did you order a piano from the Flatnote Music Store?" asked the first piano mover.

The tenant shook his head.

"Not a piano," he corrected. "I ordered a flute."

"Accordin' to this bill of ladin'," he grumbled, "you ordered a piano."

The gentleman with the inferiority complex studied the three husky piano movers.

"Very well," he said nervously, "move it in. But if your firm makes any more errors like that, I'll have to deal somewhere else!"

796   *Correct*

TEACHER: Johnny, can you tell me the name of a city in Alaska?
JOHNNY: No'm.

797   *Understatement*

We are inclined to agree with the Connecticut newspaper which affirms that Barnum never said of suckers, "One is born every minute." The great showman seldom was guilty of understatement.

798   *Wasting Gas*

Little George was visiting his aunt. He found the cat in a sunny window purring cheerfully.

"Oh, Auntie, come quick," said Little George, "the cat has gone to sleep and left his engine running."

799   *The Reason*

An employee asked her employer if she would be good enough to advance her a few dollars out of next month's wages, and gave the reason as follows:

"You see our minister is leaving and we are collecting money so that we can give him a little 'momentum'."

800   *Confused*

"What parable in the Bible do you like best?" was the question asked of a little boy. And the answer was, "The one about the fellow that loafs and fishes."

801   *Traffic Cop*

TRAFFIC COP (producing notebook):	Name, please.
MOTORIST:	Aloysius Alastair Cyprian.
TRAFFIC COP (putting book away):	Well, don't let me catch you again.

802   *Empty Head*

"I have a cold or something in my head."
"A cold, undoubtedly."

803   *Free*

"How long are you in jail for?"
"Two weeks."
"What is the charge?"
"No charge; everything is free."

804   *Ancestors*

"Speaking of old families," said the aristocrat of the party, "one of my ancestors was present at the signing of the Magna Charta."

"And one of mine," said another, "was present at the signing of the Ten Commandments."

805   *D.D or M.D.*

The temporary member of a golf club wished to fix up a game. The secretary introduced him to one Doctor Clark.

"Now, Doctor," said the stranger with a twinkle of the eye, "it is important for me to know whether you are a doctor who preaches or one who practices."

806   *A Little Hoarse*

Aunt Prudence: "Keep away from the loudspeaker, Denny. The announcer sounds as if he had a cold.

807   *The Other Half-Pound*

"I sent my little boy for two pounds of plums and you only sent a pound and a half. Are your scales correct?"

"My scales are all right, madam. Have you weighed your little boy?"

808   *Efficiency*

The department store engaged an efficiency expert, whose obsession was to move the departments to different parts of the store every day. One day a section would be on the top floor, the next it would be in the basement, and on the third it would be placed where the restaurant had been.

After three weeks of this an old lady approached a harassed salesperson and asked him if he could tell her where the draperies department was.

"No, madam," he said wearily; "but if you'll stand here for a few minutes I'm sure you'll see it go by!"

809   *I Don't Know*

PROFESSOR: What three words are used most among college men?

FRESHMAN: I don't know.

PROFESSOR: Correct.

810   *Should Know Better*

MOTHER: Willie, why did you kick your little brother in the stomach?

WILLIE: It was his own fault. He turned around.

811   *Last Chance*

Flying over the Bay of Naples, a pilot turned to his passenger and said: "Have you ever heard that phrase, 'See Naples and Die'?"

"Yes," said the passenger.

"Well," said the pilot, "take a good look—two engines are dead."

812   *Football*

No football team is so good that it satisfies the alumni or the Monday morning quarterbacks.

813   *Usually the Case*

SMITH: So your son is in college? How is he making it?

SMITHERS: He isn't. I'm making it and he's spending it.

814   *He Was First*

Oliver was careless about his personal effects. When his mother saw clothing scattered about on the chair and floor, she inquired: "Who didn't hang up his clothes when he went to bed?"

A muffled voice from under the covers murmured, "Adam."

815   *Afraid*

MOTHER: Has William come in yet?

SISTER: I think so. I haven't seen him, but the cat is hiding.

816   *Rural Free Delivery*

A Kansas farmer stopped at a bank to see if he could get a loan on his farm.

"It might be arranged," said the banker. "I'll drive out with you and appraise it."

"You don't need to bother," said the farmer, noticing a huge cloud of dust rolling up the road. "Here it comes now."

817   *My Mistake*

SHE: Sorry, darling, I'm afraid I'm late.

HE: Only half an hour.

SHE: Oh, I thought I was late.

818   *Drastic Change*

"Father," said the minister's son, "my teacher says that 'collect' and 'congregate' mean the same thing. Do they?"

"Perhaps, my son; perhaps they do," said the clergyman. "But there is a vast difference between a 'congregation' and a 'collection.'"

819   *Ancient Egypt*

The main thing that the ruins of ancient Egypt prove is that ancient Egyptian children insisted on having a shot at backing the chariot into the garage.

820   *Subtraction*

The schoolteacher was endeavoring to drum into her small pupils the fundamentals of arithmetic.

"Now, listen," she said rather desperately, "in order to subtract, things have to be the same denomination. This is what I mean. Now, you couldn't take three apples from four bananas, or six plums from eight peaches. It must be three apples from four apples, six plums from eight plums, and so on. Do you understand now?"

The majority of the children seemed to grasp the idea. One chubby-faced youngster very near the bottom of the class, however, raised a timid hand.

"Please, teacher," he said rather timidly, "you can take three quarts of milk from two cows."

821 *Trivial Pursuit*

HOTEL GUEST:	Is there an *Encyclopedia Britannica* in the hotel?
CLERK (with polite attention and regret):	There is not, sir; but what is it you wish to know?

822 *Style Note*

"I see where a Chicago man proposed that a badge be given every person who pays his taxes promptly."

"Huh! A barrel would be more appropriate."

823 *Fugitive*

Headline: "Husband Leaves in Midst of Wife's Bridge Party; Disappears." Just a fugitive from the chin gang.

824 *Qualified to Talk*

Mr. J. B. Forgan, in an address before a convention of the American Red Cross, indicated that he felt the members of the audience were more qualified to talk on the subject than he—"like the boy whose father thought he ought to be told something about the facts of life. It took considerable courage, but finally the father invited the boy into the living room after dinner, and after some hesitation said, 'Son, I should like to discuss with you some of the facts of life.' The boy said, 'Father, that is fine, what would you like to know?' "

825 *Whose Remarks*

Tony dropped a piece of heavy metal on his foot. His employer had to fill out a long form under the workingmen's compensation plan. He filled everything out down to the last question, which simply said, "Remarks." He was stumped, and went out and asked the foreman, "What do they want in here—Tony's remarks, or mine?" (Can be used in asking an audience whose remarks they want on a specific subject.)

826 *Crime*

We pay a tremendous crime bill each year, but we do get a lot of crime for our money.

827 *A Few Remarks*

If you wish to make a few unrelated preliminary remarks, you can say in good humor, as did the late Dr. Emory W. Luccock at the beginning of an address: "I should like to make a few remarks before I say anything."

828   *Unaccustomed As I Am*

When giving an address, many appreciate the comment of the college student who was writing an examination and who had simply drawn the design of a tombstone in the upper right-hand corner of his paper. On the tombstone he placed these words—"Sacred to the memory which leaves me on occasions like this."

829   *Beginning an Address*

In opening an address, one might say: If I lived in this great city (state, splendid community) with its magnificent mountains, beautiful lakes, cultured people, etc., I know I could repeat what the lady from Boston said. She said—"I live in Boston, so I never have to travel, because I am already there."

830   *Camera Action*

"Did they take an X-ray of your wife's jaw at the hospital?"

"They tried to, but they got a moving picture."

831   *Raiment Does Sound the Same*

Little Raymond came home beaming from Sunday school. "The Superintendent said something awfully nice about me in his prayer this morning. He said, 'O Lord, we thank thee for our food and Raymond.' "

832   *Sensible*

BOY: You look like a nice sensible girl. Let's get married.

GIRL: No. I'm just as nice and sensible as I look.

833   *Ideal?*

"What is your ideal man?"

"One who is clever enough to make money and foolish enough to spend it!"

834   *Careful*

He was a careful driver. At the railroad crossing he stopped, looked, and listened. All he heard was the car behind him crashing into his gas tank.

835   *She Tried*

The young man sneaked up behind her, covered her eyes with his hands, and announced:

"I'm going to kiss you if you can't tell who this is in three guesses."

"George Washington, Thomas Jefferson, Abraham Lincoln," she guessed.

836 *Honest Answer*

GOLFER TO CADDY: Why didn't you watch where my ball went?

CADDY: I'm sorry. Your ball doesn't usually go anywhere, and this took me completely by surprise.

837 *Courtesy*

In one German city, a foreign motorist who is guilty of a minor offense receives a card which reads: "You have broken the traffic regulations, but we want you to feel at home in _____."

838 *Could Be*

After several synonyms had been given for the word "jubilant," one little boy added: "Oh, I know what it means now—it's like jubilant delinquency!"

839 *Frankness*

"Thanks very much for the beautiful necktie," said Junior, kissing Grandma dutifully on the cheek.

"Oh, that's nothing to thank me for," she murmured.

"That's what I thought, but Mother said I had to."

840 *Is That Clear?*

Smart young man to the simple young girl: "Why does a black cow that eats green grass give white milk that makes yellow butter?"

Said the simple young girl: "For the same reason that black raspberries are red when they are green."

841 *Success*

A little girl had a birthday party and it was a highly successful event. She said, "It was wonderful. Nineteen out of twelve came."

842 *Good Prospects*

"What makes you think the baby is going to be a great politician? asked the young mother, anxiously.

"I'll tell you," answered the young father, confidently. "He can say more things that sound well and mean nothing at all than any youngster I ever saw."

843 *English in Australia*

Australian entering hospital:

" 'Ullow, Steve."

" 'Ullow, Jim."

"Come in to die?"

"No, yesterdy."

844 *Taking No Chances*

A kind old gentleman seeing a small boy who was carrying a lot of newspapers under his arm said: "Don't all those papers make you tired, my boy?"

"Naw, I don't read 'em," replied the lad.

845 *In the Press*

We clip the following for the benefit of those who doubt the power of the press: "Owing to the overcrowded conditions of our columns, a number of births and deaths are unavoidably postponed this week."

846 *Be Careful*

"When I was a young man," said Mr. Jones, "I thought nothing of working twelve or fourteen hours a day."

"Father," replied the young man, "I wish you wouldn't mention it. Those nonunion sentiments are liable to make you unpopular."

847 *Why?*

Two mosquitoes were watching blood donors giving their blood in a mobile truck. Said one to the other: "Just fancy. They'll come in here and lie down placidly while someone takes a pint of their blood, but they'll yell blue murder if we just take a couple of nips!"

848 *Easy Credit*

A man was asked if he lived within his income. "Certainly not," he replied. "It is all I can do to live within my credit cards."

849 *Has to Go Back Another Day*

MOTHER (to her daughter back from her first day at school): Well, dear, what did they teach you?

DAUGHTER: Not much, I've got to go again tomorrow.

850 *Natural Friction*

A certain friction between the generations is inevitable. After all, the young and the old have all the answers and those in between are stuck with all the questions.

851   *All of Them*

PRIVATE: How many successful jumps must a paratrooper make before he graduates?

SERGEANT: All of 'em—or else he's in big trouble!

852   *Hard to Understand.*

BURGLAR: What are you laughing at?

HOMEOWNER: That you come at night without a light to look for money when I can't find any in broad daylight.

853   *That's Different*

An oil tycoon appeared at a local golf links to make a fourth, followed by a servant pulling an adjustable, foam-cushioned chaise lounge behind him.

"Are you going to make that poor caddy lug that couch all over the golf course after you?" he was asked.

"Caddy, my eye," he said. "That's my psychiatrist."

854   *Awful Story*

An old-time prospector listened each morning for his pack animal to bray. When the donkey brayed once, he knew it would be clear and a good day for seeking gold. When the animal brayed twice, he knew the weather would be bad, a day to stay in camp.

The donkey was his weather burro.

855   *His Choice*

After an efficiency expert received his check for services rendered, he noticed that it was one cent short. A stickler for details, he called his client and insisted that the difference be paid. When the check for one cent arrived, he took it to his bank. The teller carefully studied the check, then leaned forward and whispered, "How would you like it, heads or tails?"

856   *Prompt Response*

PROFESSOR (rapping
on his desk):   Order, please!

VOICE FROM THE
BACK ROW: I'll take a hamburger and large fries.

857   *Too Bad*

Said the farmer mournfully: "I'm sorry I can't pay you, Doc. I slowed down like you told me and lost my farm."

858   *Grateful for Small Favors*

Our streets aren't exactly paved with gold, but occasionally you can find a parking space with a little time left on the meter.

859   *Bilingual*

A customer in an elegant Montreal restaurant went to the washroom, turned on the tap, and got scalded.

"This is an outrage," he complained. "Why aren't your taps properly marked? I turned on the faucet marked C thinking it would be cold, and got scalding-hot water."

The manager tried to be patient. "Look," he said. "The tap marked C is correct. That stands for *chaude*—French for hot. You should know that if you live in Montreal."

"Wait a minute," roared the patron. "The other tap is marked C also. How do you explain that?"

"Ah," said the manager. "That stands for 'cold.' You see, my friend, this is a bilingual establishment."

860   *Why Not?*

The young photographer had just taken a portrait of an elderly gentleman on his 98th birthday. He thanked the old man, adding, "I hope I'll be around to take your picture when you hit 100."

"Why not?" replied the patriarch. "You look healthy."

861   *Different Problem*

In a shoe store on Fifth Avenue, a clerk was reprimanded by his employer. "What's the matter—can't you serve this customer?" he growled.

"No, sir," replied the clerk. "He's Mr. Toscanini, the orchestra conductor, and he's trying to find two shoes that squeak in the same key."

862   *Thrift*

A nickel goes a long way today—you can carry it around for weeks before you find something to buy with it.

863   *One Way of Putting It*

Minister to garage mechanic, who had just finished his examination of the car for repairs: "Your estimate runneth over."

864   *Difficult Choice*

The final show for the evening was over and one flea said to the other: "Should we walk home or take the dog?"

865   *Eternal*

If you want to write something that has a good chance of living on forever, sign a home mortgage.

866   *The Right Idea*

Looking at the report on the financial condition of most nations today, we are inclined to think the old idea that the world was flat had some merit.

867   *How Cold Was It?*

It was so cold last night, the thermometer knocked on the door and wanted to come in.

868   *How Bad Was It?*

The fishing was so bad on our vacation that even the liars didn't catch any.—*Herbert V. Prochnow*

869   *Be Careful*

The little old lady entered the department store. Instantly, a band began to play, an orchid was pinned on her dress, a $100 bill placed in her hand. She found herself being photographed from all sides, and a TV camera beamed down at her.

"You're the one-millionth customer," said the master of ceremonies, smiling broadly. "And now can you tell us why you came to our store today?"

"Yes," said the little old lady. "I'm on my way to the complaint department."

870   *Beauty*

"My aunt stands in front of the mirror with her eyes closed."

"How come?"

"She wants to see how she looks when she is asleep."

871   *For Any Owner*

In an antique shop several tourists spotted a pair of early American portraits and questioned the proprietor about them.

"They're ancestors," he said.

"Whose ancestors?" one of the travelers inquired.

"Anyone who's a mind to have them," replied the proprietor.

872   *She Needed Them*

A woman in Chicago reported the theft of her Cadillac, $5,000 worth of jewelry, a TV set, stereo system, $1,000 in cash, and $50 in food stamps.

873   *Straight Talk*

A surveyor made the following report after surveying some land for an athletic field:

"It is obvious from the difference in relation to the short depth of the property that the contour is such as to preclude any reasonable development potential for active recreation."

He meant to say that the tract of land was not suitable for an athletic field.—*Sunshine Magazine*

874   *Plain English*

On the door of a government building in Washington, D.C., is the following inscription:

General Services Administration, Region 3, Public Building Service, Building Management Division, Utility Room "Custodial."

In plain English, it means "broom closet."—*Sunshine Magazine*

875   *Would He Go for It?*

A champion athlete in bed with a cold was told that he had a high temperature.

"How high is it?" he asked the attending physician.

"A hundred and one."

"What's the world's record?"

876   *Advice*

"Something's wrong with me, Grandma," sighed a young lady. "I've been a bridesmaid twice; I caught the bouquet, too, but I'm still single."

"Next time," advised Grandma, "don't reach for the flowers; reach for the best man."

877   *Practice Makes Perfect*

A man was having trouble balancing his checkbook. He shouted at his wife, "Why can't you learn to manage money?"

She shot back, "Because you never give me enough to practice with!"

878   *On Safari*

A couple were in deepest Africa hunting big game. Suddenly a huge, snarling lion jumped out of the bushes and attacked the husband. As he tried desperately to keep his head out of the lion's mouth, he yelled to his wife, "Shoot! Shoot!"

"I can't," she cried, "I just ran out of film."

879 *Looking Ahead*

A dapper gentleman introduced himself to an attractive woman at a senior dance. "You look like my third wife," he said with a smile.

"Oh, how nice. And how many times have you been married?" she asked.

"Twice," he said with a twinkle in his eye.

880 *Space Age*

Asked what he planned to do when he grew up, one fourth-grader replied, "After I go to the moon, I'd like to travel."

881 *He Didn't Say*

A disconsolate-looking farmer stood on the steps of the town hall during the progress of a political meeting.

"Who's talking in there now?" demanded a stranger briskly, "or are you just going in?"

"I've just come out," said the farmer. "Congressman Smiffkins is talking in there."

"What about?" asked the stranger.

"Well," continued the farmer, puzzled, "he didn't say."

882 *Only Three Problems*

A businessman was telling his friend about the worries plaguing him, declaring: "They're beginning to smother me, dozens closing in from all sides."

"The thing for you to do," consoled the friend, "is to simplify by lumping the related ones. That's what I did, and now I have only three problems—nagging creditors, profitless business, and the fact that I'm broke."

883 *What They Say*

It takes only eighty-four days for the average boy in grade school to outgrow a pair of shoes.

884 *Not Necessary*

TOASTMASTER: And now, our featured speaker is a fellow who needs no introduction—he didn't show up!

885 *Love*

The young wife complained, "You love football more than you love me!"

"Maybe so darling," her husband replied, "but I love you more than I love basketball."

886   *Satisfied*

"I cannot understand you," said the spinster's nephew. "You seem so happy and contented, and yet I've been under the impression that unmarried ladies usually are grouchy and irritable."

"Well," she explained, smiling, "I've got a fireplace that smokes, a parrot that swears, a cat that stays out half the night, and a dog that barks. What more do I want?"

887   *Right Answer*

The little girl's visiting aunt said to her, "You're pretty dirty, aren't you?"

"Yes," the little girl said. "But I'm prettier clean."

888   *Smart Farmer*

A canny Maine farmer was approached by a stranger and asked how much he thought his prize Jersey cow was worth. The farmer thought for a moment, looked the stranger over, then said: "Well, that depends. Are you the tax assessor or has she been hit by your car?"

889   *Nothing Interesting*

An artist was traveling in New Hampshire in search of a scenic spot for a vacation. He stopped in a roadside store and asked a farmer about his place.

"Is there any interesting scenery up your way?" he asked.

"Not much," the farmer said. "Across the road you can see our neighbor's barn, but beyond that you can't see anything but mountains for about thirty miles."

890   *Haven't Checked*

Credit manager to an applicant: "Do you have much money in the bank?"

"I don't know," replied the applicant. "I haven't shaken it lately."

891   *Fair*

An employee revealed the absolute fairness of the boss. At a meeting the other day, the boss put several ideas before the staff.

"All of you who find yourselves in disagreement with the suggestions I have made," she announced at the finish, "will please signify by saying 'I resign.'"

892   *Too Late*

A farmer determined to rehabilitate an old barn called in a carpenter to give him an estimate. After examination of the framing with an icepick, the carpenter turned to the farmer and said: "George, if I were you, I'd tear this building down and build another one."

"Why?" asked the farmer.

"Well, to tell you the truth," replied the carpenter, "the only thing that keeps it from falling down now is that the termites are holding hands."

893 *Truth*

TEACHER: What do the philosophers call truth?

STUDENT: When one fisherman calls another fisherman a liar.

894 *Peers*

Nine-year-old disdainfully to seven-year-old: "I like to talk to adults my own age."

895 *He Liked the Ice Cream*

A music teacher took his pupils to a concert to develop musical appreciation in their young minds. After the program he took them out to tea and they had cakes, ice cream, and other dainties.

Just as the youngsters were ready to go home, the teacher asked the youngest of them: "Well, Jim, did you enjoy the concert?"

"Oh, yes," Jim replied, happily. "All but the music."—*Tit-Bits, London*

896 *No Excuse*

My small grandson had to apologize for forgetting his aunt's birthday. He wrote: "I am sorry I forgot your birthday. I have no excuse and it would serve me right if you forgot mine on Friday."

897 *Yes*

"Are you a yes-man or a know-man?"—*Wall Street Journal advertisement*

898 *Sorry*

Three wise men of Gotham went to sea in a bowl;
If the bowl had been stronger my song would have been longer.

899 *We Have Doubts*

A lawyer was cross-examining a witness. "You have just testified that you heard the shot at exactly 11:32 P.M. How did you know what time it was? Did you look at your watch?"

"No," the witness said, "I looked at the sundial in the garden."

"That's stupid," accused the lawyer. "How could you tell time by a sundial at 11:32 at night?"

"Well, I had a flashlight," the witness admitted.

900   *Don't Blame Him*

One blistering hot day when they had guests for dinner, a mother asked her four-year-old son to say the blessing.

"But, Mother, I don't know what to say," he protested.

"Just say what you've heard me say, dear," she answered.

Obediently he bowed his little head and said, "Oh, Lord, why did I invite these people here on a hot day like this?"

901   *He Is in Trouble*

"I know I have my faults."

"Of course you have."

"Oh, I have, have I? Perhaps you'll tell me what they are."

902   *This Will Work*

"I'm suffering dreadfully from insomnia. I've tried all sorts of remedies, but I can find nothing that puts me to sleep."

"Try talking to yourself."

903   *Puzzled*

LITTLE BOY: Was George Washington as honest as they say?

FATHER: Yes, of course.

LITTLE BOY: Then why do they close the banks on his birthday?

904   *A Different Problem*

The senior golfer was in a pro shop for the first time. "Just make sure my caddy has good eyesight. I hit the ball farther than I can see," he announced. When the caddy appeared, he seemed older than the golfer.

"How well do you see?" asked the golfer.

"Like an eagle," replied the caddy.

After the first shot, the golfer asked, "See that one?"

"Sure did. All the way."

"Where did it go?"

"I don't remember."

905   *Familiar Refrain*

In Wisconsin, a license plate reads: EIEIO. It is owned by an old farmer named MacDonald.

906   *He Knew*

The first-grade student drew a picture of a stagecoach which was well done, except that it lacked wheels.

"Oh, it's wonderful!" exclaimed the teacher. "But I see no wheels. What holds it up?"

The little artist promptly replied, "Bad men."

907   *Quiet Please*

A young man was practicing his guitar in the small hours of the morning when the landlord came in. "Do you know there's a little lady sick upstairs?" asked the landlord.

"No," answered the musician. "Hum a little of it. Maybe I'll recall it."

908   *The Machine Was Working*

The manager of the movie theater was surprised to see a dog sitting in the front row eating popcorn. "Where did you get the popcorn?" the manager asked. "I thought the machine was broken."

909   *His Problem*

A man was arrested for stealing a hog. The trial was short, and as there was no concrete evidence against the man, the judge dismissed the case. For some reason, the man seemed not to understand.

"The case is dismissed," the judge said. "It is over. You are acquitted. You can go."

"Well, thanks, Judge," the man said, "but do I have to give him back his hog?"

910   *Fast Learner*

One day a professor saw printed on the window of a small restaurant, "Today's special: Lam Stew."

The proprietor noticed the professor's smile of amusement and asked for an explanation. He accepted gratefully the professor's suggestion to add "B".

The next time the professor passed the restaurant, he looked for the window sign. This time, the special of the day was "Clamb Chowder."

911   *New Idea*

"I'm tired of this routine existence," exclaimed the fraternity brother to his roommate. "Let's do something extraordinary, startling, magnificent; something that will make our brains whirl and our hearts leap."

"Okay," replied the roommate. And so they studied.

912   *Don't Cross the Line*

There is a line on the ocean where you lose a day after crossing it. There's also a line on most highways where you can lose a lot more if you cross it.

913   *Only Two Books*

The newlyweds were asking the advice of an older couple on how to keep a marriage running smoothly.

"Well," replied the husband, "we've always based our marriage on the resources of two very good books."

"Yes," said his wife, "the cookbook and checkbook."

914   *It's Spring, Brother!*

When the crocuses are crocing, and the daffodills are dilly; when the boys and girls of every age look moon-eyed, and act silly; when the big strong men—all known as Bill—prefer to be called Billllly . . . it's Spring, brother, it's Spring!

When landscape "artists" put the bee on you for shrubs and sodding; when wifey orders yard work, and keeps prodding, prodding, prodding; when you gaze at the azure sky and soon your head starts nodding . . . it's Spring, brother, it's Spring!—*Nomad in Cincinnati Telephone Bulletin*

915   *Good Medicine*

When the police arrested a medicine hawker for selling eternal youth pills, it was discovered that he was a repeat offender. He'd been arrested on the same charge in 1772, 1829, and 1904.

916   *Speak Slowly*

A customer hurriedly entered a store and rushed up to a clerk. "Do you have any gloves in this store?" she asked.

The clerk answered, "Aisle C."

After waiting several minutes, the customer asked again, "Do you have any gloves in this store?"

Again the clerk said, "Aisle C."

Whereupon the irate customer said, "Now, listen here, that's the second time you've told me, 'I'll see.' When are you going to go look for them?"

917   *Experience*

The hit-and-run driver was brought to trial. His lawyer pleaded eloquently and at great length in his behalf.

"Your honor," he concluded, "The plaintiff must have been walking carelessly. My client is a very careful driver. He has been driving a car for fifteen years."

"Your honor," stated the counsel for the plaintiff, "if experience is an argument, my client should win this case. He has been walking for forty-five years."

918   *Not Holes*

"What are those holes in the wood?"

"They're knotholes."

"If they're not holes, then what are they?"

919   *Good Question*

The driver was concentrating on the traffic, but he felt he had forgotten something. He stopped, checked his packages and his wallet, but couldn't decide what he'd forgotten.

When he reached his destination, his little grandson ran to the car and said, "Hi Grandpa, where's Grandma?"

920   *Literate*

Sergeant to recruit: "Have you completed high school?"

"Yes sir," he replied. "I also graduated cum laude from college and have completed three years toward my doctorate."

The sergeant nodded, reached for a rubber stamp, and slapped it on the questionnaire. It consisted of one word: "Literate."

921   *A New World*

The clerk at the drive-in bank had pulled down her sunshade. The customer couldn't see her, although she could see him. He looked cautiously at the drawer, dropped in his check, and quickly withdrew his hand. A moment later she pushed the drawer out again with his deposit slip and thanked him. He looked around as if to make sure no one was watching, then leaned out of the car and said, "I know you're automated, but thank you anyway."

922   *What Happens Then?*

One little boy said to another as they watched the escalator going down: "What happens when the basement gets full of steps?"

923   *He Was Helpful*

"Just what good have you done for humanity?" asked the judge before passing sentence on the pickpocket.

"Well," replied the confirmed criminal thoughtfully, "I've kept three or four detectives working regularly."

924   *Technology*

"Modern technology," remarked the college student to his pal, "is amazing. It has developed a thirty-cent soda can that when discarded will last forever—and a $10,000 car which, even when well taken care of, will start to rust out in a few years."

925   *Two Opinions*

The doctor recommended surgery. The patient said, "I want a second opinion." "Certainly," the doctor replied, "You're also overweight."

926   *They Never Die*

Old politicians never die—they just run once too often.

927   *Simple*

The professor of mathematics and his fiancee were out roaming in the fields when she plucked a flower. Looking coyly at him, she began to pull off the petals, saying sweetly, "He loves me, he loves me not . . ."

"You are giving yourself a lot of unnecessary trouble," said the professor. "You should count up the petals and if the total is an even number the answer will be in the negative; if an uneven number, in the affirmative."

928   *Say That Again*

A lawyer appearing in a case asked the witness: "Now, Mr. Jones, did you or did you not, on the date in question, or at any other time, previously or subsequently, say or even intimate to the defendant or anyone else, whether friend or acquaintance or in fact a stranger, that the statement imputed to you, whether just or unjust, and denied by the plaintiff, was a matter of no consequence or otherwise? Answer the question! Did you or did you not?"

The witness pondered for a little while and then said, "Did I or did I not what?"

929   *Just Yield*

The hesitant driver, waiting for traffic to clear, came to a complete stop on a freeway ramp. The traffic thinned, but the intimidated driver still waited. Finally, an infuriated voice yelled from behind, "The sign says to yield, not to give up."

930   *Just Like Us*

The people are divided into two groups—the ignorant, illogical, prejudiced, emotional group, and the intelligent, sound-thinking, reasonable people like us.—*Herbert V. Prochnow*

931   *He Should Have Served*

Recently a Kalamazoo, Michigan, resident was excused from jury duty for one of the best of all reasons—he was the defendant.

932   *A Hole-in-One*

As the sweet young thing said when she took a golf lesson, "Now which club do I use for a hole-in-one?"—*Herbert V. Prochnow*

933   *The Complaint*

A kangaroo went to his doctor and complained, "I'm not feeling jumpy."

934   *Hard Decision*

A shipwrecked sailor spent five years on a deserted island. One day he was overjoyed to see a ship drop anchor in the bay. A dinghy approached, and a ship's officer handed the sailor *The New York Times*, the *Wall Street Journal*, and three issues of *Time* magazine.

"The captain suggests," said the officer, "that you read what's going on in the world before you decide if you wish to be rescued."

935   *Nantucket*

> There was an old man of Nantucket
> Who kept all his cash in a bucket;
>   But his daughter, named Nan,
>   Ran way with a man—
> And as for the bucket, Nantucket.

> —*Anonymous (in the Princeton*
>   *Tiger)*

936   *Modern Personal Service*

The new bank officer was welcoming a lady who had just opened an account. "Be assured, Madam, to us you are never merely a number. You are two digits, a dash, a letter of the alphabet and three more digits."

937   *A Hybrid*

"What do you get," a guy asked his friend, "when you cross an owl and a goat?"

"Anybody knows that," his friend said, "a hootenanny."

938   *Written Guarantee*

The jeweler's assistant was getting married. When the time came for him to present the bride with the ring, he hesitated.

"With this ring," prompted the minister.

"With this ring," said the bridegroom, "we give a written guarantee that the price will be refunded if it is not as represented."

939   *It Happens*

"Did the play have the usual happy ending?"

"Oh, yes; everybody was glad when it was over!"

940   *He Had a Suggestion*

"Those poor children next door have no Mommy or Daddy, and no Aunt Jane," said a mother to her little boy. "Wouldn't you like to give them something?"

"Yes," replied the little boy. "Let's give them Aunt Jane."

941   *Good Reason*

MARISSA: Was your father a college man?

MAGGY: Yes, but he never mentions it. His football team didn't win a
game the last three years he was there.

942   *No Culture*

A teacher took a group of school children to the museum, where they
were shown a seventeenth-century French drawing room, correct in
every detail. Later, the teacher said to them: "Think carefully and tell
me what impressed you most."

One little girl said disapprovingly, "It didn't have television!"

943   *It Depends*

"Is it true," the reporter asked of the explorer, "that wild animals in the
jungle will not harm you if you carry a torch?"

"It all depends," said the explorer, "on how fast you carry it."

944   *The Toastmaster's Instructions*

May I ask the photographers not to take pictures of the speaker during
his address. Shoot him as he approaches the platform.

945   *Politics as Usual*

A municipal official says he ran for office again because he thought his
possible opponent, if successful, might be even more corrupt than
he was.

946   *Perfect*

A local grammar school pupil, when asked by the teacher to write a
composition on "The Effects of Laziness," turned in a blank sheet of
paper.

947   *An Unwise Question*

A budding young writer was talking to the book publisher who had
turned down a book of his poetry.

"Would you say that I should put more fire into my poetry?" the
young man asked.

"No," said the publisher, "I think you should put more of your poetry
into the fire."

948   *To the Point*

The English composition lesson was on brevity. "I want you to write the
shortest, most dramatic sentence you can think of," the teacher said.

So one of his young students wrote: "Help! Help!"

949   *Modern Practice*
Indians used to scalp their enemies. Now the Internal Revenue Service officials do the skinning.

950   *How You Look at It*
The luggage-laden husband stared miserably out the window of the airline terminal at the departing jet.

"If you hadn't taken so long getting ready," he complained to his wife, "we would have caught that plane."

"Yes," she replied, "and if you hadn't hurried me along, we wouldn't have so long to wait for the next one!"

951   *At Election Time*
There is no doubt this is a land of promise—when we hear the candidates who are seeking the votes of the people.

952   *Hard to Fix*
A woman summoned a TV repairman to fix her set. After spreading his tools out, the serviceman inquired: "What seems to be the trouble?"

Replied the woman, "Well, for one thing, the programs are lousy."

953   *Be Careful*
The junior executive went into the president's office and said: "Sir, I just received this memo 'From the desk of John J. Rogers' and I'd like to speak to your desk about it."

954   *She Loved Him*

HE: When did you first notice you loved me?
SHE: When I began to get angry when people said you were stupid.

955   *Right Answer*
The shoe dealer was hiring a clerk. "Suppose," he said, "a lady customer asked, 'Don't you think one of my feet is bigger than the other?' What would you say?"

"I'd say," promptly replied the clerk, "I'd say, 'On the contrary, Madam, one is smaller than the other.'"

The clerk was hired.

956   *A Funny Thing*
A funny thing is love. It cometh from above, and lighteth like a dove—on some.

And some whom it hits, it nearly gives them fits, and scatters all their wits—Oh hum!

957   *What He Promised*

"Darling," asked the bride, "will you still love me if I grow fat?"

"Heck, no," the groom informed her. "I promised for better or for worse, not through thick and thin."

958   *Punctuation Is Important*

"Woman without her man is helpless." (Put a comma after "woman" and after "her.")

959   *Point of View*

SUBURBAN RESIDENT: It's simply wonderful to wake up in the morning and hear the leaves on the trees and bushes whispering outside your window.

CITY RESIDENT: I guess it's all right to hear the leaves whisper, but I never could stand hearing the grass mown.

960   *He Didn't Know*

A soldier and a professor were on a plane. Tiring of conversation, the professor suggested a game of riddles to pass the time.

"A riddle you can't guess, you give me a dollar, and vice versa."

"Okay," agreed the soldier, "but you are better educated. I'll only give you fifty cents."

"All right," said the professor, "you go first."

"Well, what bird has four legs swimming and two legs flying?"

The professor thought hard. He did not want to miss the very first question. The soldier's face lit up with a wide grin. Finally the professor said, "I don't know; here's a dollar. What's the answer?"

The soldier hesitated for a moment, then said slowly, "I don't know either; here's your fifty cents!"

That ended the game.

961   *Sound Advice*

Someone once said, "If you are going to soar with the eagles in the morning, you can't hoot with the owls all night."

962   *Be Quiet*

Two cockroaches lunched in a dirty sewer and excitedly discussed the spotless, glistening new restaurant in the neighborhood from which they had been barred.

"I hear," said one, "that the refrigerators shine like polished silver. The shelves are clean as a whistle. The floors sparkle like diamonds. It's so clean . . ."

"Please," said the second in disgust, nibbling on a moldy roll. "Not while I'm eating."

963   *Not Allowed*

FIRST DOG: I feel so poorly lately—tired all the time.

SECOND DOG: Have you thought of going to a psychiatrist?

FIRST DOG: No! I'm not allowed on couches.

964   *Could Be*

A spouse who unexpectedly serves a thick, sizzling steak for dinner hasn't necessarily wrecked the car, broken a valuable antique, or overdrawn the checking account—he or she may have just run out of leftovers.

965   *Is That Clear?*

A little girl asked her Sunday school teacher: "Why do they always say 'amen' after they pray in church? Why don't they ever say 'a-women'?" Before the teacher could think of an answer to that one, a little boy in the class spoke up and said: "They do that for the same reason that all the songs they sing are 'hymns.' "

966   *Too Noisy*

The tenant complained to his landlord that the couple in the upstairs apartment annoyed him again last night with their stamping and banging on the floor until well after midnight.

"Did they awaken you?" inquired the landlord.

"Well, no," answered the tenant. "As it happened, I was still up practicing on my tuba."

967   *We Were Perfect*

Wouldn't it be wonderful if all young children behaved the way you think you did when you were the same age?

968   *Put It Back*

Not long ago a mother and her young son were shopping in a supermarket. The child, trying to be helpful, picked up a package and brought it to her.

"Oh, no, honey," protested the mother. "Go put it back. You have to cook that."—*Indianapolis News*

969   *Too Late*

This country would not be in such a mess today if the Indians had adopted more stringent immigration laws.

970   *Hard to Find*

It would be great to live in the town on television where the hero always finds a parking place in front of the bank, the supermarket, and the Post Office.

971   *Observant*

NEWLY ENGAGED YOUNG MAN: Darling, I'm not worthy of you!

HIS FIANCEE: That's why I like you. You're so observant.

972   *He Had Him There*

A farmer was bragging to some city visitors about what a good farmer he was. "I'm the old-fashioned type of farmer," he said. "I can plow, milk cows, prune trees, feed hogs and anything else that has to be done around the place. I don't guess there is anything that goes on that I can't do."

"Can you lay an egg?" one of the visitors asked.

973   *Agreement*

Psychiatrists say it's not good for a person to keep too much to himself. The Internal Revenue Service says the same thing.

974   *Don't Worry*

An airplane pilot addressed his passengers over the intercom system to tell them he had lost his way. He explained that the radar was not working, the radio beam could not be picked up, and the compass was broken. "But," he added encouragingly, "you will be glad to know that we are making very good time."

975   *Naturally*

The first Scotsman to use free air at a service station blew out four tires.

976   *TLC*

Modern medical treatment is based on three simple letters: TLC—Takes Lotsa Cash!

977   *Family Necessity*

No family should have less than three children because if there is one genius among them, there should be two to support him.

978   *Unreasonable*

PEDESTRIAN: Sorry, my good man, but I just don't give money to men on the street.

BEGGAR: Do you expect me to open an office?

979   *The Long and Short of It*
Medical people claim that we are taller in the morning than we are in the evening. We're shorter around the end of the month.

980   *More Bubble Gum*
The fact that Americans chew a million dollars' worth of gum shows how much work we will do for practically nothing.

981   *$1,000-a-Plate Dinner*
I love that phrase "$1,000-a-Plate Dinner." It always sounds like a burger that's being billed to the Pentagon.

982   *Dodged the Issues*
Admirer to political candidate: "Great speech, sir! I really like the straightforward way you dodged those issues."

983   *Reveille*
Discussing problems about teenagers, one woman asked her neighbor, "Do you find it difficult to get Stevie out of bed in the morning?"

"No," replied the other, "I just open the door and throw the cat onto his bed."

The neighbor, somewhat puzzled, asked how that helped. "Easy. Stevie sleeps with the dog."

984   *Be Careful*
"What's the idea going seventy-five miles an hour in a twenty-five mile zone?"

"I wasn't going seventy-five miles an hour—I wasn't going sixty, I wasn't going fifty. I wasn't even going forty—I wasn't . . ."

"Look out! In a minute you'll be backing into something."

985   *Seasonal*
A teacher asked her second-graders if anyone could tell her the four seasons of the year. A little boy said, "Yes, hockey, baseball, football, and basketball."

986   *Colossal*

A film salesman trying to dispose of one of his products to an independent exhibitor assured him it was "colossal."

"Oh, come now." said the exhibitor, "I saw the trade show and I'd hardly call the film 'colossal.'"

"Well," the salesman amended, "it's colossal in a small way."—*Tit-Bits, London*

987   *Speaking "Brum"*

Brummies, as folk in the area call Birmingham, England, residents, have a colorful dialect all their own, and educator and poet Ray Tennant, a native-son version of Professor Henry Higgins, has researched and collected choice samples of Brumslang in a handy reference book called *The Book of Brum*. Here are some useful phrases from it:

acawss	of course
cummoffit	you're joking
julyka?	would you like? as in *julyka cuppa tea woil yer witing?*
oidernow	I don't know

988   *Can't Recall*

In the course of a sanity trial the lawyer was cross-examining a witness. "And would you say," he asked, "that it was the defendant's habit to talk to himself when alone?"

The witness pondered this for a moment, and then answered with due caution: "That's hard to say. You see, I can't recall ever being with him when he was alone."

989   *Only One Possible Cause*

An executive purchased his first Rolls Royce. About a week after it had been delivered, he telephoned the dealer to complain that strange, wheezing noises were emanating from the front end of the car.

"There's only one possible explanation," the dealer said to him stuffily. "Your chauffeur must have asthma."

990   *The Absent-minded Professor*

—Said he had three pairs of glasses. One was for near-sightedness, one for far-sightedness, and the third to look for the other two.

—Went through the revolving door and couldn't remember whether he was going in or coming out.

—Said there were three things he couldn't remember—first, names; second, faces; and he couldn't remember what the third was.

991   *New Measures*

JEWELER: How would you like a quartz watch?
CUSTOMER: I'd like to know, does it come in pintz?

992   *Something Wrong Here*
"Mom," said a little boy, "is it all right to say you are going to 'water the horse' when you are going to give him a drink of water?"

"Yes," said his mother, "that is the correct thing to say."

"Then," said the little boy as he opened the refrigerator door and got out a carton of milk, "I'm going to milk the cat."

993   *That's Different*
"Why did you break off your engagement?"

"I no longer have a strong feeling for Herman."

"Will you give back the ring?"

"Oh, no, I still have a strong feeling for the ring."

994   *Good Idea*
Eager little Billy was determined to try the diving board. When he jumped and landed with a whacking belly-flop, he struggled ashore to announce, "Well, I did it—but that lake could sure use some water softener!"

995   *Keeping Up with the Joneses*
An ambitious young woman who sought to rise on the social ladder made her husband's life miserable trying to get him to rent a more expensive apartment. One evening he came home in a wonderfully good humor.

"What's the matter, dear?" the wife exclaimed. "Anything gone wrong?"

"Good news, dearest, good news," he shouted; "we don't have to move. The landlord has raised the rent."

996   *Goo Goo and Potsie Coo*

To this the baby listens
By the hour, day and week,
And yet his mother wonders
Why he doesn't learn to speak!

997   *A Long Time*
An army private, filling out a questionnaire for a correspondence course, was stymied a bit by the question: "How long has your present

employer been in business?" But after a few moments' worried thought, his eyes lighted up. He wrote: "Since 1776."

998   *In a Small Town*
You know you are in a small town when:
   You speak to a dog that you pass and he wags his tail.
   Someone asks how you feel, then listens to what you say.
   You dial a wrong number and talk for fifteen minutes anyway.
   You miss church and receive "get well" cards.
   You skid into a ditch on a rural road and the word gets back to town before you do.
   You write a check on "insufficient funds" and the bank covers it for you.—*The Rotarian*

999   *The Three Rs*
   At 25—Romance
   At 45—Rent
   At 65—Rheumatism

1000   *Experienced*
"Pa," chirped little Ted, "what does a man's better half mean?"
"Usually," his father said, "she means exactly what she says."

1001   *Keep Away*
One elevator to another: "Look out! I think I'm coming down with something!"

1002   *Real Foresight*
Nature is wonderful! A million years ago she didn't know we were going to wear spectacles, yet look at the way she placed our ears.

1003   *Improvement*
A wealthy industrialist was the center of attention at the fiftieth reunion of his high school class.
   "How marvelous," said a former classmate, "acquiring so much money hasn't changed you!"
   "Actually, it has," the candid millionaire told her. "I'm now 'eccentric' where I used to be impolite, and 'delightfully amusing' where I used to be a pain in the neck."

1004   *Take It Back*
Then there was the moron who took the bus home but his mother made him take it back.

1005 *His Choice*

JUDGE: You can let me try your case or be tried by a jury of your peers.

PRISONER: What's peers?

JUDGE: Peers are persons of your own kind—your equals.

PRISONER: Well, I sure don't think I wanna be tried by bank robbers!

1006 *Some Think This Is Kute*

In Kokomo they laugh in glee about the name of Kankakee,
In Kankakee they pass the buck by poking fun at Keokuk.

1007 *There Is a Large Market*

What this country needs is a telephone that doesn't ring when you are in the shower.

1008 *For Latin Students*

He who praises in praesentia,
And dispraises in absentia,
May he get the pestilentia.

1009 *Our Real Need*

What this country needs is fewer people who know what this country needs.

1010 *Try Again*

STUDENT: The government of England is a limited mockery.

1011 *Do Not Disturb*

At the side of a road, a young woman looked hopelessly at a flat tire. A friendly motorist stopped to help her.

After the tire was changed, the woman said: "Please let the jack down easily. My husband is sleeping in the back seat."

1012 *Student Comment*

Shakespeare married Anne Hathaway, but he mostly lived at Windsor with his merry wives. This is quite usual with actors.

1013 *Different Now*

FATHER TO
SCHOOLBOY (who
has come out below
a school girl in the
exams): Surely you haven't been beaten by a mere girl?

SCHOOLBOY: But, you know, Dad, girls aren't so mere now as they were in your young days!

1014 *As the Toastmaster Said*

"Welcome to our luncheon, Senator. All of us are waiting to hear the dope from Washington."

1015 *Examination Answer*

The Matterhorn was a horn blown by the ancients when anything was the matter.

1016 *Tact*

The dessert was delicious. Did you buy it yourself?

1017 *How Was the Movie Rated*

When she entered a movie theater with her dog in her arms, an attendant stepped forward. "Excuse me, madam," he said, "but you can't take your dog inside."

"How absurd!" protested the woman. "What harm could the pictures do to a tiny dog like this?"

1018 *Considerate*

ACTRESS: Now let's talk about you. What did you think of my latest picture?

1019 *Too Late*

You never really know how many parts an automobile has until it hits a tree.

1020 *The Ultimate Critic*

A movie patron arose from his seat while viewing a picture and shot himself. We believe we have seen that picture.

1021 *Shocking Good Manners*

On a bus a man gave his seat to a woman. She fainted. On recovering, she thanked him. Then he fainted.

1022 *Remember*

There are two occasions especially when one should keep his mouth shut—when swimming and when angry.

1023 *How It Happened in Verse*

Slippery ice, very thin; pretty girl tumbled in. Saw a boy upon the bank—gave a shriek, and then she sank.

Boy on bank heard her shout, jumped right in—helped her out. Now he's hers—very nice; but she had to break the ice.

1024 *Busy Then*

A motorist after being bogged down in a muddy road paid a passing farmer $20 to pull him out with a tractor. After he was on the road again, he remarked to the farmer: "I should think at that price you'd be pulling people out of this stuff day and night."

"Nope," drawled the farmer, "at night's when I tote the water for the holes."—*Capper's Weekly*

1025 *Too Inquisitive*

"Mummy" asked the child, "Why doesn't Daddy have hair on his head?"

"Daddy thinks a great deal, dear,"

The child mulled this over and then said, "Mummy, why do you have so much hair on your head?"

"Keep quiet and eat your breakfast."

1026 *Probably Not*

Young Bill had just introduced his blond and glamorous girl friend to his family.

"What do you think?" he whispered proudly. "Some dish, huh?"

"That she is!" the mother agreed, "but is she kitchen-tested?"

1027 *They Are Still Wondering*

The operator was about to close the doors of the crowded elevator when a tipsy gentleman pushed his way in. As the car started up, he tried to turn around to face the door, but was wedged in so tightly that he couldn't move. The other passengers stared into his rather bleary eyes with growing embarrassment. Finally, when the strain became quite painful, the tipsy one cleared his throat and remarked: "I expect you are wondering why I called this meeting."—*American Salesman*

1028 *Warning*

Waters on the rampage resulted in this warning at the edge of a stream in a Western state:

"NOTICE: When this sign is out of sight, it is unsafe to cross this river."

1029   *Quite a Spell!*

Said the young man, "First I got tonsillitis, then appendicitis and pneumonia. After that I got erysipelas with hemochromatosis. Following that, I got poliomyelitis, and finally ended up with hypodermics and inoculations. I certainly thought I never would get through that spelling test!"

1030   *A Great Contribution*

Next to TV, one of the greatest contributions to mankind is the knob that turns it off.

1031   *Way Ahead of Him*

TEENAGER TO SCIENTIST:	What do you do?
SCIENTIST:	I study astronomy.
TEENAGER:	I'm lucky. I finished astronomy last year.

1032   *We Are Puzzled*

Why do we always describe a doctor as "practicing"?

1033   *To Show Her Mother*

Three bank examiners walked into a bank to make an audit. It was nearly nine in the evening when one of them exclaimed, "A shortage of $500,000!"

After a careful checking of the balance sheets, the other examiners agreed. Early the following morning the bank was a beehive of investigation. The shortage was soon traced to one department.

The department head rushed up to a new employee who was hanging up her coat, and asked excitedly: "Miss Smith, do you recall canceling a check for $500,000 yesterday?"

"Oh, that check," the girl replied, opening her purse. "I took that home last night to show my mother the kind of work I do."

1034   *He Won't Buy It*

POLICEMAN:	You're under arrest for speeding.
MOTORIST:	I wasn't speeding, officer. But I passed a couple of fellows who were.

1035　*A Fine Distinction*

According to Frank Case's *Tales of a Wayward Inn,* the following saying originated with Wilson Mizner: "When you take stuff from one writer, it's plagiarism, but when you take it from many writers, it's called research."

1036　*Temptation*

The trouble with resisting temptation is that it may never come again.

1037　*Not on the Golf Course*

GOLFER:　I never played such a course in my life.

CADDIE:　Sir, you left the course twenty minutes ago. You are now in the Smith's rock garden.

1038　*A Nominal Bill*

Said the client to his lawyer, "I trust your fee is nominal." And when he got the lawyer's bill it was just that—phe-nominal!

1039　*Probably*

Do fish ever go home and talk about the size of the hook they got away from?

1040　*Saving His Money*

ROBBER:　Your money or your life.

VICTIM:　Take my life. I'm saving my money for my old age.

1041　*Nothing Unusual*

BILL:　I made a fool of myself last night at the dinner.

SAM:　My friend, don't worry. I assure you I noticed nothing unusual.

1042　*Back by Popular Demand*

The young boy brought his report card home to his father, who was a nationally known television personality.

"Were you promoted?" the man asked his son.

"Oh, better than that, Dad," the boy said. "I was held over for another 26 weeks."

1043   Student Answers

An easel is a small but vicious rodent.
A deacon is a mass of inflammable material.
Some fish swim around in shawls.
Ali Baba means being away when the crime was committed.
An alibi is the safest thing to say when you have told a lie.
An epitaph is a horse with the head of a man.
Spoonerism is a love affair, a proposal of marriage.
M.A. is what a B.A. becomes when he gets married.
A spinster is a bachelor's wife.

1044   Gossip

"It's easy to make a mountain out of a molehill. Just add a little dirt."

1045   Long After Gray's Elegy

The curfew tolls the knell of parting day
A line of cars winds slowly o'er the lea;
The pedestrian plods his absent-minded way.
And leaves the world quite unexpectedly.

—*Michigan Educational Journal*

1046   Wonderful, Except

Children are wonderful except when one asks, "Dad, what is a coaxial cable," and waits for a reply.

1047   How about Garbage Can?

TEACHER: Name three collective nouns, please.
PUPIL: Dustpan, wastebasket, and vacuum cleaner.

1048   The Problem

History wouldn't have to repeat itself so often if the world would listen.

1049   Do You Agree?

The Eiffel Tower in Paris looks like the 100-story Sears Tower after taxes.

1050   A Wonderful Family

There's a wonderful family called Stein—
There's Gert, and there's Epp, and there's Ein;
    Gert's poems are bunk,

Epp's statues are junk
And no one can understand Ein.

—Anonymous

1051   *Fast Thinker*

Wishing to encourage a young actress having a radio debut in Los Angeles, a New York admirer phoned her long distance and assured her that her broadcast had been wonderful.

"You were grand!" he declared. "You have a great future in radio."

"But," protested the actress weakly, "there must be some mistake. You see—I haven't gone on the air yet!"

The admirer was stunned, but only for a few seconds. "Ah," he said, "you forget the three hours' difference in time. You are all through here."—*Sunshine Magazine*

1052   *What They Want to Know*

Your creditors want to know when you'll come across—not when your ancestors did.—*Pierce Country (Wisconsin) Herald*

1053   *Pretty Good*

They were discussing the new typist.

MANAGER: What do you think of her?

CHIEF CLERK: Well, I don't know. She seems nice enough, but she spells atrociously.

MANAGER: Really? She must be pretty good. I'm sure I couldn't spell it.

1054   *A Toast*

To the arms of war, may they rust in peace.—*Ed Story*

1055   *Not That Way*

A man and his small son were on a bus. The boy, his nose pressed against the window, keeps asking questions: "What's on that truck, Dad?"

"I dunno," mumbles the father, immersed in his paper.

"Where does rain come from?"

"Don't bother me!"

"What does that sign say?"

"Quit pestering me!"

A passenger behind them taps the father on the shoulder, "Curious little guy you've got there."

"Sure," says the father. "How else will he learn?"

1056   *What Could He Say*

A well-meaning lady held a cookie above a dog and commanded, "Speak! Speak!"

"Why," said the dog modestly, "I hardly know what to say!"

1057   *Wrap It Carefully*

The wife of a Texas oil zillionaire decided to give her spouse a new sixty-eight-foot yacht for Christmas. She instructed the salesman: "I want this to be a surprise. Be sure to wrap it so he can't guess what it is."—*Bennett Cerf, in Esquire*

1058   *Frankness*

What the average father would really like to say to his kid at the table is, "Eat my spinach, Junior."

1059   *Hard Job*

The personnel manager said to the job applicant: "Yes, what we need is a person of vision; with drive, determination and fire; a person who can inspire others; a person who can pull our bowling team out of last place!"

1060   *She Had Awards*

The man was decorating his new den and decided it was a good place to display all the awards he and his two sons had won at various athletic competitions. When he had filled two whole walls, he remarked to his wife that it was a shame she had no awards to contribute.

The following day, she produced, neatly framed, the birth certificates of their two sons and added them to the display.

1061   *Understandable*

A new father went to the hospital to see his new offspring. Looking through the window, he saw row upon row of new arrivals, and every one of them was crying.

"Why are they all crying?" he asked the nurse.

She replied, "If you were only a few hours old, without any clothes, out of work, and owed the government $7,000 on the national debt, you'd be howling, too."

1062   *Repartee*

"You needn't think you're so wonderful. The night you proposed to me, you looked absolutely silly."

"I was absolutely silly."

1063   *Under Tall*

The woman was weighing herself while her husband looked on. She made a face.

He asked, "What's the matter? Are you overweight?"

"No, not that," she replied, "but according to this chart, I should be six inches taller."

1064   *His Difficulty*

"Children," said the teacher, "be diligent and steadfast, and you will succeed. Take the case of George Washington. Do you remember my telling you of the great difficulty George Washington had to face?"

"Yes, ma'am," said a boy. "He couldn't tell a lie."

1065   *He Is Reasonable*

TEACHER: What's the shape of the earth, Johnny?

JOHNNY: It is round.

TEACHER: How do you know it's round?

JOHNNY: All right, it's square, then. I don't want to start an argument about it.

1066   *My Bank Wrote Me*

Roses are red, and violets are blue; please come and talk to us—you overdrew.—*Tom L. Gibson*

1067   *Whose Towels*

A choir director has his towels marked Hymn and Her.

1068   *Ain't It the Truth!*

We heard about a place where "ain't" is used properly—in a roadside grocery store.

CUSTOMER: Ain't got no fresh eggs, is you?

CLERK: I ain't said I ain't!

CUSTOMER: Ain't asked you ain't you ain't. I asked you ain't you is.

1069   *Parking Problem*

An exasperated doctor parked his car in a No Parking zone, with this message on the windshield: "I have circled this block twenty times. I have an appointment to keep—'Forgive us our trespasses.'"

When he returned, he found this note: "I have circled this block for twenty years. If I don't give you a ticket, I'll lose my job—'Lead us not into temptation.'"

1070   *Warned*

"Tell me what you eat, and I'll tell you what you are," said a lunch-counter philosopher.

Whereupon a meek little man, sitting a few stools away, called to the waitress: "Cancel my order for shrimp salad, please."

1071   *Tact*

DEPARTING GUEST:	Well, good-night—hope I haven't kept you up too late.
HOST:	Not at all. We'd have been getting up soon, anyway.

1072   *Who's Shakespeare?*

AUCTIONEER:	Now what am I offered for this beautiful bust of Robert Browning?
MAN IN THE CROWD:	That isn't Browning—that's Shakespeare!
AUCTIONEER:	Well, folks, the joke's on me. Just goes to show you how much I know about the Bible.

1073   *This Must Stop*

MOTHER:	Junior, stop using such bad words.
JUNIOR:	But, Mother, Shakespeare used them.
MOTHER:	Then you'll have to quit playing with him.

1074   *Dream Come True*

"Gentlemen," stated the member of the study club, "I now firmly believe in dreams—in their reality and in the power of prophecy. Last night, while sound asleep, I dreamed that I was at a concert, and when I awoke, I was at a concert."

1075   *Considerate*

PROFESSOR:	If there are any dumbbells in the room, please stand up. (A long pause. Then a lone freshman stood up in the rear.) What—do you consider yourself a dumbbell?
FRESHMAN:	No, I just didn't want you to feel lonesome being the only person in the room standing.

1076   *Try It*

A garage man answered the distress call of a motorist whose car had stalled. He made an examination and informed her it was out of gas.

"Will it hurt," she asked, "if I drive it home with the gas tank empty?"

1077   *Correct*

PROFESSOR:	Joseph, describe hibernation to the class.
JOE:	To hibernate is to pass the winter in a state of torpor, as do certain animals. It is a sort of suspended animation during which life flickers low, and the animal barely exists through the cold, dark part of the year.
PROFESSOR:	Correct. Give us an example.
JOE:	A baseball fan.

1078   *Smart Lad*

At a children's party there were just enough cookies for each to have three. But young Bobby took four.

"You're supposed to get only three, Bobby," said his hostess, "You ought to put the fourth one back."

"Can't," exclaimed Bobby. "I ate that one first."

1079   *You Can't Beat Texas*

A group of Texans were visiting Niagara Falls. "I bet you don't have anything like this in Texas," the tour guide teased. "No," agreed one of the Texans, "but we sure have plumbers who could fix it."

1080   *No Dime Novels*

Two persons were discussing inflation in the public library. Said one, "I wonder where the dime novel has gone." The other answered cynically, "It's gone to $5.95."

1081   *Among Those Present*

The bridal veil was fragile net, the bridal gown was lace. The bride wore slippers on her feet, a smile upon her face.

The bride wore gloves of softest silk, and garlands in her hair. The bride's bouquet was white.

P.S. The groom was also there.

1082   *Remember*

FOOTBALL COACH: Men, I want you to remember this if you forget everything else I tell you: Football develops individuality, initiative, and leadership. It teaches you teamwork but it also teaches you to think and act on your own, to use your own brain to do the job. Now get out there and do exactly what I tell you.

1083   *Lonely*

A middle-aged couple were sunning themselves on a vacation beach.

"Do you know, Arthur," said the wife dreamily, "This is the first time we've ever been anywhere without the children?"

"Yes, Penelope, and believe it or not, I kind of miss them. Throw some sand in my face."

1084   *A Difficult Problem*

A tailor suffering from insomnia finally agreed to try out the old remedy of counting sheep. Next morning he turned up for business more tired than ever. "What a night," he confessed. "I counted 3,000 sheep. Then I figured that was 8,000 yards of wool. That would make 2,500 suits—and where was I going to get buttons and all that lining?"

1085   *Just a Suggestion*

The parents of a little boy either couldn't control him or didn't want to during a flight from New York to Los Angeles. The child was running up and down the aisle and getting in the way. Finally, as the stewardess was serving coffee, he bumped into her and caused her to spill her tray.

As she was cleaning up the mess, she eyed the boy and said: "Why don't you be a good boy and run outside and play awhile?"

1086   *Sure Test*

A professor was lecturing his physics class. "If molecules can be split into atoms and the atoms split into electrons, can the electrons be broken down any further?"

"I'm not certain," replied one of his pupils, "but a sure way to find out would be to mail some of them in a Christmas package marked 'fragile'."

1087   *Sorry about That*

At a rehearsal for a Sunday school Christmas tableau, the teacher carefully lined up four little "cherubs." Each carried a huge cut-out letter. As they stood side by side, the letters would spell out "STAR." A slight mixup occurred, and those present in the church auditorium nearly fell out of their pews as the four little performers took their places—in reverse.

1088   *Modern Manners*
Mother, admonishing a little girl who has been handed an orange by Santa: "Now, what do we say to Santa, dear?" Little girl, extending the orange, "Peel it."

1089   *Noah Had Problems Too*
When Noah sailed the waters blue, he had his troubles same as you. For forty days he drove the Ark before he found a place to park.

1090   *Strange*
Did'ja ever stop to ponder at mankind's peculiar ways, and why it seems most famous men were born on holidays?

1091   *The Price*

HAPPIEST MAN ON EARTH:	How much is this sparkling diamond?
JEWELER:	That one is $1,000.
MAN:	(Whistles.) And this one?
JEWELER:	That one is two whistles.

1092   *Short Recital*

JACK:	When I sat down to play the piano, they all laughed.
TIM:	Why?
JACK:	There wasn't any piano bench.

1093   *Gracie Allen and George Burns*

GRACIE:	My sister had a new baby this morning.
GEORGE:	A boy or a girl?
GRACIE:	Certainly. What else could it be?

1094   *Hard Luck for Joe*
Joe saw the train but didn't stop. They dragged his flivver to the shop. It only took a week or two to make the car as good as new; but though they hunted high and low, they found no extra parts for Joe.

1095   *Quite Slow*

They tell a story at the Empire State Building in New York about a man who dropped his watch from the top floor, took an express elevator down, and caught it before it hit the pavement. It seems his watch was slow.

1096   *They Never Die*

Old mufflers never die—they just get exhausted.—*Herbert V. Prochnow*

1097   *Hard to Find*

WOMAN (to bank teller):	I'd like to open a joint account.
TELLER:	With your husband?
WOMAN:	Heavens, no! With someone who has some money.

1098   *His Usual Problem*

GOLF PRO:	Just go through the motions and don't bother to hit the ball.
BEGINNER:	But that's the trouble I'm trying to cure!

1099   *Might Help*

JOHNNIE:	This liniment makes my arm smart.
BROTHER JIM:	That's good. Rub some on your head, too.

1100   *Problem Solver*

At last, the perfect computer. You just feed in your problems—and they never come out again.

1101   *A Hard Life*

The modern youngster's idea of roughing it is to live in a house with only one phone.

1102   *Fast Growing*

The fastest growing thing in nature is a fish—from the time a guy catches it until he tells about it.

1103   *Taking No Chance*

In the days of covered bridges, a farmer approached one with a load of hay. Taking one look down the long, dark tunnel, he turned his team around and drove off. Upon meeting another farmer and being asked why he had turned around, he answered, "Well, I could get in all right, but I'd never squeeze through that little hole at the other end!"

1104 *Wait a Minute*

The farmer told the preacher he had "got religion."

"That's fine," said the preacher, "but are you sure you're going to put aside all sin?"

"Yes, sir," said the farmer, "I'm through with sin."

"And are you going to pay up all your debts?" asked the preacher.

"Now wait a minute," said the farmer. "You aren't talking religion now; you're talking business."

1105 *Faith*

Blessings on thee, little man, barefoot boy with cheeks of tan, trudging down a dusty lane with no thought of future pain. You're our one and only bet to absorb our National Debt.

Little man with cares so few, we've got lots of faith in you. Guard each merry whistled tune, you are apt to need it soon. Have your fun, boy, while you can, you may be a barefoot man!

1106 *What If We Already Have It?*

The manager of a department store put this notice in the window: "If you need it, we have it."

But in the window of a rival, a sign appeared stating: "If we don't have it, you don't need it."

1107 *Just in Time*

Ephraim, storekeeper in a small Vermont town, was greeted by a neighbor who consoled him on the loss of some of his merchandise in a fire.

"Did you lose much?" asked the friend.

"Not too much," came the laconic reply. "I'd just marked most of my stock down twenty percent."

1108 *He Understood*

The Sunday School teacher was describing how Lot's wife looked back and turned into a pillar of salt.

Little Johnny was much interested. "My Dad looked back once," he explained, "while he was driving, and he turned into a telephone pole!"

1109 *Making It Clear*

"Just what did the man say about me?" asked the lawyer of the witness on the stand.

"He said that you were a sculptor," the witness testified, "but that you should wash more often."

"I don't understand," scowled the lawyer. "Give me his exact words."

"Well," he answered the witness hesitatingly, "he said that you were a dirty chiseler."

1110 *Christmas Drawing*
In Jane's Christmas drawing, two of the camels were approaching the inn, over which was pictured a huge star. The third camel and its rider were going directly away from it. "Why is the third man going in a different direction?" her mother asked. Jane replied, "Oh, he's looking for a place to park."

1111 *Over There*

DUM: Say, tell me, which is the other side of the street?

DIM: Why, the other side is over there.

DUM: Funny thing. That's what I thought. But I was over there and asked an old lady, and she said it was over here.

1112 *Ambitious*
She is ambitious. She reads all of Shakespeare's stuff as soon as it is published.

1113 *Happens Occasionally*
Eight-year-old Joan, anxiously watching the sunny sky for rain, suddenly asked her mother: "Mommy, didn't the weatherman on television last night say it would rain?" "Yes, dear," Mother replied. "Well," daughter responded with a sigh, "I guess God didn't hear him."

1114 *Way Back Then*
Remember when a break was an opportunity, not time for coffee?

1115 *Good Girl*
Grandpa noticed his five-year-old granddaughter out in the backyard brushing the family dog's teeth. When he asked her what in the world she was doing, she replied quickly: "I'm brushing Scotty's teeth. But don't worry, Grandpa, I'll put your toothbrush back, like I always have."

1116 *Names Make News*
Here's a list of towns with odd names, which with abbreviations of their states make interesting combinations:
    Ash, Kan.; Carpet, Tex.; Mount, Wash.; Ogoo, Ga.; Odear, Me.; Skelton, Ky.; Shoo, Fla.; Kay, O.; Houdy, Miss.; Fiver, Tenn.

1117 *Hard to Understand*
Tyler, age five, was graduated from the Beginners' Department at Sunday School. He was happy, but puzzled: "Mother," he said, "I don't understand why my teacher wasn't promoted too. She knows almost as much as I do."

1118 *Smart Lad*

TEACHER: How many zones does the earth have?

JOHNNY: Temperate zone, intemperate zone, no parking, and O.

1119 *The Way It Is*

The rain, though raining every day, upon the just and unjust fella, falls chiefly on the just, because the unjust has the just's umbrella.

1120 *One Advantage*

Whatever trouble Adam had, no man in days of yore could say, when Adam cracked a joke, "I've heard that one before."

1121 *Be Careful*

"You seem to have plenty of intelligence for a man in your position," sneered the attorney to the man on the witness stand.

"Thank you," answered the witness. "If I weren't under oath I'd return the compliment."

1122 *Still Wrong Number*

WOMAN (over telephone):   Are you the game warden?

GAME WARDEN: Yes, madam.

WOMAN: Well, thank goodness, I have the right person at last! Would you mind suggesting some games suitable for a children's party?

1123 *One Less*

A boy was sent by his parents to a private school a long distance from his home. He had been strictly enjoined to write home regularly and tell them all about himself and his new life. At the end of a week, his first letter arrived: "There are 370 boys here. I wish there were 369."

1124 *Heap Big Winner*

A deserted farmhouse in a gullied field was pictured in a farm magazine some time ago, and a prize was offered for the best 100-word description. The award was given to an Indian, who submitted the following:

Picture show white man crazy. Cut down trees. Make big tepee. Plow hill. Water wash. Wind blow soil. Grass gone. Door gone. Window gone. Whole place gone. Buck gone. Papoose gone. Squaw too. No chuckaway. No pigs. No corn. No plow. No hay. No pony. Indian no plow land. Keep grass. Buffalo eat grass. Indian eat buffalo. Hide make tepee. Make moccasin. Indian make no terrace. No make dam. All time eat. No hunt job. No hitchhike. No ask relief. No shoot pig. Great Spirit make grass.

Indian no waste anything. Indian no work. White man loco.—*Sunshine Magazine*

1125 *Truthful*

MOTHER:	Did you eat those tarts I had in the pantry?
JACK:	I didn't touch one.
MOTHER:	Well, there is only one left.
JACK:	That's the one I didn't touch.

1126 *Harem Scarem*

A sultan at odds with his harem thought of a way he could scare 'em; he caught him a mouse, which he freed in the house, thus starting the first harem scarem.

1127 *His Problem*

DINER:	I can't eat this soup.
WAITER:	I'll call the manager, sir. (Manager arrives.)
DINER:	This soup—I can't eat it.
MANAGER:	I regret that. I'll call the chef. (Chef arrives.)
DINER:	I can't eat this soup.
CHEF:	What's the matter with it?
DINER:	Nothing; no spoon.

1128 *Changed*

He shouted of the curse of wealth and made the rich man wince. But an uncle left him money—and he hasn't shouted since!

1129 *Just Walking*

I'll bicycle, ski, and fence for hours. I'll do all the sports that require hot showers. I'll play golf and love missing all my putts, but walking—just walking—drives me NUTS!

1130 *The Nation's Problem*

"The beauty of it all is," says the mayor, "it won't cost anyone a cent; we'll get it all out of a federal grant."

SIGNS OF THE TIMES

1131 *Sign in school hallway:* Free Monday through Friday: knowledge. Bring your own container.

1132   *Sign in a local hospital:* Give blood—it was meant to circulate.

1133   *Sign on an automobile wrecking establishment:* Drive carefully. We're overstocked.

1134   *Sign in a TV repair shop:* Do it yourself—then call us.

1135   *Bumper sticker:* Pedestrians don't have bumpers, so give them a brake.

1136   *Sign in a Dallas restaurant:* We sell antiques—coffee at 10¢.

1137   *Poultry farm sign:* Better laid than ever.

1138   *Sign at a service station:* We collect taxes—federal, state, local. We also sell gasoline and oil.

1139   *Cleaning shop sign:* Bring us your pressing problems.

MALAPROPS: MISUSING A WORD

1140   She has a nice sense of rumor.—*John H. Cutler*

1141   Lamb chops cooked to your likeness.

1142   I rode an alligator to the top of the First National Building.

1143   The king wore a robe trimmed with vermin.

1144   A quorum is a place to keep fish in.

1145   A vegetarian is a horse doctor.

1146   The watchwords of the French Revolution were: Liberty, Equality, and Maternity.

1147   A metaphor is something you shout through.

1148   Some areas are cultivated by irritation.

1149   A gentleman tips his hat. He should know enough to decapitate to a lady.

1150   "You and I," as a Hollywood director said, "know what an optimist is, but how many of the public know it's an eye doctor?"

SPOONERISMS: SOUNDS OR SYLLABLES OF
TWO WORDS ACCIDENTALLY CONFUSED

1151   *Professor to student:* You hissed my mystery lectures.

1152   *Minister at cathedral:* Is the bean dizzy?

1153   *Church usher to lady:* Mardon me padam, but you are occupewing the wrong pie.

FERHOODLED ENGLISH: AMUSING COMMENTS OF THE
PENNSYLVANIA DUTCH

1154   The beans is all already, so many got et.

1155   Smear me all over with jam a piece of bread.

1156   Look the window out and see if it's puttin' down somesing still
(rain).

1157   There's two roads to Johnstown. They are both the same as far,
but one is more the hill up.

1158   We walked the town over and looked the windows through.

1159   Does Chake want to go fer steady or chust for so.

1160   Hurry yourself onct and get well quick.

1161   Ve get too soon oldt un too late schmart.

10
WITTICISMS
AND EPIGRAMS

1162 With the exception of world unrest, nothing breaks out in more places than an old garden hose.

1163 Thirty minutes is long enough for any man to tell what he knows, but he doesn't become interesting until after that when he tells what he doesn't know.

1164 In some Latin American countries any man with a good voice, a large vocabulary, and a microphone is certain to develop into a political party.

1165 You can't fool all the people all the time but most of us try.

1166 A typical American is one who has his home mortgaged, owes 30 instalments on his car, plays golf when he ought to work, and looks forward to a happy old age with social security.

1167 One of the benefits of inflation is that children no longer get sick on a nickel's worth of candy.

1168 Another good test of blood pressure is to watch a man being liberal with the money he owes you.

1169 If you build a big business, you're a sinister influence; if you don't, you're a failure.

1170 The modern idea of roughing it is to have no television in the camp.

1171 A political plank is what a candidate stands on before election and sits down on afterward.

1172 Children have become so expensive that only the poor can afford them.

1173   In the old days, it was two chickens in every pot, and now it's two government employees for every taxpayer.

1174   What we need is a child labor law to keep them from working their parents to death.

1175   If all the college students who slept in class were placed end to end, they would be much more comfortable.

1176   In every one of our universities, there are a number of aggressive, clean-cut young men who are diligently working their dads through college.

1177   It is easy to pick out the best people. They'll help you do it.

1178   There must be a destiny to shape our ends, but our middles are of our own chewsing.

1179   Many an argument is sound—merely sound.

1180   The only thing that can keep on growing without nourishment is an ego.

1181   A college education seldom hurts a person if he's willing to learn a little something after he graduates.

1182   As a rule, a man who doesn't know his own mind hasn't missed so much at that.

1183   A woman doesn't hire domestic help now; she marries it.

1184   Often it's the mink in the closet that is responsible for the wolf at the door.

1185   Looking at modern art is like trying to follow the plot in a bowl of alphabet soup.

1186   A few more deductions and your take-home pay isn't going to be enough to get you there.

1187   It doesn't matter whose payroll you are on, you are working for yourself.

1188   If you would like to live a quiet, peaceful, uneventful life, you are living at the wrong time.

1189   You have heard of the person who said he always felt bad even when he felt good, for fear he would feel worse tomorrow.

1190   Education is not given for the purpose of earning a living. Education is learning what to do with a living after you earn it.

1191   Everyone now works for the government, either on the payroll or on the tax roll.

1192   The weaker the argument, the stronger the words.

1193   We like a man who comes right out and says what he thinks, when he agrees with us.

1194   A simple fact that is difficult to learn is that the time to save money is when you have some.

1195   There are two sides to every question that we're not interested in.

1196   Too much of the world is run on the theory that you don't need road manners if you are a five-ton truck.

1197   He had been dead long enough to be great.

1198   There are two sides to every question, and if you want to be popular you take both.

1199   By the time father gets the vacation bills paid, it is time to think about Christmas presents.

1200   If you want to find out what's wrong with a man, elect him to public office.

1201   The only possible reason we can see why old fools are the biggest fools is because they have had more practice.

1202   A real football fan is one who knows the nationality of every player on the All-American team.

1203   Friends are folks who excuse you when you have made a fool of yourself.

1204   We expect modern youth to be strong, courageous, and prepared to pay even more taxes than their fathers.

1205   Occasionally you see a man driving a car so carefully that you conclude it must be paid for.

1206   An honest confession is good for the soul, but bad for the reputation.

1207   Note to hunters: If it stands on its hind legs and has a pipe in its mouth, it isn't a deer.

1208   There is a lot of history that isn't fit to repeat itself.

1209   The law presumes a man innocent until he is found guilty, and then if he has any money left, his lawyer continues the presumption.

1210   The fact that Congress is no better and no worse than the country is something to worry about.

1211 Benjamin Franklin wrote: "Only two things in this life are certain —death and taxes." What the taxpayer resents is that they don't come in that order.

1212 When you see a married couple coming down the street, the one who is two or three steps ahead is the one that's mad.

1213 If you can buy a house for nothing down, you don't have to stay home to get your money's worth.—*Herbert V. Prochnow*

1214 Indians on a western reservation are reported to be showing symptoms of uneasiness. Maybe someone has been telling them that the whites want to give the country back to them.

1215 There's a bright side to everything, but there's no joy when it's on your blue suit.

1216 If the milk business ever becomes a public utility, we suppose that will make a cow a holding company.

1217 One nice thing about spending an evening at home is that you never have to redeem your hat after it's over.

1218 The only trouble with doing your Christmas shopping early is to get your wherewithal on the same schedule.

1219 A cynic says that a saver is a far-sighted person who lays money aside for the government's rainy day.

1220 You may get along at Christmas time without the holly, but you must have the berries.

1221 Bragging may not bring happiness, but no man having caught a large fish goes home through an alley.

1222 Money is an article which may be used as a universal passport to everywhere except Heaven, and as a universal provider of everything except happiness.

1223 A sharp tongue and a dull mind are usually found in the same head.

1224 Defeat is for those who acknowledge it.

1225 Common sense is the ability to detect values.

1226 The meanest habit in the world is that of self-pity.

1227 Our grandchildren are going to have a hard time paying for the good times we didn't have.

1228 Any idea a college professor has about money is almost certain to be theoretical.—*Grand Rapids Press*

1229 Talent knows what to do, tact knows how to do it.

1230 You are born in a hospital, marry in a church, die in a car—what do you need a home for?

1231 A physician says the way to keep young is to work, and that's just what we've been afraid of all the time.

1232 Talent makes a man respectable, tact makes him respected.

1233 No sooner do they get the athletes off the gridiron than they begin putting the coaches on the pan.

1234 Now and then a collision occurs when two motorists go after the same pedestrian.

1235 Nothing influences a congressman like ten thousand telegrams written by the same person.

1236 Law gives the pedestrian the right of way, but makes no provision for flowers.

1237 You can't fool all the people all the time, but it isn't necessary. A majority will do.

1238 The main thing we have learned from our shortwave set is that nearly every country in the world is full of sopranos.

1239 A physician recommends for the middle-aged light exercise and a siesta each day. Daily dozen and daily dozing.

1240 An astronaut said the earth looked blue from space. Well, it often looks that way on the ground also.

1241 Blessed are the peacemakers; they will never be unemployed.

1242 "Those who have hobbies rarely go crazy," asserts a psychiatrist. Yeah, but what about those who have to live with those who have hobbies?

1243 The drama critic's meat is the ham actor.

1244 The trouble with a husband who works like a horse is that all he wants to do evenings is hit the hay.

1245 The steps of the dining hall have become considerably worn by the treading of so many heels.—*Professor Botts, Notre Dame University*

1246 Human diseases are the same as they were a thousand years ago, says an authority. Yes, but doctors have selected more expensive names for them.

1247 The man who boasts he never made a mistake is often married to a woman who did.

1248 The fellow who gets on a high horse is riding for a fall.

1249 One hitchhiker to the other—"That's right, just sit there and let me work my finger to the bone."

1250 Another danger about one-arm driving is that a man may skid right down the center aisle of a church.

1251 Taking my economic theory course may not keep you off the bread lines, but at least you'll know why you're there.—*Professor Robert Michel, Hunter (N.Y.) College*

1252 Never miss an opportunity to make others happy—even if you have to let them alone to do it.

1253 You may write your term papers in any manner you choose—only, please observe the copyright laws.—*Professor F. G. March, San Francisco Junior College*

1254 A man never gets so confused in his thinking that he can't see the other fellow's duty.

1255 He who laughs last may laugh best, but he soon gets a reputation for being a dummy.

1256 Dad may not be able to appraise the worth of a college career, but he can tell you the cost.

1257 She was all will and a yard wide.

1258 The nice thing about a dull party is that you get to bed at a decent hour.

1259 Many of us spend half our time wishing for the things we could have if we didn't spend so much time wishing for them.

1260 A man laughs at a woman who puts on eyebrow makeup, but he spends ten minutes trying to comb two hairs across a bald spot.

1261 Actually there is no distinct class trodden underfoot except those who hold aisle seats.

1262 An Iowa professor says he finds five different kinds of dumbness. It seems incredible that a prominent man like that should have met so few people.

1263 The real problem concerning your leisure is how to keep other people from using it.

1264 A sportswriter says there are 300 kinds of games played with balls. There are more than that many played with golf balls alone.

1265 It should be easy to make an honest living—there's so little competition.

1266   Many a woman who goes on a diet finds that she is a poor loser.

1267   The political pot never boils much. The old applesauce is only warmed over.

1268   There are two kinds of voters. Those who will vote for your candidate, and a lot of ignorant prejudiced fools.

1269   Social tact is making your company feel at home, even though you wish they were.

1270   All kinds of social knowledge and graces are useful, but one of the best is to be able to yawn with your mouth closed.

1271   A politician is a person who urges you to vote for him and then sends you a bill for doing it.

1272   A Communist is a person who has given up hope of becoming a capitalist.

1273   We can't understand why goods sent by ship is called a cargo, while goods sent in a freight car is a shipment.

1274   If both sides make you laugh, you are broadminded.

1275   When you sell yourself, be sure that you don't misrepresent the goods.

1276   Some folks would rather blow their own horn than listen to the Marine band.

1277   When you argue with a fool, be sure he isn't similarly engaged.

1278   The two most important muscles which operate without the direction of the brain are the heart and the tongue.

1279   "A vegetarian diet is best for those who would be beautiful," we read. Well, it does not seem to have done much for the elephant.—*Punch (London)*

1280   All we know about "hard" and "easy" money is that any kind is both—hard to get and easy to spend.

1281   The Smithsonian Institution reveals that there is 45 trillion dollars' worth of gold in the ocean, but we don't suppose it will comfort a seasick guy much to know he's rolling in wealth.—*Boston Herald*

1282   What this country needs is a dollar which will be not so much elastic as adhesive.

1283   In giving till it hurts, some people are extremely sensitive to pain.

1284   The meanest guy in the world is the fellow who was deaf and never told his barber.

1285   The new computers do everything but think, which we must admit makes them almost human.

1286   It is much more dignified to say we're moving in cycles rather than running around in circles, although it comes to about the same thing.

1287   Man is the only animal that laughs. He is also the only animal that has a legislature.

1288   Common sense would avoid divorces and quite a few marriages too.—*Herbert V. Prochnow*

1289   A whale's tongue is found to contain 8 percent of the oil in his system. In politicians, the proportion is even higher.

1290   One can't help admiring the fellow who is stupid and knows it.

1291   It takes at least forty-eight rabbits to make a sealskin coat for a woman.

1292   Ideas are such funny things; they never work unless you do.

1293   Time wounds all heels.

1294   The fact that silence is golden may explain why there is so little of it.

1295   By the time a man learns to stand up for his rights, his arches have caved in.

1296   Worry is the interest you pay on trouble before it comes.

1297   If you think chickens are dumb, try planting some vegetables.

1298   Experience is one thing you can't get on the easy payment plan.

1299   One touch of scandal makes the whole world chin.

1300   What constitutes a living wage depends upon whether you are giving it or getting it.

1301   There are two kinds of people, the good and the bad, and the good ones are like you and me.

1302   Sometimes we're not sure whether some people are lighthearted or lightheaded.

1303   Now that the telephone company has started to introduce television phones, we may get a lot of pleasure from calling the wrong numbers.

1304   One person in every eight has an accident. The other seven have accident insurance.

1305   There are two sides to every question, and a politician usually takes both.

1306   There are only two kinds of pedestrians—the quick and the dead.

1307   The car to watch is the car behind the car in front of you.

1308   You really have insomnia if you can't sleep when it's time to get up.

1309   An article in an English journal tells how to start an amateur glee club. The real need, however, is an article telling how to stop one.

1310   Everything in the modern home is controlled by switches except the children.

1311   To tell the temperature in summer you can count the number of times a tree cricket chirps in a second and add forty, or you can look at the thermometer.

1312   They call it the sea of matrimony because husbands have such a hard job keeping their heads above water.

1313   When a reporter has nothing to write about, he writes about nothing to write about.

1314   A person seldom makes the same mistake twice. Generally it's three times or more.

1315   Patent medicine ads are so attractive that it makes a man who has his health feel as though he were missing something.

1316   The cost of living is always about the same—all a person has.

1317   An English neurologist says that a man who owns a car seldom walks in his sleep. If he has a family, he does it when he's awake.

1318   They say that every bride who is married isn't happy—just triumphant.

1319   When a man begins to realize the truth about himself, it frequently retards his program for reforming his neighbors.

1320   Some coeds said they intend to marry "men of brains, character, adequate incomes, and a nice sense of humor." It sounds like bigamy.

1321   A recent bride had six bridesmaids in hyacinth blue silk and two pages in rich crimson velvet, with gold lace. A pale bridegroom completed the color scheme.

1322   There are only a few nations left that are so backward they mind their own business.

1323   If all the candid camera fiends were placed end to end, they would probably take a picture.

1324   According to a doctor, singing warms the blood. We have heard some that has made ours positively boil.

1325   Love at first sight is possible, but it is always well to take a second look.

1326   Now and then one picks up a magazine on the stands that makes one curious to see the stuff the editor rejected.

1327   So far no one has invented an intelligence test to equal matrimony.

1328   Sign in wallpaper and paint store: "Husbands choosing colors must have note from wives."

1329   An optimist sees only the initial payment; the pessimist sees the future installments and the upkeep.

1330   A good deal of our prosperous appearance is due to driving a mortgaged car over a bonded road.

1331   It may be understandable if Junior believes in Santa Claus, but it's unpardonable if a politician leads Grandpa to believe it.

1332   Only Americans have mastered the art of being prosperous though broke.

1333   An advertisement for a lecturer says he "speaks straight from the shoulder." Too bad some of these talks can't originate a little higher up.

1334   Reforms come from below. No man with four aces howls for a new deal.

1335   We have the highest standard of living in the world. Too bad we can't afford it.

1336   When a man says, "I run things at my house," he may mean the washing machine, the vacuum cleaner, and the furnace.

1337   Many a man stays home nights because he has the house to himself.

1338   A man who sits in a swamp all day waiting to shoot a duck will kick if his wife has dinner ten minutes late.

1339   There's no justice. If you make out your income tax correctly, you go to the poorhouse. If you don't, you go to jail.

1340   Probably the world's greatest humorist was the man who called installments "easy payments."

1341   Only an average person is always at his best.

1342   The paramount question before the country today is, "How much is the down payment?"

1343   A teacher asked a precocious youngster what he was going to be when he grew up, and he said a taxpayer.

1344   Our laundryman has the wisdom of a Solomon. When he can't decide to whom a certain shirt belongs, he splits it in half.

1345   A man left the bulk of his fortune to his lawyer. If everybody did this, a lot of time would be saved.

1346   "Just think," exclaimed the enthusiastic young husband, "by the time we get all this furniture paid for we'll have genuine antiques!"

1347   Golf liars have one advantage over the fishing kind—they don't have to show anything to prove it.

1348   About the time one learns how to make the most of life, the most of it is gone.

1349   Among the things that seem to grow by leaps and bounds are the children in the apartment overhead.

1350   The best things in life are free. It's the worst things that are so expensive.

1351   You may not know when you are well off, but the Internal Revenue Service does.

1352   What this country needs is a man who can be right and President at the same time.

1353   "An Eskimo woman is old at forty," says an explorer. An American woman is not old at forty. In fact, she's not even forty.

1354   Behind every successful man, there's a woman telling him he doesn't amount to much.

1355   It takes three generations or one good guess in the stock market to make a gentleman.

1356   A wizard is the person who can keep up with the neighbors and the installments, too.

1357   It is very difficult to stand prosperity, especially your neighbor's.

1358   Statistics show Americans spent several billions on vacations last year, but they don't say at which resort hotel.

1359   It's nice to have four years between elections. It takes people that long to regain their faith.

1360   All work and no play makes jack for the nerve specialist.

1361   You can fool some of the people all of the time and all of the people some of the time and the rest of the time somebody else will fool them.

1362   We used to worry about future generations becoming soft, but no more. Not when we think of the bond issues they're going to have to pay off.

1363   A college professor declares that contrary to scientific opinion, the interior of the earth is not so hot. In our opinion, the same thing is true of the exterior.

1364   Problems in marriage often arise because a man too often shows his worst side to his better half.

1365   It's sort of depressing to think that most of us are just like the rest of the people.

1366   What any government needs is more pruning and less grafting.

1367   A good many human dynamos are short-circuited in a few years.

1368   Someday we hope to be wise enough to get the vitamins that wild animals get by eating what they like.

1369   A politician doesn't stand on his record; he jumps on the other fellow's.

1370   The optimist may be wrong, but he has a lot more fun than the pessimist.

1371   The two agencies that redistribute great fortunes are taxation and offspring.

1372   The human race seems to have improved everything except people.

1373   The great leader is one who never permits his followers to discover that he is as dumb as they are.

1374   We wonder if the eloquent founders of this nation would have talked so glowingly of posterity if they had known we were going to be it.

1375   On the political menu too, applesauce is served with pork.

1376   A small town is one where the folks know all the news before the paper comes out, but take it to see whether the editor got the stories the way they heard them.

1377   "The first lie detector," says Sam Hill in the Cincinnati *Enquirer,* "was made out of the rib of a man." And no improvement has ever been made on the original machine.

1378   A businessman is judged by the company he keeps solvent.

1379   The idea of fingerprinting children is a good one. It will settle the question as to who used the guest towel in the bathroom.

1380   A kiss is a peculiar proposition. Of no use to one, yet absolute bliss to two. The small boy gets it for nothing, the young man has to lie for it, and the old man has to buy it. The baby's right, the lover's privilege, and the hypocrite's mask. To a young girl, faith; to a married woman, hope.

1381   The great difficulty in amplifiers is that they amplify the speaker's voice, but not his ideas.

1382   When a boy marries, two opinions prevail at the home he is leaving: His mother thinks he is throwing himself away, and his sisters think the girl is.

1383   Some people are like French bread—little dough, but lots of crust.

1384   Inflation or no inflation, the cost of living seems to remain about the same—all that we earn.

1385   Every man is a hero in his own home—until the company leaves.

1386   The young man who worked so hard to graduate later wonders what the hurry was.

1387   We send our actors to England and England sends her actors to us. It's getting to be hams across the sea.

1388   One thing all nations have in common is the ability to see each other's faults.

1389   It's a good thing that politicians are generally paid by the year. They would starve to death on piecework.

1390   When everybody tends to his own business, news is scarce.

1391   One reason we are a great nation is because we have been unable to exhaust our natural resources in spite of our best efforts.

1392   Pat a man on the back and you may make his head swell.

1393   Sometime the restaurants may retaliate by putting in a line of drugs and toilet articles.

1394   The man who saves money nowadays isn't a miser; he's a wizard.

1395   You should try to save something while your salary is small. It is almost impossible to save after you begin earning more.

1396   The bigger the bankroll, the tighter the rubber band.

1397   The trouble with self-made men is that they quit the job too early.

1398   A sordid money-grabber is anybody who grabs more money than you can grab.

1399   The subways are so crowded that even the men can't all get seats.

1400   Never bet on a sure thing unless you can afford to lose.

1401   If all the autos in the world were laid end to end, it would be Sunday afternoon.

1402   A pessimist is one who, given the choice between two evils, chooses both of them.

1403   The trouble with these "Do You Want Money?" ads is that when you read them you always discover you either have to work for it or mortgage something to get it.

1404   It's worth the taxi fare to feel you don't care what happens to the fenders.

1405   One guy who always goes to the top is a barber.

1406   There are tens of millions of telephones in the United States, so when you make it in two dials you aren't doing so badly at that.

1407   A lot of nice, fat turkey gobblers would strut less if they could see into the future.

1408   The theater at the present time is not holding a mirror up to life, but a keyhole.

1409   The camera never lies, and it takes a family album to convince some people that the truth is a terrible thing.

1410   The broad general rule is that a man is about as big as the things that make him mad.

1411   The greatest consolation for many vacationers is that they have found where not to go next time.

1412   The polls are places where you stand in line for a chance to decide who will spend your money.

1413   Man wants but little here below, but he usually gets along on less.

1414   Most people agree with the person who keeps his mouth shut.

1415   The greatest paradox of them all is still civilized warfare.

1416   A resort is a place where the natives live on your vacation money until next summer.

1417   The poet Heine once said to a caller, "My head today is perfectly barren, and you will find me stupid enough; for a friend has been here, and we exchanged ideas."

1418 U.S. now stands for Unlimited Spending.—*Tampa Tribune*

1419 The bigger a man's head gets, the easier it is to fill his shoes.

1420 The fact that no one knows anything about the future makes a business forecaster more confident.

1421 Evolution: dress, $40.75; frock, $75.95; gown, $250; creation, $350.

1422 A man can blow his own horn nowadays before he completes all the payments.

1423 All things come to him who waits, but they are apt to be pretty well shopworn.

1424 The man's insomnia was so bad that the sheep were picketing him for shorter hours.

1425 He made a nickel go so far the buffalo got sore feet.

1426 Judging from the amount of the public debt, it is no longer much of a compliment to tell a lady she looks like a million dollars.

1427 If you can spend a perfectly useless afternoon in a perfectly useless manner, you have learned how to live.—*Lin Yutang*

1428 The diploma you get from the school of experience is inscribed in marble, but you won't be able to read it.

1429 A woman is a man's solace, but if it wasn't for her, he wouldn't need any solace.

1430 According to a survey, the most dangerous traffic hour is between seven and eight o'clock at night. That's when everyone is through dinner and hurrying to get nowhere.

1431 He's so stingy that when the boys give three cheers, he only gives two.

1432 To enjoy garden work, put on a wide hat and gloves, hold a little trowel in one hand, and tell the man where to dig.

1433 There will always be a multitude who are congenitally unable to think straight.—*Charles Evans Hughes*

1434 You can't fall out of bed if you sleep on the floor.

1435 A golf player is a person who can drive seventy miles an hour in any traffic with perfect ease, but blows up on a two-foot putt if somebody coughs.

1436 It is getting harder and harder to find a courteous person who isn't trying to sell you something.

1437   A real friend will not visit you in prosperity unless he is invited, but when you are in adversity he will call without invitation.

1438   The cautious suitor who stays on the fence too long usually ends up getting the gate.

1439   The greatest inspiration is often born of desperation. The fellow who thinks he can't is probably right.

1440   The advantage about working day and night is that you earn enough to pay the doctor when you break down.

1441   When a fellow's too much in love with himself, he's not likely to have much competition.

1442   It's the fellow in the office who blows his horn the loudest who is generally in a fog.

1443   The neighbor's son is very active in church—he squirms, wiggles, and fidgets.

1444   Sixty million people go to the movies every week, and almost all of them file past our seats at the most exciting part of the picture.

1445   When Uncle Sam plays Santa Claus, it's the taxpayer who holds the bag.

1446   Professor Warren of Harvard Law School concedes modern youth a little: "An A.B. degree nowadays means that the holder has mastered the first two letters of the alphabet."

1447   The trick in campaigning is to give them platitudes without fear or favor and straight-from-the-shoulder generalities.

1448   One advantage in being stupid is that you never get lonely.

1449   Many persons do not leave their footprints on the sands of time, but they leave their skidmarks at the traffic intersections.

1450   A perpetual optimist is a person who has nothing to worry about because he has nothing to worry with.

1451   When success turns a man's head, he faces failure.

1452   Some persons have tact, others tell the truth.

1453   There are two kinds of fishermen; those who fish for sport and those who catch something.

1454   Buying what you do not need is an easy road to needing what you cannot buy.

1455   Weak knees come from a weak head.

1456   What is mind? No matter. What is matter? Never mind.—
Thomas Hewitt Key

1457   Riches are no menace if we do not divorce dollars from sense.

1458   The chief fault of American audiences is that they see the point
before you get there, which is disconcerting.—*Jerome K. Jerome*

1459   The man whose conscience never troubles him must have it pretty
well trained.

1460   Some persons pray for more things than they are willing to work
for.

1461   Tomorrow never comes, but the morning after certainly does.

1462   There are some who call it the Sock Market.

1463   We would be glad to pay as we go if we could catch up paying for
where we have been.

1464   At a banquet of firemen recently, the chief proposed the toast:
"The ladies! Their eyes kindle the only flame which we cannot extin-
guish, and against which there is no insurance."

1465   The real test of golf and in life is not keeping out of the rough . . .
but getting out after we are in.

1466   Life has a way of evening up things. For every woman who makes
a fool out of some man, there's another who makes a man out of some
fool.

1467   The difference between a groove and a grave is only a matter of
depth.

1468   A luxury on which you can make the down payment becomes a
necessity.

1469   Nothing handicaps you so much in golf as honesty.

1470   The only reason a great many American families don't own an
elephant is that they have never been offered an elephant for a dollar
down and a dollar a week.

1471   A politician thinks of the next election; a statesman of the next
generation.

1472   No matter how bad prose is, it might be verse.

1473   Everytime he looks in the mirror he takes a bow.

1474   The difference between most men is small, but that little difference is large.

1475 The difference between a prejudice and a conviction is that you can explain a conviction without getting mad.

1476 As a man grows wiser, he talks less and says more.

1477 The average American works himself to death so he can live.

1478 Someone wants to know if there is any cure for waking up with a severe headache. We can only think of insomnia.

1479 When a girl reduces, she is going out of her weigh to please some man.

1480 By the streets of "by and by," one arrives at the house of "never."—*Cervantes*

1481 If you wish to be miserable, you must think about yourself, what you want, what you like, what respect people ought to pay you, and what people think of you.

1482 The truth is the opinion that survives.

1483 Minimize friction and create harmony. You can get friction for nothing, but harmony costs courtesy and self-control.

1484 Nature makes blunders, too. She gives the biggest mouth to those who have the least to say.

1485 It should be easy for any government to please the people. All they want is lower taxes and more spending.

1486 A man may have more money than brains, but not for long.

1487 It is commendable, to be sure, for a college to offer a course in "What Contemporary Civilization Is," but a little information as to where it is would help a lot too.

1488 If you want to flatter somebody, just look serious and ask him what he thinks of the general situation.

1489 If the colleges continue to get more and more finicky, pretty soon an amateur won't be able to make a decent living in any sport.

1490 Sign in a library: Only low talk permitted here.

1491 We live in a free country where a man can say what he thinks if he isn't afraid of his wife, his neighbors, his boss, his customers, or the government.

1492 Making a fool of yourself is not so bad if you realize who did it.

1493 Man isn't so smart. Thousands of years before he began to have afternoon headaches from trying to think, the turtle had a streamlined body, hard top, retractable landing gear, and a mobile home.

1494 Money talks and it never says anything so often as "goodby."

1495 The first essential for leadership is a group of dumb people to follow you.

1496 There is nothing more difficult than the art of making advice agreeable.

1497 At twenty the will reigns, at thirty the wit, and at forty the judgment.

1498 This is a free country, and a good many people are getting it that way by agreeing to pay later.

1499 A rabbit's foot is a poor substitute for horse sense.

1500 It is possible that the man who wakes up to find himself famous has been sleeping all the while with one eye open.

1501 A friend forgives your defects, and if he is very fond of you, he doesn't see any.

1502 Nowadays every man wants life, liberty, and two cars in which to pursue happiness.

1503 Simile—R is silent as in Harvard.

1504 Our eyes are placed in front because it is more important to look ahead than look back.

1505 If you can't think of any other way to flatter a man, tell him he's the kind that can't be flattered.

1506 If parents haven't learned something from experience, they can always learn it from their children.

1507 A rich uncle always has nieces and nephews named after him.

1508 Sign at Jonestown, Pa., store on New York to Harrisburg highway: Modern Antiques.

1509 It certainly pays to advertise. There are twenty-six mountains in Colorado higher than Pike's Peak.

1510 Some people just can't unbend and be human until misfortune has taken the starch out of them.

1511 If time heals, it shouldn't be necessary to go beyond the waiting room into the doctor's office.

1512 Some people are born great, some achieve greatness, and some just grate.

1513 In the old days a bad man would go around with nicks in his gun handle, instead of in his fenders.

1514 You might as well do your Christmas hinting early.

1515 The man who thinks he has no faults has at least one.

1516 I had a little dog. I called him August. August was fond of jumping at conclusions, especially at the wrong conclusion. One day he jumped at a mule's conclusion. The next day was the first of September.

1517 There are three applause periods in a speech. Applause by the audience at the beginning of a speech expresses faith. Applause in the middle of a speech expresses hope. Applause at the end of a speech expresses charity.

1518 We have often wondered why Nature didn't construct a man so he could kick himself occasionally.

1519 A recession is a period in which you tighten up your belt. A depression is a time in which you have no belt to tighten. When you have no trousers to hold up, it's a panic.

1520 In some cities they tear down buildings to save taxes. They might try tearing down some taxes to save buildings.

1521 He who hesitates probably turned into a one-way street.

1522 The government not only has the bad habit of living beyond its income, but also beyond ours.

1523 It's hard to keep up with the neighbors without falling behind with the creditors.

1524 "Many of the compositions that have been handed in are trite—or should I say tripe!"—*Professor in English class*

1525 Customer (to headwaiter): "Just for a point of information, did the waiter who took my order leave any family?"

1526 If they ever close up the Metropolitan Opera, where will society go to talk while opera is being sung?

1527 A good many car drivers don't need seatbelts as much as they need straitjackets.

1528 We have far too many divorces. Too many persons marry in haste and repent at leisure. A wedding is the only prerequisite for a divorce now.

1529 The other day, the newspapers were showing the pictures of an old man who had reached the age of ninety-eight. But there is nothing so wonderful about that. Look at how long it took him to get there.

1530 The reason some of us find it difficult to think is that we haven't had any previous experience.

1531   "The surtax on any amount of surtax net income not shown in the table is computed by adding to the surtax for the largest amount shown which is less than the income, the surtax upon the excess over the amount of the rate indicated in the table."—*Instruction on income-tax blank.* We contend that the government should supply a slide rule, prayer book, and Ouija board with each income-tax return form.

1532   When you hear some folks you know blow and brag, you are reminded of the time the flea said to the elephant, "Boy, didn't we shake that bridge when we crossed it?"

1533   A thoughtful economist has just written a 100-page "Short History of Money." We could write a history of ours in six words: "Here it is; there it goes!"

1534   It is not only unkind to speak of a wasteful bureaucracy—it is also repetitious.

1535   *Found on a freshman's registration card:* Name of parents: Mamma and Papa.

1536   "A toast," exclaimed the hobo lifting his tomato can. "Here's to de holidays! Bless de hull t'ree hundred and sixty-five of 'em!"

1537   *Sign in a self-service elevator:* Eighth Floor Button Out of Order. Please Push Three and Five Instead.

1538   Most of us are confident we could move the mountains if somebody would clear the hills out of our way.

1539   Making love is like making pie. All you need is a lot of crust and some applesauce. (Then mix it with a spoon.)

1540   A famous old inn claims to own a sixty-year-old cheese. It is, of course, still going strong.

1541   *Sign on a Scottish golf course:* Members will refrain from picking up lost balls until they have stopped rolling.

1542   In the old days child guidance was something parents were expected to provide and not submit to.

1543   "Multiple births are more frequent in larger families," declares a statistician. It's mighty hard to fool these statisticians.

1544   In trying to convey an important idea to another person, the Irishman said: "If I can get this one idea into your head, you will have it in a nutshell."—*Dr. Emory W. Luccock*

1545   A good speech has a good beginning and a good ending, both of which are kept very close together.

1546   Nothing gives you quite the thrill of treading in the darkness on a step that isn't there.

1547   It is just as well that justice is blind; she might not like some of the things done in her name if she could see them.

1548   The world has facilities enough now for transmitting intelligence rapidly—that is, until we get more intelligence to transmit.

1549   Somebody always backs down when the public gets its back up.

1550   "The slow thinkers live longest," says a prominent psychologist. Not if they cross the street.

1551   If a man wants his dreams to come true, he must wake up.

1552   The difficulty in turning immigrants into good Americans is to find a model to work by.

1553   A magazine writer says we need a new religion. But let's not do anything rash until we try the old ones.

1554   If he dodges cars, he is a pedestrian; if he dodges taxes, he is a financier; if he dodges responsibility, he is a statesman.

1555   The modern girl may have her little weaknesses, but she isn't effeminate.

1556   There is nothing but ill-fortune in a habit of grumbling, which requires no talent, no self-denial, no brains, no character.—*O. S. Marden*

1557   One advantage of being poor is that it doesn't take much to improve your situation.

1558   A depression is a period when people do without the things their parents never had.

1559   One nice thing about a one-way street is that you can only be bumped in the rear.

1560   If you make a better mousetrap now, you're just in the old rat race.

1561   A sensible girl is not so sensible as she looks because a sensible girl has more sense than to look sensible.

1562   One half of knowing what you want is knowing what you must give up before you get it.—*Sidney Howard*

1563   A seventh-grade pupil won first prize in his class for the best short baseball story: "Rain, no game."

1564   When prices are high, money doesn't talk; it whispers.

1565   The longest way home is on the old expense account.

1566   Experience is what you get when you're looking for something else.

1567   Snobbery is the pride of those who are not sure of their position.—*Berton Braley*

1568   Be pretty if you can, be witty if you must, be agreeable if it kills you.—*Elsie De Wolfe*

1569   Some folks seem to get the idea they're worth a lot of money just because they have it.

1570   A young girl came into a bank to buy some savings bonds. When the teller asked her what denomination, she replied, "Presbyterian."

1571   The average fire is put out before any considerable damage is done by the fire department.

1572   Before television, no one ever knew what a headache looked like.

1573   If we should lock up all the feebleminded, who would write our hit songs?

1574   Alarmists seemingly regard the rising generation as a falling one.

1575   Remember the old days when people killed time by working instead of by coffee breaks?

1576   Man is an able creature, but he has made 32,600,000 laws and hasn't yet improved on the Ten Commandments.

1577   The world never will be wholly civilized. Some areas have no natural resources worth seizing.

1578   The members of the smart set never get that way by listening to one another.

1579   The evil that men do lives after them. The saxophone was made in 1846.

1580   Success is getting what you want; happiness is wanting what you get.

1581   The greatest service that could be rendered the Christian peoples would be to convert them to Christianity.

1582   When the salesclerk tells you the price of the article, you can grin and bear it, or smile and charge it.

1583   If you think trifles won't be noticed, just let a catsup bottle drip on white trousers at a picnic.

1584   If you are sure you are right, you can afford to keep quiet.

1585   Scientists say we are what we eat. Nuts must be a commoner diet than we had thought.

1586   The reason ideas die quickly in some heads is because they can't stand solitary confinement.

1587   It's queer that men should take up a life of crime when there are so many legal ways to be dishonest.

1588   Patrick Henry said, "Give me liberty or give me death," but now we leave out the words "liberty" and "death."

1589   Francis Scott Key deserved fame because he knew all the verses of "The Star-Spangled Banner."

1590   Next to automation nothing beats a wastebasket for speeding up work.

1591   It's surprising how many persons unselfishly will neglect their own work in order to tell you how to run your affairs.

1592   "It's me" is called poor English, but we really think it ain't so bad.—*Herbert V. Prochnow*

1593   Never put off until tomorrow what you can do today, because by that time there will be a tax on it.—*Herbert V. Prochnow*

1594   The person who never worries may not be smart enough to know what's going on.—*Herbert V. Prochnow, Jr.*

1595   It isn't easy to love your neighbor as your pelf.—*Herbert V. Prochnow*

1596   You can say what you want to around home because no one pays any attention to you.

1597   Flattery is telling the other person what he thinks of himself.—*Herbert V. Prochnow, Jr.*

1598   When there is nothing to be said, some person prepares a speech on it.

1599   The man who never makes a mistake must get tired of doing nothing.

1600   It's strange how you can hear a rattle in your car easier than one in your head.—*Herbert V. Prochnow, Jr.*

1601   It has taken three generations to go from farm to garden to can opener.—*Herbert V. Prochnow*

1602   After the first hour a large cocktail party sounds like a zoo at feeding time.—*Herbert V. Prochnow*

1603 A husband looked at his house, his car and his furniture and said it was wonderful so many people made a living on what he had not paid for.—*Herbert V. Prochnow*

1604 It's not hard to be an executive. Things change so fast you can't be wrong all the time.—*Herbert V. Prochnow*

1605 If you think no ones cares if you're alive, try missing a few installment payments.

1606 Today a dollar earned is a nickel saved.—*Herbert V. Prochnow, Jr.*

1607 You can fool all the people some of the time, but you can fool yourself all the time.—*Herbert V. Prochnow*

1608 Have you ever been at a party when you were too tired to listen and too courteous to leave?

1609 One half of the world knows how the other half lives, but they don't know how many installments they are behind.

1610 An honest man is never a successful fisherman.

1611 A sign says "Drive slow—you may meet a fool." Better say, "Drive slow—two fools may meet."—*Herbert V. Prochnow*

1612 A good thing about the world is that conditions never get so bad they couldn't get worse.—*Herbert V. Prochnow*

1613 An empty head almost always goes with a stuffed shirt.

1614 Many of us know how to say nothing—few of us know when.

1615 Somehow we couldn't help but like the boy who said he climbed the tree to put back an apple that had fallen down.—*Herbert V. Prochnow, Jr.*

1616 Whenever you feel depressed with what life has done to you, take a look at the family album.—*Herbert V. Prochnow*

1617 It pays to smile, but if you want to enjoy a good laugh look in the mirror.—*Herbert V. Prochnow*

1618 Nothing is more powerful than hope. One little nibble will keep a person fishing all day.—*Herbert V. Prochnow, Jr.*

1619 Nowadays, kids just have to go to college. How else are they going to get a good high school education?

1620 If you have the determination to keep everlastingly at it, you will attain success as well as a nervous breakdown.—*Herbert V. Prochnow*

1621 There are 5,280 feet in a mile, except when you detour there are 10,560.—*Herbert V. Prochnow, Jr.*

1622   To entertain some people all you have to do is sit and listen.—*Herbert V. Prochnow*

1623   The best way to drive a nail without mashing your fingers is to hold the hammer with both hands.

1624   First men fight for freedom, and then they make laws to gradually take it away.—*Herbert V. Prochnow, Jr.*

1625   If one person can do a job in one hour, four persons can do it in four hours.—*Herbert V. Prochnow*

1626   A conviction is what a vice president has when he knows what the president thinks.—*Herbert V. Prochnow, Jr.*

1627   Money doesn't make fools of persons, but it does tend to show them up.—*Herbert V. Prochnow*

1628   If I understand what the economists are saying, the situation is hopeless—but improving.—*Herbert V. Prochnow, Jr.*

1629   Nature abhors a vacuum, and she sometimes fills an empty head with conceit.—*Herbert V. Prochnow*

1630   Half the world consists of people who have something to say and don't; the other half have nothing to say and keep on saying it.

1631   What the world needs is a tabloid Bible.—*Herbert V. Prochnow*

1632   All men are born equal, but what they are equal to is the important thing.—*Herbert V. Prochnow*

1633   Very few of us take advantage of opportunities to keep quiet.—*Herbert V. Prochnow, Jr.*

1634   A vacationer caught a fish so big he dislocated both shoulders in describing it.—*Herbert V. Prochnow*

1635   A modern parent is one who promises his son an automobile if he behaves until he is fifteen years old.—*Herbert V. Prochnow*

1636   We can fly jet airplanes, broadcast color television, and make atomic power, but we're not so sure about how to bring up children.—*Herbert V. Prochnow*

1637   The way to stay poor is to pretend to be rich.—*Herbert V. Prochnow, Jr.*

1638   No person ever had so many faults he couldn't fall in love with himself.—*Herbert V. Prochnow*

1639   It's hard to suffer in silence, because that takes all the pleasure out of the suffering.—*Herbert V. Prochnow, Jr.*

1640   Most people are always ready to say a good word about themselves.—*Herbert V. Prochnow*

1641 One person you have to watch if you are going to save money is yourself.—*Herbert V. Prochnow, Jr.*

1642 When you begin to wonder if something is worth what it costs, you have reached middle age.—*Herbert V. Prochnow*

1643 If you ask some people what they are thinking about, it's a compliment.—*Herbert V. Prochnow*

1644 A punctual person is patient, because he gets that way waiting for those who are not punctual.—*Herbert V. Prochnow, Jr.*

1645 Holding a political candidate to the facts is impossible. It's like asking Beethoven where he got the statistics for his Fifth Symphony.—*Herbert V. Prochnow*

1646 If all the toastmasters in the world were placed end to end, the silence would be restful.—*Herbert V. Prochnow*

1647 The fellow who argues that all religions should unite probably doesn't speak to his brother-in-law.—*Herbert V. Prochnow*

1648 A pedagogue works against ignorance, but a demagogue gets a profit out of it.—*Herbert V. Prochnow*

1649 Most of us would prefer to be miserably rich than happily poor.—*Herbert V. Prochnow, Jr.*

1650 When we hear some popular songs, we are sure the illiteracy rate is still pretty high.—*Herbert V. Prochnow*

1651 There may be songs that never die, but it isn't the fault of TV or radio.—*Herbert V. Prochnow*

1652 Not only are the sins of the fathers visited upon the children but nowadays the sins of the children are visited upon the fathers.—*Herbert V. Prochnow*

1653 No one knows how to save money as well as the person who hasn't any.—*Herbert V. Prochnow, Jr.*

1654 Many politicians are for and against an issue and they don't care who knows it.—*Herbert V. Prochnow*

1655 It isn't easy for an idea to squeeze into a head filled with prejudices.—*Herbert V. Prochnow, Jr.*

1656 In the old days a delinquent was a youngster who owed a few cents on an overdue library book.—*Herbert V. Prochnow, Jr.*

1657 Always borrow from a pessimist. He never expects to be repaid.—*Herbert V. Prochnow*

1658 We nominate for the Hall of Fame the scientist who said dead leaves help a lawn in the fall.—*Herbert V. Prochnow, Jr.*

1659   We have relatively few illiterates in the United States, but millions of people who can't read traffic signs.—*Herbert V. Prochnow*

1660   Dumb animals are the ones that can satisfy their appetites without a cocktail hour before dinner.

1661   Don't worry what people are thinking about you. They aren't thinking about you, but about themselves.—*Herbert V. Prochnow, Jr.*

1662   Why criticize a person for talking about himself, when that may be the subject about which he is best informed.—*Herbert V. Prochnow*

1663   It is very difficult to like a person with whom you can't find any fault.—*Herbert V. Prochnow, Jr.*

1664   We have seen more pictures of college students engaged in various sports than we have pictures of students taking home books from the library.

1665   You can lead high school graduates to college, but you cannot make them think.—*Herbert V. Prochnow, Jr.*

1666   A yawn may be considered bad manners, but it can also be considered an honest opinion.

1667   By the time you have enough experience to be smart, your memory is shorter, your stamina is lower, and you are bald.—*Herbert V. Prochnow*

1668   *Prochnow's law:* Regardless of how many items there are on the agenda, a committee meeting takes the same amount of time.—*Herbert V. Prochnow*

1669   Most people can't save because their neighbors are always doing something they can't afford.—*Herbert V. Prochnow, Jr.*

1670   Things never seem so bad if you know your neighbor is having a worse time.—*Herbert V. Prochnow, Jr.*

1671   Most families don't mind paying the piper if they can do it on the installment plan.—*Herbert V. Prochnow, Jr.*

1672   A soft answer may turn away wrath, but never a door-to-door salesman.—*Herbert V. Prochnow*

1673   Many a fisherman has found they bite, but mostly on the neck and legs.—*Herbert V. Prochnow*

1674   The only thing worse than an alarm clock that goes off is one that doesn't.—*Herbert V. Prochnow*

1675   Is a lame duck a politician whose goose has been cooked?

1676   What gives people trouble is itching for what they want instead of scratching for it.

1677   In the old days men blazed trails. Now they burn up the roads.—*Herbert V. Prochnow*

1678   Our international troubles must be serious because it takes hundreds of luncheon speakers every week to solve them.—*Herbert V. Prochnow*

1679   No person is humble who thinks he is.—*Herbert V. Prochnow, Jr.*

1680   Only one animal—man—can be skinned and live.—*Herbert V. Prochnow*

1681   Enthusiasm without intelligence is disaster.—*Herbert V. Prochnow, Jr.*

1682   Two can live as cheaply as one, but nowadays it takes both of them to earn enough to do it.

1683   The line is often busy when your conscience tries to speak.—*Herbert V. Prochnow*

1684   One thing we ought to keep as sound as a dollar is the dollar.—*Herbert V. Prochnow*

1685   A politician advocates rigid economy with free spending.

1686   A precocious child doesn't take a second piece of cake when he goes visiting. He takes two the first time.—*Herbert V. Prochnow, Jr.*

1687   Nations that live by the sword perish by the pensions.—*Herbert V. Prochnow*

1688   It's all right for children to have original ideas, but not in mathematics.—*Herbert V. Prochnow, Jr.*

1689   When both the speaker and the audience are confused, the speech is "profound."

1690   If an infant can't think, why does it yell as soon as it sees the kind of world it's in?—*Herbert V. Prochnow, Jr.*

1691   If you were to list the ten smartest people in town, who would be the other nine?

1692   Teachers are never fully appreciated by parents until it rains all day Saturday.

1693   Those who say you can't take it with you never saw a car packed for a vacation trip.

1694   Experience is a wonderful thing, for it enables you to recognize a mistake when you make it again.

1695   The easiest way to tell the difference between young plants and weeds is to pull up everything. If they come up again, they're weeds.

11
AMUSING AND UNUSUAL DEFINITIONS

1696 *Acrobat:* The only person who can do what everyone else would like to do—pat himself on the back.

1697 *Actors:* The only honest hypocrites.—*Hazlitt*

1698 *Adam:* The one man in the world who couldn't say, "Pardon me, haven't I seen you before?"

1699 *Adjective:* The banana peel of the parts of speech.—*Clifton Fadiman, The Reader's Digest*

1700 *Adolescence:* The period when children are certain they will never be as stupid as their parents.

1701 *Advice:* What you take for a cold. The suggestions you give someone else which you believe will work to your benefit. Something most of us "give until it hurts."

1702 *All-expense tour:* The perfect example of truth-in-advertising.

1703 *Amateur athelete:* An athlete who is paid in cash—not by check.

1704 *Amateur carpenter:* A carpenter who resembles lightning. He never strikes twice in the same place.

1705 *Amateur golfer:* The man who moves heaven and earth to play golf.

1706 *Ambidextrous:* When you are clumsy with both hands.

1707 *American:* A person who is always ready to discuss the Constitution although he has never read it.

1708 *Antique collector's song:* "You take the highboy and I'll take the lowboy."

1709 *Appendix:* What you have out before the doctor decides it is your gall bladder that is making you sick.—*Herbert V. Prochnow*

1710 *Architecture:* Frozen music.

1711 *Ash trays:* A dish you put where the ash strays.

1712 *Attic:* A place where you keep the things you will never want until after you throw them away.

1713 *Average intelligence:* To be less stupid than half of the people and more stupid than the other half.—*Herbert V. Prochnow*

1714 *Babysitter:* A person you pay who invites friends to your house to keep your children awake.

1715 *Bachelor:* A person who never quite gets over the idea that he is a thing of beauty and a boy forever.

1716 *Bargain:* When two people are sure they got the better of each other.

1717 *Bargain:* It's easy to tell when you've got a bargain—it doesn't fit.

1718 *Bigotry:* The disease of ignorance.—*Thomas Jefferson*

1719 *Block:* The distance between some people's ears.

1720 *Boaster:* A person with whom it is no sooner done than said.—*Milwaukee Journal*

1721 *Body:* An envelope.—*Dr. Alexis Carrel*

1722 *Bottoms up:* A toast you never make to the crew in a boat race.

1723 *Boyhood:* A summer sun.—*Edgar Allan Poe*

1724 *Bridge:* Next to hockey the most dangerous shin-bruising game in America.

1725 *Budget:* A family's attempt to live below its yearnings.

1726 *Buffer state:* One between two biffer states.

1727 *Bureau:* In the old days a bureau was a place you hid your money so you would save it. Now a government bureau is a place they take your money so they can spend it.

1728 *Bus driver:* The person who tells you where to get off.

1729 *Business:* The playthings of our elders.—*St. Augustine*

1730 *Business:* Like riding a bicycle. Either you keep moving or you fall down.—*John David Wright*

1731 *Business economy:* A reduction in some other employee's salary.

1732   *Busy doctor:* A doctor who has so many patients that when there is nothing the matter with you, he will tell you so.

1733   *Canoe:* An object that acts like a small boy—it behaves better when paddled from the rear.

1734   *Careful driver:* The fellow who has made the last payment on his car.

1735   *Caricature:* The tribute that mediocrity pays to genius.—*Oscar Wilde*

1736   *Car sickness:* The feeling some people get when each month's installment comes due.—*Herbert V. Prochnow, Jr.*

1737   *Cauliflower:* A cabbage with a college education.—*Mark Twain*

1738   *Centenarian:* A person who has lived to be 100 years old. He never smoked or he smoked all his life. He used whiskey for eighty years or he never used it. He was a vegetarian or he wasn't a vegetarian. Follow these rules carefully, and you too can be a centenarian.

1739   *Charm:* The ability to make someone else think that both of you are quite wonderful.

1740   *Cheese:* Milk's leap toward immortality.—*Clifton Fadiman*

1741   *Chewing gum:* A dentiferous treadmill.—*Thomas A. Edison*

1742   *Chiropodist:* A fellow who, when given an inch, will take a foot. A man who is down at the heel even when he is prosperous.

1743   *Christmas jewelry:* The first thing to turn green in the spring.—*Kin Hubbard*

1744   *City life:* Millions of people being lonesome together.—*Thoreau*

1745   *Civil service:* The kind you get when your tip is big enough.

1746   *Civilization:* The time when men learn to live off each other instead of off the land.—*Mort Sahl*

1747   *Classic:* Something that everybody wants to have read and nobody wants to read.—*Mark Twain*

1748   *Classical music:* The kind you "keep on hoping will turn into a tune."—*Kin Hubbard*

1749   *Climate:* Something that lasts all the time, whereas weather lasts only a few days.

1750   *Cold feet:* The ailment you get when you know what the consequences are going to be.

1751   *College:* The land of the midnight sons.

1752   *College English department:* The chamber of commas.

1753   *College football team:* An organization the American boy joins in order to see the United States.

1754   *Communist:* A fellow who likes what he doesn't have so well he doesn't want you to have it either.

1755   *Commuter:* A person who has a complaint of longstanding.

1756   *Conceit:* God's gift to little men.—*Bruce Barton*

1757   *Conference:* The confusion of one person multiplied by the number present.

1758   *Conference:* A meeting of a group of men who singly can do nothing, but who collectively agree that nothing can be done.—*Fred Allen*

1759   *Conscience:* (A small boy's definition) Something that makes me tell my mother before my sister does.

1760   *Conscience:* The sixth sense that comes to our aid when we are wrong and tells us that we are about to get caught.

1761   *Cooperation:* Doing with a smile what you are compelled to do.

1762   *Corruption:* An evil that grows respectable with age.—*Voltaire*

1763   *Courage:* Fear that has said its prayers.—*Karle Baker, as reported in Better Homes and Gardens, June 1955*

1764   *Coward:* One who, in a perilous emergency, thinks with his legs.—*Ambrose Bierce*

1765   *Crank:* A man with a new idea until the idea succeeds, then he is a genius.—*Mark Twain*

1766   *Critic, drama:* A man who gives the best jeers of his life to the theater.

1767   *Critic, literary:* A person who will discuss the social objectives of a book that never had any.—*Herbert V. Prochnow*

1768   *Crooked dough:* Something handled by counterfeiters and pretzel manufacturers.

1769   *Crooner:* A fellow who uses his mouth to sing through his nose.—*Groucho Marx*

1770   *Cunning:* When you get the best bargain; when the other fellow gets the best of it, it's cheating.

1771   *Cynic:* A man who knows the price of everything, and the value of nothing.—*Oscar Wilde*

1772   *Cynicism:* Intellectual dandyism.—*George Meredith*

1773 *Dangerous surgical operation:* An operation that costs more than $1,000.

1774 *Death:* The one thing no one can survive.—*Oscar Wilde*

1775 *Defeated politician:* The candidate who never has to explain why he is unable to keep his campaign promises.

1776 *Deficit:* What you've got when you haven't as much as if you had nothing.

1777 *Delay:* The greatest remedy for anger.—*Seneca*

1778 *Delegate-at-large:* A man who goes to a convention without his wife.

1779 *Delicatessen operator:* A man who has women eat out of his hand.

1780 *Dentist:* A man who runs a filling station.

1781 *Dentist:* A collector of old magazines.

1782 *Depression:* A period when you can't spend money you don't have.

1783 *Desk:* A wastebasket with drawers.

1784 *Detour:* The roughest distance between two points.

1785 *Detour:* A road that teaches you how and where the other half lives.—*Herbert V. Prochnow*

1786 *Dieting:* The penalty for exceeding the feed limit.

1787 *Diets:* For people who are thick and tired of it.

1788 *Dime:* A dollar after taxes.

1789 *Diplomat:* Forever poised between a cliché and an indiscretion.—*Harold Macmillan.*

1790 *Diplomat:* A person who straddles an issue when he isn't dodging one.

1791 *Discontent:* The first step in the progress of a man or a nation.—*Oscar Wilde*

1792 *Discretion:* When a husband is sure he is right and then asks his wife.

1793 *Dishonorable:* Any action committed by a competitor.—*Elbert Hubbard*

1794 *Doctor:* A man who has his tonsils, adenoids, and appendix.

1795 *Doorman:* A genius who can open the door of your car with one hand, help you in with the other, and still have one left for the tip.—*Dorothy Kilgallen*

1796   *Dough:* A misnomer for money; dough sticks to your fingers.

1797   *Draw:* A term used to describe the result of a battle between a dentist and a patient.

1798   *Dutch treat:* When two businessmen have dinner and each uses his own expense account.

1799   *Duty:* What you expect from other people.—*Oscar Wilde*

1800   *Eager beaver:* A person who works twice as hard but doesn't know why.

1801   *Economist:* A guy with a Phi Beta Kappa key on one end of his watch chain and no watch on the other end.—*Alben W. Barkley*

1802   *Economist:* A person who can tell you what is going to happen next month and explain later why it didn't.

1803   *Economist:* A person who tells you what to do with your money after you have done something else with it.

1804   *Editor:* A person employed on a newspaper, whose business it is to separate the wheat from the chaff, and to see that the chaff is printed.—*Elbert Hubbard*

1805   *Education:* Reeling and writhing and different branches of arithmetic—ambition, distraction, uglification, and derision.—*Lewis Carroll*

1806   *Education:* Something that may help a person get along without intelligence.

1807   *Education:* The inculcation of the incomprehensible into the ignorant by the incompetent.—*Sir Josiah Stamp.*

1808   *Education:* The only thing a man is willing to pay for, and hopes he doesn't get.

1809   *Education:* Training that helps one to make more money unless he becomes an educator.

1810   *Egotist:* A person who is fascinated with himself.

1811   *Egotist:* A person of low taste who is more interested in himself than in you.

1812   *Egotist:* A person who suffers from too much vitamin I.—*Outdoor Indiana*

1813   *Election year:* One year in four when the great dish is applesauce.

1814   *Electrician:* A man who wires for money.

1815   *Elephant:* A mouse put together on a cost-plus basis.

1816   *Elephant:* A useful animal with a vacuum cleaner in front and a rug beater at the back.

1817   *Epigram:* A half truth so stated as to irritate the person who believes the other half.—*Shailer Mathews*

1818   *Error in judgment:* Thinking you have an open mind when it's merely vacant.

1819   *Evening:* The time of day when people do anything to keep from going to bed and getting eight hours' sleep.—*Herbert V. Prochnow*

1820   *Example:* An illustration. The teacher asked the student to give an example of the word "boycott." The student said, "The wind blew down my brother's neck and the boycott an awful cold."

1821   *Executive:* A person who can without the facts make quick decisions which occasionally are right.

1822   *Executive:* A person who never even dreamed of earning the salary he can't get along on today.

1823   *Executive ability:* The faculty of earning your bread by the work of other people.

1824   *Executive ability:* Deciding quickly and getting somebody else to do the work.—*J. G. Pollard*

1825   *Faints:* What they call a fence in the South.

1826   *Faith:* What makes you look at a colored seed catalog.

1827   *Fanaticism:* Redoubling your effort when you have forgotten your aim.—*George Santayana*

1828   *Farm:* A portion of land covered by a mortgage.

1829   *Farmer:* A person who makes money in the country and spends it in town. An agriculturist is a person who makes his money in town and spends it in the country.

1830   *Farsighted:* A term used to describe a man who wouldn't take a chance on an auto raffle because he didn't have a garage.

1831   *Farsighted:* When one buys two lawn mowers—one for the neighbors to use.

1832   *Farsighted:* To order three eggs in a restaurant—one for your vest.

1833   *Fashion:* A form of ugliness so intolerable that we have to alter it every six months.—*Oscar Wilde*

1834   *Fatalist:* A person who jumps just as far as the rest of us when a car honks in his ear.

1835 *Father:* A fellow who is put on the pan if he doesn't bring home the bacon.

1836 *Female archer:* A girl who works on eyebrows in a beauty parlor.

1837 *Fifth marriage:* The triumph of hope over experience.

1838 *Fisherman:* One who drops the fish a line but seldom hears from them.

1839 *Flatter:* To feed with an empty spoon.—*Italian proverb*

1840 *Flaw:* What the Harvard graduate thinks you walk on in a house. In Georgia it is pronounced *flow.*

1841 *Floating debt:* A yacht that hasn't been paid for.

1842 *Folk singer:* A person who sings through his nose by ear.

1843 *Fox:* A wolf who sends flowers.—*Hugh Weston*

1844 *Friend:* What you call a person who dislikes the same people you dislike.—*Herbert V. Prochnow*

1845 *Frog:* The only living thing that has more lives than a cat. It croaks every night.

1846 *Genius:* The ability to evade work by doing something right the first time it has been done.

1847 *Genius:* A person who could tell you about his operation but doesn't.

1848 *Gentleman:* One who never hurts another's feelings unintentionally.—*Oliver Herford*

1849 *Gentleman:* A person who has home movies of his vacation, but doesn't insist on showing them to you.—*Herbert V. Prochnow*

1850 *Gentleman:* One who holds the door open while his wife carries in the groceries.—*Puck, Tit-Bits, London*

1851 *Golf:* A game that has produced more liars than anything else except the income tax. Most golfers have taken up the wrong sport. They should have taken up trap shooting.

1852 *Golf:* A game in which the balls lie on the ground and the players lie in the clubhouse.

1853 *Golf optimist:* The fellow who said he made fifteen on the first hole, fourteen on the second, thirteen on the third, and then blew up.

1854 *Government expert:* One who complicates simple things.

1855 *Grapefruit:* An eye tonic.

1856 *Gratitude:* Merely a secret hope of greater favors.—*La Rochefoucauld*

1857 *Gratitude:* The most painful thing to bear, next to ingratitude.—*Henry Ward Beecher*

1858 *Guest towel:* A towel you look at but never use.

1859 *Hair:* The only acceptable substitute for baldness.

1860 *Hamburger:* The last roundup.

1861 *Happiness:* The result of being too busy to be miserable.

1862 *Hard work:* An accumulation of easy things you should have done earlier.—*Herbert V. Prochnow, Jr.*

1863 *Hero:* The person who moves that the minutes of the last meeting be accepted without reading them.

1864 *Hero:* One who is afraid to run away.—*English proverb*

1865 *Hero:* A soldier lucky enough to be seen while doing his duty.

1866 *Hide and sick:* A game played on any ocean liner by the passengers.

1867 *Historian:* An author who seeks to give you what was important in yesterday's news.

1868 *History:* A confused heap of facts.—*Lord Chesterfield*

1869 *Hitchhiker:* The only person who could be completely incapacitated by the loss of his thumb.

1870 *Hobby:* An endless amount of hard work that you would be ashamed to do for a living.

1871 *Hog:* Corn that walks.

1872 *Home:* The place where, when you have to go there, they have to take you in.—*Robert Frost*

1873 *Home:* The place where you can enjoy corn on the cob and soup.

1874 *Hospital:* The only place you can get into without having baggage. They don't hold the trunk like a hotel does . . . they just hold the body.—*Will Rogers*

1875 *Housewife's problem:* Having too much month left over at the end of the money.

1876 *Human beings:* The only animals of which I am thoroughly and cravenly afraid.—*George Bernard Shaw*

1877 *Human nature:* The thing which makes some men hewers of wood and others drawers of dividends.

1878 *Humor in advertising:* "We welcome complaints." "We trust you." "Home cooking."

1879 *Imagination:* What makes some politicians think they are statesmen.

1880 *Immigration:* The sincerest form of flattery.

1881 *Impatience:* Waiting in a hurry.

1882 *Inflation:* When everybody is so rich that no one can afford anything.

1883 *Inflation:* Being broke with money in your pocket.

1884 *Inflation:* Instead of not having the money you haven't got, you have twice as much, but it's worth only half of what you haven't got.

1885 *Insomnia:* When you keep a lot of innocent sheep jumping over a fence all night because you can't go to sleep.

1886 *In the money:* A condition many hope for, but only a bank teller experiences.

1887 *Intuition:* What enables a woman to contradict her husband before he says anything.

1888 *I owe it all to:* An expression commonly used in connection with one's wife, landlord, or pawnbroker.

1889 *Jack:* A thing that lifts a car and also keeps it going.

1890 *Janitor:* A man who never puts out any excess hot air.

1891 *Jay:* A bird of the crow family, which can be found in fields and meadows. A jaywalker, on the other hand, is a bird of the Schmoe family who can be found in traffic jams and morgues.—*Phyllis Battelle, in New York Journal American, November 28, 1955*

1892 *Journalist:* A newspaperman out of a job.—*Elbert Hubbard*

1893 *Jugoslavia:* A case of dictated but not red.—*Herbert V. Prochnow*

1894 *June:* The month for weddings—when you have perfect daze.

1895 *Jury:* The only thing that doesn't work right when it's fixed.

1896 *Jury:* Twelve persons chosen to decide who has the better lawyer.—*Robert Frost*

1897 *Kangaroo:* Nature's initial effort to produce a cheerleader.

1898 *Kibitzer:* A person with an inferiority complex.

1899 *Kindness:* A language which the dumb can speak, and the deaf can understand.—*C. N. Bovee*

1900 *Laughter:* The sound you hear when you stumble, or lose your hat in the wind.

1901 *Laundry:* A place where they produce clothes without buttons.

1902 *Law:* A net to catch the fly and let the hawk go free.—*Spanish proverb*

1903 *Law of diminishing returns:* An economic law familiar to laundry-men.

1904 *Layman:* What they call a lemon in the South.

1905 *Lean years ahead:* What every woman hopes for.

1906 *Lend me your ears:* A phrase used by Marc Antony and by the mothers of ten million six-year-olds.

1907 *Library:* A place where the dead live.

1908 *Library of Congress:* The most complete library in this country except that it has no books on balancing the budget.—*Herbert V. Prochnow*

1909 *Life:* Trouble.

1910 *Life insurance:* A plan that keeps you poor all your life so you can die rich.

1911 *Listener, good:* A silent flatterer.

1912 *Love:* The last word in a letter or telegram.

1913 *Luxury:* Something you don't really need and can't do without.

1914 *Major general:* An army officer who has his men behind him before the battle and ahead of him during it.

1915 *Major speech:* An address in which a candidate calls his opponent a big bum instead of a little one.—*Boston Journal*

1916 *Man:* The only animal that blushes. Or needs to.—*Mark Twain*

1917 *Man:* The only animal with brains enough to find a cure for the diseases caused by his own folly.

1918 *Management:* The ability to let other people have your way.—*Herbert V. Prochnow*

1919 *Manners:* The person who has good manners can put up with someone who has bad manners.

1920 *Man of few words:* One who takes three hours to tell you he is a man of few words.

1921 *Man of few words:* A husband.

1922   *Marriage:* Requires falling in love many times—always with the same person.

1923   *Marriage:* A period when you make progress if you break even. The most dangerous year in married life is the first; then comes the second, third, fourth, fifth, etc.

1924   *Marriage:* Has three states—cooing—wedding—billing.

1925   *Melancholy:* The pleasure of being sad.—*Victor Hugo*

1926   *Meter maid:* A person who always does a fine day's work.

1927   *Microscope expert:* A person who magnifies everything.

1928   *Middle age:* The period when you begin to wonder what it was you ate the day before yesterday.

1929   *Middle age:* When you know your way around, but you don't feel like going.

1930   *Middle age:* That difficult period between juvenile delinquency and senior citizenship when you have to take care of yourself.

1931   *Minor operation:* One performed on someone else.

1932   *Miser:* A person who lives within his installment payments.—*Herbert V. Prochnow*

1933   *Monday morning:* When we look back wistfully on the good old days—Saturday and Sunday.—*Catholic Digest*

1934   *Monologue:* A conversation between a traffic cop and an automobile driver.—*Herbert V. Prochnow*

1935   *Mouth:* The grocer's friend, the dentist's fortune, the orator's pride, and the fool's trap.

1936   *Music:* The speech of angels.—*Thomas Carlyle*

1937   *Naive person:* Anyone who thinks you are interested when you ask how he is.

1938   *Necessary evil:* One we like so much we refuse to do away with it.

1939   *Necessity:* Something you can't get along without, but do. A luxury is something you can get along without, but don't.—*Herbert V. Prochnow*

1940   *New idea:* An impossibility until it is born.

1941   *Newspaper:* The means by which one half the world enjoys the troubles of the other half.

1942 *No-hit pitcher:* A ballplayer who can throw a ball faster than you can shake a stick at it.

1943 *Nostalgia:* Trimming the Christmas tree with popcorn made in the microwave oven.

1944 *Oboe:* A kind of American tramp.

1945 *Oculist:* A man with an eye for business.

1946 *Old age:* When you wonder whether the thumping sound could be a loose fan belt in the car, or your heart.—*Richmond Times-Dispatch*

1947 *Old age:* When it takes you twice as long to rest and only half as long to get tired.

1948 *Old age:* When you know all the answers, but no one asks you the questions.

1949 *On the rocks:* A phrase meaning a person is either bankrupt or working in jail. The difference is inconsequential.

1950 *Open mind:* The mind of a man who has the willpower to get rid of his present prejudices and take on a new set of prejudices. Sometimes, a case of a person merely rearranging his prejudices.

1951 *Open mindedness:* The pathway to wisdom; close your mind and you dwell in ignorance.

1952 *Opera:* An exotic and irrational entertainment.—*Dr. Samuel Johnson*

1953 *Opera:* When a guy gets stabbed in the back and instead of bleeding he sings.—*Ed Gardner*

1954 *Opera:* A form of entertainment where there's always too much singing.—*Claude Debussy*

1955 *Operation:* Something that took a surgeon an hour to perform and the patient years to describe.

1956 *Optimist:* A person who thinks he can get by with saying "thanks" to the headwaiter.—*Herbert V. Prochnow*

1957 *Optimist:* One who takes a frying pan on a fishing trip.

1958 *Optimist:* One who thinks he will never do anything stupid again.

1959 *Optimist:* A person who thinks there are some big berries in the bottom of the box.

1960 *Optimist:* Someone who doesn't care what happens as long as it happens to someone else.

1961 *Optimist:* A person who tells you to cheer up when things are going his way.

1962   *Optimist:* A person who believes that a housefly is looking for a way to get out.—*George Jean Nathan*

1963   *Optimist:* A cheerful guy who is blissfully unaware of what is going on.

1964   *Optimist:* A person who is waiting for his ship to come in but hasn't sent one out.

1965   *Overeating:* The destiny that ends our shapes.

1966   *Packing:* Parking in Boston.

1967   *Paper clips:* A product used as pipecleaners, radio connections, garter clasps, toothpicks, necktie clasps, costume jewelry, for twisting when nervous and sometimes even for clipping a few papers together.

1968   *Parking lot:* The place where you take your car to have little dents put in the fenders.

1969   *Parking space:* An unoccupied space about seven feet wide and fifteen feet long next to the curb—on the other side of the street.

1970   *Patriot:* A person who saves enough of his salary each week to pay his income tax.—*Herbert V. Prochnow*

1971   *Pay dirt:* In the old days it referred to gold-bearing soil, not to novels.—*Herbert V. Prochnow*

1972   *Pedestrian:* A person who isn't safe even when he is riding.

1973   *Perfection:* An alarm clock that doesn't ring.

1974   *Perspiration:* The best solvent of all for solving your problems.

1975   *Pessimism:* The determination to see less than there is in anything; optimism is the ability to see more than there is in everything.

1976   *Pessimist:* A person who would commit suicide if he could do it without killing himself.

1977   *Pessimist:* A person who is happy when he is wrong.—*Herbert V. Prochnow, Jr.*

1978   *Philosophy:* The ability to bear with calmness the misfortunes of our friends.—*French proverb*

1979   *Physician:* He collects when God has cured.—*Spanish proverb*

1980   *Pickpocket:* A man who generally lives alone, but occasionally goes out in a crowd for a little change.

1981   *Pickpocket:* The optimist in a crowd.

1982   *Playing by note:* To learn to play the piano by note instead of by ear. Twelve payments on the note and the piano is yours to learn to play.

1983   *Poet:* What you do in the South when you pour a liquid.

1984   *Poetry:* It's some sort of make-believe that's got some sort of truth in it—a little bit that's so fascinating you can't get rid of it.—*Robert Frost*

1985   *Poise:* The ability to keep talking while someone else picks up the check.

1986   *Political campaign:* A war in which everybody shoots from the lip.—*Raymond Moley*

1987   *Political plum:* One result of careful grafting.

1988   *Politician:* A fellow who shakes your hand before the election and shakes you after the election.

1989   *Politics:* The career of plundering and blundering.—*Disraeli*

1990   *Positive:* Being wrong at the top of your voice.—*Ambrose Bierce*

1991   *Precocious child:* The child who took his nose apart to see what made it run.

1992   *Prejudice:* Being down on what you are not up on.

1993   *Procrastination, creative:* The deliberate gift of time to yourself each day to do what gives you the greatest satisfaction, even if that means doing nothing at all.

1994   *Prodigal son:* One who left his home but took everything else.

1995   *Profanity:* The effort of a feeble mind to express itself forcibly.—*Paul E. Holdcraft*

1996   *Profanity:* A way of escape for the man who runs out of ideas.

1997   *Professor:* One who talks in someone else's sleep.—*W. H. Auden*

1998   *Progress:* The exchange of one nuisance for another.—*Havelock Ellis*

1999   *Prosperity:* A period in which you spend money you haven't got.—*Herbert V. Prochnow*

2000   *Prosperity:* A period when there are a lot of dinners for after-dinner speakers to speak after.

2001   *Prosperity:* Something private citizens create for which politicians take credit.

2002   *Prosperity, modern:* Two cars in the garage, a boat in the driveway, and a large debt due at the bank.

2003   *Proverb:* Any short saying that states a great truth. Examples: Birds of a feather catch a cold. A thing of beauty keeps you broke forever.

2004   *Prune:* A discouraged plum.

2005   *Psychiatrist:* A person who doesn't have to worry, so long as others do.

2006   *Public library building:* The tallest building in town—it has more stories than any other.

2007   *Rabbit:* A little animal that grows the fur other animals get credit for when it's made into a lady's coat.

2008   *Radical:* A man with both feet firmly planted in the air.—*Franklin D. Roosevelt*

2009   *Reactionary:* A somnambulist walking backwards.—*Franklin D. Roosevelt*

2010   *Reception:* An ordinary party without chairs.

2011   *Recession:* When you begin to have some stall in installment.

2012   *Reckless driver:* A person who passes you when you are exceeding the speed limit.

2013   *Reckless driver:* The other motorist.

2014   *Reckless driver:* Do not confuse a reckless driver with a wreckless driver.

2015   *Reckless driving:* A husband or wife with a hammer and some nails working on a freshly painted living room wall.

2016   *Reducing machine:* A machine that costs so much you have to starve yourself to keep up the payments.

2017   *Reformer:* One who insists on his conscience being your guide.

2018   *Reformer:* One who makes his associates feel miserable about their pleasures.

2019   *Reindeer:* Horses with hatracks.

2020   *Rejected play manuscript:* A case of all work and no play.

2021   *Reunion:* When you meet people your own age who all look a lot older than you.

2022   *Rich man:* A man who isn't afraid to ask the clerk to show him something cheaper.

2023   *Rich man:* Only a poor man with money.

2024   *Rich man:* A man who has so much money he doesn't even know his son is in college.

2025   *Riding:* The art of keeping a horse between yourself and the ground.—*London Times*

2026   *Righteous indignation:* Your own wrath as compared to the shocking bad temper of others.—*Elbert Hubbard*

2027   *Rounder:* The fellow who can't look his wife squarely in the eye.

2028   *Rush hour:* When the traffic stands still.

2029   *Salary:* An amount of money that, no matter how large it is, some people spend more than.

2030   *Sales resistance:* The triumph of mind over patter.—*Boston Transcript*

2031   *Salesman:* A good salesman is the fellow who can convince his wife that she looks fat in a fur coat.

2032   *Scandal:* A breeze stirred up by a couple of windbags.

2033   *Scotsman:* The only golfer who wouldn't knock a golf ball out of sight.

2034   *Scoundrel:* A man who won't stay bought.—*William Marcy "Boss" Tweed*

2035   *Self-confidence:* A personal quality that is closely related to conceit.—*Herbert V. Prochnow*

2036   *Self-made man:* An individual who might have done better by letting out the contract. An admission that one is a self-made man makes one a martyr; it relieves the conscience of the rest of the world.

2037   *Sense of humor:* What makes you laugh at something which would make you mad if it happened to you.

2038   *Sewing circle:* A group that darns husbands.—*Herbert V. Prochnow*

2039   *Sheepskin:* Something presented to a college graduate to cover his intellectual nakedness.—*Robert M. Hutchins*

2040   *Short vacation:* Half a loaf.—*Vesta M. Kelly*

2041   *Sickness:* Means not to feel well. There are three stages: (1) ill; (2) pill; (3) bill. Sometimes there is another: (4) will.

2042   *Silence:* What would follow if the average politician spoke his mind.

2043   *Silence:* The wit of fools.—*LaBruyere*

2044   *Silence:* The art of conversation.—*William Hazlitt*

2045   *Silence:* A conversation with an Englishman.—*Heinrich Heine*

2046   *Skeptic:* One who won't take know for an answer.

2047 *Sleep:* An excellent way of listening to an opera.—*James Stephens*

2048 *Small town:* A place where everybody knows whose check is good.

2049 *Smallest man in history:* The soldier who went to sleep on his watch.

2050 *Smart fellow:* A man who says what he thinks, provided, of course, he agrees with us.

2051 *Smile:* Something that adds to your face value.

2052 *Snorer:* A sound sleeper.

2053 *Snoring:* The last of the personal liberties.

2054 *Socialist:* An unsuccessful person who figures his last chance to get something is to get a part of yours.

2055 *Sophistication:* To be too smart to feel guilty about anything you do.

2056 *Sophistication:* The art of convincing others that you are well informed on things about which you know nothing.

2057 *SOS:* A musical term meaning same, only softer.

2058 *Spaghetti:* A psychological necessity.—*Sophia Loren*

2059 *Spanking:* A case of punishing one extremity to get sense in the other.

2060 *Specialist:* A person with a one-track mind.

2061 *Spendthrift:* A person who gets more out of life than there is in it.

2062 *Spring:* A time when boys feel gallant and girls feel buoyant.

2063 *Statistician:* A man who can go directly from an unwarranted assumption to a preconceived conclusion.

2064 *Straight line:* Most of the time the shortest distance between two points is under construction.

2065 *Success:* Being able to afford spending what you are already spending.

2066 *Success:* To get as much money as the other fellow wishes he could have got.

2067 *Success:* The ability to get along with some people and ahead of some others.

2068 *Successful man:* One who can earn more than his wife can spend.

2069 *Successful wife's motto:* If at first you don't succeed, cry, cry again.

2070 *Sugar daddy:* A fellow who calls his sweetie a little sugar and later pays her a lump sum.

2071 *Summertime:* When you don't pay your bills and the creditors think you're on vacation.

2072 *Sympathizer:* A fellow that's for you as long as it doesn't cost anything.—*Kin Hubbard*

2073 *Tact:* The ability to describe others as they see themselves.—*Abraham Lincoln*

2074 *Tact:* The ability to shut your mouth before someone else wants to.

2075 *Tailor:* An occupation that suits everyone.

2076 *Tax:* The price of civilization.—*Justice Oliver Wendell Holmes*

2077 *Tax collector:* A person who has what it takes to take what you have.

2078 *Tax cut:* The kindest cut of all.

2079 *Tax, income:* The fine for reckless thriving.

2080 *Taxpayer:* A person who has the whole government on his payroll.

2081 *Taxpayer:* The meek people who are going to inherit the earth and pay off the mortgage we leave them.

2082 *Tea:* An affront to luncheon and an insult to dinner.—*Mark Twain*

2083 *Television:* A device that permits people who haven't anything to do to watch people who can't do anything.—*Fred Allen*

2084 *Term aider:* Tomato in New York.

2085 *Thinking:* The talking of the soul with itself.—*Plato*

2086 *Third putt:* The most difficult shot in golf.

2087 *Thrift:* A virtue in your ancestors.

2088 *Tin sin stow:* A five and ten store in the South.

2089 *Toastmaster:* Someone who introduces those who need no introduction.

2090 *Toe:* A part of the foot used to find furniture in the dark.

2091 *Tomorrow:* The day that comes before you have finished solving all of today's problems.

2092 *Toot ensemble:* Two hundred cars waiting for a green light at a busy intersection on a Sunday afternoon.

2093   *Toreador:* The power behind the thrown.—*Elbert Hubbard*

2094   *Totem pole:* An Indian's family tree.—*R. L. Ripley*

2095   *Tourist:* A person who drives 1,000 miles to see some beautiful scenery and litters the road all the way.

2096   *Tourist:* A guy who travels 5,000 miles to have his picture taken in front of his car.

2097   *Tradition:* The widespread acceptance of something which was at first of questionable merit—and still is.

2098   *Traffic cop:* Someone who never loses an argument.

2099   *Traffic light:* A green light that changes to red as your car approaches.

2100   *Traffic light:* A trick to get pedestrians halfway across the street safely.

2101   *Tragedy:* A bride without a can opener.

2102   *Tragedy:* A California citizen dying in Florida, or a Florida citizen dying in California.

2103   *Travel:* An experience that fills the mind and empties the purse.

2104   *Travel:* A fool's paradise.—*Ralph Waldo Emerson*

2105   *Truth:* The first casualty in time of war.—*Boake Carter*

2106   *Truthful woman:* A woman who does not lie about anything except her age, her weight, and her husband's salary.

2107   *Twilight:* All the difference between day and night.

2108   *Typographical error:* A misstatement. Illustration: A newspaper carried the notice that John Doe was a "defective" on the police force. This was a typographical error. It should have said, "Mr. John Doe is a detective on the police farce."

2109   *Ukulele:* The link that's missing between music and noise.

2110   *Umbrella:* A movable roof.

2111   *Umpire:* A retired baseball player whose eyesight fails him.

2112   *Uneducated:* To get by on your brains.

2113   *Unhappiness:* Not knowing what we want and killing ourselves to get it.—*Don Herold*

2114   *University:* A college with a stadium seating over 50,000.

2115   *Upper crust:* A number of persons stuck together by their dough.

2116 *Vacation:* An all-expense tour.

2117 *Vacation:* Something you take when you can't take what you've been taking.

2118 *Vacation:* The period of time when you get too active and too tired on your own time.

2119 *Vacation resort:* Where you go when you are worn out and where you come back a complete wreck.

2120 *Vacation resort:* A place that overlooks a lake, and also overlooks comfortable beds and good food.

2121 *Velocity:* What a person puts a hot plate down with.

2122 *Ventriloquist:* One who talks straight from the tummy.

2123 *Ventriloquist:* A man who talks to himself for a living.—*Quentin Reynolds*

2124 *Veterinarian:* A doctor who can't ask his patient questions.—*David Harum*

2125 *Vice:* A sin that has become a habit.

2126 *Vice president:* A title given to a bank officer in place of a raise in salary.

2127 *Viola:* An instrument played by a disappointed second violinist.—*Deems Taylor*

2128 *Vote:* To choose the lesser of evils.

2129 *Waffle:* A pancake with a nonskid tread.—*American Boy*

2130 *Waiter:* A guy who believes that money grows on trays.—*Walter Winchell*

2131 *War:* A racket.—*Major General Smedley D. Butler*

2132 *War:* A continuation of politics by other means.—*Clausewitz*

2133 *Washington:* The city bureauful.—*G. C. Ebbert*

2134 *Weather:* The discourse of fools.—*English proverb*

2135 *Webster, Noah:* The author who had the biggest vocabulary.

2136 *Weed:* A plant whose virtues have not been discovered.—*Emerson*

2137 *West Pointer:* A boy who wasn't too proud to speak to a Congressman.—*Will Rogers*

2138 *Whoa:* What Paul Revere said at the end of his ride.

2139 *Willpower:* The ability to eat one salted peanut and stop.

2140   *Winter:* The time of year when it gets later earlier.

2141   *Woman's ambition:* To be weighed and found wanting.

2142   *Women:* Those who think more with their hearts than with their heads.

2143   *Wretched:* The name Richard in the South.

2144   *X:* The signature of a person who failed his Ph.D. examination.

2145   *Yes:* The answer to any question your employer asks.

2146   *Yes man:* One who stoops to concur.—*Greta Christiansen*

2147   *Yours:* Anything which up to the present others have not been able to get away from you.

2148   *Zoo:* A place devised for animals to study the habits of human beings.—*Oliver Herford*

12
INTERESTING LIVES AND INTERESTING FACTS

2149 *No Vacation*

The late columnist Arthur Brisbane declined to accept William Randolph Hearst's offer of a six months' paid vacation in appreciation for his good work.

"There are two reasons why I will not accept your generous offer, Mr. Hearst," said Brisbane. "The first is that if I quit writing my column for half a year, it might affect the circulation of your newspapers. The second reason is that it might not!"

2150 *Say It*

When you've got a thing to say, say it—don't take half a day; life is short, a fleeting vapor—don't you fill the entire paper with a tale, which at a pinch, could be cornered in an inch. Boil her down until she simmers. Polish her until she glimmers.

When you've got a thing to say, say it—don't take half a day.—*Sunshine Magazine*

2151 *Mark Twain*

Mark Twain once asked a neighbor if he might read a set of his books. The neighbor replied ungraciously that he was welcome to read them in his library, but he had a rule never to let a book leave the house. Some weeks later the same neighbor sent over to ask for the loan of his lawnmower.

"I shall be very glad to lend you my lawnmower," said Mark Twain, "but since I made it a rule never to let it leave my lawn, you will be obliged to use it there."

2152   *Work Break*

A harried businessman, reflecting on the coffee break, pasted this notice on the company's bulletin board:

"Due to increased competition, and a keen desire to remain in business, we find it necessary to institute a new policy. We are asking that somewhere between starting and quitting time, and without infringing on the time devoted to lunch, coffee breaks, rest periods, story telling, ticket selling, vacation planning, and rehashing of gossip, each employee endeavor to find some time that can be set aside and known as the 'Work Break.' This may seem a radical innovation, but we believe that the idea has possibilities. It can conceivably be an aid to steady employment and regular pay checks. While adoption of the 'Work Break' is not compulsory, it is hoped that each employee will find time to give it a fair trial."

2153   *Discipline for Freedom*

Lovers of freedom often overlook this paradox: There is no true freedom without discipline. An ordered and disciplined life gives us freedom to do the things we want to do. . . .

Life offers a choice between self-discipline and imposed discipline. The advocates of dictators would have all discipline imposed by outside force to produce efficient lives. But those of us who love the freedom of democracy do not care to have our lives regulated by some dictator.

Yet discipline is essential. Have it we must, whether we like it or not. If we do not want dictators, we must impose upon ourselves discipline to bring order out of social chaos.

2154   *What's in a Man*

Longfellow was once introduced to a man named Longworth and when the latter commented on the similarity of names, the poet said: "Here is a case, I fear, where Pope's line will apply—'worth makes the man—want of it the fellow.' "

2155   *Disraeli*

Disraeli, when prime minister of England, was known, among many other things, as having an excellent memory. One day he was asked how he managed to remember all those names and never offend anyone by appearing not to recognize members of Parliament on sight. The prime minister replied: "When I meet a man whose name I cannot remember, I give myself two minutes; then if it is a hopeless case, I always say: 'And how is the old complaint?' "

2156   *Patience*

Infinite patience is the price that many a man has paid for success. Gibbon worked twenty years on his *Decline and Fall of the Roman Em-*

pire. Noah Webster spent thirty-six years on his dictionary. George Bancroft spent twenty-six years on his *History of the United States.*

2157 *Schubert*

Schubert's C Major Symphony, familiarly known as the Sixth Symphony, is conceded by many musicians to be his masterpiece. This work was first performed in Vienna in 1828, but London and Paris did not hear it until thirty years later. The Paris Orchestra, under Habeneck, refused to play it, and the London Philharmonic laughed at the composition. The conductor withdrew it from rehearsal. Sir August Manns placed it on a program in London in 1856, and after the first movement was finished the horn player called to the first violin sitting close to him:

"Tom, have you been able to discover a tune yet?"

"Heck, no. This hasn't any tune," the violinist replied.

2158 *Hawthorne*

The greatest literary artist in American history, our foremost novelist, Nathaniel Hawthorne, not only owed his success to the daily inspiration of his wife, but also his only opportunity to compose first his mind, and then his masterpiece. If it had not been for Sophia, perhaps we should not now remember Nathaniel. He lost his job in the customhouse. A broken-hearted man, he went home to tell his wife that he was a failure. To his amazement, she beamed with joy, and said: "Now you can write your book!" To his bitter rejoinder, "Yes, and what shall we live on while I am writing it?" the astounding woman opened a drawer and took out an unsuspected hoard of cash. "Where on earth did you get that?" She answered, "I have always known that you were a man of genius. I knew that some day you would write an immortal masterpiece. So every week, out of the money you have given me for housekeeping, I have saved something; here is enough to last us one whole year." Hawthorne sat down and wrote one of the finest books ever written in the Western Hemisphere—*The Scarlet Letter.*

2159 *His Greatest Thought*

Daniel Webster, when asked what was the greatest thought that had ever entered his mind, replied: "My accountability to Almighty God."

2160 *Lincoln*

The Battle of Gettysburg had just been fought. Lincoln sensed an opportunity to end the war by driving hard against Lee's rear in retreat. A swift, daring attack might do it. As commander-in-chief of the army, he ordered General Meade to pursue. A friendly note in the president's handwriting accompanied the instructions:

"The order I enclose is not of record. If you succeed, you need not publish the order. If you fail, publish it. Then, if you succeed, you will have all the credit of the movement. If not, I'll take all the responsibility."

That was Abraham Lincoln, brave, self-effacing, a nobleman in thought and deed.

2161 *Benjamin Franklin*
Printer, editor, publisher, businessman, financier, economist, and teacher of thrift, philosopher, moralist, and advocate of the simple life, scientist and patron of education, philanthropist, statesman, diplomat —and above all a man and a patriot, he is claimed as their own by more groups than any other person in our history. With truth he has been characterized as: "A Man" so various, that he seemed not one but all mankind's epitome. Someone has called him a typical American; rather might we think of him as a composite American. Born in poverty, he was apprenticed in a print shop and always thought of himself as a printer. "He that hath a trade, hath an estate" is one of his famous maxims. By thrift and industry he accumulated a competency which enabled him to devote the latter half of his life to public service. By one fitted to judge, Franklin has been referred to as "the greatest of all diplomatic representatives of this country." As the collector of funds for the Revolutionary War, he might be known as the originator of the Liberty Loan. He has been called the Father of our Navy; and as Postmaster General of the Colonies founded the first adequate postal system here. Not only does our government recognize his great services, but more and more are we coming to realize how much we owe to Benjamin Franklin's genius in all manner of human relationships and endeavors.—*Calvin Coolidge*

2162 *Tact*
Charles Schwab walked through a factory. He saw three men smoking. He did not reprimand them. He merely reached in his pocket, took out three cigars and said, "Boys, have a cigar on me, but I should appreciate it if you would not smoke it during working hours."

2163 *Winston S. Churchill*
A story of Winston S. Churchill—told by Gertrude Atherton:

"Shortly after he left the Conservative side of the House (of Commons) for the Liberal, he was taking a certain young woman down to dinner, when she looked up at him coquettishly, and remarked with the audacity of her kind:

" 'There are two things I don't like about you, Mr. Churchill.'

" 'And what are they?'

" 'Your new politics and mustache.'

" 'My dear madam,' he replied suavely, 'pray do not disturb yourself. You are not likely to come in contact with either.' "—*Atlanta Journal*

2164   *What I Ought to Do*

> I am only one, but I am one;
> I cannot do everything
> But I can do something.
> What I can do, I ought to do
> And what I ought to do
> By the grace of God, I will do.
>
>   *—Canon Farrar*

2165   *Lord Chesterfield*

Lord Chesterfield, attending an entertainment in France, appeared to be gazing about at the brilliant circle of ladies which surrounded him, when he was approached by Voltaire.

"My lord," laughingly remarked the great Frenchman, "I know you are a well-qualified judge. Tell me, who are more beautiful—the English or the French ladies?"

In the face of such a ticklish question most men might have quailed; but not the adroit Chesterfield. Looking about at the sea of feminine faces made lovely by the liberal use of rouge and other artificial colorings, he replied, "Upon my word, I cannot tell. I am really no connoisseur of paintings."

2166   *Benjamin Franklin*

Did you ever stop to wonder who invented the old-fashioned stove—or bifocal glasses—who first advocated the use of copper for roofs—who conceived of a damper for chimneys—who first pointed out that white is the coolest thing to wear in summer—who invented the long pole that is now used in grocery stores to reach articles on top shelves—who thought of a combined chair and step-ladder—who was responsible for the paving and lighting of streets—who thought it would be nice to have trees bordering both sides of streets—who formed the first library company—the first fire company—the first American fire insurance company—who founded the dead letter office and the penny post—who was responsible for American university education? Well, it was Benjamin Franklin, who incidentally was the first president of one of America's oldest universities—the University of Pennsylvania.—*The Fusion Point*

2167   *Discovery*

> Who never walks save where he sees
> Men's tracks, makes no discoveries.
>
>   *—J. G. Holland*

2168   *Charles I*

Although it was Ferdinand V of Spain who dispatched Hernando Cortez on an exploration of the New World, it was to his son, Charles I, that the redoubtable explorer returned to make his report. Cortez recommended that a passage to India be effected by digging a canal across the Isthmus of Panama.

Charles consulted his advisers and then rejected the recommendation. Asked to explain the reason for his decision, the King sternly replied: "It would be a violation of the biblical injunction: 'What God hath joined together let no man put asunder.' "

2169   *Lafayette*

One day at a public function, the admirers of General Lafayette, desiring to show the love and admiration they felt for their idol, unhitched his horses from the carriage and pulled the vehicle to the hotel themselves.

Some weeks later, a friend of the general, recalling the stirring event, remarked: "You must have been very much pleased."

Lafayette regarded him quietly for a moment, then, with a whimsical smile, replied, "Yes, it was delightful, delightful; but one thing disturbs me a little—I never saw anything more of my horses."

2170   *Sir Walter Scott*

Long after Sir Walter Scott had gained renown as a writer, he endeavored to conceal his literary fame from his children, even attempting to keep them from reading his works.

One day his publisher, Ballantyne, came to congratulate him upon the success of his *Lady of the Lake,* and seeing the author's twelve-year-old daughter alone in the library, said, "And how do you like *The Lady of the Lake?*"

"Oh," she replied, "I haven't read it. Father says that nothing is so harmful for young people as reading bad books."

2171   *Respect*

Charles V admired and respected the great Titian. One day, when the brush dropped from Titian's hand, Charles V picked it up for him, saying: "You deserve to be served by an emperor."

2172   *Mozart and Haydn*

Mozart once said to a critic, "If you and I were both melted down together, we should not furnish materials for one Haydn."

And Haydn said of Mozart that if every friend of music, and great men in particular, appreciated Mozart's genius as he did, "Nations would vie with each other to possess such a jewel within their frontiers."

2173   *Your Neighbor*

Sometimes a neighbor whom we have disliked a lifetime for his arrogance and conceit lets fall a single commonplace remark that shows us another side, another man, really; a man uncertain, puzzled, and in the dark like ourselves.—*Willa Cather*

2174   *Respect a Burden*

One time when Napoleon was walking at St. Helena with Mrs. Balcombe, some servants approached carrying a load. Mrs. Balcombe ordered them out of the way, but Napoleon interrupted and said, "Respect the burden, madam."

2175   *A Livelihood and Letters and Arts*

Many writers, scientists, and distinguished men have had to make a living in business, government, and various fields while they pursued their other interests as time permitted. Chaucer was a soldier and later comptroller of petty customs. Spencer was secretary to the Lord Deputy of Ireland; Bacon was a lawyer before he became Lord Keeper and Lord Chancellor. Addison was Secretary of State. Shakespeare managed a theater and was but an ordinary actor. Dante and Boccaccio were in embassies. Galileo was a physician; Schiller a surgeon. Defoe was a brick and tile maker and a shopkeeper. John Stuart Mill was an examiner in the East India House, and Charles Lamb also worked there. Macaulay wrote the *Lays of Ancient Rome* while holding the position of Secretary of War. Ricardo was a banker. Sir Isaac Newton was a Master of the Mint.

2176   *An Estimate of the Value of Character and Leadership*

In 1798, Washington was an old man living in retirement at Mount Vernon. It seemed possible that France might declare war against us. President Adams wrote Washington, "We must have your name, if you will permit us to use it; there will be more efficacy in it than in many an army." Here was an estimate of the great esteem in which the people held Washington's character and leadership.

2177   *Men and Movements*

Great institutions and movements grow out of men of great character. So we think of Quakerism and Fox, Methodism and Wesley, Puritanism and Calvin, Jesuitism and Loyola.

2178   *Mothers*

George Herbert said a good mother equaled a hundred schoolmasters. George Washington, the eldest of five children, was only eleven years old when his father died. His mother was a woman of extraordinary ability who handled her responsibilities with such success that her children grew up to reflect honor upon themselves and upon her. Goethe, Scott, Gray, Schiller, Wesley, Bacon, Erskine, all were particularly influenced by the intelligent guidance of their mothers.

2179 *Counting the House*

At the end of a concert at Carnegie Hall, Walter Damrosch asked Rachmaninoff what sublime thoughts had passed through his head as he stared out into the audience during the playing of his concerto. Said Rachmaninoff: "I was counting the house."—*David Ogilvy*

2180 *Absentminded*

Henry Erskine, Lord Advocate of Scotland toward the close of the eighteenth century, had a tutor who was very absentminded. So much so that Erskine, who thought a great deal of the old man, was one day flabbergasted to hear him say: "I was very sorry, my dear boy, you have had the fever in your family; was it you or your brother who died of it?" "It was I," Erskine replied. "Ah, dear me, I thought so—very sorry for it—very sorry for it." And the old man walked away.

2181 *In God We Trust*

The motto "In God We Trust" first appeared on a coin of the United States in 1864. It was on a two-cent piece, and two years later, it was placed on the nickel, quarter, half, and silver dollar. It was added to the penny in 1909, to the dime in 1916, and having been dropped from the nickel in 1883, it was restored to that coin in 1938. Originally it was used because of high religious sentiment during the Civil War. The Secretary of the Treasury authorized it after receiving a number of appeals from devout citizens urging that the Deity be recognized suitably on our coins.

2182 *No Reason for Dislike*

Years on Wall Street failed to rob the late Dwight Morrow of a shy, whimsical humor. Being told that a certain business acquaintance had acquired a marked dislike for him, Mr. Morrow lapsed into a puzzled silence, then plaintively exclaimed: "I don't see why he should feel hard toward me. I don't remember ever doing anything for him."

2183 *Only Lacked Poverty*

A nobleman, who was an enthusiastic amateur painter, once took a sample of his best work to the great Turner for his candid opinion of it. The artist examined it carefully and, turning to the gentleman, said: "My lord, you lack nothing but poverty to become a very excellent painter."

2184 *Who Owns America?*

Not the politicians. They are public servants, paid by the people to serve the people.

Not the rich. The corporations of America are owned by more than thirty million people.

Not the labor unions, even though some of their leaders act that way.

It is the savers who own America. By doing without things, by self-denial, they built homes and started stores, bought government bonds, invested money in American industry—money which buys machines and provides jobs. Most of what their savings earn is taken away from them in taxes, but because it is in their character never to waste, they still save. If they ever stopped, there would be no new capital to create new jobs, no new machinery to make better jobs, no profitable enterprise whose taxes help keep America going.

It is indeed the savers who keep America alive. Let's be sure the laws keep savers alive, too.—*Warner & Swasey, Cleveland*

2185 *Inspiration*

Boswell and Johnson were at Drury Lane Theatre together watching the great actor Garrick. Boswell said to Johnson, "Garrick is not himself tonight," and the great man replied, "No."

All at once Garrick commenced to act superbly, and Boswell remarked, "Do you notice how he has changed and changed for the better?" "Yes," said the old sage, "and did you notice at what point he changed? He took a higher style when Edmund Burke came into the theatre."

2186 *Youth*

Alfred Tennyson wrote his first volume at eighteen.

Alexander was a mere youth when he rolled back the Asiatic hordes that threatened to overwhelm European civilization almost at its birth.

Napoleon had conquered Italy at twenty-five.

Byron, Raphael, and Poe died at thirty-seven after writing their names among the world's immortals.

Newton made some of his greatest discoveries before he was twenty-five.

It is said that no English poet ever equaled Chatterton at twenty-one.

Victor Hugo wrote a tragedy at fifteen. Many of the world's greatest geniuses never saw forty years.

2187 *Sorrow*

To live through a period of stress and sorrow with another human being creates a bond which nothing seems able to break. People can be happy together and look back on their contacts very pleasantly, but such contacts will not make the same kind of bond that sorrow lived through together will create.—*Eleanor Roosevelt*

2188 *Benjamin Franklin*

Famous was the toast given by Benjamin Franklin when he was dining, as the American emissary, with the English Ambassador and the French Minister at Versailles. The story was first published in 1797.

"George the Third," proposed the British Ambassador, "who, like the sun in its meridian, spreads a luster throughout and enlightens the world."

"The illustrious Louis the Sixteenth," proposed the French Minister, "who, like the moon, sheds his mild and benignant rays on and influences the globe."

"George Washington," thereupon proposed witty Benjamin Franklin, "commander of the American armies, who, like Joshua of old, commanded the sun and the moon to stand still, and they obeyed him."

2189 *Webster and Crockett*

After hearing Daniel Webster speak, Davy Crockett said to him: "I had heard that you were a very great man, but I don't think so. I heard your speech and understood every word you said."

2190 *Mark Twain*

Mark Twain, as Samuel Langhorne Clemens (1835–1910) chose to call himself, was known to be eccentric—Mrs. Clemens called him "careless"—in his dress. As many a man did before him, and many another has done since, Mark Twain went calling one day without his necktie. He had been visiting Harriet Beecher Stowe, of "Uncle Tom" fame, and he was not aware of his lack of haberdashery until Mrs. Clemens called attention to it on his return.

A little later Mrs. Stowe answered her door to find a messenger, who gave her a small package. Opening it, she found a black silk necktie inside and a brief note:

"Here is a necktie. Take it out and look at it. I think I stayed half an hour this morning without this necktie. At the end of that time, will you kindly return it, as it is the only one I have. Mark Twain."

2191 *Rudyard Kipling*

When the report went around that Rudyard Kipling was getting a shilling a word for his writings, some Oxford students sent him a shilling, accompanied by this message:

"Please send us one of your words."

And right back came the unexpected answer:
"Thanks."

2192   *Houdini*

Florenz Ziegfeld and Charles Dillingham, the famous Broadway producers, were pallbearers at the funeral of Houdini, the great magician. As they carried the coffin of the famed handcuff and escape wizard out of the church, Dillingham leaned over and said, "Ziggie, I bet you a hundred dollars he ain't in here!"—*Ladies Home Journal*

2193   *A Difference*

A musical student visited Mozart one day and said: "I want to write a concerto. Will you tell me how to go about it?"

"You are too young," replied the great composer. "Wait until you are a few years older."

"But," objected the young man, "you composed when you were seven or eight."

"Yes," agreed Mozart, "but I didn't have to ask anyone how to do it."

2194   *Not His Attire*

For some reason Bret Harte frequently found himself credited with the authorship of the popular poem "Little Breeches," a distinction properly belonging to John Hay.

"My dear Mr. Harte, I am so delighted to meet you," exclaimed a gushing young lady. "I want to tell you how much I enjoyed reading your 'Little Breeches'."

"I thank you very kindly, madam," replied Harte, "but permit me to say—you have put the little breeches on the wrong man."

2195   *Frederick the Great*

Frederick the Great was a master diplomat, and able to compliment those whom he wished to please. In 1770, when the interviews were being held at court, he noticed General Laudohn, one of his most able adversaries, seated across the table. Speaking up in a loud voice, he said: "Pray, sir, take place here at my right; I do not feel at ease to have you opposite me even at the table."

2196   *Wellington*

At the Battle of Waterloo, the colonel commanding the British artillery observed to the Duke of Wellington: "I have got the exact range of the spot where Bonaparte and his staff are standing. If your grace will allow me, I think I can pick some of them off." "No, no," replied Wellington, "Generals-in-chief have something else to do in a great battle besides firing at each other."

2197   *Brandeis*

Louis D. Brandeis, Associate Justice of the United States Supreme Court, was one evening attending a dinner party, and a discussion of lawsuits and trials came about. After listening for several minutes to the discussion, which centered on the causes of arguments which wound up in the Court for termination, the Justice said: "Arguments seem so futile to me, for behind every argument I have ever heard lies the astounding ignorance of someone."

2198   *Being Different*

Woolworth conceived the idea of the five and ten cent store.

That was different. His fortune was measured by millions when he passed away.

Wanamaker conceived the idea of one price to everybody in his retail stores.

That was different, for at the time he put this policy into effect it was directly contrary to the accepted practice throughout the country.

Ford determined to build a light, cheap car for the millions.

That was different. His reward came in greatly increased automobile output.

Human progress has often depended on the courage of a man who dared to be different.

2199   *The Challenge of Tom Dooley*

The late Dr. Thomas Dooley, who gained world acclaim in sacrifices to relieve suffering in the outer reaches of the world, wrote as follows to a young doctor, challenging him to spend his life in service:

"Dedicate some of your life to others. Your dedication will not be a sacrifice. It will be an exhilarating experience because it is intense effort applied toward a meaningful end."

2200   *Failures*

Lord Bulwer's life was a succession of failures, crowned with final triumph. His first novel was a failure; his first drama was a failure; so were his first speeches and poems. But he fought both defeat and ridicule and finally won a place with Thackeray and Dickens.

Savonarola's first efforts were dismal failures. His brave heart eventually made him Italy's greatest orator.

Daniel Webster could not make a speech until after years of persistent effort. Finally, he became one of America's greatest orators.

Washington lost more battles than he won. But he triumphed in the end.

Franklin, Patrick Henry, Clay, Jackson, Douglas, Lincoln, Grant, all were sons of poor parents. They faced many obstacles, but they finally surmounted them successfully.

2201   *Time*

Voltaire, the famous Frenchman, was a dwarf in body and a giant in intellect.

In his *Zadig, a Mystery of Fate,* is found the following question put to Zadig by the Grand Magi:

"What, of all things in the world, is the longest and the shortest, the swiftest and the slowest, the most divisible and the most extended, the most neglected and the most regretted, without which nothing can be done, which devours all that is little, and enlivens all that is great?"

Here is Zadig's answer:

"Time."

"Nothing is longer, since it is the measure of eternity.

"Nothing is shorter, since it is insufficient for the accomplishment of your projects.

"Nothing is more slow to him that expects; nothing more rapid to him that enjoys.

"In greatness it extends to infinity, in smallness it is infinitely divisible.

"All men neglect it; all regret the loss of it; nothing can be done without it.

"It consigns to oblivion whatever is unworthy of being transmitted to posterity, and it immortalizes such actions as are truly great."

Time is man's most precious asset.

2202   *No Passes*

In the days when the late Colonel Edward H. R. Green, railroad industrialist and banker, was managing the Texas Midland Railroad for his mother, the astute Hetty Green—known to fame as the "richest woman in America"—he was having a lot of trouble with applicants for passes over the line, and so consulted his mother about it. She mentioned the matter to her friend Chauncey M. Depew, who knew all about railroads, being a high official of the New York Central. Depew gave her a list of biblical quotations, which she forwarded to her son.

The list was arranged as a calender in this manner:

Monday—"Thou shalt not pass." (Num. 20:18)

Tuesday—"Suffer not a man to pass." (Judg. 3:28)

Wednesday—"The wicked shall no more pass." (Nah. 1:15)

Thursday—"This generation shall not pass." (Mark 13:30)

Friday—"By a perpetual decree it cannot pass." (Jer. 5:22)

Saturday—"None shall pass." (Isa. 34:10)

Sunday—"So he paid the fare thereof and went." (Jonah 1:3)

2203   *Parental Praise*

When Edward Bok asked Lockwood Kipling, the father of Rudyard Kipling, what he thought of his son's work, the elder Kipling replied, "Creditable."

Surprised, Bok persisted, "But surely you must consider that Rud has done some great work?" He was thinking of *The Jungle Book*, "If," *Captains Courageous*, and other immortal works.

"Creditable," repeated Kipling's father briefly.

Bok was almost ready to give up. "But you think him capable of great work, do you not?"

"He has a certain grasp of the human instinct," Lockwood Kipling admitted. "That some day will lead him to write a great work."

Kipling was never in danger of meaningless praise from his father.— *Christian Science Monitor*

2204   *One Must Eat*

Daniel Webster, the great American statesman, was once sued by his butcher for a bill of long standing. Before the suit was settled he met the butcher on the street, and to that worthy's embarrassment said: "Why have you not sent around my order?" "Why, Mr. Webster," said the man. "I did not think you wanted to deal with me when I brought this suit."

"Tut, tut," said Webster, "sue all you wish, but for heaven's sake, don't try to starve me to death."

2205   *A Long Speech*

In an early American Congress, General Alexander Smythe of Virginia and Henry Clay were members. Smythe was a studious man, but a very laborious speaker who worried the House with prolonged speeches. One day in particular he was being very tedious, and turning to Mr. Clay, said: "You, sir, speak for the present generation; but I speak for posterity." Clay without smiling, retorted: "Yes, and you seem resolved to speak until the arrival of your audience."

2206   *Joseph Choate*

When Joseph Choate was American ambassador to Great Britain, many amusing incidents arose. For one, he had gained quite a lot of weight while in England. When he returned to his country, some of his friends, remembering his slight build, remarked about his corpulence. "Why, Mr. Choate," said one, "you have been getting stout since you went abroad." "Oh, yes," replied he, "I found it necessary to meet the Englishmen halfway."

2207 *Westinghouse*

Two freight trains collided, and a young man set to work to prevent a repetition of such an accident. The result was the invention of the air brake and the beginning of a great industry.

Railroad executives took the attitude of Commodore Vanderbilt, who, when George Westinghouse explained the superiority of the air brake over the dangerous hand brakes, exclaimed: "Do you mean to tell me that you expect to stop a train with wind? I have no time to waste on damn fools."

Westinghouse did not give up and complain that his ability was not appreciated. He invented a railroad frog which appealed to the railroad officials and eventually gave him an opportunity to have the air brake tested. It is that air brake and Westinghouse's system of railway signaling which made all travel safer.

2208 *Ole Bull*

When Ole Bull, the famous Norwegian violinist, came to play in America, there were some jealous musicians here who attacked him through the press. Mr. James Gordon Bennett very graciously offered him the columns of the *Herald,* so that he might make his reply. But wise Ole Bull knew that he possessed a far better weapon than a printing press.

"I tink, Mr. Bennett," he replied in his broken English, "it is best tey writes against me, and I plays against tem."

The great acclaim he received at the hands of the American public proved that he was right.

2209 *Einstein*

Professor Albert Einstein gave what he considered the best formula for success in life. "If a is success in life, I should say the formula is a equals x plus y plus z, x being work and y being play."

"And what is z?" inquired the interviewer.

"That," he answered, "is keeping your mouth shut."—*Christian Register*

2210 *Madame de Stael*

Madame de Stael, whose plain features and blunt manner caused many men discomfiture, one night was dining at the home of the beautiful Madame Recamier. The astronomer Lalande found himself seated between these two women. Thinking he would please both, he exclaimed: "How happy I am to find myself between wit and beauty."

Not lacking in spirit was Madame de Stael, whose prompt reply was: "And without possessing either."

2211 *Royalty*

Nicholas I of Russia had asked Liszt, the great pianist, to play at court. Right in the middle of the opening number, the great musician looked at the Czar and saw him talking to an aide. He continued playing, but was very much irritated. As the Czar did not stop, Liszt finally quit playing. The Czar sent a messenger to ask why he was not playing, and Liszt said: "When the Czar speaks, everyone should be silent." Thereafter there was no interruption in the concert.

2212 *Dr. Everett's Advice*

An indignant Bostonian once rushed to Dr. Everett's house. One of the local papers had published an article severely criticizing this man. Should he demand a public apology, or file a suit for damages?

Dr. Everett listened quietly, then interrupted. "What should you do? My dear sir, do nothing. Half the people who read that paper never saw that article. Half of those who read it do not understand it. Half of those who did understand it did not believe it. Half of those who believed it were of no consequence anyway."—*Christian Science Monitor*

2213 *The Truly Wise*

The man who knows not that he knows not aught—
He is a fool; no light can ever reach him.
Who knows he knows not and would fain be taught—
He is but simple; take thou him and teach him.
And whoso, knowing, knows not that he knows—
He is asleep; go thou to him and wake him.
The truly wise both knows and knows he knows—
Cleave thou to him and nevermore forsake him.

—*Arab proverb*

2214 *Simple or Complex Economy*

We are told that when Washington, Jefferson, and company originally assigned tasks to governmental and business leaders, we had in this country a "simple economy" and that now we have a "complex economy," though I have never been able to see why one is complex and the other is simple. When my grandmother had to build a fire out of buffalo chips and make a pot of soup out of nothing, that wasn't so simple. My daughter can turn on the gas, open up a tin can, and there is the soup. I would like to know which is the complex and which is the simple.—*B. E. Heacock*

2215   *Compound Interest*

Here are four rules that will help anyone who wants to know just what money will do:

At 4 percent compound interest, money will double itself in a little less than eighteen years.

At 5 percent compound interest, money will double itself in approximately fourteen years.

At 6 percent compound interest, money will double itself in approximately twelve years.

At 8 percent compound interest, money will double itself in about nine years.

When these facts are understood, large fortunes are not so wonderful after all, and a person only wonders that more families do not possess them.

2216   *Epitaph*

A tombstone in an English village cemetery has the following inscription:

> "Here lies a miser who lived for himself,
> And cared for nothing but gathering pelf,
> Now, where he is or how he fares,
> Nobody knows and nobody cares."

2217   *Code of Conduct*

Written in 1858 for the four employees of Carson, Pirie & Company, now Carson, Pirie, Scott & Company, Chicago.

"Stores must be open from 6 A.M. to 9 P.M. the year round. Store must be swept; counter base and showcases dusted, lamps trimmed, filled and chimneys cleaned; pens made; doors and windows opened; a pail of water, also a bucket of coal brought in before breakfast (if there is time to do so and attend to customers who call).

"Store must not be opened on the Sabbath, unless necessary to do, and then only for a few minutes.

"The employee who is in the habit of smoking Spanish cigars, being shaved at the barber shop, going to dances and other places of amusement, will surely give his employer reason to be suspicious of his integrity and honesty.

"Each employee must pay not less than $5 per year to the church and must attend Sunday school regularly.

"Men employees are given one evening a week for courting and two if they go to prayer meeting.

"After fourteen hours of work in the store, the leisure hours should be spent mostly in reading."

Some of these rules may seem a bit humorous now, but there are great lessons in this code for all of us.

2218   *Words*

Of the 400,000 words in the English language, the working journalist is accredited with use of the largest number, something less than 20,000. Clergymen, lawyers, and doctors use an average of about 10,000 words. Skilled workers of ordinary education know about 5,000, farm laborers about 1,600. The sciences and professions have large numbers of words the layman never hears of. For instance, medical men and women must know the names of 433 muscles, 193 veins, 707 arteries, 500 pigments, 295 poisons, 109 tumors, 700 tests, over 200 diseases, and over 1,300 bacteria.

Yet with all these words, think of the people who still have trouble expressing themselves. Think of the people who constantly wonder what they are all about.

2219   *Evolution of Man*

To be a circus clown.
To be like dad.
To be a fireman.
To do something noble.
To get wealthy.
To make ends meet.
To get an old age pension.

2220   *America in the Early Nineteenth Century*

There was not a public library in the United States.
Almost all the furniture was imported from England.
An old copper mine in Connecticut was used as a prison.
There was one hat factory, and that made cocked hats.
Every gentleman wore a queue, and powdered his hair.
Crockery plates were objected to because they dulled the knives.
Virginia contained a fifth of the whole population of the country.
A gentleman bowing to a lady always scraped his foot on the ground.
The whipping post and pillory were still standing in Boston and New York.
Beef, pork, salt fish, potatoes, and hominy were the staple diet all year round.

Buttons were scarce and expensive, and the trousers were fastened with pegs or laces.

When a man had enough to eat, he placed his spoon across his cup to indicate that he wanted no more.

The church collection was taken in a bag at the end of a pole, with a bell attached to arouse sleepy contributors.

2221 *Premonition*

Georges Bizet was ill. At the opera house, his own *Carmen* was being performed. Madame Galli-Marie, in the title role, was shuffling the cards in that scene where Carmen has a premonition of her death.

Two hours later Bizet, the composer, was dead!

2222 *Giving*

The grave of Christopher Chapman in Westminster Abbey, bearing the date 1680, says:

> What I gave, I have,
> What I spent, I had,
> What I left, I lost
> By not giving it.

2223 *Cold Feet*

Measuring six feet four himself, Lincoln once met a soldier several inches taller than himself. "Say, friend," said the President, looking up in admiration, "does your head know when your feet are cold?"

2224 *Epitaph 1827*

A seventeenth-century tombstone in an English churchyard contains this inscription:

> Here lies the body of Ethan Bevan,
> Killed by lightning sent from heaven
> For trading horses on Sunday, June eleven,
> In the year Eighteen Hundred Twenty-seven.

2225 *Free Man*

Thomas Jefferson, with all his brilliance and great confidence in the future of the Republic, thought it would take a thousand years to settle the West. He underestimated what free men can accomplish, given the opportunity to create for themselves with minimum government interference and restrictions.—*William A. Patterson, former president, United Airlines*

2226 *The End in View*

Thackeray knew how to puncture the ego of a snob as well with his tongue as with his famous pen.

One day at his club, he was accosted by an officer of the Guards notorious for both his vanity and his pomposity, who, in a tone of patronizing familiarity, exclaimed: "Haw, Thackeray, old boy, I hear Lawrence has been painting your portrait!"

"So he has," replied Thackeray.

"Haw! Full length?"

"No. Full-length portraits are for soldiers that we may see their spurs. But with authors, the other end of the man is the principal thing."—*Wall Street Journal*

2227 *Outwitted*

Rufus Choate, in association with Daniel Webster, was handling an important case for a Boston shipping house. Before him in the witness box was an Irish shipowner, whom he was trying to confuse by asking him a long and involved question. According to a spectator, the question wound all round the case and straggled through every street in Boston. But the witness remained calm and unruffled.

When Mr. Choate had finished, the Irishman leaned forward and quietly asked: "Mr. Choate, will ye be afther repating that question again?"—*Wall Street Journal*

2228 *A Great Debt*

During forty-seven years of intermittent government service, Herbert Hoover turned all of his federal salary checks over to charitable causes and institutions, including his $20,000 annual pension as a former President. He made his fortune as a mining engineer early in his career. He has given away all his governmental income, he once explained, to acknowledge "a great debt" to his country for the many advantages and opportunities that it had conferred upon him.

2229 *Lincoln's Measure*

At a White House reception the Russian Ambassador was talking to President Lincoln when the chief executive asked: "Would you have taken me for an American if you had met me anywhere else than in this country?"

The Muscovite, who was something of a wag, surveyed the President's tall frame, and replied: "No, I should have taken you for a Pole."

"And so I am," exclaimed Lincoln, drawing himself up to his full height, "and a Liberty Pole at that."—*Wall Street Journal*

2230 *Equipped for a Lecture Tour*

A good story concerns Erich Maria Remarque, the author of *All Quiet on the Western Front,* and a pretty American girl to whom he was introduced in Berlin.

The American, speaking in German, asked Remarque why he had never visited the United States. His answer was that he knew only a few sentences in English.

"What are the sentences?" inquired the girl.

Whereupon Remarque, speaking slowly in somewhat gutteral English, said: "How do you do? I love you. Forgive me. Forget me. Ham and eggs, please."

"Sakes alive!" ejaculated the girl. "Why, with that vocabulary you could tour my country from Maine to California."

2231 *How's That?*

Anyone can do any amount of work provided it isn't the work he is supposed to be doing at that moment.—*Robert Benchley*

2232 *Depew's Choice*

At a dinner given in his honor, Chauncey Depew was the recipient of many compliments from various speakers.

Replying, Mr. Depew began: "It's pleasant to hear these nice words while I'm still alive. I'd rather have the taffy than the epitaphy."

2233 *Misplaced*

Bernard Shaw was a past master at the ready retort. A young woman sitting next to him at dinner remarked: "What a wonderful thing is youth!"

"Yes—and what a crime to waste it on children," G.B.S. replied sagely.

2234 *Disengaged*

At one time during the American Civil War, General George B. McClellan, then in command of the Union forces, was conducting a waiting campaign. He was so careful to avoid mistakes that little headway was evident. President Lincoln thereupon wrote him a letter:

"My dear McClellan: If you don't want to use the Army, I should like to borrow it for a while. Yours respectfully, A. Lincoln"

2235 *Woodrow Wilson*

Someone asked Woodrow Wilson how long he would prepare for a ten-minute speech. He said, "Two weeks." "How long for an hour speech?" "One week." "How long for a two-hour speech?" "I am ready now."

2236   *Charles Lamb and Whist*

Charles Lamb tells of a chronic grumbler who always complained at whist because he had so few trumps. By some artifice his companions managed to deal him the whole thirteen, hoping to extort some expression of satisfaction, but he only looked more wretched than ever as he examined his hand. "Well, Tom," said Lamb, "haven't you trumps enough this time?" "Yes," grumbled Tom, "but I've no other cards."

2237   *Fulton and Napoleon*

An American inventor had come to Paris and had offered the French admiralty two inventions: one of them a ship to be propelled by steam instead of by the wind; the other a submarine boat which was to sink ships by the discharge of a kind of torpedo. "The man is a charlatan," was Napoleon's comment on Fulton, after an experiment in which the inventor's "plunging boat" had had a partial success; and he brushed the whole matter aside. If the American had brought him models of a machine gun and field telegraph, he would have opened his purse.—*Emil Ludwig, in Napoleon*

2238   *Humility*

Tho I am truly sensible of the high honor done me in this appointment, yet I feel great distress from a consciousness that my abilities and military experience may not be equal to the extensive and important trust. However, as the Congress desire it, I will enter upon the momentous duty, and exert every power I possess in their service and for the support of the glorious cause. I beg they will accept my most cordial thanks for this distinguished testimony of their approbation.

But lest some unlucky event should happen unfavorable to my reputation, I beg it may be remembered by every gentleman in the room that I this day declare, with the utmost sincerity, I do not think myself equal to the command I am honored with.

As to pay, sir, I beg leave to assure the Congress that as no pecuniary consideration could have tempted me to accept this arduous employment at the expense of my domestic ease and happiness, I do not wish to make any profit from it. I will keep an exact account of my expenses. These I doubt not, they will discharge, and that is all I desire.—*George Washington, on his appointment as commander-in-chief*

2239   *Harvard College*

The first college in this country was Harvard College, now Harvard University. Established in Cambridge, Massachusetts, in 1636, the college was surrounded by a tall fence to keep out wolves and Indians.

2240   *Humble Beginnings*

Even after the J. C. Penney Company was doing a volume of business of hundreds of thousands of dollars, its office equipment remained cheap and austere. Mr. Penney recalls in his book, *Fifty Years with the Golden Rule,* that the office was a room measuring 30 by 35 feet, with a cement floor, one flat-top desk loaned to him by a friend, and one old-fashioned standing desk. Merchants in the early days devised this type of desk on the principle that a bookkeeper who had to stand up at his work would not likely fall asleep.

When mail came in, Mr. Penney personally slit the envelopes and used the blank sides for scratch paper. There was no typewriter, and all work was done in longhand. When a pencil was needed, one of the men went out and bought one for a penny. They bought ink a bottle at a time, and a nickel's worth of pen points.

They kept all overhead expenses down so that the price of all merchandise could remain as low as possible. Eventually, of course, they learned that in modern merchandising it is necessary to make use of the newest and most efficient office equipment. But they showed in the beginning that poverty and poor equipment are never barriers if people work hard and employ right principles.—*Sunshine Magazine*

2241   *Cleanliness*

It has always been called "the White House." But it was not until 1850 that the first bathtub was installed in the presidential residence. Millard Fillmore was the brave executive who took this great step toward cleaner politics.

2242   *Failure*

Bizet, the great composer, died at the age of thirty-seven, brokenhearted over the supposed failure of his opera *Carmen.*

2243   *The Ten Commandments*

Someone has tabulated that we have put 35 million laws on the books trying to enforce the Ten Commandments.—*Bert Masterson, in the Wall Street Journal*

2244   *Middle Age*

Middle age is when a man figures he has enough financial security to wear the flashy sports coats he didn't have the courage to wear when he was young.—*Bill Vaughan, in Milwaukee Journal*

2245   *Easy*

Clarence Darrow, noted criminal lawyer and dissenter since youth, was to participate in a debate with another attorney.

"Are you familiar with the subject?" Darrow was asked.

"No," he confessed.

"Then how can you engage in a debate?"

"Easily," said Darrow. "I'll take the negative side. I can argue AGAINST anything."

2246 *Sounds Expensive*

We live in a land where a lazy loafer is often referred to as an "under-achiever," and the smallest size olive on the shelf is described as "medium." Hence it won't surprise anyone to hear of a dentist who refers to the new set of choppers he gives his clients when their teeth wear out as an "aesthetic restoration."—*Presbyterian Life*

2247 *God and Man*

The Founding Fathers believed devoutly that there was a God and that the unalienable rights of man were rooted—not in the state, nor the legislature, nor in any other human power—but in God alone.—*Tom G. Clark, Associate Justice, U.S. Supreme Court*

2248 *Home*

Booth Tarkington traveled widely, but home to him was his native Indiana.

One night, when he was on a Pacific cruise, a companion said to him: "Why don't you turn in? It's midnight."

"I'm not sleepy," said the author. "It's only eight o'clock in Indiana."

2249 *Don't Interrupt*

Sir Winston Churchill rehearsed his speeches at every opportunity.

One morning, when Sir Winston was in his tub, his valet heard his voice above the splashing. Opening the door, he asked:

"Were you speaking to me, sir?"

"No," replied Churchill, annoyed at the interruption, "I was addressing the House of Commons."

2250 *Not Easy*

The late Justice Cardozo, it seems, was a bad sailor. An acquaintance found him leaning over the rail of a ship as it swayed to the heavy roll of the sea.

"Can I do something for you, Judge?" the friend asked.

"Yes," pleaded the Justice. "Overrule the motion."

2251 *Common Sense*

Dr. Carl Compton of MIT used to tell the story of his sister who lived in Burma.

She was having some wiring installed by a native electrician. Again and again he would come to her for instructions and finally, in exasperation, she said: "You know what I want done. Why don't you use your common sense and do it?"

He made a grave bow and said, "Madam, common sense is a rare gift of God. I have only a technical education."

2252   *The Bible*

A skeptic in London said, in speaking of the Bible, that it was quite impossible in these days to believe in any book whose authority was unknown. A Christian asked him if the compiler of the multiplication table was known. "No," he answered.

"Then, of course, you do not believe in it?"

"Oh, yes, I believe it because it works so well."

"So does the Bible," was the rejoinder, and the skeptic had no answer.—*Katherine Bevis, in Watchman-Examiner*

2253   *Sir Josiah Stamp*

The late Sir Josiah Stamp, in a speech at the Chicago Club, expressed a hope that he wasn't talking too long. "I shouldn't like to be in the position of the parson," he explained, "who, in the midst of an interminable sermon, suddenly broke off his discourse to chide: 'You know I don't mind a bit having you look at your watches to see what time it is, but it really annoys me when you put them up to your ears to hear if they are still running!' "

2254   *A Difference of Two Commas*

Margaret Anglin, the story goes, left this message stuck in the mirror of Mrs. Fiske's dressing room:

"Margaret Anglin says Mrs. Fiske is the best actress in America."

Mrs. Fiske read it, added two commas, stuck it in an envelope, and sent it back to Miss Anglin. It read: "Margaret Anglin, says Mrs. Fiske, is the best actress in America."

2255   *Couldn't Avoid Him*

The handwriting of Nathaniel Hawthorne was so illegible that some of his manuscripts remained unpublished because nobody could read them. This was likewise true of Thomas Carlyle.

The story is told of a type compositor who was employed by a London printing office because of a strong recommendation which he brought from Scotland. The first piece of manuscript given him to set was by Carlyle.

"Great Scott!" said the new typesetter. "Have you that man here, too? I fled from Scotland to avoid him!"—*The Uplift*

2256   *The Sistine Madonna*

The art of interpretation is great and rare. Raphael was walking along a road in the outskirts of Rome upon one occasion; he met a peasant woman passing by with a shawl on her head lapping over one shoulder. He paused: there he saw motherhood, patience, love, sympathy, courage, suffering; he asked her to go to his studio, and he placed upon the canvas a work of art that thousands of people go thousands of miles yearly to see, the "Sistine Madonna."

2257   *Meters for Our Minds*

If we had any meters which could record the movements of our minds as we have meters to clock our taxicabs, we would find they keep running every waking moment. . . . Sometimes our inner thoughts eventually affect our facial expression. When Gilbert Stuart, the experienced painter of portraits, met Talleyrand, the wily French politician, he is reported to have said: "If that man is not a scoundrel, God does not write a legible hand."—*Ralph W. Sockman*

2258   *That Explains It*

One of the world's most famous bells, the great Big Ben in the clock tower of the House of Parliament in London, England, weighs thirteen and one-half tons. It is nine feet in diameter and seven and one-half feet high. The bell was installed while tall, stout Sir Benjamin Hall was serving as Commissioner of Works. He was called Big Ben, and members of Parliament named the bell for him.

2259   *A Wise Judge*

In a book about the life of renowned Englishman Cecil Rhodes, there is a story of a judge who was called upon to settle a dispute between two brothers about the inheritance of the family land. Said the wise old judge: "Let one brother divide the land, then let the other brother have first choice."

2260   *Courage Conquers*

Whenever we are confronted with a bad situation, we should say to ourselves: "This is the reality with which I have to live and I must figure out a way in which I can meet my situation bravely and heroically." There are many examples in history that show us life can be met bravely and effectively whatever tragedy has befallen us. Demosthenes, the great Greek orator, stuttered, and it was his inclination to hide from people and not use his great talents. Finally he realized that only as he spoke stutteringly would he learn to conquer his handicap. The great scientist Steinmetz was so terribly deformed that it took him a long time to accept that his handicap in no way really kept him from contributing much to scientific progress. Milton had to learn, painfully, to believe that he could make his life sing with his poetry in spite of his blindness. Robert Louis Stevenson seemed to produce his greatest works when he was suffering most physically. Beethoven had to be satisfied with composing beautiful music even though he couldn't hear it. And even after a stroke, Louis Pasteur made his greatest discovery. Likewise when we have what we consider are unsurmountable handicaps we should be challenged to devise ways of conquering our handicaps.—*The Better Way*

2261   *Creative Loafing*

Have you ever noticed how some of your best ideas have popped into your head while you have been sitting in a boat fishing, playing a round of golf, or sitting on the beach watching the waves roll in?

Newton was loafing under an apple tree when he saw an apple fall and got the gravitation idea.

While loafing and finding peace for his soul, Galileo watched the great swinging lamp. It gave him the idea of a pendulum swinging to and fro as a means of measuring the passage of time.

Watt was loafing in the kitchen when he noticed the steam lifting the top of the teakettle, and conceived the idea of a steam engine.

Vacations are valuable investments. We should take little vacations every day. Many times we will get more ideas and better ideas in two hours of creative loafing than in eight hours at the desk.—*Wilferd Peterson*

2262   *George Burns and Gracie Allen*

GRACIE: I did the silliest thing today. I dropped the baby's blanket out the window.

GEORGE: That was careless. The baby's likely to catch pneumonia.

GRACIE: Oh, no, he won't. He was in the blanket.

2263   *Eleven Who Were Poor*

John Adams, second President of the United States, was the son of a grocer of very moderate means. The only start he had was a good education.

Andrew Jackson was born in a log hut in North Carolina, and was reared in the beautiful pine woods for which the state is famous.

James K. Polk spent the earlier years of his life helping to dig a living out of a new farm in North Carolina. He was afterward a clerk in a country store.

Millard Fillmore was the son of a New York farmer, and his home was a humble one. He learned the business of a clothier.

James Buchanan was born in a small town in the Allegheny Mountains. His father cut the logs and built the house in what was then a wilderness.

Abraham Lincoln was the son of a wretchedly poor farmer in Kentucky, and lived in a log cabin until he was twenty-one years old.

Andrew Johnson was apprenticed to a tailor at the age of ten by his widowed mother. He was never able to attend school, and picked up all the education he ever had.

Ulysses S. Grant lived the life of a village boy, in a plain house on the banks of the Ohio River, until he was seventeen years of age.

James A. Garfield was born in a log cabin. He worked on the farm until he was strong enough to use carpenter's tools, when he learned the trade. He afterward worked on a canal.

Grover Cleveland's father was a Presbyterian minister with a small salary and a large family. The boys had to earn their living.

William McKinley's early home was plain and comfortable, and his father was able to keep him at school.—*Rocky Mountain Advocate*

2264　*In the Hands of God*

On the night of July 10, 1943, General Eisenhower watched the vast armada of 3,000 ships sailing across from Malta to the shores of Sicily for a great battle. The General saluted his heroic men and then bowed his head in prayer. To an officer beside him, Eisenhower explained: "There comes a time when you've used your brains, your training, your technical skill, and the die is cast and the events are in the hands of God, and there you have to leave them."—*Charles L. Allen*

2265　*Age and Accomplishment*

Since when has age become a disqualifying factor in human endeavor and accomplishments? Between the ages of 70 and 83, Commodore Vanderbilt added ten million dollars to his fortune. Verdi, at 83, produced his magnificent "Te Deum," his "Stabat Mater," and "Ave Maria." Oliver Wendell Holmes, at 79, wrote his "Over the Teacups," and Tennyson, at 83, wrote "Crossing the Bar."

2266　*Youth*

Macaulay was a historian at eight. Byron wrote verses at ten. The immortal Mozart made his debut as a composer and musician at six. Douglas Jerrold scored a success on the stage with a farce when he was only fourteen. Some of Robert Burns' best poems were written while he was a ploughboy. And Ruskin had written *Modern Painters* at twenty-four.—*William Strong*

2267   *No Compliments*

"Do you like your portrait?" Whistler asked the celebrity whose portrait he had painted.

"No, I don't," replied the other. "You must admit, Mr. Whistler, it's a bad work of art."

"Yes," retorted the painter, "but then you must admit you are a bad work of nature."

2268   *Quick Wit*

It was one of the late Lloyd George's campaigns in England. Someone threw a brick through a window and it fell on the platform at his feet. Picking it up, he cried: "Behold the only argument of our opponents."

In another gathering, a man shouted: "Oh, you're not so much; your dad used to peddle vegetables with a donkey and cart." "Yes," replied the orator, "that is true. My father was a very poor man. The cart has long since disappeared, but I see the donkey is still with us."

2269   *Way Back Then*

When a federal income tax was being advocated back in 1913, under President Wilson's administration, its backers promised that the tax rate would never go beyond ten percent.

2270   *Touché!*

An actress congratulated Ilka Chase on her book, *Past Imperfect*. "Who wrote it for you?"

"Darling," clawed back Ilka, "I'm so glad you like it. Who read it to you?"—*Washington Times-Herald*

2271   *For Rehearsals*

That great maestro Arturo Toscanini was, I think, almost as well known for his ferocious temper as for his outstanding musicianship. When members of his orchestra played badly, he would pick up anything in sight and hurl it to the floor.

During one rehearsal, a flat note caused the genius to grab his valuable watch and smash it beyond repair.

Shortly afterward he received from his devoted musicians a luxurious velvet-lined box containing two watches—one a beautiful gold timepiece, the other a cheap one on which was inscribed: "For rehearsals only."—*Puck, London*

2272   *The First Flight*

On the morning of the 18th of December, 1903, the Dayton (Ohio) *Journal* carried a banner headline, "Stores Filled With Christmas Shoppers," and not a word concerning the historic flight of two local boys, Orville and Wilbur Wright.

Lorin, younger brother of the fliers, had tried to inform the press, upon receipt of a telegram. "Fifty-seven seconds, eh?" yawned Frank Tunison, of the *Journal* staff. "If it had been fifty-seven minutes it might be a news item."

2273   *The Difference*

A philosopher has said that it is not so much a matter of what we have as what we do with what we have that makes the difference in this world.

Longfellow could take a worthless sheet of paper, write a poem on it and make it worth $6,000. That's genius.

Rockefeller could sign his name to a piece of paper and make it worth a million. That's capital.

Uncle Sam can take silver, stamp an emblem on it, and make it worth a dollar. That's money.

A mechanic can take metal that is worth only five dollars and make it worth fifty dollars. That's skill.

An artist can take a piece of canvas, paint a picture on it and make it worth $1,000. That's art.

2274   *Tough Question*

John Barrymore, watching a tense football game, was distracted by the man next to him, who bragged: "When I was in college I helped Harvard beat Yale three times in succession!"

"That so?" snapped Barrymore. "Which team were you playing on?"

2275   *Your Best Friend*

Once, while sitting in a restaurant, the late Henry Ford was asked: "Who is your best friend?"

Ford thought for a moment, then took out his pencil and wrote in large letters on the tablecloth: "He is your best friend who brings out of you the best that is in you."—*Norman Vincent Peale*

2276   *No Degrees*

The late Speaker of the House, Sam Rayburn, was once asked how honorable a certain Congressman was. Rayburn stared in astonishment and replied: "There are no degrees of honorable. You are or you aren't."

2277   *A High Title*

Cardinal-designate Archbishop Richard Cushing, Boston: "I really don't know whether I should be termed 'your excellency' or 'your eminence.' It doesn't make much difference to me after what happened the other day. I met a woman who addressed me as 'your elegance' and I don't know that any other title can quite match that."

2278 *When You Go*

Eugene Field once was forced to rent a room in a boarding house so incredibly dirty that he was amused by a sign tacked to the front door: "Please wipe your feet."

Field stayed only a week in the place, and as he was about to leave, he put his luggage down long enough to add a line to the placard on the door. He wrote: "When you go out!"

2279 *Daring Believers*

Three friends—Henry Ford, Harvey Firestone, and Thomas A. Edison —were companions who hitched the gasoline engine to a buggy, cushioned the wheel to destructive road shocks, and lighted the road to the darkest night. They were great and daring believers.—*Ira E. Carney*

2280 *The Father of Lincoln*

Like many other people, I had thought Abraham Lincoln's father was a shiftless, unambitious sort of man. I had given Lincoln's mother, and some other mystic influence, chief credit for his greatness.

In the beautiful memorial building in Hodgenville, Kentucky, which shelters the little cabin in which Lincoln was born, is evidence which throws a new light on the father of this great man. I learned these facts:

That Thomas Lincoln was orphaned at six years and grew up homeless in the wild woods of Kentucky.

That at twenty-five he was the possessor of his cabin home and its neighboring acres.

That he built with his own hands five homes, each better than the preceding one.

That he was a good carpenter for the times and had the best set of tools in Washington County.

That he had a cow and a calf, milk and butter, and a good feather bed.

That he had a home-woven "kiverlid," big and little pots, a loom and a wheel.

That he was a peaceful, industrious, respected citizen; an honest and contented pioneer.

That he won and held the love and faith of two noble women.

That Abraham Lincoln said of him: "My father insisted that none of his children should suffer for lack of education as he did."

Certainly, there is a picture of a strong man! Of a man who faced and conquered great obstacles. Of a man possessing courage, character, and energy. A man who was, for his time, a success, and who visioned greater and finer things for his children.

Thomas Lincoln, my hat is off to your memory!—*Wilferd A. Peterson, in Associated Dispatcher*

2281   *What an Author Named Anonymous Wrote over the Years*
Nobody knows the trouble I've seen.
   Men may work from sun to sun, but women's work is never done.
   Do not fold, spindle or mutilate.
   That's the way the cookie crumbles.
   America, love it or leave it.
   Such rhymes as "London Bridge Is Falling Down," "Mary, Mary,
Quite Contrary" and "Jack Sprat."

> Now I lay me down to sleep;
> I pray the Lord my soul to keep.
> If I should die before I wake
> I pray the Lord my soul to take.

2282   *His Training*
I was trained from the beginning to work, to save, and to give.—*John D. Rockefeller, Jr.*

2283   *Accomplishments of Older Persons*
Jessica Tandy, at age 74, opened triumphantly on Broadway in the demanding role of Amanda in a revival of "The Glass Menagerie," by Tennessee Williams. Rex Harrison, age 75, opened successfully as the lead in the revival of "Heartbreak House"—a drama by George Bernard Shaw who, incidentally, continued to write plays late into life. At age 81, Barbara McClintock won the Nobel Prize for medicine, while Indian-born Subrahmanyan Chancrasekhar, 73, and William Fowler, 72, shared the prize for physics.

2284   *Charles Spurgeon's Advice to Speakers*
When you speak of Heaven, let your face light up, let it be irradiated by a heavenly gleam, let your eyes shine with reflected glory. But when you speak of Hell, your ordinary expression will do.

2285   *Humility*
A comparatively unknown, struggling young pianist was giving his first performances in London. His concert was a sellout, but when his manager hurried to tell him the good news, he found the virtuoso huddled in a dingy corner, practicing. As he heard the report that every seat in the house had been sold, and people were clamoring for standing room, the pianist wept and said: "It's wrong! I can't take their money! I can't play at all!" He was Ignace Jan Paderewski.—*Journal of Living*

2286   *Lincoln's Faith*

Abraham Lincoln was a student of the Bible from his childhood, and reverently believed in its teachings. He once said, "Whenever any church will inscribe over its altar as a qualification for membership the Savior's statement of the substance of the law and gospel, 'Thou shalt love the Lord Thy God with all thy heart, and with all thy soul, and with all thy mind, and thy neighbor as thyself,' that church will I join with all my heart and soul."

2287   *Edison's Vacation*

One evening when Thomas A. Edison returned home from work, his wife said: "You have worked long enough without a rest. You must go on a vacation."

"But where will I go?" he asked.

"Decide where you would rather be than anywhere else on earth, and go there," was the answer.

"Very well," promised Edison. "I will go tomorrow."

The next morning he went back to work in his laboratory.

2288   *Next Question*

Franklin Roosevelt once asked Harry Hopkins, "Harry, where is the population most dense in the United States?"

Harry grinned a moment, and then said, "From the neck up!"

2289   *Repartee*

"I never saw sunsets like yours, Mr. Turner," said a lady to the famous artist.

"Don't you wish you did?" he replied.

2290   *The Scrap Pile*

The marble block was cast away. It had been spoiled in the quarry. There was a tiny crack, so it was cast aside. That was, however, before Michelangelo came wandering along. His keen eye detected the beauty of the rejected stone. He began to chip it, a little off here, and some there, and more of its beauty was revealed. One day an heroic David emerged from the rejected stone, a figure to amaze the world. The scrap rejected of men had been glorified forever.—*Sunshine Magazine*

2291   *Lincoln's Goal*

I desire so to conduct the affairs of this administration that if at the end, when I come to lay down the reins of power, I have lost every other friend on earth, I shall at least have one friend left, and that friend shall be down inside of me.—*Abraham Lincoln*

2292   *Horace Mann Speaks*

Horace Mann, one of the founders of the public school system, wrote: "A house without books is like a room without windows. No man has a right to bring up his children without surrounding them with books, if he has the means to buy them. It is a wrong to his family. Children learn to read by being in the presence of books. The love of knowledge comes with reading and grows upon it. And the love of knowledge, in a young mind, is almost a warrant against the inferior thrill of passions and vices."

2293   *He Didn't Know*

A doctor hesitated when a call for help came on a particularly inclement night, but his love for humanity was strong, and he went through a drenching rain to the distant home of a farmer. His services saved the life of a small child. Years later, the doctor said: "I never dreamed that in saving the life of that farm child I was saving the life of the leader of England." That child was David Lloyd-George, onetime British prime minister.—*Charles L. Wallis, Treasury of Sermon Illustrations*

2294   *A Risk*

Isadora Duncan, famous dancer, once wrote to George Bernard Shaw with the proposal that, according to eugenics, a child of whom they could be the parents would be a superhuman.

"Think what a child it would be, with my body and your brain."

Shaw replied, "But suppose the child was so unlucky as to have my body and your brain."

2295   *Thomas Jefferson*

A gentleman of thirty-two who could calculate an eclipse, survey an estate, tie an artery, plan an edifice, try a cause, break a horse, dance a minuet and play the violin.—*James Parton, Life of Jefferson*

2296   *Epitaphs*

Die when I may, I want it said of me by those who knew me best, that I always plucked a thistle and planted a flower where I thought a flower would grow.—*Abraham Lincoln*

> The Body of Benjamin Franklin, Printer
> (Like the cover of an old book,
> Its contents torn out
> And stript of its lettering and gilding),
> Lies here, food for worms;
> But the work shall not be lost,
> For it will (as he believed) appear once more

In a new
And more elegant edition,
Revised and corrected
by the Author.

Benjamin Franklin

Here was buried Thomas Jefferson, author of the Declaration of American Independence, of the statute of Virginia for religious freedom, and father of the University of Virginia.—*Jefferson, epitaph written for himself.*

2297 *Nor Be Afraid*

It was Robert Browning who a hundred years ago said: "Grow old along with me. The best is yet to be; the last of life, for which the first was made. Our times are in His hands who saith, 'A whole I planned, youth shows but half. Trust God; see all, nor be afraid.'"

13
BIBLICAL QUOTATIONS

OLD TESTAMENT

Genesis

2298 God created man in his own image. 1:27

2299 It is not good that man should be alone. 2:18

2300 In the sweat of thy face shalt thou eat bread. 3:19

2301 For dust thou art, and unto dust shalt thou return. 3:19

2302 Am I my brother's keeper? 4:9

2303 There were giants in the earth in those days. 6:4

2304 Whoso sheddeth man's blood, by man shall his blood be shed. 9:6

2305 The voice is Jacob's voice, but the hands are the hands of Esau. 27:22

Exodus

2306 Who made thee a prince and a judge over us? 2:14

2307 A land flowing with milk and honey. 3:8

2308 The land of Egypt, when we sat by the flesh-pots, and when we did eat bread to the full. 16:3

The Ten Commandments 20:3–17

2309 I. Thou shalt have no other gods before me.

2310 II. Thou shalt not make unto thee any graven image, or any likeness of any thing that is in heaven above, or that is in the earth beneath, or that is in the water under the earth: thou shalt not bow down thyself to them, nor serve them: for I the Lord thy God am a jealous God, visiting the iniquity of the fathers upon the children unto the third and fourth generation of them that hate me; and shewing mercy unto thousands of them that love me, and keep my commandments.

2311 III. Thou shalt not take the name of the Lord thy God in vain; for the Lord will not hold him guiltless that taketh his name in vain.

2312 IV. Remember the sabbath day, to keep it holy. Six days shalt thou labor, and do all thy work; but the seventh day is the sabbath of the Lord thy God: in it thou shalt not do any work, thou, nor thy son, nor thy daughter, thy manservant, nor thy maidservant, nor thy cattle, nor the stranger that is within thy gates: for in six days the Lord made heaven and earth, the sea, and all that in them is, and rested the seventh day: wherefore the Lord blessed the sabbath day, and hallowed it.

2313 V. Honor thy father and thy mother: that thy days may be long upon the land which the Lord thy God giveth thee.

2314 VI. Thou shalt not kill.

2315 VII. Thou shalt not commit adultery.

2316 VIII. Thou shalt not steal.

2317 IX. Thou shalt not bear false witness against thy neighbor.

2318 X. Thou shalt not covet thy neighbor's house, thou shalt not covet thy neighbor's wife, nor his manservant, nor his maidservant, nor his ox, nor his ass, nor anything that is thy neighbor's.

Deuteronomy

2319 Man doth not live by bread only. 8:3

2320 Eye for eye, tooth for tooth, hand for hand, foot for foot. 19:21

2321 Thou shalt not muzzle the ox when he treadeth out the corn. 25:4

Joshua

2322 I am going the way of all the earth. 23:14

Judges

2323 The stars in their courses fought against Sisera. 5:20

First Samuel

2324   Be strong, and quit yourselves like men. 4:9

2325   A man after his own heart. 13:14

Second Samuel

2326   How are the mighty fallen! Tell it not in Gath, publish it not in the streets of Askelon. 1:19, 20

2327   And Nathan said to David, Thou art the man. 12:7

First Kings

2328   How long halt ye between two opinions? If the Lord be God follow him: but if Baal, then follow him. 18:21

2329   A still small voice. 19:12

First Chronicles

2330   Our days on the earth are as a shadow. 29:15

2331   And he died in a good old age, full of days, riches, and honour. 29:28

Job

2332   One that feared God, and eschewed evil. 1:1

2333   The Lord gave, and the Lord hath taken away; blessed be the name of the Lord. 1:21

2334   Skin for skin, yea all that a man hath will he give for his life. 2:4

2335   Shall a man be more pure than his Maker? 4:17

2336   Although affliction cometh not forth of the dust, neither doth trouble spring out of the ground: yet man is born into trouble as the sparks fly upward. 5:6, 7

2337   Man that is born of a woman is of few days, and full of trouble. 14:1

2338   I am escaped with the skin of my teeth. 19:20

2339   The price of wisdom is above rubies. 28:18

2340   Behold my desire is . . . that mine adversary had written a book. 31:35

2341 But there is a spirit in man; and the inspiration of the Almighty giveth them understanding. 32:8

2342 He multiplieth words without knowledge. 35:16

2343 He saith among the trumpets, Ha, ha; and he smelleth the battle afar off. 39:25

Psalms

2344 Yea, though I walk through the valley of the shadow of death, I will fear no evil: for thou art with me; thy rod and thy staff they comfort me. 23:4

2345 Many are the afflictions of the righteous: but the Lord delivereth him out of them all. 34:19

2346 The wicked borroweth, and payeth not again: but the righteous showeth mercy, and giveth. 37:21

2347 He heapeth up riches, and knoweth not who shall gather them. 39:6

2348 Blessed is he that considereth the poor. 41:1

2349 As the hart panteth after the water brooks. 42:1

2350 Deep calleth unto deep. 42:7

2351 Oh that I had wings like a dove! for then would I fly away, and be at rest. 55:6

2352 We took sweet counsel together. 55:14

2353 The words of his mouth were smoother than butter, but war was in his heart; his words were softer than oil, yet were they drawn swords. 55:21

2354 Cast thy burden upon the Lord, and he shall sustain thee: he shall never suffer the righteous to be moved. 55:22

2355 Vain is the help of man. 60:11

2356 For a thousand years in thy sight are but as yesterday when it is past, and as a watch in the night. 90:4

2357 As for man, his days are as grass: as a flower of the field, so he flourisheth. 103:15

2358 They that go down to the sea in ships, that do business in great waters; these see the works of the Lord, and his wonders in the deep. 107:23, 24

2359   The stone which the builders refused is become the headstone of the corner. 118:22

2360   Lo, children are an heritage of the Lord: happy is the man that hath his quiver full of them. 127:3, 5

2361   Behold, how good and how pleasant it is for brethren to dwell together in unity! 133:1

2362   If I forget thee, O Jerusalem, let my right hand forget her cunning. 137:5

2363   I am fearfully and wonderfully made. 139:14

Proverbs

2364   The fear of the Lord is the beginning of knowledge, but fools despise wisdom and instruction. 1:7

2365   Surely in vain the net is spread in the sight of any bird. 1:17

2366   Withhold not good from them to whom it is due, when it is in the power of thine hand to do it. 3:27

2367   Go to the ant, thou sluggard; consider her ways, and be wise. 6:6

2368   As an ox goeth to the slaughter. 7:22; Jer. 11:19

2369   A wise son maketh a glad father. 10:1

2370   In the multitude of counsellors there is safety. 11:14; 24:6

2371   He that is surety for a stranger shall smart for it. 11:15

2372   A virtuous woman is a crown to her husband. 12:4

2373   The way of the transgressors is hard. 13:15

2374   He that walketh with wise men shall be wise: but a companion of fools shall be destroyed. 13:20

2375   He that spareth his rod hateth his son. 13:24

2376   Righteousness exalteth a nation. 14:34

2377   A soft answer turneth away wrath: but grievous words stir up anger. 15:1

2378   A merry heart maketh a cheerful countenance. 15:13

2379   Pride goeth before destruction, and an haughty spirit before a fall. 16:18

2380   The hoary head is a crown of glory, if it be found in the way of righteousness. 16:31

2381   He that is slow to anger is better than the mighty: and he that ruleth his spirit than he that taketh a city. 16:32

2382   He that repenteth a matter separateth very friends. 17:9

2383   He that hath knowledge spareth his words. 17:27

2384   Even a fool, when he holdeth his peace, is counted wise. 17:28

2385   A man's gift maketh room for him, and bringeth him before great men. 18:16

2386   He that hath pity upon the poor lendeth unto the Lord. 19:17

2387   Wine is a mocker, strong drink is raging. 20:1

2388   It is naught, it is naught, saith the buyer—but when he is gone his way, then he boasteth. 10:14

2389   A good name is rather to be chosen than great riches. 22:1

2390   Train up a child in the way he should go: and when he is old, he will not depart from it. 22:6

2391   The rich ruleth over the poor, and the borrower is servant to the lender. 22:7

2392   Seest thou a man diligent in his business? he shall stand before kings; he shall not stand before mean men. 22:29

2393   As he thinketh in his heart, so is he. 23:7

2394   Drowsiness shall clothe a man with rags. 23:21

2395   If thou faint in the day of adversity, thy strength is small. 24:10

2396   Rejoice not when thine enemy falleth, and let not thine heart be glad when he stumbleth. 24:17

2397   Debate thy cause with thy neighbor himself; and discover not a secret to another. 25:9

2398   A word fitly spoken is like apples of gold in pitchers of silver. 25:11

2399   Whoso boasteth himself of a false gift is like clouds and wind without rain. 25:14

2400   Seest thou a man wise in his own conceit? there is more hope of a fool than of him. 26:12

2401   The sluggard is wiser in his own conceit than seven men that can render a reason. 26:16

2402   As coals are to burning coals, and wood to fire; so is a contentious man to kindle strife. 26:21

2403   Boast not thyself of tomorrow; for thou knowest not what a day may bring forth. 27:1

2404   The wicked flee when no man pursueth: but the righteous are bold as a lion. 28:1

2405   He that maketh haste to be rich shall not be innocent. 28:20

2406   He that giveth unto the poor shall not lack: but he that hideth his eyes shall have many a curse. 28:27

2407   A fool uttereth all his mind: but a wise man keepeth it in till afterward. 29:11

2408   The ants are a people not strong, yet they prepare their meat in the summer. 30:25

2409   Favor is deceitful, and beauty is vain. 31:30

Ecclesiastes

2410   One generation passeth away, and another generation cometh; but the earth abideth forever. 1:4

2411   All the rivers run into the sea; yet the sea is not full. 1:7

2412   In much wisdom is much grief. 1:18

2413   Better is an handful with quietness, than both hands full with travail and vexation of spirit. 4:6

2414   A living dog is better than a dead lion. 9:4

2415   The race is not to the swift, nor the battle to the strong, neither yet bread to the wise, nor yet riches to men of understanding, nor yet favour to men of skill; but time and chance happeneth to them all. 9:11

2416   He that diggeth a pit shall fall into it. 10:8

2417   Cast thy bread upon the waters: for thou shalt find it after many days. 11:1

2418   Remember now thy Creator in the days of thy youth, while the evil days come not. 12:1

2419   Of making many books there is no end; and much study is a weariness of the flesh. 12:12

Song of Solomon

2420   Many waters cannot quench love. 8:7

Isaiah

2421   The ox knoweth his owner, and the ass his master's crib. 1:3

2422   Bring no more vain oblations; incense is an abomination unto me. 1:13

2423   They shall beat their swords into ploughshares, and their spears into pruning hooks. 2:4

2424   What mean ye that ye . . . grind the faces of the poor. 3:15

2425   Therefore the Lord himself shall give you a sign; Behold, the virgin shall conceive, and bear a son, and shall call his name Immanuel. 7:14

2426   The wolf also shall dwell with the lamb, and the leopard shall lie down with the kid. 11:6

2427   How art thou fallen from heaven, O Lucifer, son of the morning! 14:12

2428   Babylon is fallen, is fallen. 21:9

2429   Watchman, what of the night? 21:11

2430   Let us eat and drink, for tomorrow we shall die. 22:13

2431   We have made a covenant with death. 28:15

2432   Behold, the nations are as a drop of a bucket, and are counted as the small dust of the balance. 40:15

2433   Shall the clay say to him that fashioneth it, What makest thou? 45:9

2434   A man of sorrows and acquainted with grief. 53:3

2435   We all do fade as a leaf. 64:6

Jeremiah

2436   Saying, Peace, peace; when there is no peace. 6:14

Lamentations

2437   She that was great among the nations, and princess among the provinces, how is she become tributary! 1:1

Hosea

2438   For they have sown the wind, and they shall reap the whirlwind. 8:7

Joel

2439 Your sons and your daughters shall prophesy, your old men shall dream dreams, your young men shall see visions. 2:28

Zechariah

2440 Prisoners of hope. 9:12

2441 I was wounded in the house of my friends. 13:6

NEW TESTAMENT

The Gospel According to St. Matthew

2442 And now also the axe is laid unto the root of the trees. 3:10

2443 Repent; for the kingdom of heaven is at hand. 4:17

2444 Blessed are the poor in spirit: for theirs is the kingdom of heaven.

2445 Blessed are they that mourn: for they shall be comforted.

2446 Blessed are the meek: for they shall inherit the earth.

2447 Blessed are they which do hunger and thrist after righteousness: for they shall be filled.

2448 Blessed are the merciful: for they shall obtain mercy.

2449 Blessed are the pure in heart: for they shall see God.

2450 Blessed are the peacemakers: for they shall be called the children of God.

2451 Blessed are ye, when men shall revile you, and persecute you, and shall say all manner of evil against you falsely, for my sake.

2452 Rejoice, and be exceeding glad: for great is your reward in heaven: for so persecuted they the prophets which were before you. 5:3–12

2453 Ye are the salt of the earth: but if the salt have lost his savour, wherewith shall it be salted? (See Mark 9:50; Luke 14:34) 5:13

2454 Ye are the light of the world. A city that is set on a hill cannot be hid. 5:14

2455 Neither do men light a candle, and put it under a bushel. (See Mark 4:21) 5:15

2456 Whosoever is angry with his brother without a cause shall be in danger of the judgment. 5:22

2457 And if thy right eye offend thee, pluck it out, and cast it from thee; for it is profitable for thee that one of thy members should perish, and not that thy whole body should be cast into hell. 5:29

2458   Whosoever shall smite thee on thy right cheek, turn to him the other also. (See Luke 6:20) 5:39

2459   Give to him that asketh thee, and from him that would borrow of thee turn not thou away. 5:42

2460   Love your enemies. (See Luke 6:27) 5:44

2461   Let not thy left hand know what thy right hand doeth. 6:3

2462   Use not vain repetitions. 6:7

2463   Where moth and rust doth corrupt, and where thieves break through and steal. 6:19

2464   For where your treasure is, there will your heart be also. (See Luke 12:34) 6:21

2465   No man can serve two masters. (See Luke 16:13) 6:24

2466   Ye cannot serve God and mammon. (See Luke 16:13) 6:24

2467   Consider the lilies of the field, how they grow; they toil not, neither do they spin: And yet I say unto you, That even Solomon in all his glory was not arrayed like one of these. (See Luke 12:27) 6:28, 29

2468   Take therefore no thought for the morrow: for the morrow shall take thought for the things of itself. Sufficient unto the day is the evil thereof. 6:34

2469   Judge not, that ye be not judged. (See Luke 6:37) 7:1

2470   Ask, and it shall be given you; seek, and ye shall find; knock, and it shall be opened unto you: for every one that asketh receiveth; and he that seeketh findeth; and to him that knocketh it shall be opened. 7:7, 8

2471   What man is there of you, whom if his son ask bread, will he give him a stone? (See Luke 11:11) 7:9

2472   Therefore all things whatsoever ye would that men should do to you, do ye even so to them. (See Luke 6:31) 7:12

2473   Wide is the gate, and broad is the way, that leadeth to destruction. 7:13

2474   Beware of false prophets, which come to you in sheep's clothing, but inwardly they are ravening wolves. 7:15

2475   A good tree cannot bring forth bad fruit, neither can a corrupt tree bring forth good fruit. 7:18

2476   And the rain descended, and the floods came, and the winds blew and beat upon that house, and it fell not; for it was founded upon a rock. 7:25

2477 A foolish man, which built his house upon the sand. (See Luke 6:49) 7:26

2478 I am a man under authority, having soldiers under me: and I say to this man, Go, and he goeth; and to another, Come, and he cometh. 8:9

2479 The foxes have holes, and the birds of the air have nests; but the Son of man hath not where to lay his head. 8:20

2480 Follow me; and let the dead bury their dead. (See Luke 9:60) 8:22

2481 No man putteth a piece of new cloth unto an old garment. (See Mark 3:21) 9:16

2482 The harvest truly is plenteous, but the labourers are few. (See Luke 10:2) 9:37

2483 The very hairs of your head are all numbered. (See Luke 21:18) 10:30

2484 A man's foes shall be they of his own household. 10:36

2485 Come unto me, all ye that labour and are heavy laden. 11:28

2486 He that is not with me is against me. (See Mark 9:40; Luke 9:50; 11:23) 12:30

2487 The tree is known by his fruit. (See Luke 6:44) 12:33

2488 Out of the abundance of the heart the mouth speaketh. (See Luke 6:45) 12:34

2489 Whosoever hath, to him shall be given, and he shall have more abundance: but whosoever hath not, from him shall be taken away even that he hath. 13:12

2490 When he had found one pearl of great price. 13:46

2491 If the blind lead the blind, both shall fall into the ditch. 15:14

2492 Get thee behind me Satan. (See Mark 8:33) 16:23

2493 For what is a man profited, if he shall gain the whole world and lose his own soul? (See Mark 8:36; Luke 9:25) 16:26

2494 What therefore God hath joined together, let not man put asunder. (See Mark 10:9) 19:6

2495 It is easier for a camel to go through the eye of a needle, than for a rich man to enter into the kingdom of God. (See Mark 10:25) 19:24

2496 But many that are first shall be last; and the last shall be first. (See Mark 10:31; Luke 13:30) 19:30

2497 For many are called, but few are chosen. 22:14

2498 Render therefore unto Caesar the things which are Caesar's; and unto God the things that are God's. (See Mark 12:17; Luke 20:25) 22:21

2499 And whosoever shall exalt himself shall be abased; and he that shall humble himself shall be exalted. (see Luke 14:11) 23:12

2500 Ye blind guides, which strain at a gnat, and swallow a camel. 23:24

2501 Ye are like unto whited sepulchres, which indeed appear beautiful outward, but are within full of dead men's bones, and of all uncleanness. 23:27

2502 War and rumours of wars. 24:6

2503 Well done, thou good and faithful servant. 25:21

2504 Reaping where thou hast not sown, and gathering where thou hast not strawed. (See Luke 19:21) 25:24

2505 There shall be weeping and gnashing of teeth. 25:30

2506 I was a stranger, and ye took me in. 25:35

2507 Inasmuch as ye have done it unto one of the least of these my brethren, ye have done it unto me. 25:40

2508 So the last error shall be worse than the first. 27:64

2509 Lo, I am with you always, even unto the end of the world. 28:20

The Gospel According to St. Mark

2510 He that hath ears to hear, let him hear. 4:9

2511 Lord, I believe; help thou mine unbelief. 9:24

2512 Whosoever shall offend one of these little ones that believe in me, it is better for him that a millstone were hanged about his neck, and he were cast into the sea. 9:42

2513 Suffer the little children to come unto me, and forbid them not: for of such is the kingdom of God. (See Matt. 19:13; Luke 18:15) 10:14

2514 Which devour widows' houses, and for a pretence make long prayers. (See Matt. 23:14) 12:40

The Gospel According to St. Luke

2515 On earth peace, good will towards men. 2:14

2516 Be content with your wages. 3:14

2517 Physician, heal thyself. 4:20

2518 The labourer is worthy of his hire. 10:7

2519 He passed by on the other side. 10:31

2520 Go, and do thou likewise. 10:37

2521 Every kingdom divided against itself is brought to desolation; and a house divided against a house falleth. 11:17

2522 Friend, go up higher. 14:10

2523 I have married a wife, and therefore I cannot come. 14:20

2524 Wasted his substance with riotous living. 15:13

2525 How hardly shall they that have riches enter into the kingdom of God! 18:24

2526 God be merciful to me a sinner. 18:13

2527 The Son of man is come to seek and to serve that which was lost. 19:10

The Gospel According to St. John

2528 He came unto his own, and his own received him not. 1:11

2529 Can there any good thing come out of Nazareth? 1:46

2530 Men loved darkness rather than light, because their deeds were evil. 3:19

2531 He was a burning and a shining light. 5:35

2532 Judge not according to the appearance. 7:24

2533 The truth shall make you free. 8:32

2534 The night cometh, when no man can work. 9:4

2535 Let not your heart be troubled. 14:1

2536 In my father's house are many mansions. 14:2

2537 I am the way, the truth, and the life. 14:6

2538 Greater love hath no man than this, that a man lay down his life for his friends. 15:13

2539 What I have written I have written. 19:22

2540 Come and dine. 20:12

Acts of the Apostles

2541 Of a truth I perceive that God is no respecter of persons: but in every nation he that feareth him, and worketh righteousness, is accepted with him. 10:34, 35

2542 It is more blessed to give than to receive. 20:35

2543 Much learning doth make thee mad. 26:24

Epistle to the Romans

2544 To be carnally minded is death. 8:6

2545 He that giveth, let him do it with simplicity; he that ruleth, with diligence; he that sheweth mercy, with cheerfulness. 12:8

2546 Abhor that which is evil; cleave to that which is good. 12:9

2547 Mind not high things, but condescend to men of low estate. Be not wise in your own conceits. 12:16

2548 If it be possible, as much as lieth in you, live peaceably with all men. 12:18

2549 Vengeance is mine; I will repay, saith the Lord. 12:19

2550 In so doing thou shalt heap coals of fire on his head. (See Proverbs 25:22) 12:20

2551 Owe no man anything. 13:8

2552 The night is far spent, the day is at hand: let us therefore cast off the works of darkness, and let us put on the armour of light. 13:12

2553 None of us liveth to himself, and no man dieth to himself. 14:7

First Epistle to the Corinthians

2554 Eye hath not seen, nor ear heard, neither have entered into the heart of man, the things which God hath prepared for them that love him. 2:9

2555 The wisdom of this world is foolishness with God. 3:19

2556 Absent in body, but present in spirit. 5:3

2557 A little leaven leaveneth the whole lump. 5:6

2558 The fashion of this world passeth away. 7:31

2559 Knowledge puffeth up, but charity edifieth. 8:1

2560 Let him that thinketh he standeth take heed lest he fall. 10:12

2561 The earth is the Lord's and the fullness thereof. 10:26, 28

2562 Though I bestow all my goods to feed the poor, and though I give my body to be burned, and have not charity, it profiteth me nothing. 13:3

2563　Charity suffereth long, and is kind; charity envieth not; charity vaunteth not itself, is not puffed up, doth not behave itself unseemly, seeketh not her own, is not easily provoked, thinketh no evil; rejoiceth not in iniquity, but rejoiceth in the truth; beareth all things, believeth all things, hopeth all things, endureth all things. 13:4–7

2564　Charity never faileth. 13:8

2565　When I was a child, I spake as a child, I understood as a child, I thought as a child: but when I became a man, I put away childish things. 13:11

2566　And now abideth faith, hope, charity, these three; but the greatest of these is charity. 13:13

2567　Christ died for our sins. 15:3

2568　Be not deceived: Evil company corrupts good morals. 15:33

Second Epistle to the Corinthians

2569　A thorn in the flesh. 12:7

Epistle to the Galatians

2570　Ye are all the children of God by faith in Christ Jesus. 3:26

2571　Whatsoever a man soweth, that shall he also reap. 6:7

2572　Let us not be weary in well-doing: for in due season we shall reap, if we faint not. 6:9

Epistle to the Ephesians

2573　Carried about with every wind of doctrine. 4:14

2574　Let not the sun go down upon your wrath. 4:26

2575　Let no man deceive you with vain words. 5:6

2576　Children, obey your parents in the Lord: for that is right. 6:1

Epistle to the Philippians

2577　For to me to live is Christ, and to die is gain. 1:21

2578　The peace of God, which passeth all understanding. 4:7

2579　Whatsoever things are true, whatsoever things are honest, whatsoever things are just, whatsoever things are pure, whatsoever things are lovely, whatsoever things are of good report; if there be any virtue, and if there be any praise, think on these things. 4:8

2580   I have learned, in whatsoever state I am, therewith to be content. 4:11

2581   I can do all things through Christ which strengthened me. 4:13

Second Epistle to the Thessalonians

2582   Yet count him not as an enemy but admonish him as a brother. 3:15

First Epistle to Timothy

2583   Every creature of God is good. 4:4

2584   Neglect not the gift that is in thee. 4:14

2585   And having food and raiment let us be therewith content. 6:8

2586   For the love of money is the root of all evil. 6:10

2587   Rich in good works. 6:18

Second Epistle to Timothy

2588   I have fought the good fight, I have finished the course, I have kept the faith. 4:7

Epistle to the Hebrews

2589   Faith is the substance of things hoped for, the evidence of things not seen. 11:1

2590   Whom the Lord loveth he chasteneth, and scourgeth every son whom he receiveth. If ye endure chastening, God dealeth with you as with sons; for what son is he whom the father chasteneth not? 12:6, 7

Epistle of James

2591   Let every man be swift to hear, slow to speak, slow to wrath. 1:19

2592   Faith without works is dead. 2:20

2593   For what is your life? It is even a vapour, that appeareth for a little time and then vanisheth away. 4:14

First Epistle of Peter

2594   Love covereth a multitude of sins. 4:8

Second Epistle of Peter

2595   The dog is turned to his own vomit again; and the sow that was washed to her wallowing in the mire. 2:23

First Epistle of John

2596   The world passeth away, and the lust thereof: but he that doeth the will of God abideth forever. 2:17

The Revelation

2597   Be thou faithful unto death, and I will give thee a crown of life. 2:10

2598   I am Alpha and Omega, the beginning and the end, the first and the last. 22:13

14

A RICH TREASURE HOUSE OF SELECTED QUOTATIONS

ABILITY

2599 He is always the severest censor of the merits of others who has the least worth of his own.—*E. L. Magoon*

2600 The winds and waves are always on the side of the ablest navigators.—*Edward Gibbon*

ABUSE

2601 Abuse is the weapon of the vulgar.—*S. G. Goodrich*

ACHIEVEMENT

2602 First say to yourself what you would be; and then do what you have to do.—*Epictetus*

2603

Heaven is not reached at a single bound;
But we build the ladder by which we rise
From the lowly earth to the vaulted skies,
And we mount to its summit round by round.

—*Josiah Gilbert Holland*

2604

Oh may I join the choir invisible
Of those immortal dead who live again
In minds made better by their presence.

—*Marian Evans Cross*

2605   An ill-favoured thing, sir, but mine own.—*Shakespeare*

2606   Finish every day and be done with it. You have done what you could; some blunders and absurdities crept in; forget them as soon as you can. Tomorrow is a new day; you shall begin it well and serenely and with too high a spirit to be encumbered with your old nonsense.—*Ralph Waldo Emerson*

2607   We judge ourselves by what we feel capable of doing; others judge us by what we have done.—*Longfellow*

2608

> Men at some time are masters of their fates:
> The fault, dear Brutus, is not in our stars,
> But in ourselves, that we are underlings.
>
> —*Shakespeare*

2609   Nothing will come of nothing.—*Shakespeare*

2610   No great thing is created suddenly, any more than a bunch of grapes or a fig. If you tell me that you desire a fig, I answer you that there must be time. Let it first blossom, then bear fruit, then ripen.—*Epictetus*

2611   My greatest inspiration is a challenge to attempt the impossible.—*Albert A. Michelson*

2612   "Give me a standing place," said Archimedes, "and I will move the world." Goethe has changed the postulate into the precept. "Make good thy standing place, and move the world."—*S. Smiles*

2613   A brain is known by its fruits.—*H. G. Wells*

ACTION

2614   Awake, arise, or be forever fallen!—*John Milton*

2615   Thought is the seed of action.—*Emerson*

ADMIRATION

2616   Admiration: our polite recognition of another man's resemblance to ourselves.—*Ambrose Bierce*

2617   Admiration is the daughter of ignorance.—*Benjamin Franklin*

ADVERSITY

2618   I'll say this for adversity: people seem to be able to stand it, and that's more than I can say for prosperity.—*Kin Hubbard*

2619   You can bear anything if it isn't your own fault.—*K. F. Gerould*

2620   Happy those who, knowing they are subject to uncertain changes, are prepared and armed for either fortune; a rare principle, and with much labor learned in wisdom's school.—*Massinger*

2621   In this thing one man is superior to another, that he is better able to bear prosperity or adversity.—*Philemon*

2622   Most of our comforts grow up between our crosses.—*Young*

2623   The greater the difficulty, the more glory in surmounting it. Skillful pilots gain their reputation from storms and tempests.—*Epicurus*

2624   Let us be of good cheer, remembering that the misfortunes hardest to bear are those which never come.—*J. R. Lowell*

2625   It has done me good to be somewhat parched by the heat and drenched by the rain of life.—*Longfellow*

2626   Adversity has the effect of eliciting talents which in prosperous circumstances would have lain dormant.—*Horace*

ADVICE

2627   A bad cold wouldn't be so annoying if it weren't for the advice of our friends.—*Kin Hubbard*

2628   A good scare is worth more to a man than good advice.—*Edgar Watson Howe*

AGE

2629   When one finds company in himself and his pursuits, he cannot feel old, no matter what his years may be.—*A. B. Alcott*

2630   Age will not be defied.—*Francis Bacon*

2631   Men of age object too much, consult too long, adventure too little, repent too soon.—*Francis Bacon*

2632   It is not by the gray of the hair that one knows the age of the heart.—*Sir Henry Bulwer*

2633   It is usual to associate age with years only because so many men and women somewhere along in what is called middle age stop trying.— *Henry Ford*

2634   A poor, infirm, weak, and despised old man.—*Shakespeare*

2635   The ripest fruit first falls.—*Shakespeare*

2636   Crabbed age and youth cannot live together.—*Shakespeare*

2637   Nobody loves life like an old man.—*Sophocles*

2638   We hope to grow old, yet we fear old age; that is, we are willing to live, and afraid to die.—*LaBruyere*

2639

> Age is a quality of mind;
> If you've left your
> Dreams behind,
> If hope is cold,
> If you no longer look ahead
> If your ambitious fires
> Are dead,
> Then, you are old!

AMBITION

2640 Every man is said to have his peculiar ambition. . . . I have no other so great as that of being truly esteemed by my fellow-men, by rendering myself worthy of their esteem.—*Lincoln*

2641 Most people would succeed in small things if they were not troubled by great ambitions.—*Longfellow*

2642 Hitch your wagon to a star.—*Emerson*

2643 When that the poor have cried, Caesar hath wept: Ambition should be made of sterner stuff.—*Shakespeare*

AMERICA

2644 There is nothing wrong with America that the faith, love of freedom, intelligence, and energy of her citizens cannot cure.—*Dwight D. Eisenhower*

2645 We've got our problems, I know, but it's my strong conviction that there's a lot more good about America than there is wrong.—*Gerald Ford*

2646 America is a willingness of the heart.—*F. Scott Fitzgerald*

2647 Our greatness is built upon our freedom—is moral, not material. We have a great ardor for gain; but we have a deep passion for the rights of man.—*Woodrow Wilson*

ANCESTORS

2648 Every man is an omnibus in which his ancestors ride.—*O. W. Holmes*

ANTICIPATION

2649 Nothing is so good as it seems beforehand.—*George Eliot*

2650 Uncertainty and expectation are the joys of life. Security is an insipid thing, though the overtaking and possessing of a wish discovers the folly of the chase.—*William Congreve*

APPETITE

2651   Any young man with good health and a poor appetite can save up money.—*J. M. Bailey*

APPRECIATION

2652   Next to excellence is the appreciation of it.—*William M. Thackeray*

2653   I have yet to find the man, however exalted his station, who did not do better work and put forth greater effort under a spirit of approval than under a spirit of criticism.—*Charles Schwab*

ART

2654   Real art is illumination. . . . It adds stature to life.—*Brooks Atkinson*

2655   In art the hand can never execute anything higher than the heart can inspire.—*Emerson*

BABY

2656   Here we have a baby. It is composed of a bald head and a pair of lungs.—*Eugene Field*

BEAUTY

2657   A thing of beauty is a joy for ever.—*John Keats*

2658   In all ranks of life the human heart yearns for the beautiful; and the beautiful things that God makes are his gift to all alike.—*Harriet Beecher Stowe*

2659   Unless we find beauty and happiness in our backyard, we will never find them in the mountains.

BIBLE

2660   I call the Book of Job, apart from all theories about it, one of the grandest things ever written with pen.—*Thomas Carlyle*

2661   The Bible is a window in this prison-world, through which we may look into eternity.—*Timothy Dwight*

2662   The English Bible—a book which, if everything else in our language should perish, would alone suffice to show the whole extent of its beauty and power.—*Thomas B. Macaulay*

BIOGRAPHY

2663   Biography is the only true history.—*Carlyle*

2664   Every great man nowadays has his disciples, and it is always Judas who writes the biography.—*Oscar Wilde*

BOOKS

2665   All that Mankind has done, thought, gained or been: it is lying as in magic preservation in the pages of books. They are the chosen possession of men.—*Carlyle*

2666   Everywhere I have sought rest and found it not except sitting apart in a nook with a little book.—*Thomas à Kempis*

2667   As good almost kill a man as kill a good book: who kills a man kills a reasonable creature, God's image; but he who destroys a good book kills reason itself, kills the image of God, as it were, in the eye.—*Milton*

BORE

2668   The secret of boring people lies in telling them everything.—*Anton Chekhov*

2669

> He says a thousand pleasant things,
> But never says "Adieu."
>
> —*J. G. Saxe*

BREVITY

2670   This is the short and the long of it.—*Shakespeare*

BRIBERY

2671   Few men have virtue to withstand the highest bidder.—*George Washington*

BUSINESS

2672   We demand that big business give people a square deal; in return we must insist that when anyone engaged in big business honestly endeavors to do right, he shall himself be given a square deal.—*Theodore Roosevelt*

2673   The greatest meliorator of the world is selfish, huckstering trade.—*Emerson*

2674   To my mind the best investment a young man starting out in business could possibly make is to give all his time, all his energies to work, just plain, hard work.—*C. M. Schwab*

CAUTION

2675   Little boats should keep near shore.—*Franklin*

2676   Caution is the eldest child of wisdom.—*Victor Hugo*

CHANGE

2677

> The world goes up and the world goes down,
> And the sunshine follows the rain;
> And yesterday's sneer and yesterday's frown
> Can never come over again.

> *—Charles Kingsley*

CHARACTER

2678 The end of a dissolute life is, most commonly, a desperate death. *—Bion*

2679 It is hardly respectable to be good nowadays.*—Edith Sitwell*

2680 We boil at different degrees.*—Emerson*

2681 Condemn the fault, and not the actor of it?*—Shakespeare*

2682 Make it thy business to know thyself, which is the most difficult lesson in the world.*—Cervantes*

2683 Be such a man, and live such a life, that if every man were such as you, and every life a life like yours, this earth would be God's Paradise.*—Phillips Brooks*

2684 I would to God thou and I knew where a commodity of good names were to be bought.*—Shakespeare*

2685 Smooth runs the water where the brook is deep.*—Shakespeare*

2686 To reform a man, you must begin with his grandmother.*—Victor Hugo*

2687 What the heart has once owned and had, it shall never lose.*—H. W. Beecher*

2688 The holiest of all holidays are those kept by ourselves in silence and apart, the secret anniversaries of the heart, when the full tide of feeling overflows.*—Longfellow*

2689 Envy's memory is nothing but a row of hooks to hang up grudges on. Some people's sensibility is a mere bundle of aversions; and you hear them display and parade it, not in recounting the things they are attached to, but in telling you how many things and persons "they cannot bear."*—John Foster*

2690 The hardest trial of the heart is, whether it can bear a rival's failure without triumph.*—Aikin*

2691

Our deeds still travel with us from afar,
And what we have been makes us what we are.

—*George Eliot*

2692   Secret, and self-contained, and solitary as an oyster.—*Charles Dickens*

2693   Be and continue poor, young man, while others around you grow rich by fraud and disloyalty; be without place or power, while others beg their way upward; bear the pain of disappointed hopes, while others gain the accomplishment of theirs by flattery; forego the gracious pressure of the hand for which others cringe and crawl. Wrap yourself in your own virtue, and seek a friend and your daily bread. If you have in such a course grown gray with unblenched honor, bless God, and die.—*Heinzelmann*

2694   Talents are best nurtured in solitude; character is best formed in the stormy billows of the world.—*Goethe*

2695   Our character is but the stamp on our souls of the free choices of good and evil we have made through life.—*Geikie*

2696   In the destiny of every moral being there is an object more worthy of God than happiness. It is character. And the grand aim of man's creation is the development of a grand character—and grand character is, by its very nature, the product of probationary discipline.—*Austin Phelps*

2697   Leaves seem light, useless, idle, wavering and changeable—they even dance; yet God has made them part of the oak. So he has given us a lesson, not to deny stout-heartedness within, because we see lightsomeness without.—*Leigh Hunt*

CHARITY
2698   My poor are my best patients. God pays for them.—*Boerhaave*

2699   He who waits to do a great deal of good at once, will never do anything.—*Samuel Johnson*

CHILDREN
2700   Children are the anchors that hold a mother to life.—*Sophocles*

2701   How sharper than a serpent's tooth it is to have a thankless child!—*Shakespeare*

2702 If I could get to the highest place in Athens, I would lift up my voice and say: "What mean ye, fellow citizens, that ye turn every stone to scrape wealth together, and take so little care of your children, to whom ye must one day relinquish all?"—*Socrates*

2703 Childhood has no forebodings; but then it is soothed by no memories of outlived sorrow.—*George Eliot*

2704 The first duty to children is to make them happy. If you have not made them so, you have wronged them. No other good they may get can make up for that.—*C. Buxton*

2705 What's done to children, they will do to society.—*Karl Menninger*

2706

> We have the nicest garbage man,
> He empties out our garbage can;
> He's just as nice as he can be
> He always stops and talks with me,
> My mother doesn't like his smell,
> But then, she doesn't know him well.
>
> —*From Sermons and Prayers of*
> *Peter Marshall*

CHOICE

2707 There's small choice in rotten apples.—*Shakespeare*

2708 The question is this: Is man an ape or an angel? I, my lord, I am on the side of the angels.—*Disraeli*

CHRIST

2709 If the life and death of Socrates were those of a sage, the life and death of Jesus were those of a God.—*J. J. Rousseau*

CIVILIZATION

2710 3 Fish: "Master, I marvel how the fishes live in the sea."
1 Fish: "Why, as men do a-land: the great ones eat up the little ones."
—*Shakespeare*

2711 Better fifty years of Europe than a cycle of Cathay.—*Tennyson*

2712

> Yet I doubt not through the ages one increasing purpose runs,
> And the thoughts of men are widened with the process of the suns.
>
> —*Tennyson*

2713   The history of the world is the record of man in quest of his daily bread and butter.—*Hendrik Willem Van Loon*

2714   A conviction that what is called fashionable life was compound of frivolity, of fraud and vice.—*Disraeli*

2715   Ring in the nobler modes of life with sweeter manners, purer laws.—*Tennyson*

2716

> Ring out old shapes of foul disease,
> Ring out the narrowing lust of gold;
> Ring out the thouand wars of old,
> Ring in the thousand years of peace!
>
> —*Tennyson*

2717   The true test of civilization is, not the census, nor the size of cities, nor the crops—no, but the kind of man the country turns out. —*Emerson*

2718   No true civilization can be expected permanently to continue which is not based on the great principles of Christianity.—*Tryon Edwards*

CLOTHES

2719   Good clothes open all doors.—*Thomas Fuller*

2720   She wears her clothes as if they were thrown on her with a pitch-fork.—*Jonathan Swift*

COMMON SENSE

2721   Good health and good sense are two of life's greatest blessings.— *Publius Syrus*

2722   Common sense does not ask an impossible chessboard, but takes the one before it and plays the game.—*Wendell Phillips*

COMMUNISM

2723   The theory of Communism may be summed up in one sentence: Abolish all private property.—*Karl Marx and Friedrich Engels*

2724   Communism is the exploitation of the strong by the weak. In Communism, inequality springs from placing mediocrity on a level with excellence.—*Proudhon*

CONCEIT

2725   He who is always his own counsellor will often have a fool for a client.—*Hunter*

2726   He was like a cock who thought the sun had risen to hear him crow.—*George Eliot*

2727   I am not in the roll of common men.—*Shakespeare*

2728   An egotist is a man who talks so much about himself that he gives me no time to talk about myself.—*H. L. Wayland*

2729   Conceit in weakest bodies strongest works.—*Shakespeare*

2730   Truly, this world can get on without us, if we would but think so.—*Longfellow*

CONDUCT

2731   We are growing serious, and, let me tell you, that's the very next step to being dull.—*Addison*

2732   Sometimes we may learn more from a man's errors, than from his virtues.—*Longfellow*

2733   It is not enough that you form, and even follow the most excellent rules for conducting yourself in the world; you must, also, know when to deviate from them, and where lies the exception.—*Greville*

2734   A bone to the dog is not charity. Charity is the bone shared with the dog, when you are just as hungry as the dog.—*Jack London*

CONQUEST

2735   I came, I saw, I conquered.—*Julius Caesar*

2736   Self-conquest is the greatest of victories.—*Plato*

CONSCIENCE

2737   A guilty conscience never feels secure.—*Publius Syrus*

2738   Guilty consciences always make people cowards.—*Pilpay*

2739   A peace above all earthly dignities, a still and quiet conscience.—*Shakespeare*

2740   Conscience is merely your own judgment of the right or wrong of our actions, and so can never be a safe guide unless enlightened by the word of God.—*Tryon Edwards*

2741   There is no class of men so difficult to be managed in a state as those whose intentions are honest, but whose consciences are bewitched.—*Napoleon I*

2742   It is astonishing how soon the whole conscience begins to unravel if a single stitch drops. One single sin indulged in makes a hole you could put your head through.—*C. Buxton*

CONSERVATISM

2743   A Conservative is a statesman who is enamored of existing evils, as distinguished from the Liberal, who wishes to replace them with others.—*Ambrose Bierce*

CONTENTMENT

2744   Poor and content is rich and rich enough.—*Shakespeare*

2745   The despotism of custom is on the wane. We are not content to know that things are; we ask whether they ought to be.—*J. S. Mill*

2746   One should be either sad or joyful. Contentment is a warm sty for eaters and sleepers.—*Eugene O'Neill*

2747   Since we cannot get what we like, let us like what we can get.—*Spanish proverb*

CONVERSATION

2748   Let thy speech be better than silence, or be silent.—*Dionysius the Elder*

2749   Gratiano speaks an infinite deal of nothing; his reasons are as two grains of wheat hid in two bushels of chaff; you shall seek all day ere you find them, and when you have them they are not worth the search.—*Shakespeare*

2750   Know how to listen, and you will profit even from those who talk badly.—*Plutarch*

2751   Men of few words are the best men.—*Shakespeare*

2752   Language is the dress of thought.—*Samuel Johnson*

2753

> And when you stick on conversation's burrs,
> Don't strew your pathway with those dreadful urs.
>
>   —*Oliver Wendell Holmes*

2754   A kind of excellent dumb discourse.—*Shakespeare*

COURAGE

2755   We should do by our cunning as we do by our courage, always have it ready to defend ourselves, never to offend others.—*Greville*

2756   Cowards do not count in battle; they are there, but not in it.—*Euripides*

2757   Courage is grace under pressure.—*Ernest Hemingway*

2758 No man is worth his salt who is not ready at all times to risk his body . . . to risk his well-being . . . to risk his life . . . in a great cause. —*T. Roosevelt*

2759 For courage mounteth with occasion.—*Shakespeare*

2760 The better part of valour is discretion.—*Shakespeare*

2761 I will utter what I believe today, if it should contradict all I said yesterday.—*Wendell Phillips*

2762 No man can answer for his own valor or courage, till he has been in danger.—*LaRochefoucauld*

2763 The brave man is not he who feels no fear, for that were stupid and irrational; but he whose noble soul subdues its fear, and bravely dares the danger nature shrinks from.—*Joanna Baillie*

2764 At the bottom of a good deal of the bravery that appears in the world there lurks a miserable cowardice. Men will face powder and steel because they cannot face public opinion.—*E. H. Chapin*

CREATIVITY

2765 Originality is nothing but judicious imitation. The most original writers borrowed one from another. The instruction we find in books is like fire. We fetch it from our neighbor's, kindle it at home, communicate it to others, and it becomes the property of all.—*Voltaire*

2766 It is better to create than to be learned; creating is the true essence of life.—*Niebuhr*

2767 If you would create something, you must be something.—*Goethe*

CRIME

2768 Punishment is lame, but it comes.—*Herbert*

2769 Those who are themselves incapable of great crimes, are ever backward to suspect others.—*LaRochefoucauld*

2770 The devil knoweth his own, and is a particularly bad paymaster. —*F. M. Crawford*

2771 The consequences of our crimes long survive their commission, and, like the ghosts of the murdered, forever haunt the steps of the malefactor.—*Sir Walter Scott*

2772

Nor florid prose, nor honied lines of rhyme,
Can blazon evil deeds, or consecrate a crime.

—*Byron*

CRITICISM

2773   Sarcasm is the language of the devil; for which reason I have long since as good as renounced it.—*Carlyle*

2774   The pleasure of criticism takes from us that of being deeply moved by very beautiful things.—*LaBruyere*

2775   If we had no failings ourselves, we should not take so much pleasure in finding out those of others.—*LaRochefoucauld*

2776   There is an unfortunate disposition in man to attend much more to the faults of his companions that offend him, than to their perfections which please him.—*Greville*

2777   Endeavor to be always patient of the faults and imperfections of others; for thou hast many faults and imperfections of thine own that require forebearance. If thou are not able to make thyself that which thou wishest, how canst thou expect to mold another in conformity to thy will?—*Thomas à Kempis*

2778   For I am nothing, if not critical.—*Shakespeare*

2779   Those who have free seats at the play hiss first.—*Chinese proverb*

CURIOSITY

2780   Where necessity ends, desire and curiosity begin; no sooner are we supplied with everything nature can demand, than we sit down to contrive artificial appetites.—*Samuel Johnson*

DEATH

2781   Out of the jaws of death.—*Shakespeare*

2782   He that dies pays all debts.—*Shakespeare*

2783   When death, the great reconciler, has come, it is never our tenderness that we repent of, but our severity.—*George Eliot*

2784   Let's talk of graves, of worms, and epitaphs.—*Shakespeare*

2785   Did any man at his death, ever regret his conflicts with himself, his victories over appetite, his scorn of impure pleasure, or his sufferings for righteousness' sake?—*W. E. Channing*

2786

But oh for the touch of a vanished hand,
And the sound of a voice that is still!

—Tennyson

2787   Each in his narrow cell forever laid, the rude forefathers of the hamlet sleep.—*Thomas Gray*

2788   Cowards die many times before their deaths; the valiant never taste of death but once.—*Shakespeare*

2789   Dear as remembered kisses after death.—*Tennyson*

2790   Vicissitude of fortune, which spares neither man nor the proudest of his works, but buries empires and cities in a common grave.—*Gibbon*

2791   Why fear death? It is the most beautiful adventure in life.—*Charles Frohman*

2792   Man wants but little, nor that little long. How soon must he resign his very dust, which frugal nature lent him for an hour.—*Young*

2793   The boast of heraldry, the pomp of pow'r, and all that beauty, all that wealth e'er gave, await like the inevitable hour; the paths of glory lead but to the grave.—*Gray*

2794   In every parting, there is an image of death.—*George Eliot*

2795   Who knows but life be that which men call death, and death what men call life?—*Euripides*

2796   I know of but one remedy against the fear of death that is effectual and that will stand the test either of a sick-bed or of a sound mind—that is, a good life, a clear conscience, an honest heart, and a well-ordered conversation; to carry the thoughts of dying men about us, and so to live before we die as we shall wish we had when we come to it.—*Norris*

2797   Death has nothing terrible which life has not made so. A faithful Christian life in this world is the best preparation for the next.—*Tryon Edwards*

2798   A dislike of death is no proof of the want of religion. The instincts of nature shrink from it, for no creature can like its own dissolution. But though death is not desired, the result of it may be, for dying to the Christian is the way to life eternal.—*W. Jay*

2799   Time for him had merged itself into eternity; he was, as we say, no more.—*Thomas Carlyle*

2800   The grave buries every error, covers every defect, extinguishes every resentment. From its peaceful bosom spring none but fond regrets and tender recollections. Who can look down upon the grave of an enemy, and not feel a compunctious throb that he should have warred with the poor handful of dust that lies moldering before him. —*Washington Irving*

DECEPTION

2801   Half the work that is done in the world is to make things appear what they are not.—*E. R. Beadle*

2802   The very essence of assumed gravity is design, and consequently deceit; a taught trick to gain credit with the world for more sense and knowledge than a man is worth.—*Laurence Sterne*

2803   The cunning livery of hell.—*Shakespeare*

2804   It is a shameful and unseemingly thing to think one thing and speak another, but how odious to write one thing and think another.—*Seneca*

2805   It goes far toward making a man faithful to let him understand that you think him so; and he that does but suspect I will deceive him, gives me a sort of right to do it.—*Seneca*

DECISION

2806   Decision of character will often give to an inferior mind command over a superior.—*W. Wirt*

2807   Tomorrow I will live, the fool does say: today itself's too late; the wise lived yesterday.—*Martial*

DEEDS

2808   We have left undone those things which we ought to have done; and we have done those things which we ought not to have done.—*Book of Common Prayer*

DEFEAT

2809   What is defeat? Nothing but education, nothing but the first step to something better.—*Wendell Phillips*

DESIRE

2810   Our desires always increase with our possessions. The knowledge that something remains yet unenjoyed impairs our enjoyment of the good before us.—*Samuel Johnson*

DETERMINATION

2811   I'll not budge an inch.—*Shakespeare*

2812   The best lightning-rod for your protection is your own spine.—*Emerson*

2813   Man has his will, but woman has her way.—*O. W. Holmes*

2814   He who is firm and resolute in will moulds the world to himself.—*Goethe*

2815   Either I will find a way, or I will make one.—*Sir Philip Sidney*

2816   The truest wisdom, in general, is a resolute determination.—*Napoleon I*

2817 Toil, feel, think, hope; you will be sure to dream enough before you die, without arranging for it.—*J. Sterling*

DOING

2818 Do not then be afraid of defeat. You are never so near to victory as when defeated in a good cause.—*H. W. Beecher*

2819 None are so busy as the fool and knave.—*John Dryden*

2820 If to do were as easy as to know what were good to do, chapels had been churches, and poor men's cottages princes' palaces.—*Shakespeare*

2821 Our grand business is not to see what lies dimly in the distance, but to do what lies clearly at hand.—*Carlyle*

2822 Doing is the great thing. For if resolutely people do what is right, in time they come to like doing it.—*Ruskin*

DOUBT

2823

Our doubts are traitors
And make us lose the good we oft might win
By fearing to attempt.

—*Shakespeare*

DUTY

2824 He on whom Heaven confers a sceptre knows not the weight till he bears it.—*Corneille*

2825 I do perceive here a divided duty.—*Shakespeare*

2826 Every duty which we omit, obscures some truth which we should have known.—*Ruskin*

2827 We live in a world which is full of misery and ignorance, and the plain duty of each and all of us is to try to make the little corner he can influence somewhat less miserable and somewhat less ignorant than it was before he entered it.—*Huxley*

2828 An ambassador is an honest man sent to lie and intrigue abroad for the benefit of his country.—*Sir H. Wotton*

2829

Not once or twice in our rough-island story
The path of duty was the way to glory.

—*Tennyson*

EARNESTNESS

2830   Earnestness is the salt of eloquence.—*V. Hugo*

2831   Earnestness is enthusiasm tempered by reason.—*Pascal*

ECONOMY

2832   Socrates said, "Those who want fewest things are nearest to the gods."—*Diogenes Laertius*

2833   He seldom lives frugally who lives by chance. Hope is always liberal, and they that trust her promises make little scruple of reveling today on the profits of tomorrow.—*Samuel Johnson*

2834   A sound economy is a sound understanding brought into action. It is calculation realized; it is the doctrine of proportion reduced to practice; it is foreseeing contingencies and providing against them; it is expecting contingencies and being prepared for them.—*Hannah More*

2835   Nothing is cheap which is superfluous, for what one does not need is dear at a penny.—*Plutarch*

2836   There are but two ways of paying a debt; increase of industry in raising income, or increase of thrift in laying out.—*Carlyle*

EDUCATION

2837   There is a time in every man's education when he arrives at the conviction that envy is ignorance; that imitation is suicide; that he must take himself for better, for worse, as his portion; that though the wide universe is full of good, no kernel of nourishing corn comes to him but through his toil bestowed on that plot of ground which is given him to till. The power which resides in him is new in nature, and none but he knows what that is which he can do, nor does he know until he has tried.—*Emerson*

2838   Human history becomes more and more a race between education and catastrophe.—*H. G. Wells*

2839   The great end of education is, to discipline rather than to furnish the mind; to train it to the use of its own powers, rather than fill it with the accumulations of others.—*Tryon Edwards*

2840   He is to be educated not because he is to make shoes, nails, and pins, but because he is a man.—*Channing*

2841   Culture is "To know the best that has been said and thought in the world."—*Matthew Arnold*

2842   A mixture of misery and education is highly explosive.—*Herbert Samuel*

2843   Out of monuments, names, words, proverbs, traditions, private records and evidences, fragments of stories, passages of books and the like, we do save and recover somewhat from the deluge of time.—*Bacon*

2844   The real object of education is to give children resources that will endure as long as life endures; habits that time will ameliorate, not destroy; occupations that will render sickness tolerable, solitude pleasant, age venerable, life more dignified and useful, and death less terrible.—*Sydney Smith*

2845   All who have meditated on the art of governing mankind have been convinced that the fate of empires depends on the education of youth.—*Aristotle*

2846   I consider the human soul without education like marble in a quarry, which shows none of its inherent beauties until the skill of the polisher fetches out the colors and makes the surface shine.—*Joseph Addison*

2847   Education makes people easy to lead, but difficult to drive; easy to govern, but impossible to enslave.—*Lord Brougham*

2848   "What! He is now going to try to teach me!" Why not? There is nobody from whom you cannot learn. Before God, who speaks through all men, you are always in the bottom class of nursery school.—*Dag Hammarskjold*

2849   Personally I'm always ready to learn, although I do not always like being taught.—*Winston Churchill*

ELOQUENCE
2850   Eloquence is the child of knowledge.—*Disraeli*

2851   The manner of speaking is full as important as the matter, as more people have ears to be tickled than understandings to judge.—*Chesterfield*

ENEMY
2852   Observe thyself as thy greatest enemy would do, so shalt thou be thy greatest friend.—*Jeremy Taylor*

2853   He makes no friend who never made a foe.—*Tennyson*

2854   If we could read the secret history of our enemies, we should find in each man's life sorrow and suffering enough to disarm all hostility.—*Longfellow*

2855   It is much safer to reconcile an enemy than to conquer him; victory may deprive him of his poison, but reconciliation of his will.—*Feltham*

2856   However rich or powerful a man may be, it is the height of folly to make personal enemies; for one unguarded moment may yield you to the revenge of the most despicable of mankind.—*Lyttleton*

2857   If you want enemies, excel others; if friends, let others excel you.—*Colton*

ENTHUSIASM

2858   Violent zeal even for truth has a hundred to one odds to be either petulancy, ambition, or pride.—*Swift*

2859   Every production of genius must be the production of enthusiasm.—*Disraeli*

2860   Every man is enthusiastic at times. One man has enthusiasm for thirty minutes—another man has it for thirty days, but it is the man who has it for thirty years who makes a success in life.—*Edward B. Butler*

EQUALITY

2861   There is nothing that so strikes men with fear as the saying that they are all the sons of God.—*G. K. Chesterton*

2862   As men, we are all equal in the presence of death.—*Publius Syrus*

ERROR

2863   When every one is in the wrong, every one is in the right.—*LaChaussee*

2864   The man who makes no mistakes does not usually make anything.—*Edward J. Phelps*

EVIL

2865   He will give the devil his due.—*Shakespeare*

2866   The devil can cite Scripture for his purpose.—*Shakespeare*

2867   The world is grown so bad, that wrens make prey where eagles dare not perch.—*Shakespeare*

2868   All the perfumes of Arabia will not sweeten this little hand.—*Shakespeare*

2869   There is some soul of goodness in things evil, would men observingly distil it out.—*Shakespeare*

2870   There is this good in real evils, they deliver us, while they last, from the petty despotism of all that were imaginary.—*Colton*

EXAMPLE

2871   I am a part of all that I have met.—*Tennyson*

2872   My advice is, to consult the lives of other men as we would a looking-glass, and from thence fetch examples for our own imitation.—*Terence*

2873   If you would convince a man that he does wrong, do right. Men will believe what they see. Let them see.—*Thoreau*

2874   Man is an imitative creature, and whoever is foremost leads the herd.—*Schiller*

2875   People seldom improve when they have no other model but themselves to copy after.—*Goldsmith*

2876   No man was ever great by imitation.—*Samuel Johnson*

2977   No man is so insignificant as to be sure his example can do no hurt.—*Lord Clarendon*

2878   We are all of us more or less echoes, repeating involuntarily the virtues, the defects, the movements, and the characters of those among whom we live.—*Joubert*

EXPERIENCE

2879   I had rather have a fool to make me merry than experience to make me sad.—*Shakespeare*

2880   I know the past, and thence will assay to glean a warning for the future, so that man may profit by his errors, and derive experience from his folly.—*Shelley*

2881   There is no merit where there is no trial; and till experience stamps the mark of strength, cowards may pass for heroes, and faith for falsehood.—*A. Hill*

2882   No man was ever endowed with a judgment so correct and judicious, but that circumstances, time, and experience would teach him something new, and apprise him that of those things with which he thought himself the best acquainted, he knew nothing; and that those ideas which in theory appeared the most advantageous were found, when brought into practice, to be altogether impracticable.—*Terence*

EYES

2883   Eyes will not see when the heart wishes them to be blind. Desire conceals truth, as darkness does the earth.—*Seneca*

FAITH

2884   For they conquer who believe they can.—*Virgil*

2885

> Howe'er it be, it seems to me,
> 'Tis only noble to be good,
> Kind hearts are more than coronets,
> And simple faith than Norman blood.
>
> —*Tennyson*

2886   Here I stand; I can do no otherwise. God help me. Amen!—*Martin Luther*

2887   It is cynicism and fear that freeze life; it is faith that thaws it out, releases it, sets it free.—*Harry Emerson Fosdick*

2888   Fanatic faith, once wedded fast to some dear falsehood, hugs it to the last.—*Moore*

2889   Goodness thinks no ill where no ill seems.—*Milton*

2890   Strike from mankind the principle of faith, and men would have no more history than a flock of sheep.—*Bulwer*

2891   All the scholastic scaffolding falls, as a ruined edifice, before one single word—faith.—*Napoleon I*

2892   Faith in order, which is the basis of science, cannot reasonably be separated from faith in an ordainer, which is the basis of religion.—*Asa Gray*

FALSEHOOD

2893   A lie never lives to be old.—*Sophocles*

2894   Lie not, neither to thyself, nor man, nor God. It is for cowards to lie.—*Herbert*

2895   The practice of politics in the East may be defined by one word—dissimulation.—*Disraeli*

2896   The most terrible of lies is not that which is uttered but that which is lived.—*W. G. Clarke*

2897   Never chase a lie; if you let it alone, it will soon run itself to death. You can work out a good character faster than calumny can destroy it.—*E. Nott*

2898   A liar should have a good memory.—*Quintilian*

FAME

2899   Toil, says the proverb, is the sire of fame.—*Euripides*

2900   Those who despise fame seldom deserve it. We are apt to undervalue the purchase we cannot reach, to conceal our poverty the better. It is a spark that kindles upon the best fuel, and burns brightest in the bravest breast.—*Jeremy Collier*

2901   To judge of the real importance of an individual, we should think of the effect his death would produce.—*Levis*

2902   How men long for celebrity! Some would willingly sacrifice their lives for fame, and not a few would rather be known by their crimes than not known at all.—*Sinclair*

2903   Our admiration of a famous man lessens upon our nearer acquaintance with him; and we seldom hear of a celebrated person without a catalogue of some of his weaknesses and infirmities.—*Addison*

FAMILY

2904   Who serves his country well has no need of ancestors.—*F. Voltaire*

2905   As are families, so is society. If well ordered, well instructed, and well governed, they are the springs from which go forth the streams of national greatness and prosperity—of civil order and public happiness.—*Thayer*

2906   It is a wise father that knows his own child.—*Shakespeare*

2907   A man cannot leave a better legacy to the world than a well-educated family.—*Thomas Scott*

2908   It is indeed a desirable thing to be well descended, but the glory belongs to our ancestors.—*Plutarch*

2909   Every man is his own ancestor, and every man is his own heir. He devises his own future; and he inherits his own past.—*H. F. Hedge*

2910   Mere family never made a man great. Thought and deed, not pedigree, are the passports to enduring fame.—*Skobeleff*

FARMING

2911   Those who labor in the earth are the chosen people of God, if He ever had a chosen people, whose breasts He has made His peculiar deposit for substantial and genuine virtue.—*Jefferson*

2912   A farmer is always going to be rich next year.—*Philemon*

FASHION

2913   Fashion is that by which the fantastic becomes for a moment the universal.—*Oscar Wilde*

FAULT

2914   When a man is wrong and won't admit it, he always gets angry.—
Haliburton

2915   The absent are never without fault, nor the present without excuse.—*Franklin*

2916   Men do not suspect faults which they do not commit.—*Samuel
Johnson*

2917

> But friend, to me
> He is all fault who hath no fault at all.
> For who loves me must have a touch of earth.
>
> —*Tennyson*

FEAR

2918   No one loves the man whom he fears.—*Aristotle*

2919   One of the greatest artifices the devil uses to engage men in vice
and debauchery is to fasten names of contempt on certain virtues, and
thus fill weak souls with a foolish fear of passing for scrupulous, should
they desire to put them in practice.—*Blaise Pascal*

2920   The two great movers of the human mind are the desire of good,
and the fear of evil.—*Samuel Johnson*

2921

> They are slaves who fear to speak
> For the fallen and the weak.
>
> —*J. R. Lowell*

2922

> They are slaves who dare not be
> In the right with two or three.
>
> —*J. R. Lowell*

FLAG

2923   Let it rise! let it rise, till it meet the sun in his coming: let the
earliest light of the morning gild it, and the parting day linger and play
on its summit.—*Daniel Webster*

FLATTERY

2924   If we would not flatter ourselves, the flattery of others could not
harm us.—*LaRochefoucauld*

2925 When our vices quit us, we flatter ourselves with the belief that it is we who quit them.—*LaRochefoucauld*

FLOWERS

2926 Flowers have an expression of countenance as much as men or animals. Some seem to smile; some have a sad expression; some are pensive and diffident; others again are plain, honest and upright, like the broad-faced sunflower and the hollyhock.—*H. W. Beecher*

FOOD

2927 He hath eaten me out of house and home.—*Shakespeare*

2928 One meal a day is enough for a lion, and it ought to be for a man.—*G. Fordyce*

2929 They are as sick that surfeit with too much, as they that starve with nothing.—*Shakespeare*

FOOLS

2930 However big the fool, there is always a bigger fool to admire him.—*Nicholas Boileau*

2931 As if anything were so common as ignorance! The multitude of fools is a protection to the wise.—*Cicero*

2932 Fortune, to show us her power, and abate our presumption, seeing she could not make fools wise, has made them fortunate.—*Montaigne*

2933 Ridicule is the first and last argument of fools.—*C. Simmons*

2934 A fool flatters himself; the wise man flatters the fool.—*Bulwer*

2935 In all companies there are more fools than wise men, and the greater part always gets the better of the wiser.—*Rabelais*

2936 A learned fool is more foolish than an ignorant fool.—*Molière*

2937 He who thinks himself wise, O heavens! is a great fool.—*Voltaire*

FORGIVENESS

2938 It is easier for the generous to forgive, than for the offender to ask forgiveness.—*Thomson*

2939 They who forgive most, shall be most forgiven.—*Bailey*

2940 Nothing in this lost and ruined world bears the meek impress of the Son of God so surely as forgiveness.—*Alice Cary*

FORGOTTEN

2941 Who is the Forgotten Man? He is the clean, quiet, virtuous, domestic citizen, who pays his debts and his taxes and is never heard of out of his little circle.—*William Graham Sumner*

FORTUNE

2942 Fortune is not on the side of the faint-hearted.—*Sophocles*

2943 Fortune is like glass, the brighter the glitter, the more easily broken.—*Publius Syrus*

2944

There is a tide in the affairs of men
Which taken at the flood, leads on to fortune:
Omitted, all the voyage of their life
Is bound in shallows and in miseries.

—*Shakespeare*

FRANKNESS

2945 There are few, very few, that will own themselves in a mistake.—*Swift*

2946 I can promise to be candid, though I may not be impartial.—*Goethe*

FREEDOM

2947 The cause of freedom is the cause of God.—*Samuel Bowles*

2948 Personal liberty is the paramount essential to human dignity and human happiness.—*Bulwer-Lytton*

2949 Free enterprise has produced more of everything for everyone than any other way of life known to mankind, any place on earth since the beginning of recorded history. It is the right of an individual to pursue any endeavor so long as he operates in accordance with the laws—local, state and federal—governing such endeavor.—*Roe S. Clark, Marquette Memo*

2950 Our nation was founded as an experiment in human liberty. Its institutions reflect the belief of our founders that men had their origin and destiny in God; that they were endowed by Him with inalienable rights and had duties prescribed by moral law, and that human institutions ought primarily to help men develop their God-given possibilities.—*John Foster Dulles*

2951 The liberty of discussion is the chief safeguard of all other liberties.—*Thomas Babington Macaulay*

FRIENDSHIP
2952 What you dislike in another, take care to correct in yourself.—*Sprat*

2953 Reprove thy friend privately; commend him publicly.—*Solon*

2954 The greatest comfort of my old age, and that which gives me the highest satisfaction, is the pleasing remembrance of the many benefits and friendly offices I have done to others.—*Cato*

2955 We gain nothing by being with such as ourselves: we encourage each other in mediocrity. I am always longing to be with men more excellent than myself.—*Charles Lamb*

2956 If a man does not make new acquaintances as he advances through life, he will soon find himself left alone; one should keep his friendships in constant repair.—*Samuel Johnson*

2957 Thou mayest be sure that he that will in private tell thee of thy faults, is thy friend, for he adventures thy dislike, and doth hazard thy hatred; there are few men that can endure it, every man for the most part delighting in self-praise, which is one of the most universal follies that bewitcheth mankind.—*Sir Walter Raleigh*

2958 We take care of our health, we lay up money, we make our roof tight and our clothing sufficient, but who provides wisely that he shall not be wanting in the best property of all—friends?—*Emerson*

FUTURE
2959 When all else is lost, the future still remains.—*Bovee*

2960 The present is great with the future.—*Leibnitz*

GENIUS
2961 The true genius is a mind of large general powers, accidentally determined to some particular direction.—*Samuel Johnson*

2962 Doing easily what others find difficult is talent; doing what is impossible for talent is genius.—*Henri-Frederic Amiel*

2963 Every man who observes vigilantly, and resolves steadfastly, grows unconsciously into genius.—*Bulwer*

2964 Times of general calamity and confusion have ever been productive of the greatest minds. The purest ore is produced from the hottest furnace, and the brightest thunderbolt is elicited from the darkest storm.—*Colton*

2965   Men give me some credit for genius. All the genius I have lies in this: when I have a subject in hand, I study it profoundly. Day and night it is before me. I explore it in all its bearings. My mind becomes pervaded with it. Then the effort which I make the people are pleased to call the fruit of genius. It is the fruit of labor and thought.—*Alexander Hamilton*

2966   There is no great genius without tincture of madness.—*Seneca*

GENTLEMEN

2967   Men of courage, men of sense, and men of letters are frequent: but a true gentleman is what one seldom sees.—*Steele*

2968   Good-breeding shows itself most, where to an ordinary eye it appears the least.—*Addison*

2969   One of the marks of a gentleman is his refusal to make an issue out of every difference of opinion.—*Arnold H. Glasow*

GIVING
2970

> There was a man, though some did count him mad,
> The more he cast away the more he had.
>
> —*John Bunyan*

2971   Shall we call ourselves benevolent, when the gifts we bestow do not cost us a single privation?—*Degerando*

2972   He who is not liberal with what he has, does not deceive himself when he thinks he would be liberal if he had more.—*W. S. Plumer*

GOD
2973

> A mighty fortress is our God,
> A bulwark never failing;
> Our helper He amid the flood
> Of mortal ills prevailing.
>
> —*Martin Luther*

2974   That is best which God sends; it was his will; it is mine.—*O. Meredith*

2975   The world is God's epistle to mankind—his thoughts are flashing upon us from every directions.—*Plato*

2976   God tempers the wind to the shorn lamb.—*Sterne*

2977   Gawd knows, an' 'E won't split on a pal.—*Rudyard Kipling*

2978   Anything that makes religion a second object makes it no object. He who offers to God a second place offers him no place.—*Ruskin*

2979   How often we look upon God as our last and feeblest resource! We go to Him because we have nowhere else to go. And then we learn that the storms of life have driven us, not upon the rocks, but into the desired haven.—*George Macdonald*

2980   Two men please God—who serves Him with all his heart because he knows Him; who seeks Him with all his heart because he knows Him not.—*Panin*

2981   Of all men these are the most odd—they who say there is no God! Have they asked the evening sky what hand placed the stars on high? Not alone at time of prayer, God is present everywhere.—*W. J. Thompson*

GOSSIP

2982   We cannot control the evil tongues of others; but a good life enables us to disregard them.—*Cato*

2983   Done to death by slanderous tongues.—*Shakespeare*

2984

> And there's a lust in man no charm can tame
> Of loudly publishing our neighbor's shame;
> On eagles' wings immortal scandals fly,
> While virtuous actions are but born and die.
>
> —*Stephen Harvey*

GOVERNMENT

2985   If Karl Marx were alive today, his problem would be to find parking spaces for the American proletariat rather than break their chains of economic slavery.—*G. K. Reddy, Times of India*

2986   As I sat opposite the Treasury Bench, the Ministers reminded me of those marine landscapes not unusual on the coasts of South America. You behold a range of exhausted volcanoes.—*Disraeli*

2987   Freedom of religion, freedom of the press, and freedom of person under the protection of the habeas corpus, these are principles that have guided our steps through an age of revolution and reformation.—*Jefferson*

2988   A State, to prosper, must be built on foundations of a moral character; and this character is the principal element of its strength and the only guaranty of its permanence and prosperity.—*J. Currie*

2989 The greater the power the more dangerous the abuse.—*Edmund Burke*

2990 What is the best government? That which teaches us to govern ourselves.—*Goethe*

2991 Every wanton and causeless restraint of the will of the subject, whether practised by a monarch, a nobility, or a popular assembly, is a degree of tyranny.—*William Blackstone*

2992 The four pillars of government . . . religion, justice, counsel and treasure.—*Francis Bacon*

2993 In that fierce light which beats upon a throne.—*Tennyson*

2994 A man must first govern himself ere he is fit to govern a family; and his family ere he be fit to bear the government of the commonwealth.—*Sir Walter Raleigh*

2995 Our rulers will best promote the improvement of the nation by strictly confining themselves to their own legitimate duties, by leaving capital to find its most lucrative course, commodities their fair price, industry and intelligence their natural reward, idleness and folly their natural punishment, by maintaining peace, by defending property and by observing strict economy in every department of the state. Let the Government do this—the people will assuredly do the rest.—*Thomas Babington Macaulay*

2996 No man undertakes a trade he has not learned, even the meanest; yet everyone thinks himself sufficiently qualified for the hardest of all trades, that of government.—*Socrates*

2997 We must warn ourselves, over and over, that we cannot have something for nothing. The wages of state welfare is the tyranny of the state.—*Raymond Moley*

GRATITUDE

2998 Ingratitude, thou marble-hearted fiend!—*Shakespeare*

2999 Most men remember obligations, but not often to be grateful; the proud are made sour by the remembrance and the vain silent.—*Simms*

3000 It is generally true that all that is required to make men unmindful of what they owe to God for any blessing, is, that they should receive that blessing often and regularly.—*Whately*

3001 He who receives a benefit should never forget it; he who bestows should never remember it.—*Charron*

GREATNESS

3002 From the sublime to the ridiculous there is but one step.—*Napoleon I*

3003   The mightiest powers by deepest calms are fed.—*B. W. Procter*

3004   No man is so great as mankind.—*Theodore Parker*

3005   Let him that would move the world first move himself.—*Socrates*

3006   In the heraldry of heaven goodness precedes greatness, and so on earth it is more powerful. The lowly and lovely may often do more good in their limited sphere than the gifted.—*Bp. Horne*

3007   The lives of great men all remind us, we can make our lives sublime.—*Longfellow*

3008   Speaking generally, no man appears great to his contemporaries, for the same reason that no man is great to his servants—both know too much of him.—*Colton*

3009   The greatest man in history was the poorest.—*Emerson*

3010   A great many men—some comparatively small men now—if put in the right position, would be Luthers and Columbuses.—*E. H. Chapin*

3011   I would much rather that posterity should inquire why no statues were erected to me, than why they were.—*Cato*

3012   There are three marks of a superior man: being virtuous, he is free from anxiety; being wise, he is free from perplexity; being brave, he is free from fear.—*Confucius*

GRIEF

3013   If you have tears, prepare to shed them now.—*Shakespeare*

3014   There is no grief which time does not lessen and soften.—*Cicero*

HABIT

3015   How use does breed a habit in man!—*Shakespeare*

3016   Sow an act, and you reap a habit; sow a habit, and you reap a character; sow a character, and you reap a destiny.—*G. D. Boardman*

HAPPINESS

3017   How bitter a thing it is to look into happiness through another man's eyes!—*Shakespeare*

3018   Silence is the perfectest herald of joy: I were but little happy, if I could say how much.—*Shakespeare*

3019   The most unhappy of all men is he who believes himself to be so.—*Hume*

3020   Only the spirit of rebellion craves for happiness in this life. What right have we human beings to happiness?—*Henrik Ibsen*

3021   The fountain of content must spring up in the mind; and he who has so little knowledge of human nature as to seek happiness by changing anything but his own disposition, will waste his life in fruitless efforts, and multiply the griefs which he purposes to remove.—*Samuel Johnson*

3022   I have learnt to seek my happiness in limiting my desires rather than in attempting to satisfy them.—*John Stuart Mill*

HARDSHIP

3023   There are some defeats more triumphant than victories.—*Michel de Montaigne*

3024   Fire is the test of gold; adversity of strong men.—*Seneca*

3025   Nature is upheld by antagonism. Passions, resistance, danger, are educators. We acquire the strength we have overcome.—*Emerson*

HEALTH

3026   God heals, and the doctor takes the fee.—*Franklin*

3027   Life is not to live, but to be well.—*Martial*

3028   He who has health, has hope; and he who has hope, has everything.—*Arab proverb*

HEART
3029

Still stands thine ancient sacrifice—
An humble and a contrite heart.

—*Rudyard Kipling*

3030   Whatever America hopes to bring to pass in the world must first come to pass in the heart of America.—*Dwight D. Eisenhower*

HEAVEN

3031   Earth hath no sorrow that Heaven cannot heal.—*Thomas Moore*

3032   God has two dwellings: one in heaven, and the other in a meek and thankful heart.—*Izaak Walton*

3033   Men are all groping for infinity—every effort to prove there is no God is in itself an effort to reach for God.—*Bishop Charles Edward Locke*

3034   There's none but fears a future state; and when the most obdurate swear they do not, their trembling hearts belie their boasting tongues.
—*John Dryden*

HISTORY

3035   History, a distillation of rumor.—*Carlyle*

3036   There is properly no history, only biography.—*Emerson*

3037   History is indeed little more than the register of the crimes, follies, and misfortunes of mankind.—*Edward Gibbon*

HOME

3038   The strength of a nation, especially of a republican nation, is in the intelligent and well-ordered homes of the people.—*Mrs. Sigourney*

3039   To most men their early home is no more than a memory of their early years. The image is never marred. There's no disappointment in memory, and one's exaggerations are always on the good side.—*George Eliot*

HONESTY

3040   I am afraid we must make the world honest before we can honestly say to our children that honesty is the best policy.—*George Bernard Shaw*

3041   Money dishonestly acquired is never worth its cost, while a good conscience never costs as much as it is worth.—*J. P. Senn*

HONOR

3042

> For Brutus is an honourable man;
> So are they all, all honourable men.
>
>   —*Shakespeare*

3043   Great honours are great burdens.—*Ben Jonson*

HOPE

3044   He who loses hope, may then part with anything.—*Congreve*

3045   Hope is the only good that is common to all men; those who have nothing else possess hope still.—*Thales*

HUMANITY

3046   After all there is but one race—humanity.—*George Moore*

3047   Humanity is the Son of God.—*Theodore Parker*

HUMILITY

3048   Humility is the solid foundation of all the virtues.—*Confucius*

3049   I believe the first test of a truly great man is his humility.—*John Ruskin*

HUMOR

3050 Honest good humor is the oil and wine of a merry meeting, and there is no jovial companionship equal to that where the jokes are rather small and the laughter abundant.—*Washington Irving*

3051 Where judgment has wit to express it, there is the best orator.—*Penn*

3052 Wit loses its respect with the good, when seen in company with malice; and to smile at the jest which places a thorn in another's breast, is to become a principal in the mischief.—*Richard B. Sheridan*

3053 The little foolery that wise men have makes a great show.—*Shakespeare*

IDEAS

3054 No army can withstand the strength of an idea whose time has come.—*Victor Hugo*

3055 It is only liquid currents of thought that move men and the world.—*Wendell Phillips*

3056 Imagination is more important than knowledge.—*Albert Einstein*

3057 New ideas can be good or bad, just the same as old ones.—*Franklin D. Roosevelt*

IGNORANCE

3058 Against stupidity the very gods themselves contend in vain.—*J. C. F. von Schiller*

3059 An ass may bray a good while before he shakes the stars down.—*George Eliot*

3060 The more we study the more we discover our ignorance.—*Shelley*

3061 The common curse of mankind, folly and ignorance.—*Shakespeare*

IMMORTALITY

3062 Immortality is the glorious discovery of Christianity.—*William Ellery Channing*

3063 Life is the childhood of our immortality.—*Goethe*

3064 The nearer I approach the end, the plainer I hear around me the immortal symphonies of the worlds which invite me. It is marvelous, yet simple.—*Victor Hugo*

INDEPENDENCE

3065   There is no dignity quite so impressive and no independence quite so important as living within your means.—*Calvin Coolidge*

INFLATION

3066   Inflation, which, unless checked, will impoverish a people and destroy a nation, is denounced regularly, like sin. But, unfortunately, like sin, it is tolerated, encouraged and indeed enjoyed by many.—*Bernard Baruch*

INJURY

3067   If the other person injures you, you may forget the injury; but if you injure him, you will always remember.—*Kahlil Gibran*

INSULT

3068

> Of all the griefs that harass the distressed,
> Sure the most bitter is a scornful jest;
> Fate never wounds more deep the generous heart,
> Than when a blockhead's insult points the dart.
>
> —*Samuel Johnson*

INTENTIONS

3069   Good intentions are very mortal and perishable things; like very mellow and choice fruit they are difficult to keep.—*C. Simmons*

3070   In the works of man as in those of nature, it is the intention which is chiefly worth studying.—*Goethe*

JEALOUSY

3071   In jealousy there is more of self-love, than of love to another.—*LaRochefoucauld*

3072   All jealousy must be strangled in its birth, or time will soon make it strong enough to overcome the truth.—*Davenant*

JUDGMENT

3073   Young in limbs, in judgment old.—*Shakespeare*

3074   I never knew so young a body with so old a head.—*Shakespeare*

JUSTICE

3075   As to be perfectly just is an attribute of the divine nature, to be so to the utmost of our abilities is the glory of man.—*Addison*

3076 Man is unjust, but God is just; and finally justice triumphs.— *Longfellow*

3077 How much easier it is to be generous than just! Men are sometimes bountiful who are not honest.—*Junius*

3078 Justice and power must be brought together, so that whatever is just may be powerful, and whatever is powerful may be just.—*Pascal*

KINDNESS
3079 Rich gifts wax poor when givers prove unkind.—*Shakespeare*

3080 I expect to pass through life but once. If therefore, there be any kindness I can show, or any good thing I can do to any fellow-being, let me do it now, and not defer or neglect it, as I shall not pass this way again.—*Penn*

3081 This was the most unkindest cut of all.—*Shakespeare*

3082 To cultivate kindness is a valuable part of the business of life.— *Samuel Johnson*

KNOWLEDGE
3083 To despise theory is to have the excessively vain pretension to do without knowing what one does, and to speak without knowing what one says.—*Fontenelle*

3084 If you have knowledge, let others light their candles by it.— *Margaret Fuller*

3085 Common sense is the knack of seeing things as they are, and doing things as they ought to be done.—*E. C. Stowe*

3086 Socrates said that there was one only good, namely, knowledge; and one only evil, namely, ignorance.—*Diogenes Laertius*

3087 Ignorance never settles a question.—*Disraeli*

3088 Who are a little wise, the best fools be.—*John Donne*

3089 Have the courage to be ignorant of a great number of things, in order to avoid the calamity of being ignorant of everything.—*Sydney Smith*

3090 Command large fields, but cultivate small ones.—*Virgil*

3091 We know accurately only when we know little; with knowledge doubt increases.—*Goethe*

3092 Whoso neglects learning in his youth loses the past and is dead for the future.—*Euripides*

3093

>   Wearing all that weight
>   Of learning lightly like a flower.
>
>   *—Tennyson*

3094   Lack of confidence and lack of information sleep in the same bed, locked in the closest kind of embrace. When a man has confidence he gets along in business, but without confidence he might just as well not enter business at all. For confidence is the son of vision, and is sired by information.*—Cornelius Vanderbilt, Jr.*

3095   He who has no inclination to learn more will be very apt to think that he knows enough.*—Powell*

3096   Knowledge is of two kinds. We know a subject ourselves, or we know where we can find information upon it.*—Samuel Johnson*

3097   Every branch of knowledge which a good man possesses, he may apply to some good purpose.*—C. Buchanan*

3098   The more extensive a man's knowledge of what has been done, the greater will be his power of knowing what to do.*—Disraeli*

3099   Nothing in this life, after health and virtue, is more estimable than knowledge, nor is there anything so easily attained, or so cheaply purchased, the labor, only sitting still, and the expense but time, which, if we do not spend, we cannot save.*—Sterne*

3100   All wish to possess knowledge, but few, comparatively speaking, are willing to pay the price.*—Juvenal*

3101   To be proud of learning, is the greatest ignorance.*—Jeremy Taylor*

LABOR

3102   If you divorce capital from labor, capital is hoarded, and labor starves.*—Daniel Webster*

3103   Whatever there is of greatness in the United States, or indeed in any other country, is due to labor. The laborer is the author of all greatness and wealth. Without labor there would be no government, and no leading class, and nothing to preserve.*—U. S. Grant*

LANGUAGE

3104   Words should be employed as the means, not as the end; language is the instrument, conviction is the work.*—Sir J. Reynolds*

3105   The knowledge of words is the gate of scholarship.*—Wilson*

3106   It makes a great difference in the force of a sentence whether a man be behind it or no.—*Emerson*

LAUGHTER

3107   Laff every time you pheel tickled, and laff once in awhile enyhow. —*Josh Billings*

3108   They laugh that win.—*Shakespeare*

3109   Men show their character in nothing more clearly than by what they think laughable.—*Goethe*

3110   If we consider the frequent reliefs we receive from laughter, and how often it breaks the gloom which is apt to depress the mind, one would take care not to grow too wise for so great a pleasure of life.— *Addison*

LAW

3111   No people were ever better than their laws, though many have been worse.—*J. B. Priestley*

3112   Good laws make it easier to do right and harder to do wrong.— *William E. Gladstone*

3113   We should never create by law what can be accomplished by morality.—*Montesquieu*

3114   Laws are the very bulwarks of liberty; they define every man's rights, and defend the individual liberties of all men.—*J. G. Holland*

LIBERTY

3115   The history of free men is never really written by chance but by choice—their choice.—*Dwight D. Eisenhower*

3116   Eternal vigilance is the price of liberty.—*Jefferson*

3117   The true danger is, when liberty is nibbled away, for expedients, and by parts.—*Edmund Burke*

3118   I know not what course others may take; but as for me, give me liberty or give me death!—*Patrick Henry*

3119   Liberty and union, now and forever, one and inseparable.—*Daniel Webster*

3120   Free will is not the liberty to do whatever one likes, but the power of doing whatever one sees ought to be done, even in the very face of otherwise overwhelming impulse. There lies freedom, indeed.—*G. Macdonald*

3121 It is a strong desire, to seek power, and to lose liberty.—*Francis Bacon*

3122 Liberty is the right to do what the laws allow; and if a citizen could do what they forbid, it would be no longer liberty, because others would have the same powers.—*Montesquieu*

3123 O Liberty, how many crimes are committed in thy name!—*Mme. Roland*

3124 The people never give up their liberties but under some delusion. —*Burke*

LIBRARY

3125 A great library contains the diary of the human race. The great consulting room of a wise man is a library.—*G. Dawson*

3126 The true university of these days is a collection of books.—*Carlyle*

3127 We enter our studies, and enjoy a society which we alone can bring together. We raise no jealousy by conversing with one in preference to another; we give no offense to the most illustrious by questioning him as long as we will, and leaving him as abruptly. Diversity of opinion raises no tumult in our presence; each interlocutor stands before us, speaks or is silent, and we adjourn or decide the business at our leisure.—*Landor*

LIFE

3128 The smallest worm will turn, being trodden on.—*Shakespeare*

3129 I have had my day and my philosophies.—*Tennyson*

3130 The web of our life is of a mingled yarn, good and ill together.— *Shakespeare*

3131 Press not a falling man too far!—*Shakespeare*

3132 The pleasantest things in the world are pleasant thoughts, and the great art in life is to have as many of them as possible.—*C. N. Bovee*

3133 The shell must break before the bird can fly.—*Tennyson*

3134 Life is a quarry, out of which we are to mold and chisel and complete a character.—*Goethe*

3135 Though we seem grieved at the shortness of life in general, we are wishing every period of it at an end. The minor longs to be at age, then to be a man of business, then to make up an estate, then to arrive at honors, then to retire.—*Addison*

3136 If I could get the ear of every young man but for one word, it would be this; make the most and best of yourself. There is no tragedy like a

wasted life—a life failing of its true end, and turned to a false end.—
T. T. Munger

3137 Hope writes the poetry of the boy, but memory that of the man.
Man looks forward with smiles, but backward with sighs. Such is the
wise providence of God. The cup of life is sweetest at the brim, the flavor
is impaired as we drink deeper, and the dregs are made bitter that we
may not struggle when it is taken from our lips.—*A. Monod*

3138

> Of all the words of tongue and pen,
> The saddest are, "It might have been,"
> More sad are these we daily see
> "It is, but it hadn't ought to be!"
>
> —*Bret Harte*

3139 Life resembles the banquet of Damocles; the sword is ever suspended.—*Voltaire*

3140 The vocation of every man and woman is to serve other people.—
Count Leo Nikolaevich Tolstoi

3141 The measure of a man's life is the well spending of it, and not the
length.—*Plutarch*

3142

> My life is like the summer rose
> That opens to the morning sky,
> But ere the shades of evening close
> Is scattered on the ground—to die.
>
> —*Richard Henry Wilde*

3143 Roaming in thought over the Universe, I saw the little that is
Good steadily hastening towards immortality, and the vast that is evil
I saw hastening to merge itself and become lost and dead.—*Walt
Whitman*

3144 One life; a little gleam of time between two eternities; no second
chance for us forever more.—*Carlyle*

3145 Why all this toil for the triumphs of an hour?—*Young*

3146 While we are reasoning concerning life, life is gone; and death,
though perhaps they receive him differently, yet treats alike the fool and
the philosopher.—*David Hume*

3147   We never live; we are always in the expectation of living.—
Voltaire

3148   The Wine of Life keeps oozing drop by drop, the Leaves of Life
keep falling one by one.—*Rubaiyat of Omar Khayyam, translation by
Edward FitzGerald*

3149

Oh threats of Hell and Hopes of Paradise!
One thing at least is certain—This life flies;
One thing is certain; and the rest is Lies;
The Flower that once has blown for ever dies.
—*Rubaiyat of Omar Khayyam, translation by
Edward FitzGerald*

LITERATURE

3150   In science, read, by preference, the newest works; in literature the
oldest. The classic literature is always modern.—*Bulwer*

3151   The decline of literature indicates the decline of a nation; the two
keep pace in their downward tendency.—*Goethe*

3152   Nothing lives in literature but that which has in it the vitality of
creative art; and it would be safe advice to the young to read nothing but
what is old.—*E. P. Whipple*

3153   Literature is the immortality of speech.—*Schlegel*

LOVE

3154

To do him any wrong was to beget
A kindness from him for his heart was rich—
Of such fine mould that if you sowed therein
The seed of Hate, it blossomed Charity.

—*Tennyson*

3155   The course of true love never did run smooth.—*Shakespeare*

3156   No man at one time can be wise and love.—*Robert Herrick*

3157   To be rich in admiration and free from envy; to rejoice greatly in
the good of others; to love with such generosity of heart that your love is
still a dear possession in absence or unkindness—these are the gifts of
fortune which money cannot buy and without which money can buy
nothing. He who has such a treasury of riches, being happy and valiant
himself, in his own nature, will enjoy the universe as if it were his own

estate; and help the man to whom he lends a hand to enjoy it with him.—*Robert Louis Stevenson*

3158 Then, must you speak of one that loved not wisely but too well; of one not easily jealous, but being wrong perplex'd in the extreme.—*Shakespeare*

3159 There's beggary in the love that can be reckon'd.—*Shakespeare*

3160 Men have died from time to time, and worms have eaten them, but not for love.—*Shakespeare*

3161 'Tis better to have loved and lost than never to have loved at all.—*Tennyson*

3162

> Drink to me only with thine eyes,
> And I will pledge with mine;
> Or leave a kiss but in the cup,
> And I'll not look for wine.
>
> —*Ben Jonson*

3163 I do not love thee, Sabidius, nor can I say why; this only I can say; I do not love thee.—*Martial*

3164 Next to God, thy parents.—*Penn*

3165 Never to judge rashly; never to interpret the actions of others in ill-sense, but to compassionate their infirmities, bear their burdens, excuse their weaknesses, and make up for their defects—to hate their imperfections, but love themselves, this is the true spirit of charity.—*Caussin*

3166 The conqueror is regarded with awe; the wise man commands our respect; but it is only the benevolent man that wins our affection.—*Howells*

3167 Courtship consists in a number of quiet attentions, not so pointed as to alarm, nor so vague as not to be understood.—*Sterne*

3168 In charity there is no excess.—*Francis Bacon*

3169 Love does not consist in gazing at each other but in looking together in the same direction.—*Antoine De Saint-Exupéry*

3170 Man's love is of man's life a part; it is woman's whole existence.—*Byron*

3171 There is nothing half so sweet in life as love's young dream.—*T. Moore*

3172 It is astonishing how little one feels poverty when he loves.—*Bulwer*

LUXURY

3173 Luxury makes a man so soft, that it is hard to please him, and easy to trouble him; so that his pleasures at last become his burden. Luxury is a nice master, hard to be pleased.—*Mackenzie*

3174 Avarice and luxury, those pests which have ever been the ruin of every great state.—*Livy*

3175 On the soft bed of luxury most kingdoms have expired.—*Young*

3176 War destroys men, but luxury destroys mankind; at once corrupts the body and the mind.—*Crown*

MAJORITY

3177 The voice of the majority is no proof of justice.—*Schiller*

3178 It never troubles the wolf how many the sheep may be.—*Virgil*

3179 We go by the major vote, and if the majority are insane, the sane must go to the hospital.—*H. Mann*

3180 A man in the right, with God on his side, is in the majority though he be alone.—*H. W. Beecher*

MANKIND

3181

Let each man think himself an act of God.
His mind a thought, his life a breath of God.

—Bailey

3182 We are the miracle of miracles, the great inscrutable mystery of God.—*Carlyle*

3183 Man is an animal that makes bargains; no other animal does this—one dog does not change a bone with another.—*Adam Smith*

3184 He that is good for making excuses, is seldom good for anything else.—*Franklin*

3185 Man proposes, but God disposes.—*Thomas à Kempis*

3186 What a piece of work is a man! ... in form and moving how express and admirable! in action how like an angel! in apprehension how like a god!—*Shakespeare*

3187 Lord, what fools these mortals be!—*Shakespeare*

3188   It takes a clever man to turn cynic and a wise man to be clever enough not to.—*Fannie Hurst*

3189   He was a man, take him for all in all, I shall not look upon his like again.—*Shakespeare*

3190   In counsel it is good to see dangers; but in execution, not to see them unless they be very great.—*Bacon*

3191   The tendency is to be broadminded about other people's security.—*Aristide Briand*

3192   There is no man so good, who, were he to submit all his thoughts and actions to the law, would not deserve hanging ten times in his life.—*Montaigne*

3193   So far is it from being true that men are naturally equal, that no two people can be half an hour together but one shall acquire an evident superiority over the other.—*Samuel Johnson*

3194   I do not mean to expose my ideas to ingenious ridicule by maintaining that everything happens to every man for the best; but I will contend, that he who makes the best use of it, fulfills the part of a wise and good man.—*Cumberland*

3195   There is less misery in being cheated than in that kind of wisdom which perceives, or thinks it perceives, that all mankind are cheats.—*E. H. Chapin*

3196   In my youth I thought of writing a satire on mankind, but now in my age I think I should write an apology for them.—*Walpole*

3197   Man is not the creature of circumstances. Circumstances are the creatures of men.—*Disraeli*

3198   Passion often makes fools of the ablest men, and able men of the most foolish.—*LaRochefoucauld*

3199   Nothing is so uncertain as the minds of the multitude.—*Leiz*

3200   The multitude is always in the wrong.—*Roscommon*

3201

> The Devil was sick, the Devil a monk would be;
> The Devil was well, the Devil a monk was he.
>
> —*Rabelais*

3202   Were we to take as much pains to be what we ought to be, as we do to disguise what we really are, we might appear like ourselves without being at the trouble of any disguise whatever.—*LaRochefoucauld*

3203 I can make a lord, but only the Almighty can make a gentleman. —*James I*

3204 I do not know what comfort other people find in considering the weakness of great men, but 'tis always a mortification to me to observe that there is no perfection in humanity.—*S. Montague*

3205 Not armies, not nations, have advanced the race; but here and there, in the course of ages, an individual has stood up and cast his shadow over the world.—*E. H. Chapin*

3206 The proper study of mankind is man.—*Alexander Pope*

3207 Man's inhumanity to man makes countless thousands mourn.— *Robert Burns*

3208 Man! thou pendulum betwixt a smile and tear.—*Byron*

3209 In the adversity of our best friends we often find something that is not exactly displeasing.—*LaRochefoucauld*

MARRIAGE
3210 I chose my wife, as she did her wedding gown, for qualities that would wear well.—*Oliver Goldsmith*

3211 Men should keep their eyes wide open before marriage, and half shut afterward.—*Madame Scuderi*

3212 The sanctity of marriage and the family relation make the cornerstone of our American society and civilization.—*Garfield*

MASTER
3213 If thou art a master, sometimes be blind; if a servant, sometimes be deaf.—*Fuller*

3214 Men, at some time, are masters of their fates.—*Shakespeare*

MAXIMS
3215 Maxims are the condensed good sense of nations.—*Sir J. Mackintosh*

3216 All maxims have their antagonist maxims; proverbs should be sold in pairs, a single one being but a half truth.—*W. Matthews*

3217 The two maxims of any great man at court are, always to keep his countenance, and never to keep his word.—*Swift*

MEDICINE
3218 The best of all medicines are resting and fasting.—*Franklin*

3219   Over the door of a library in Thebes is the inscription, "Medicine for the soul."—*Diodorus Siculus*

MEDIOCRITY

3220   Mediocrity is not allowed to poets, either by the gods or men.—*Horace*

3221   Nothing in the world is more haughty than a man of moderate capacity when once raised to power.—*Wessenburg*

3222   There are certain things in which mediocrity is not to be endured, such as poetry, music, painting, public speaking.—*LaBruyere*

MEDITATION

3223   Meditation is the nurse of thought, and thought the food of meditation.—*C. Simmons*

3224   It is not the number of books you read, nor the variety of sermons you hear, nor the amount of religious conversation in which you mix, but it is the frequency and earnestness with which you meditate on these things till the truth in them becomes your own and part of your being, that ensures your growth.—*F. W. Robertson*

MEMORY

3225   Memory tempers prosperity, mitigates adversity, controls youth, and delights old age.—*Lactanius*

3226   Memory is the receptacle and sheath of all knowledge.—*Cicero*

3227   The memory is a treasurer to whom we must give funds, if we would draw the assistance we need.—*Rowe*

3228   Everyone complains of his memory; nobody of his judgment.—*LaRochefoucauld*

3229   Memory seldom fails when its office is to show us the tombs of our buried hopes.—*Lady Blessington*

3230   The true art of memory is the art of attention.—*Samuel Johnson*

MERCY

3231   Among the attributes of God, although they are all equal, mercy shines with even more brilliancy than justice.—*Cervantes*

3232   Teach me to feel another's woe, to hide the fault I see; that mercy I to others show, that mercy show to me.—*Pope*

METHOD

3233   Method is like packing things in a box; a good packer will get in half as much again as a bad one.—*Cecil*

3234   Every great man exhibits the talent of organization or construction, whether it be in a poem, a philosophical system, a policy, or a strategy. And without method there is no organization nor construction.—*Bulwer*

MISER

3235   The prodigal robs his heir; the miser robs himself.—*LaBruyere*

3236   A miser grows rich by seeming poor; an extravagant man grows poor by seeming rich.—*Shenstone*

MISFORTUNE

3237   He that is down needs fear no fall.—*Bunyan*

3238   Little minds are tamed and subdued by misfortune; but great minds rise above it.—*Washington Irving*

MISTAKE

3239   The sight of a drunkard is a better sermon against that vice than the best that was ever preached on that subject.—*Saville*

3240   Any man may make a mistake, but none but a fool will continue in it.—*Cicero*

3241   No man ever became great or good except through many and great mistakes.—*Gladstone*

3242   The only people who make no mistakes are dead people. I saw a man last week who had not made a mistake for four thousand years. He was a mummy in the Egyptian department of the British Museum.—*H. L. Wayland*

MOB

3243   Human affairs are not so happily arranged that the best things please the most men. It is the proof of a bad cause when it is applauded by the mob.—*Seneca*

3244   A mob is a society of bodies, voluntarily bereaving themselves of reason, and traversing its work. The mob is man, voluntarily descending to the nature of the beast. Its fit hour of activity is night; its actions are insane, like its whole constitution.—*Emerson*

3245   We are all of us imaginative in some form or other, for images are the brood of desire.—*George Eliot*

MODERATION

3246 Moderation is the inseparable companion of wisdom, but with it genius has not even a nodding acquaintance.—*Colton*

3247 Everything that exceeds the bounds of moderation has an unstable foundation.—*Seneca*

MODESTY

3248 Bashfulness is an ornament to youth, but a reproach to old age.—*Aristotle*

3249 Modesty is a shining light; it prepares the mind to receive knowledge and the heart for truth.—*Guizot*

3250 It is no great thing to be humble when you are brought low; but to be humble when you are praised is a great and rare attainment.—*St. Bernard*

3251 Modesty seldom resides in a breast that is not enriched with nobler virtues.—*Goldsmith*

3252 The greatest ornament of an illustrious life is modesty and humility, which go a great way in the character even of the most exalted princes.—*Napoleon I*

MONEY

3253 But the jingling of the guinea helps the hurt that Honour feels.—*Tennyson*

3254 All love has something of blindness in it, but the love of money especially.—*South*

3255 Men are seldom more innocently employed than when they are honestly making money.—*Samuel Johnson*

3256 The covetous man never has money; the prodigal will have none shortly.—*Ben Jonson*

3257 To despise money is to dethrone a king.—*Chamfort*

3258 Ready money is Aladdin's lamp.—*Byron*

MONUMENT

3259 No man who needs a monument ever ought to have one.—*Hawthorne*

3260 Tombs are the clothes of the dead; a grave is but a plain suit; a rich monument is an embroidered one.—*Fuller*

MORNING

3261   The morning hour has gold in its mouth.—*Franklin*

3262   Now from night's gloom the glorious day breaks forth, and seems to kindle from the setting stars.—*D. K. Lee*

MORTALITY

3263

Oh, why should the spirit of mortal be proud?
Like a fast-flitting meteor, a fast-flying cloud,
A flash of the lightning, a break of the wave,
He passes from life to his rest in the grave.

—William Knox

MOTHER

3264   Let France have good mothers, and she will have good sons.—*Napoleon I*

3265   My mother's influence in molding my character was conspicuous. She forced me to learn daily long chapters of the Bible by heart. To that discipline and patient, accurate resolve I owe not only much of my general power of taking pains, but the best part of my taste for literature.—*John Ruskin*

3266   All that I am, or hope to be, I owe to my angel mother.—*Lincoln*

3267   A father may turn his back on his child; brothers and sisters may become inveterate enemies; husbands may desert their wives and wives their husbands. But a mother's love endures through all; in good repute, in bad repute, in the face of the world's condemnation, a mother still loves on, and still hopes that her child may turn from his evil ways, and repent; still she remembers the infant smiles that once filled her bosom with rapture, the merry laugh, the joyful shout of his childhood, the opening promise of his youth; and she can never be brought to think him all unworthy.—*Washington Irving*

MUSIC

3268   I even think that sentimentally I am disposed to harmony. But organically I am incapable of a tune.—*Charles Lamb*

3269   There is something marvelous in music. I might almost say it is, in itself, a marvel. Its position is somewhere between the region of thought and that of phenomena; a glimmering medium between mind and matter, related to both and yet differing from either. Spiritual, and yet requiring rhythm; material, and yet independent of space.—*H. Heine*

NATION

3270   Socrates said he was not an Athenian or a Greek, but a citizen of the world.—*Plutarch*

3271   The primary duty of organized society is to enlarge the lives and increase the standards of living of all the people.—*Herbert Hoover*

3272   Our purpose is to build in this nation a human society, not an economic system.—*Herbert Hoover*

3273

Praise the Power that hath made and preserved us a nation,
Then conquer we must, for our cause it is just
And this be our motto, "In God is our trust."

—*Francis S. Key*

3274   A good newspaper and Bible in every house, a good schoolhouse in every district, and a church in every neighborhood, all appreciated as they deserve, are the chief support of virtue, morality, civil liberty, and religion.—*Franklin*

3275   Patriotism is the last refuge of a scoundrel.—*Samuel Johnson*

3276   Territory is but the body of a nation. The people who inhabit its hills and valleys are its soul, its spirit, its life.—*Garfield*

3277   No nation can be destroyed while it possesses a good home life.—*J. G. Holland*

3278   Not that I love Caesar less, but that I loved Rome more.—*Shakespeare*

3279   The noblest motive is the public good.—*Virgil*

3280   After what I owe to God, nothing should be more dear or more sacred than the love and respect I owe to my country.—*De Thou*

3281   Republics come to an end by luxurious habits; monarchies by poverty.—*Montesquieu*

3282   Taxes are the sinews of the state.—*Cicero*

NATURE

3283   To him who in the love of nature holds communion with her visible forms, she speaks a various language.—*William Cullen Bryant*

3284   One touch of nature makes the whole world kin.—*Shakespeare*

3285   Nature is the living, visible garment of God.—*Goethe*

3286   Nature is the most thrifty thing in the world; she never wastes anything; she undergoes change, but there's no annihilation—the essence remains.—*T. Binney*

NECESSITY

3287   Necessity knows no law except to conquer.—*Publius Syrus*

3288   Necessity reforms the poor, and satiety the rich.—*Tacitus*

NEWSPAPER

3289   Were it left to me to decide whether we should have a government without newspapers or newspapers without government, I should not hesitate a moment to prefer the latter.—*Jefferson*

NIGHT

3290   The death-bed of a day, how beautiful!—*Bailey*

3291   I must become a borrower of the night for a dark hour or twain.—*Shakespeare*

3292   Ye stars, that are the poetry of heaven!—*Byron*

3293   The stars hang bright above, silent, as if they watched the sleeping earth.—*Coleridge*

3294

> The curfew tolls the knell of parting day,
> The lowing herd winds slowly o'er the lea,
> The ploughman homeward plods his weary way.
> And leaves the world to darkness and to me.
>
> —*Thomas Gray*

3295   The day is done, and darkness falls from the wings of night.—*Longfellow*

3296   In her starry shade of dim and solitary loveliness, I learn the language of another world.—*Byron*

3297   Wisdom mounts her zenith with the stars.—*Mrs. Barbauld*

NOBILITY

3298   Tears are the noble language of the eye.—*Robert Herrick*

3299   Virtue is the first title of nobility.—*Molière*

3300   If a man be endued with a generous mind, this is the best kind of nobility.—*Plato*

3301   It is better to be nobly remembered, than nobly born.—*Ruskin*

OBEDIENCE

3302 Let the child's first lesson be obedience, and the second may be what thou wilt.—*Fuller*

3303 Wicked men obey from fear; good men, from love.—*Aristotle*

OBLIVION

3304

Full many a gem of purest ray serene
The dark, unfathomed caves of ocean bear:
Full many a flower is born to blush unseen,
And waste its sweetness on the desert air.

—*Thomas Gray*

3305 Oblivion is the flower that grows best on graves.—*George Sand*

3306 Fame is a vapor; popularity an accident; riches take wings; and the only certainty is oblivion.—*Horace Greeley*

OBSTACLES

3307 Don't be afraid to stumble. Any inventor will tell you that you don't follow a plan far before you strike a snag. If, out of 100 ideas, you get one that works, it's enough.—*Charles F. Kettering*

OPEN-MINDED

3308 It is well for people who think to change their minds occasionally in order to keep them clean. For those who do not think, it is best at least to rearrange their prejudices once in a while.—*Luther Burbank*

3309 The great menace to the life of an industry is industrial self-complacency.—*David Sarnoff*

3310 It is always the minorities that hold the key of progress; it is always through those who are unafraid to be different that advance comes to human society.—*Raymond B. Fosdick*

3311 "Can any good come out of Nazareth?" This is always the question of the wiseacres and knowing ones. But the good, the new, comes from exactly that quarter whence it is not looked for, and is always something different from what is expected. Everything new is received with contempt, for it begins in obscurity. It becomes a power unobserved.—*Feuerbach*

OPINION

3312 I have bought golden opinions from all sorts of people.—*Shakespeare*

3313   There is no such thing as modern art. There is art—and there is advertising.—*Albert Sterner*

3314   Predominant opinions are generally the opinions of the generation that is vanishing.—*Disraeli*

3315   The eyes of other people are the eyes that ruin us. If all but myself were blind, I should want neither fine clothes, fine houses, nor fine furniture.—*Franklin*

3316   The men of the past had convictions, while we moderns have only opinions.—*H. Heine*

3317   The history of human opinion is scarcely anything more than the history of human errors.—*Voltaire*

OPPORTUNITY

3318   Art is long, life short; judgment difficult, opportunity transient.—*Goethe*

3319   Next to knowing when to seize an opportunity, the most important thing in life is to know when to forego an advantage.—*Disraeli*

3320   Great opportunities come to all, but many do not know they have met them. The only preparation to take advantage of them is simple fidelity to what each day brings.—*A. E. Dunning*

ORATORY

3321   Oratory is the power to talk people out of their sober and natural opinions.—*Chatfield*

PAIN

3322   Pain is the deepest thing we have in our nature, and union through pain and suffering has always seemed more real and holy than any other.—*Hallam*

3323   He jests at scars that never felt a wound. But, soft! What light through yonder window breaks? It is the east, and Juliet is the sun.—*Shakespeare*

PARENT

3324   The first half of our lives is ruined by our parents and the second half by our children.—*Clarence S. Darrow*

PATIENCE

3325   If I have ever made any valuable discoveries, it has been owing more to patient attention, than to any other talent.—*Sir Isaac Newton*

3326   How poor are they that have not patience!—*Shakespeare*

3327   It's easy finding reasons why other folks should be patient.—*George Eliot*

3328   Patience is bitter, but its fruit is sweet.—*Rousseau*

3329   There are times when God asks nothing of his children except silence, patience, and tears.—*C. S. Robinson*

3330   Patience is power; with time and patience the mulberry leaf becomes silk.—*Chinese proverb*

3331   Steady, patient, persevering thinking will generally surmount every obstacle in the search after truth.—*Emmons*

PEACE

3332   Peace hath her victories no less renown'd than war.—*John Milton*

3333   Peace is such a precious jewel that I would give anything for it but truth.—*M. Henry*

3334   There is but one way to tranquility of mind and happiness, and that is to account no external things thine own, but to commit all to God.—*Epictetus*

3335   Five great enemies to peace inhabit with us: viz., avarice, ambition, envy, anger, and pride. If those enemies were to be banished, we should infallibly enjoy perpetual peace.—*Petrarch*

PERFECTION

3336   It is a bad plan that admits of no modification.—*Publius Syrus*

3337   Bachelors' wives and old maids' children are always perfect.—*Chamfort*

3338   It takes a long time to bring excellence to maturity.—*Publius Syrus*

3339   It is only imperfection that complains of what is imperfect. The more perfect we are, the more gentle and quiet we become toward the defects of others.—*Fenelon*

PERSISTENCE

3340   Every noble work is at first impossible.—*Carlyle*

3341   The falling drops at last will wear the stone.—*Lucretius*

3342   And many strokes, though with a little axe, hew down and fell the hardest-timbered oak.—*Shakespeare*

3343   Take care to get what you like or you will be forced to like what you get.—*George Bernard Shaw*

PHILOSOPHY

3344   Three things too much, and three too little are pernicious to man: to speak much, and know little; to spend much, and have little; to presume much, and be worth little.—*Cervantes*

3345   There are more things in heaven and earth, Horatio, than are dreamt of in your philosophy.—*Shakespeare*

3346   It was through the feeling of wonder that men now and at first began to philosophize.—*Aristotle*

3347   The greatest object in the universe, says a certain philosopher, is a good man struggling with adversity; yet there is a still greater, which is the good man that comes to relieve it.—*Oliver Goldsmith*

3348   The discovery of what is true, and the practice of that which is good, are the two most important objects of philosophy.—*Voltaire*

3349   The first business of a philosopher is to part with self-conceit.—*Epictetus*

3350   Philosophy, when superficially studied, excites doubt; when thoroughly explored, it dispels it.—*Bacon*

PITY

3351   Pity is not natural to man. Children are always cruel. Savages are always cruel. Pity is acquired and improved by the cultivation of reason.—*Samuel Johnson*

PLEASURE

3352   The generous heart should scorn a pleasure which gives others pain.—*Thomson*

3353   If all the year were playing holidays, to sport would be as tedious as to work.—*Shakespeare*

3354   Consider pleasures as they depart, not as they come.—*Aristotle*

3355   He who can at all times sacrifice pleasure to duty approaches sublimity.—*Lavater*

POETRY

3356   A poet must needs be before his own age, to be even with posterity.—*J. R. Lowell*

3357   Poets utter great and wise things which they do not themselves understand.—*Plato*

3358   One merit of poetry few persons will deny; it says more, and in fewer words, than prose.—*Voltaire*

POLITENESS

3359   As charity covers a multitude of sins before God, so does politeness before men.—*Greville*

3360   A polite man is one who listens with interest to things he knows all about, when they are told him by a person who knows nothing about them.—*DeMorny*

POLITICS

3361   A statesman makes the occasion, but the occasion makes the politician.—*G. S. Hillard*

3362   Politics is the art of being wise for others—policy of being wise for self.—*Bulwer*

3363   There is no gambling like politics.—*Disraeli*

3364   Nothing is politically right which is morally wrong.—*Daniel O'Connell*

3365   There is an infinity of political errors which, being once adopted, become principles.—*Abbé Raynal*

3366   Every political question is becoming a social question, and every social question is becoming a religious question.—*R. T. Ely*

POVERTY

3367   Meager were his looks, sharp misery had worn him to the bones.—*Shakespeare*

3368   Let not ambition mock their useful toil, their homely joys and destiny obscure; nor grandeur hear with a disdainful smile the short and simple annals of the poor.—*Thomas Gray*

3369   Poverty is the wicked man's tempter, the good man's perdition, the proud man's curse, the melancholy man's halter,—*Bulwer*

3370   Of all the advantages which come to any young man, I believe it to be demonstrably true that poverty is the greatest.—*J. G. Holland*

3371   Poverty is uncomfortable, as I can testify: but nine times out of ten the best thing that can happen to a young man is to be tossed overboard and compelled to sink or swim for himself.—*Garfield*

3372   He is not poor that has little, but he that desires much.—*Daniel*

POWER

3373   Power will intoxicate the best hearts, as wine the strongest heads. No man is wise enough, nor good enough, to be trusted with unlimited power.—*Colton*

3374 Self-reverence, self-knowledge, self-control, these three alone lead life to sovereign power.—*Tennyson*

PRAISE

3375 Sweet is the scene where genial friendship plays the pleasing game of interchanging praise.—*O. W. Holmes*

3376 Praise undeserved is satire in disguise.—*Broadhurst*

3377 Those who are greedy of praise prove that they are poor in merit.—*Plutarch*

3378 Damn with faint praise.—*Pope*

3379 As the Greek said, many men know how to flatter; few know to praise.—*Wendell Phillips*

PRAYER

3380 I pray thee, O God, that I may be beautiful within.—*Socrates*

3381 Her eyes are homes of silent prayer.—*Tennyson*

3382 Our prayers should be for blessings in general, for God knows best what is good for us.—*Socrates*

3383 A strict belief in fate is the worst kind of slavery; on the other hand there is comfort in the thought that God will be moved by our prayers.—*Epicurus*

3384 Certain thoughts are prayers. There are moments when, whatever be the attitude of the body, the soul is on its knees.—*Victor Hugo*

3385 Let not him who prays, suffer his tongue to outstrip his heart; nor presume to carry a message to the throne of grace, while that stays behind.—*South*

3386 A prayer in its simplest definition is merely a wish turned God-ward.—*Phillips Brooks*

3387 The Lord's Prayer contains the sum total of religion and morals.—*Wellington*

3388 The Lord's Prayer is not, as some fancy, the easiest, the most natural of all devout utterances. It may be committed to memory quickly, but it is slowly learned by heart.—*Maurice*

3389 If you don't have faith, pray anyway. If you don't understand or believe the words you're saying, pray anyway. Prayer can start faith, particularly if you pray aloud. And even the most imperfect prayer is an attempt to reach God.—*Cary Grant, actor*

PREJUDICE

3390 To be prejudiced is always to be weak.—*Samuel Johnson*

3391 Never try to reason the prejudice out of a man. It was not reasoned into him and cannot be reasoned out.—*Sydney Smith*

3392 Prejudice is the reason of fools.—*Voltaire*

3393 Ignorance is less remote from the truth than prejudice.—*Diderot*

3394 When the judgment is weak, the prejudice is strong.—*O'Hara*

3395 Even when we fancy we have grown wiser, it is only, it may be, that new prejudices have displaced old ones.—*Bovee*

3396 Prejudices are what rule the vulgar crowd.—*Voltaire*

PRIDE

3397 To be vain of one's rank or place, is to show that one is below it.—*Stanislaus*

3398 Pride is seldom delicate; it will please itself with very mean advantages.—*Samuel Johnson*

3399 Of all marvellous things, perhaps there is nothing that angels behold with such supreme astonishment as a proud man.—*Colton*

3400 Haughty people seem to me to have, like the dwarfs, the stature of a child and the face of a man.—*Joubert*

3401 We mortals, men and women, devour many a disappointment between breakfast and dinner-time; keep back the tears and look a little pale about the lips, and in answer to inquiries say, "Oh, nothing!" Pride helps us; and pride is not a bad thing when it only urges us to hide our own hurts—not to hurt others.—*George Eliot*

PRINCIPLES

3402 He who merely knows right principles is not equal to him who loves them.—*Confucius*

3403 Expedients are for the hour; principles for the ages.—*H. W. Beecher*

PROGRESS

3404 Progress—the onward stride of God.—*Victor Hugo*

3405 I find the great thing in this world is not so much where we stand, as in what direction we are moving.—*O. W. Holmes*

3406 Progress comes from discontent, not complacency.—*Henry Ford II*

PROMISE

3407   The vow that binds too strictly snaps itself.—*Tennyson*

3408   Apt to promise is apt to forget.—*Thomas Fuller*

PROPERTY

3409   Property is at once the consequence and the basis of the state.—*Mikhail A. Bakunin*

3410   The instinct of ownership is fundamental in man's nature.—*William James*

3411   The reason why men enter into society is the preservation of their property.—*Locke*

PROSPERITY

3412   Treason doth never prosper; for if it prosper, none dare call it treason.—*Sir. J. Harrington*

3413   Prosperity tries the fortunate, adversity the great.—*Pliny the Younger*

3414   All sunshine makes the desert.—*Arab proverb*

3415   Everything in the world may be endured, except continual prosperity.—*Goethe*

PRUDENCE

3416   The one prudence in life is concentration; the one evil is dissipation.—*Emerson*

3417   Rashness is the characteristic of ardent youth, and prudence that of mellowed age.—*Cicero*

PURPOSE

3418   Give a man health and a course to steer; and he'll never stop to trouble about whether he's happy or not.—*George Bernard Shaw*

QUESTIONS

3419

> I keep six honest serving men
> They taught me all I knew:
> Their names are What and Why and When
> And How and Where and Who.
>
> —*Rudyard Kipling*

QUOTATIONS

3420 Next to the originator of a good sentence is the first quoter of it.—*Emerson*

3421 I quote others only the better to express myself.—*Montaigne*

3422 By necessity, by proclivity, and by delight, we quote. We quote not only books and proverbs, but arts, sciences, religions, customs, and laws; nay, we quote temples and houses, tables and chairs by imitation.—*Emerson*

READING

3423 Deep versed in books, and shallow in himself.—*Milton*

3424 Read not to contradict and confute; nor to believe and take for granted; nor to find talk and discourse; but to weigh and consider.—*Francis Bacon*

3425 Books are men of higher stature, and the only men that speak aloud for future times to hear.—*Elizabeth Barrett Browning*

3426 There is no book so bad but something valuable may be derived from it.—*Pliny*

3427 Some books are to be tasted; others swallowed; and some few to be chewed and digested.—*Bacon*

3428 When a book raises your spirit, and inspires you with noble and manly thoughts, seek for no other test of its excellence. It is good, and made by a good workman.—*LaBruyere*

3429 Reading maketh a full man; conference a ready man; and writing an exact man; and, therefore, if a man write little, he had need have a great memory; if he confer little, he had need have a present wit; and if he read little, he had need have much cunning, to seem to know that he doth not.—*Bacon*

3430 We should accustom the mind to keep the best company by introducing it only to the best books.—*Sydney Smith*

3431 That is a good book which is opened with expectation, and closed with delight and profit.—*A. B. Alcott*

REASON

3432 Blot out vain pomp; check impulse; quench appetite; keep reason under its own control.—*Marcus Aurelius Antoninus*

3433 We may take Fancy for a companion, but must follow Reason as our guide.—*Samuel Johnson*

3434 O judgment! thou art fled to brutish beasts, and men have lost their reason.—*Shakespeare*

3435 Neither rhyme nor reason.—*Shakespeare*

3436 When passion is on the throne, reason is out of doors.—*M. Henry*

3437 Never reason for what you do not know. If you do, you will soon believe what is utterly against reason.—*Ramsay*

3438 To reason correctly from a false principle, is the perfection of sophistry.—*Emmons*

3439 Neither great poverty nor great riches will hear reason.—*Fielding*

RELIGION

3440 What greater calamity can fall upon a nation than the loss of worship.—*Carlyle*

3441 A strong and faithful pulpit is no mean safeguard of a nation's life.—*St. John*

3442 Christianity is the companion of liberty in all its conflicts, the cradle of its infancy, and the divine source of its claims.—*De Tocqueville*

3443 A little philosophy inclineth man's mind to atheism; but depth in philosophy bringeth men's minds about to religion.—*Francis Bacon*

3444 Morality without religion has no roots. It becomes a thing of custom, changeable, transient, and optional.—*H. W. Beecher*

3445 The blood of the martyrs is the seed of the church.—*St. Jerome*

3446 Seems it strange that thou shouldest live forever? Is it less strange that thou shouldst live at all? This is a miracle; and that no more.—*Young*

3447 I have immortal longings in me.—*Shakespeare*

3448 The best theology is rather a divine life than a divine knowledge.—*Jeremy Taylor*

3449 Carry the cross patiently, and with perfect submission; and in the end it shall carry you.—*Thomas à Kempis*

3450 An agnostic is a man who doesn't know whether there is a God or not, doesn't know whether he has a soul or not, doesn't know whether there is a future life or not, doesn't believe that anyone else knows any more about these matters than he does, and thinks it a waste of time to try to find out.—*Dana*

3451 Some people will bring to church a hymn book or a prayer book—but not a pocket book.—*Jack Herbert*

3452   No sciences are better attested than the religion of the Bible.—*Sir Isaac Newton*

3453   The longer you read the Bible, the more you will like it; it will grow sweeter and sweeter; and the more you get into the spirit of it, the more you will get into the spirit of Christ.—*Romaine*

3454   The whole hope of human progress is suspended on the ever-growing influence of the Bible.—*William H. Seward*

3455   Do you know a book that you are willing to put under your head for a pillow when you lie dying? That is the book you want to study while you are living. There is but one such book in the world. The Bible.—*Joseph Cook*

3456   If religious books are not widely circulated among the masses in this country, and the people do not become religious, I do not know what is to become of us as a nation.—*Daniel Webster*

3457   Religion cannot pass away. The burning of a little straw may hide the stars of the sky, but the stars are there, and will reappear.—*Carlyle*

3458   Culture of intellect, without religion in the heart, is only civilized barbarism and disguised animalism.—*Bunsen*

3459   Religion is the best armor in the world, but the worst cloak.—*John Newton*

3460   Only truly Christian life will do more to prove the divine origin of Christianity than many lectures. It is of much greater importance to develop Christian character, than to exhibit Christian evidence.—*J. M. Gibson*

3461   He who shall introduce into public affairs the principles of primitive Christianity, will revolutionize the world.—*Franklin*

3462   There's not much practical Christianity in the man who lives on better terms with angels and seraphs, than with his children, servants, and neighbors.—*H. W. Beecher*

3463   A Christian church is a body or collection of persons, voluntarily associated together, professing to believe what Christ teaches, to do what Christ enjoins, to imitate his example, cherish his spirit, and make known his gospel to others.—*R. F. Sample*

3464   The problem of religion is to induce people to practice in their daily lives what they say they believe in church.—*Barnes-Ross Co.*

REMORSE

3465   Remorse is beholding heaven and feeling hell.—*Moore*

3466 Of all the sad words of tongue or pen, the saddest are these: "It might have been."—*Whittier*

REPENTANCE

3467 Of all acts of man repentance is the most divine. The greatest of all faults is to be conscious of none.—*Carlyle*

3468 To do so no more is the truest repentance.—*Luther*

3469 There is one case of death-bed repentance recorded, that of the penitent thief, that none should despair; and only one that none should presume.—*St. Augustine*

REPUTATION

3470 Reputation, reputation, reputation! Oh, I have lost my reputation! I have lost the immortal part of myself, and what remains is bestial.—*Shakespeare*

3471 The way to gain a good reputation is to endeavor to be what you desire to appear.—*Socrates*

3472 One may be better than his reputation, but never better than his principles.—*Latena*

3473 Good name in man and woman, dear my lord, Is the immediate jewel of their souls: Who steals my purse steals trash; 'tis something, nothing; 'Twas mine, 'tis his, and has been slave to thousands: But he that filches from me my good name Robs me of that which not enriches him and makes me poor indeed.—*Shakespeare, Othello*

RESPONSIBILITY

3474 Blessed is the person who sees the need, recognizes the responsibility, and actively becomes the answer.—*William Arthur Ward*

REVENGE

3475 In taking revenge a man is but equal to his enemy, but in passing it over he is his superior.—*Bacon*

3476 Revenge is the poor delight of little minds.—*Juvenal*

REVOLUTION

3477 Revolutions begin in the best heads, and run steadily down to the populace.—*Metternich*

3478 Too long denial of guaranteed right is sure to lead to revolution—bloody revolution, where suffering must fall upon the innocent as well as the guilty.—*U. S. Grant*

3479   Revolutions are not made, they come. A revolution is as natural a growth as an oak. It comes out of the past. Its foundations are laid far back.—*Wendell Phillips*

REWARD

3480   Recompense injury with justice and unkindness with kindness.—*Confucius*

3481   The evening of a well-spent life brings its lamps with it.—*Joubert*

3482   He who wishes to secure the good of others has already secured his own.—*Confucius*

RICHES

3483   We have seen better days.—*Shakespeare*

3484   Most of the luxuries and many of the so-called comforts of life are not only not indispensable, but positive hindrances to the elevation of mankind.—*Thoreau*

3485   Can one desire too much of a good thing?—*Shakespeare*

3486   There are two things needed in these days; first, for rich men to find out how poor men live; and second, for poor men to know how rich men work.—*E. Atkinson*

3487   Riches are apt to betray a man into arrogance.—*Addison*

3488   I am happy in having learned to distinguish between ownership and possession. Books, pictures, and all the beauty of the world belong to those who love and understand them. All of these things that I am entitled to, I have—I own them by divine right. So I care not a bit who possesses them. I used to care very much and consequently was very unhappy.—*James Howard Keller*

3489   My riches consist not in the extent of my possessions, but in the fewness of my wants.—*J. Brotherton*

3490   The pride of dying rich raises the loudest laugh in hell.—*John Foster*

3491   To have what we want is riches, but to be able to do without is power.—*G. Macdonald*

3492   Public sentiment will come to be, that the man who dies rich dies disgraced.—*Andrew Carnegie*

RIGHT

3493   I would rather be right than be President.—*Henry Clay*

3494 Let us have faith that right makes might, and in that faith, let us to the end, dare to do our duty, as we understand it.—*Lincoln*

SABBATH

3495 He who ordained the Sabbath loves the poor.—*J. R. Lowell*

3496 The longer I live the more highly do I estimate the Christian Sabbath, and the more grateful do I feel to those who impress its importance on the community.—*Daniel Webster*

3497 A corruption of morals usually follows a profanation of the Sabbath.—*Blackstone*

SCIENCE

3498 Every great advance in science has issued from a new audacity of imagination.—*John Dewey*

3499 Science is simply common sense at its best—that is, rigidly accurate in observation, and merciless to fallacy in logic.—*T. H. Huxley*

SECRET

3500 A truly wise man should have no keeper of his secret but himself.—*Guizot*

3501 Three may keep a secret, if two of them are dead.—*Franklin*

SELF-CONTROL

3502 Heat not a furnace for your foe so hot.—*Shakespeare*

3503 He who reigns within himself and rules his passions, desires, and fears is more than a king.—*Milton*

SERIOUSNESS

3504 It is not so important to be serious as it is to be serious about important things. The monkey wears an expression of seriousness which would do credit to any college student, but the monkey is serious because he itches.—*Robert Maynard Hutchins*

SILENCE

3505 Speech is great, but silence is greater.—*Carlyle*

3506 Silence never shows itself to so great an advantage as when it is made the reply to calumny and defamation.—*Addison*

3507 'Tis not my talent to conceal my thoughts, or carry smiles and sunshine in my face, when discontent sits heavy at my heart.—*Addison*

3508 Learn to hold thy tongue; five words cost Zacharias forty weeks of silence.—*Fuller*

3509   Speaking much is a sign of vanity, for he that is lavish in words is a niggard in deed.—*Sir W. Raleigh*

SIMPLICITY

3510   The fashion wears out more apparel than the man.—*Shakespeare*

3511   Simplicity of all things, is the hardest to be copied.—*Steele*

3512   Nothing is more simple than greatness; indeed, to be simple is to be great.—*Emerson*

3513   The greatest truths are the simplest; and so are the greatest men. —*Hare*

SIN

3514   Selfishness is the greatest curse of the human race.—*W. E. Gladstone*

3515   I am a man more sinn'd against than sinning.—*Shakespeare*

3516   Some rise by sin, and some by virtue fall.—*Shakespeare*

3517   No man ever became extremely wicked all at once.—*Juvenal*

3518   Of Man's first disobedience, and the fruit of that forbidden tree whose mortal taste brought death into the world, and all our woe.—*John Milton*

3519   Sin is essentially a departure from God.—*Luther*

3520   How immense appear to us the sins that we have not committed.—*Madame Necker*

3521   Sins are like circles in the water when a stone is thrown into it; one produces another. When anger was in Cain's heart, murder was not far off.—*Philip Henry*

SINCERITY

3522   Without earnestness no man is ever great or does really great things. He may be the cleverest of men; he may be brilliant, entertaining, popular; but he will want weight.—*Bayne*

3523   Sincerity and truth are the basis of every virtue.—*Confucius*

SLANDER

3524   Slander is a vice that strikes a double blow, wounding both him that commits, and him against whom it is committed.—*Saurin*

3525   Slander is the revenge of a coward, and dissimulation his defense.—*Samuel Johnson*

SLEEP

3526   Sleep that knits up the ravell'd sleave of care, and death of each day's life, sore labour's bath, balm of hurt minds, great nature's second course, chief nourisher in life's feast.—*Shakespeare*

3527   O sleep, O gentle sleep, nature's soft nurse! how have I frightened thee, that thou no more wilt weigh my eyelids down and steep my senses in forgetfulness?—*Shakespeare*

SOCIETY

3528   Society is composed of two great classes: those who have more dinners than appetite, and those who have more appetite than dinners.—*Chamfort*

3529   The best cure for worry, depression, melancholy, brooding, is to go deliberately forth and try to lift with one's sympathy the gloom of somebody else.—*Arnold Bennett*

3530   God has made no one absolute. The rich depend on the poor, as well as the poor on the rich. The world is but a magnificent building; all the stones are gradually cemented together. No one subsists by himself alone.—*Feltham*

SOLITUDE

3531   No one is so utterly desolate, but some heart, though unknown, responds unto his own.—*Longfellow*

3532   Eating the bitter bread of banishment.—*Shakespeare*

3533   I never found the companion that was so companionable as solitude.—*Thoreau*

3534   A wise man is never less alone than when he is alone.—*Swift*

3535   Conversation enriches the understanding, but solitude is the school of Genius.—*Gibbon*

3536   If from society we learn to live, it is solitude should teach us how to die.—*Byron*

3537   It is easy, in the world, to live after the world's opinion; it is easy, in solitude to live after your own; but the great man is he who, in the midst of the crowd, keeps with perfect sweetness the independence of solitude.—*Emerson*

SORROW

3538   The deeper the sorrow the less tongue it hath.—*Talmud*

3539   When sorrows come, they come not single spies, but in battalions.—*Shakespeare*

3540   Good night, good night! parting is such sweet sorrow, that I shall say good night till it be morrow.—*Shakespeare*

3541   Men can counsel and speak comfort to that grief which they themselves not feel.—*Shakespeare*

3542   Joys are our wings; sorrows our spurs.—*Richter*

3543   Tearless grief bleeds inwardly.—*Bovee*

3544   Tears are often the telescope by which men see far into heaven.—*H. W. Beecher*

3545   Everyone can master a grief but he that has it.—*Shakespeare*

SOUL

3546   Sensuality is the grave of the soul.—*Channing*

3547   It is the mind that makes the man, and our vigour is in our immortal soul.—*Ovid*

3548   Great truths are portions of the soul of man; great souls are portions of eternity.—*J. R. Lowell*

3549   Two souls with but a single thought, two hearts that beat as one.—*E. F. J. von Munch-Bellinghausen*

3550

> Build thee more stately mansions, O, my soul,
> As the swift seasons roll!
> Leave thy low-vaulted past!
> Let each new temple, nobler than the last
> Shut thee from heaven with a dome more vast,
> 'Till thou at length art free,
> Leaving thine outgrown shell by life's unresting sea!
>
> —*O. W. Holmes*

3551   Whatever that be which thinks, which understands, which wills, which acts, it is something celestial and divine, and on that account must necessarily be eternal.—*Cicero*

3552   I am fully convinced that the soul is indestructible, and that its activity will continue through eternity. It is like the sun, which, to our eyes, seems to set in night; but it has in reality only gone to diffuse its light elsewhere.—*Goethe*

SPEECH

3553   Charm us, orator, till the lion look no larger than the cat.—*Tennyson*

3554   Speech is a faculty given to man to conceal his thoughts.—*Talleyrand*

3555   Speeches cannot be made long enough for the speakers, nor short enough for the hearers.—*Perry*

3556   Repartee is perfect, when it effects its purpose with a double edge. Repartee is the highest order of wit, as it bespeaks the coolest yet quickest exercise of genius at a moment when the passions are roused.—*Colton*

3557   Rhetoric is nothing but reason well dressed, and argument put in order.—*Jeremy Collier*

3558   "I have heard many great orators," said Louis XIV to Massilon, "and have been highly pleased with them; but whenever I hear you, I go away displeased with myself." This is the highest encomium that could be bestowed on a preacher.—*C. Simmons*

3559   With words we govern men.—*Disraeli*

3560   What too many orators want in depth, they give you in length.—*Montesquieu*

3561   The language of the heart—which comes from the heart and goes to the heart—is always simple, graceful, and full of power, but no art of rhetoric can teach it. It is at once the easiest and most difficult language—difficult, since it needs a heart to speak it; easy, because its periods, though rounded and full of harmony, are still unstudied.—*Bovee*

SPRING

3562   In the spring a livelier iris changes on the burnished dove; in the spring a young man's fancy lightly turns to thoughts of love.—*Tennyson*

SUCCESS

3563   Nothing succeeds so well as success.—*Talleyrand*

3564   *Benjamin Franklin's secret of success:* "I will speak ill of no man, and speak all the good I know of everybody."

3565   Many shining actions owe their success to chance, though the general or statesman runs away with the applause.—*Home*

3566   The way to be nothing is to do nothing.—*Howe*

TACT

3567   It is a very hard undertaking to seek to please everybody.—*Publius Syrus*

3568 Tact comes as much from goodness of heart as from fineness of taste.—*Endymion*

3569 It is a sad thing when men have neither the wit to speak well, nor judgment to hold their tongues.—*LaBruyere*

TAXES

3570 The art of taxation consists in so plucking the goose as to obtain the largest amount of feathers with the least possible amount of hissing.—*Attributed to J. B. Colbert*

3571 The power to tax carries with it the power to embarrass and destroy.—*Supreme Court of the United States—Evans v. Gore, 1920*

TEACHER

3572 The teacher is like the candle which lights others in consuming itself.—*Ruffini*

TEMPTATION

3573 No man is matriculated to the art of life till he has been well tempted.—*George Eliot*

3574 Every temptation is great or small according as the man is.—*Jeremy Taylor*

3575 Better shun the bait than struggle in the snare.—*Dryden*

3576 Some temptations come to the industrious, but all temptations attack the idle.—*Spurgeon*

THOUGHT

3577 True, I talk of dreams, which are the children of an idle brain, begot of nothing but vain fantasy.—*Shakespeare*

3578 Thy wish was father, Harry, to that thought.—*Shakespeare*

3579 Give thy thoughts no tongue.—*Shakespeare*

3580 There is nothing either good or bad, but thinking makes it so.—*Shakespeare*

3581 Thinking is the hardest work there is, which is the probable reason why so few engage in it.—*Henry Ford*

3582 Sit in reverie, and watch the changing color of the waves that break upon the idle seashore of the mind.—*Longfellow*

3583 Every thought which genius and piety throw into the world alters the world.—*Emerson*

3584   They only babble who practise not reflection. I shall think; and thought is silence.—*Sheridan*

3585   Some persons do first, think afterward, and then repent forever.—*Secker*

3586   A picture is an intermediate something between a thought and a thing.—*Coleridge*

3587   Everything that deceives may be said to enchant.—*Plato*

3588   It is not strange that remembered ideas should often take advantage of the crowd of thoughts and smuggle themselves in as original. Honest thinkers are always stealing unconsciously from each other. Our minds are full of waifs and estrays which we think our own. Innocent plagiarism turns up everywhere.—*O. W. Holmes*

3589   The men of action are, after all, only the unconscious instruments of the men of thought.—*Heinrich Heine*

TIME
3590   The inaudible and noiseless foot of Time.—*Shakespeare*

3591   We burn daylight.—*Shakespeare*

3592   It is hoped that, with all modern improvements, a way will be discovered of getting rid of bores; for it is too bad that a poor wretch can be punished for stealing your handkerchief or gloves, and that no punishment can be inflicted on those who steal your time, and with it your temper and patience, as well as the bright thoughts that might have entered your mind, if they had not been frightened away by the bore.—*Byron*

3593   O, call back yesterday, bid time return!—*Shakespeare*

3594   Come what come may, time and the hour run through the roughest day.—*Shakespeare*

3595   In the posteriors of this day, which the rude multitude call the afternoon.—*Shakespeare*

3596   The great rule of moral conduct is, next to God, to respect time.—*Lavater*

3597   If hours did not hang heavy, what would become of scandal?—*Bancroft*

3598   Dost thou love life? Then do not squander time, for that is the stuff life is made of.—*Franklin*

3599   No hand can make the clock strike for me the hours that are passed.—*Byron*

3600   Tomorrow is the day when idlers work, and fools reform, and mortal men lay hold on heaven.—*Young*

3601   Every man's life lies within the present; for the past is spent and done with, and the future is uncertain.—*Marcus Aurelius Antoninus*

3602   Live this day as if it were the last.—*Kerr*

3603   Thou wilt find rest from vain fancies if thou doest every act in life as though it were thy last.—*Marcus Aurelius Antoninus*

3604   Time is a sort of river of passing events, and strong is its current; no sooner is a thing brought to sight than it is swept by and another takes its place, and this too will be swept away.—*Marcus Aurelius Antoninus*

3605   The whole life of man is but a point of time; let us enjoy it, therefore, while it lasts, and not spend it to no purpose.—*Plutarch*

3606   Dionysius the Elder, being asked whether he was at leisure, he replied, "God forbid that it should ever befall me!"—*Plutarch*

3607   As if you could kill time without injuring eternity!—*Thoreau*

3608   Nothing lies on our hands with such uneasiness as time. Wretched and thoughtless creatures! In the only place where covetousness were a virtue we turn prodigals.—*Addison*

3609   All my possessions for a moment of time.—*Queen Elizabeth I's last words*

TOLERANCE
3610   He who never leaves his own country is full of prejudices.—*Goldoni*

3611   Intolerance has been the curse of every age and state.—*S. Davies*

3612   Tolerance comes with age; I see no fault committed that I myself could not have committed at some time or other.—*Goethe*

TRADITION
3613   But to my mind, though I am native here and to the manner born, it is a custom more honoured in the breach than the observance.—*Shakespeare*

3614   Tradition is an important help to history, but its statements should be carefully scrutinized before we rely on them.—*Addison*

TRAGEDY
3615   The worst is not so long as we can say, "This is the worst."—*Shakespeare*

3616   A perfect tragedy is the noblest production of human nature.— *Addison*

3617   Never morning wore to evening, but some heart did break.— *Tennyson*

TRAVEL

3618   Usually speaking, the worst bred person in company is a young traveller just returned from abroad.—*Swift*

3619   The travelled mind is the catholic mind, educated out of exclusiveness and egotism.—*A. B. Alcott*

TRIFLES

3620   Small to greater matters must give way.—*Shakespeare*

3621   Good taste rejects excessive nicety; it treats little things as little things, and is not hurt by them.—*Fenelon*

3622   Trifles make perfection, but perfection itself is no trifle.— *Michaelangelo*

3623   He that despiseth small things shall fall by little and little.— *Ecclesiasticus*

3624   Most of the critical things in life, which become the starting points of human destiny, are little things.—*R. Smith*

3625   It is the little rift within the lute that by and by will make the music mute, and ever widening slowly silence all.—*Tennyson*

TROUBLES

3626   This world has cares enough to plague us; but he who meditates on others' woe, shall, in that meditation, lose his own.—*Cumberland*

3627   Troubles are often the tools by which God fashions us for better things.—*H. W. Beecher*

3628   If you see ten troubles coming down the road, you can be sure that nine will run into the ditch before they reach you.—*Calvin Coolidge*

TRUTH

3629   Logic is the art of convincing us of some truth.—*LaBruyere*

3630   Those who exaggerate in their statements belittle themselves.— *C. Simmons*

3631   Truth is truth to the end of reckoning.—*Shakespeare*

3632   The truth is always the strongest argument.—*Sophocles*

3633   A man should never be ashamed to own he has been in the wrong, which is but saying, in other words, that he is wiser today than he was yesterday.—*Pope*

3634   The telling of a falsehood is like the cut of a sabre; for though the wound may heal, the scar of it will remain.—*Saadi*

3635   Truth sits upon the lips of dying men.—*Matthew Arnold*

3636

Truth, crushed to earth, shall rise again:
The eternal years of God are hers;
    But Error, wounded, writhes with pain,
    And dies among his worshippers.

                    —*William Cullen Bryant*

3637   Truth is the foundation of all knowledge and the cement of all societies.—*John Dryden*

3638   If the world goes against truth, then Athanasius goes against the world.—*Athanasius*

3639   He who seeks truth should be of no country.—*Voltaire*

VANITY

3640   It is our own vanity that makes the vanity of others intolerable to us.—*LaRochefoucauld*

3641   Vanity is the fruit of ignorance.—*Ross*

3642   There is no arena in which vanity displays itself under such a variety of forms as in conversation.—*Pascal*

3643   There's none so homely but loves a looking-glass.—*South*

VENGEANCE

3644   The fire you kindle for your enemy often burns yourself more than him.—*Chinese proverb*

3645   No man ever did a designed injury to another, but at the same time he did a greater to himself.—*Home*

VIRTUE

3646   Of all virtues magnanimity is the rarest; there are a hundred persons of merit for one who willingly acknowledges it in another.—*Hazlitt*

3647   There is but one virtue—the eternal sacrifice of self.—*George Sand*

3648   True humility, the highest virtue, mother of them all.—*Tennyson*

3649   Confidence in another man's virtue is no slight evidence of one's own.—*Montaigne*

3650   He that is good will infallibly become better, and he that is bad will as certainly become worse; for vice, virtue, and time are three things that never stand still.—*Colton*

3651   I cannot praise a fugitive and cloistered virtue, unexercised and unbreathed, that never sallies out and sees her adversary. The virtue that knows not the utmost that vice promises to her followers, and rejects it, is but a blank virtue, not a pure.—*Milton*

VOICE

3652   The voice of the people is the voice of God.—*Hesiod*

WANT

3653

Man wants but little here below,
Nor wants that little long.

—*Goldsmith*

WAR

3654   Take my word for it, if you had seen but one day of war, you would pray to Almighty God, that you might never see such a thing again.—*Wellington*

3655   In disarming Peter, Christ disarmed every soldier.—*Tertullian*

3656   One murder makes a villain; millions a hero.—*Bishop Porteus*

3657   Who overcomes by force hath overcome but half his foe.—*John Milton*

3658   War loves to seek its victims in the young.—*Sophocles*

3659   War! that mad game the world so loves to play.—*Swift*

3660   There never was a good war, or a bad peace.—*Franklin*

3661   War is the business of barbarians.—*Napoleon I*

3662

Someone had blundered:
Theirs not to make reply,

Theirs not to reason why,
Theirs but to do and die.

—Tennyson

3663

Cannon to right of them,
Cannon to left of them,
Cannon in front of them.
. . . .
Into the jaws of death,
Into the mouth of hell
Rode the six hundred.

—Tennyson

WEALTH

3664   Rich people should consider that they are only trustees for what they possess, and should show their wealth to be more in doing good than merely in having it. They should not reserve their benevolence for purposes after they are dead, for those who give not of their property till they die show that they would not then if they could keep it any longer.—*Bishop Hall*

3665   All that glisters is not gold.—*Shakespeare*

3666   Rank and riches are chains of gold, but still chains.—*Ruffini*

3667   Supine amidst our flowing store, we slept securely, and we dreamt of more.—*John Dryden*

3668   He is richest who is content with the least, for content is the wealth of nature.—*Socrates*

3669   Wealth may be an excellent thing, for it means power, leisure, and liberty.—*J. R. Lowell*

3670   There is no society, however free and democratic, where wealth will not create an aristocracy.—*Bulwer*

3671   Wealth consists not in having great possessions but in having few wants.—*Epicurus*

WIFE

3672   For a wife take the daughter of a good mother.—*Fuller*

3673   The sum of all that makes a just man happy consists in the well choosing of his wife.—*Massinger*

All other goods by fortune's hand are given:
A wife is the peculiar gift of Heav'n.

—Pope

WILL

3675 If weakness may excuse, what murderer, what traitor, parricide incestuous, sacrilegious, but may plead it? All wickedness is weakness, that plea, therefore, with God or man will gain thee no remission.—*Milton*

3676 Man has his will, but woman has her way.—*Oliver Wendell Holmes*

3677 People do not lack strength; they lack will.—*Hugo*

3678 To deny the freedom of the will is to make morality impossible.—*Froude*

WIND

3679 The gentle wind, a sweet and passionate wooer, kisses the blushing leaf.—*Longfellow*

WISDOM

3680 Knowledge comes, but wisdom lingers.—*Tennyson*

3681 A child can ask a thousand questions that the wisest man cannot answer.—*J. Abbott*

3682 Judge of a man by his questions rather than by his answers.—*Voltaire*

3683 The years teach much which the days never know.—*Emerson*

3684 Wise men argue causes; fools decide them.—*Anacharsis*

3685 The fool doth think he is wise, but the wise man knows himself to be a fool.—*Shakespeare*

3686 When he that speaks, and he to whom he speaks, neither of them understand what is meant, that is metaphysics.—*Voltaire*

3687 He is truly wise who gains wisdom from another's mishap.—*Publius Syrus*

3688 People generally quarrel because they cannot argue.—*G. K. Chesterton*

3689 If a man will begin with certainties, he shall end in doubts; but if he will be content to begin with doubts, he shall end in certainties.—*Francis Bacon*

3690 A fool may have his coat embroidered with gold, but it is a fool's coat still.—*Rivarol*

3691 A well-cultivated mind is made up of all the minds of preceding ages; it is only the one single mind educated by all previous time.—*Fontenelle*

3692 Few minds wear out; more rust out.—*Bovee*

3693 Common-sense in an uncommon degree is what the world calls wisdom.—*Coleridge*

3694 The Delphic oracle said I was the wisest of all the Greeks. It is because that I alone, of all the Greeks, know that I know nothing.—*Socrates*

3695 The first consideration a wise man fixeth upon is the great end of his creation; what it is, and wherein it consists; the next is of the most proper means to that end.—*Walker*

3696 Perfect wisdom hath four parts, viz., wisdom, the principle of doing things aright; justice, the principle of doing things equally in public and private; fortitude, the principle of not flying danger but meeting it; and temperance, the principle of subduing desires and living moderately.—*Plato*

WIT
3697 To leave this keen encounter of our wits.—*Shakespeare*

3698 There's a skirmish of wit between them.—*Shakespeare*

3699 I am not only witty in myself, but the cause that wit is in other men.—*Shakespeare*

WOMAN
3700 Frailty, thy name is woman!—*Shakespeare*

3701 Her voice was ever soft, gentle, and low—an excellent thing in woman.—*Shakespeare*

3702 A lion among ladies is a most dreadful thing.—*Shakespeare*

3703 Woman apparently is doing everything possible to destroy in herself those very qualifications which render her beautiful, namely, modesty, purity, and chastity. It is a blindness which can only be explained by the fascination of that vanity of which the Scriptures speak with such severity.—*Pope Pius XI*

3704 No one knows like a woman how to say things which are at once gentle and deep.—*Victor Hugo*

3705 Men have sight; women insight.—*Hugo*

WORD

3706 A very great part of the mischiefs that vex this world arises from words.—*Burke*

3707 The word impossible is not in my dictionary.—*Napoleon I*

3708

But yesterday the word of Caesar might
Have stood against the world; now lies he there,
And none so poor to do him reverence.

—*Shakespeare*

WORK

3709 Rest is the sweet sauce of labor.—*Plutarch*

3710 God gives every bird its food, but he does not throw it into the nest.—*J. G. Holland*

3711 So many worlds, so much to do, so little done, such things to be.—*Tennyson*

3712 Things don't turn up in this world until somebody turns them up.—*Garfield*

3713 It is a sober truth that people who live only to amuse themselves, work harder at the task than most people do in earning their daily bread.—*H. More*

3714 Light is the task where many share the toil.—*Homer*

3715 Every man is, or hopes to be, an Idler.—*Samuel Johnson*

3716 Few men are lacking in capacity, but they fail because they are lacking in application.—*Calvin Coolidge*

3717 Temptation rarely comes in working hours. It is in their leisure time that men are made or marred.—*W. M. Taylor*

3718 Laziness grows on people; it begins in cobwebs and ends in iron chains. The more business a man has to do the more he is able to accomplish, for he learns to economize his time.—*Sir M. Hale*

3719 If you have great talents, industry will improve them; if moderate abilities, industry will supply their deficiencies. Nothing is denied to well-directed labor; nothing is ever to be attained without it.—*Sir Joshua Reynolds*

3720   Every industrious man, in every lawful calling, is a useful man. And one principal reason why men are so often useless is, that they neglect their own profession or calling, and divide and shift their attention among a multiplicity of objects and pursuits.—*Emmons*

3721   There is only one thing which will really train the human mind, and that is the voluntary use of the mind by the man himself. You may aid him, you may guide him, you may suggest to him, and, above all you may inspire him; but the only thing worth having is that which he gets by his own exertions: and what he gets is proportionate to the effort he puts into it.—*A. Lawrence Lowell*

WORLD
3722

> This world is all a fleeting show,
> For man's illusion given;
> The smiles of joy, the tears of woe,
> Deceitful shine, deceitful flow,
> There's nothing true but Heaven.
>
> —*More*

3723

> All the world's a stage,
> And all the men and women merely players.
>
> —*Shakespeare*

WORRY
3724   Nothing in the affairs of men is worthy of great anxiety.—*Plato*

WRITING
3725   The wise men of old have sent most of their morality down the stream of time in the light skiff of apothegm or epigram—*E. P. Whipple*

3726   The two most engaging powers of an author, are, to make new things familiar, and familiar things new.—*Samuel Johnson*

3727   The pen is the tongue of the mind.—*Miguel de Cervantes*

3728   The press is the foe of rhetoric, but the friend of reason.—*Colton*

3729   There are only two powers in the world, the sword and the pen; and in the end the former is always conquered by the latter.—*Napoleon I*

3730   Plagiarists have, at least, the merit of preservation.—*Disraeli*

WRONG

3731   Truth forever on the scaffold, wrong forever on the throne.—*J. R. Lowell*

YOUTH

3732   So wise so young, they say, do never live long.—*Shakespeare*

3733   He wears the rose of youth upon him.—*Shakespeare*

3734   We have some salt of our youth in us.—*Shakespeare*

3735   The excesses of our youth are drafts upon our old age, payable with interest about thirty years after date.—*Colton*

3736   Girls we love for what they are; young men for what they promise to be.—*Goethe*

15
PERTINENT PROVERBS

ABSENCE

3737 He that is absent is soon forgotten.

3738 Greater things are believed of those who are absent.—*Tacitus*

ABUNDANCE

3739 Abundance, like want, ruins man.—*Franklin*

ACHE

3740 The tongue ever turns to the aching tooth.

ACQUAINTANCE

3741 Short acquaintance brings repentance.

ACTION

3742 Action is the proper fruit of knowledge.

3743 Great actions speak great minds.—*Fletcher*

3744 In great attempts it is glorious even to fail.—*Cassius Longinus*

ADVANTAGE

3745 Every advantage has its disadvantage.—*Latin proverb*

ADVERSITY

3746 Adversity makes a man wise, not rich.

3747 There is no education like adversity.—*Disraeli*

3748 Adversity has no friends.—*Tacitus*

3749 Put your troubles in a pocket with a hole in it.

ADVICE

3750 Fools need advice most, but wise men only are the better for it.—*Franklin*

3751 Less advice and more hands.—*German proverb*

3752 When we are well, it is easy to give good advice to the sick.—*Terence*

3753 Hazard not your wealth on a poor man's advice.—*Spanish proverb*

3754 Ask advice, but use your own common sense.—*Yiddish proverb*

AFFECTION

3755 Talk not of wasted affection, affection never was wasted.—*Longfellow*

AGE

3756 All would live long, but none would be old.—*Franklin*

3757 Many foxes grow gray, but few grow old.—*Franklin*

3758 No wise man ever wished to be younger.—*Swift*

3759 The old forget, the young don't know.—*German proverb*

3760 It is hard to put old heads on young shoulders.

AMBITION

3761 Ambition is the mind's immodesty.—*D'Avenant*

3762 Ambition is the only power that combats love.—*Cibber*

3763

... fling away ambition:
By that sin fell the angels.

—*Shakespeare*

3764 Would you rise in the world, veil ambition with the forms of humanity.—*Chinese proverb*

3765 There is no eel so small but it hopes to become a whale.—*German proverb*

3766 Ambition destroys its possessor.—*Hebrew proverb*

AMUSEMENT

3767   Amusement is the happiness of those who cannot think.—*Pope*

ANGER

3768   He that is slow to wrath is of great understanding.—*Old Testament, Proverbs*

3769   Anger is never without a reason, but seldom with a good one.—*Franklin*

3770   When a man grows angry, his reason rides out.

3771   When anger blinds the eye, truth disappears.

3772   The greatest remedy for anger is delay.—*Seneca*

APPEARANCE

3773   All things are less dreadful than they seem.

3774   Men are valued not for what they are, but for what they seem to be.—*Bulwer-Lytton*

3775   O what a goodly outside falsehood hath!—*Shakespeare*

ARCHITECTURE

3776   Architecture is the art of how to waste space.—*Philip Johnson*

ARGUMENT

3777   A noisy man is always in the right.

3778   Treating your adversary with respect is giving him an advantage to which he is not entitled.—*Samuel Johnson*

3779   You have not converted a man because you have silenced him.

ARTIST

3780   An artist is a dreamer consenting to dream of the actual world.—*Santayana*

3781   Every artist writes his own autobiography.—*H. Ellis*

3782   The great artist is the simplifier.—*Amiel*

ASPIRATION

3783   No bird soars too high if he soars with his own wings.—*Blake*

3784   Heaven is not reached at a single bound.

3785   Too low they build, who build beneath the stars.—*Young*

ATHEISM

3786   The fool hath said in his heart, There is no God.—*Old Testament, Psalms*

3787   Atheism is rather in the lip than in the heart of man.—*Bacon*

BEAR

3788   Make sure of the bear before you sell his skin.—*Aesop*

BEAUTY

3789   All heiresses are beautiful.

3790   Beauty and folly are old companions.

3791   Beauty has wings, and too hastily flies.

BEGIN

3792   All glory comes from daring to begin.

3793   He who begins many things, finishes but few.

BELIEF

3794   Each man's belief is right in his own eyes.

3795   He does not believe that does not live according to his belief.

3796   A belief is not true because it is useful.—*Amiel*

BENEFIT

3797   To accept a benefit is to sell one's freedom.

3798   When you confer a benefit on a worthy man you oblige all men.

BIOGRAPHY

3799   Biography—one of the new terrors of death.—*Arbuthnot*

BIRTH

3800   Our birth made us mortal, our death will make us immortal.

3801   No man can help his birth.—*Danish proverb*

3802   He who is born, yells; he who dies is silent.—*Russian proverb*

BLAME

3803   He must be pure who would blame another.—*Danish proverb*

BLIND

3804   When the blind man carries the banner, woe to those who follow.—*French proverb*

BOLDNESS

3805   Great boldness is seldom without some absurdity.—*Bacon*

3806   Boldness has genius, power, and magic in it.—*Goethe*

3807   Fortune assists the bold.—*Latin proverb*

BOOK

3808   A book may be as great a thing as a battle.—*Disraeli*

3809   A good book is the precious life-blood of the master spirit.—*Milton*

3810   Books, the children of the brain.

3811   Word by word the great books are written.—*Voltaire*

BORROW

3812   Creditors have better memories than debtors.

3813   He who does not have to borrow lives without cares.—*Yiddish proverb*

BREAD

3814   If you have bread, don't look for cake.—*Yiddish proverb*

3815   Whose bread I eat, his song I sing.—*German proverb*

BUILD

3816   To build is to be robbed.

3817   It is easier to pull down than to build.—*Latin proverb*

BURDEN

3818   Every horse thinks his own pack heaviest.

3819   None knows the weight of another's burden.

3820   The burden is light on the shoulder of another.—*Russian proverb*

BUSINESSMAN

3821   Everyone lives by selling something.

3822   Keep thy shop and thy shop will keep thee.

3823   The market is a place set apart where men may deceive each other.—*Greek proverb*

CAESAR

3824   What millions died—that Caesar might be great!—*Campbell*

CANDOR

3825 I hate him that my vices telleth me.—*Chaucer*

CEMETERY

3826 A piece of a churchyard fits everybody.

CHARACTER

3827 Put more trust in character than in an oath.—*Greek proverb*

3828 Character is destiny.—*Greek proverb*

3829 It matters not what you are thought to be, but what you are.—*Latin proverb*

CHARITY

3830 He that gives to be seen will relieve none in the dark.

3831 He gives twice who gives quickly.—*Latin proverb*

3832 Charity begins, but doth not end, at home.

CHILDREN

3833 Children are poor men's riches.

3834 Children have wide ears and long tongues.

3835 Little children, little sorrows; big children, big sorrows.

3836 Where children are not, heaven is not.

3837 Children have more need of models than of critics.—*French proverb*

3838 Better the child should cry than the father.—*German proverb*

3839 Our neighbor's children are always the worst.—*German proverb*

CHURCH

3840 A church is God between four walls.—*French proverb*

CITY

3841 In cities vice is hidden with most ease.

3842 A great city, a great solitude.—*Greek proverb*

CLEVER

3843 Cleverness is serviceable for everything, sufficient for nothing.—*French proverb*

3844 Don't be so clever; cleverer ones than you are in jail.—*Russian proverb*

3845   He who would be too clever makes a fool of himself.—*Yiddish proverb*

3846   Too clever is dumb.—*German proverb*

COMMERCE

3847   Commerce is the great civilizer.

3848   The merchant has no country.—*Jefferson*

CONCEIT

3849   Conceit is God's gift to little men.

3850   Conceit may puff a man up, but never prop him up.

3851   He is so full of himself that he is quite empty.

CONSCIENCE

3852   A quiet conscience sleeps in thunder.

CONTENT

3853   Content lodges oftener in cottages than in palaces.

3854   Think not on what you lack as much as on what you have.—*Greek proverb*

COURAGE

3855   Courage is the most common and vulgar of the virtues—*Melville*

3856   You can't answer for your courage if you have never been in danger.—*French proverb*

3857   Fortune favors the brave.

3858   The strongest man in the world is he who stands alone.—*Ibsen*

DANGER

3859   The danger past and God forgotten.

3860   Fear the goat from the front, the horse from the rear, and man from all sides.—*Russian proverb*

DAY

3861   One of these days is none of these days.

DEATH

3862   Let the dead bury their dead.—*New Testament, Matthew*

3863   Yet a little sleep, a little slumber, a little folding of the hands to sleep.—*Old Testament, Proverbs*

3864   As soon as a man is born he begins to die.

3865

> Death is but a path that must be trod
> If man would ever pass to God.
>
> —*Parnell*

3866   Six feet of earth make all men equal.—*Italian proverb*

3867   Death—the gate of life.—*Latin proverb*

DEBT

3868   That is but an empty purse that is full of other men's money.

DECEIT

3869

> O what a tangled web we weave,
> When first we practice to deceive!
>
> —*Sir Walter Scott*

3870   The easiest person to deceive is one's self.

DEMOCRACY

3871   Democracy becomes a government of bullies tempered by editors.—*Emerson*

3872   Democracy substitutes election by the incompetent many for appointment by the corrupt few.—*G. B. Shaw*

DESTINY

3873   What will be, will be.—*Italian proverb*

DISPUTE

3874   He who disputes with the stupid must have sharp answers.—*German proverb*

DOCTOR

3875   A man who is his own doctor has a fool for his patient.

3876   In a good surgeon, a hawk's eye; a lion's heart; and a lady's hand.

3877   Every doctor thinks his pills the best.—*German proverb*

DOUBT

3878   Doubt makes the mountain which faith can move.

DRESS

3879   If all the world went naked, how could we tell the kings?

3880   No fine clothes can hide the clown.

3881   That man is best dressed whose dress no one observes.

DUTY

3882   Duty determines destiny.

EARLY

3883   Get a name to rise early, and you may lie all day.

ECONOMY

3884   Without frugality none can be rich, and with it very few would be poor.

3885   Frugality is misery in disguise.—*Latin proverb*

EDUCATION

3886   Without a gentle contempt for education no gentleman's education is complete.—*G. K. Chesterton*

3887   There is no royal road to geometry.—*Euclid*

EGOTISM

3888   Every man is of importance to himself.

3889   When a man tries himself, the verdict is in his favor.

ELOQUENCE

3890   By persuading others we convince ourselves.—*Junius*

3891   It is the heart which makes men eloquent.—*Latin proverb*

ENEMY

3892   A man's greatness can be measured by his enemy.

3893   None but myself ever did me any harm.—*Napoleon I*

3894   Better a good enemy than a bad friend.—*Yiddish proverb*

ENVY

3895   Envy is the sincerest form of flattery.

EQUALITY

3896 Equality begins in the grave.—*French proverb.*

3897 Time is the only thing we all possess equally.

ERROR

3898 When the learned man errs, he errs with a learned error.—*Arab proverb*

3899 Who errs and mends, commends himself to God.—*Spanish proverb*

ETERNITY

3900 In the presence of eternity, the mountains are as transient as the clouds.

EVIL

3901 Evil often triumphs but never conquers.

3902 An evil life is a kind of death.—*Spanish proverb*

EXAMPLE

3903 A good example is the best sermon.

3904 Example is a lesson that all men can read.

3905 Example is the school of mankind, and they will learn at no other.—*Burke*

EXPERIENCE

3906 He knows the water best who has waded through it.—*Danish proverb*

3907 It is costly wisdom that is bought by experience.

3908 Experience is the teacher of fools.—*Latin proverb*

FACT

3909 Facts do not cease to exist because they are ignored.

3910 You can't alter facts by filming them over with romance.

FAME

3911 All fame is dangerous: good brings envy; bad, shame.

3912 Fame is but an inscription upon a grave.

3913 Fame . . . that last infirmity of noble minds.—*Milton*

FATHER

3914   One father is more than a hundred schoolmasters.

FEAR

3915   Fear is the offspring of ignorance.

3916   Fear makes lions tame.—*German proverb*

3917   Our fears always outnumber our dangers.—*Latin proverb*

3918   If the thunder is not loud, the peasant forgets to cross himself.—*Russian proverb*

FIGHT

3919   We fight to great disadvantage when we fight with those who have nothing to lose.—*Italian proverb*

3920   Do not fight against two adversaries.—*Latin proverb*

FORTUNE

3921   A man's own manners do shape his fortune.

3922   Seldom are men blessed with good fortune and good sense at the same time.—*Latin proverb*

FRIEND

3923   Friendship is love without his wings.—*Lord Byron*

3924   A faithful friend is an image of God.—*French proverb*

GIVING

3925   The wise man does not lay up treasure. The more he gives, the more he has.—*Chinese proverb*

3926   He that gives his heart will not deny his money.

3927   He who can give has many a good neighbor.

GOD

3928   God often visits us, but most of the time we are not at home.—*French proverb*

3929   God is patient because eternal.—*St. Augustine*

GOVERNMENT

3930   No man is good enough to govern another without that other's consent.—*Lincoln*

3931   Every country has the government it deserves.—*French proverb*

HAPPINESS
3932 Man is not born for happiness.

3933 Happiness is made to be shared.—*French proverb*

HEART
3934 When there is room in the heart there is room in the house.—*Danish proverb*

HISTORY
3935 History repeats itself.

HONESTY
3936 An honest man does not make himself a dog for the sake of a bone.—*Danish proverb*

3937 They are all honest men, but my cloak is not to be found.—*Spanish proverb*

HONOR
3938 Let us do what honor demands.—*French proverb*

HOPE
3939 Hope is the poor man's income.—*Danish proverb*

3940 Great hopes make great men.

HUMILITY
3941 There is no true holiness without humility.

3942 Humble thyself in all things.—*Thomas à Kempis*

HUSBAND
3943 A good husband makes a good wife.

3944 A good wife makes a good husband.

IGNORANCE
3945 The tragedy of ignorance is its complacency.

3946 He who knows nothing is confident of everything.

3947 Ignorance is a voluntary misfortune.

3948 It is impossible to defeat an ignorant man by argument.—*William McAdoo*

IMMORTALITY

3949   All men desire to be immortal.

3950   He hath not lived that lives not after death.

INDEPENDENCE

3951   Paddle your own canoe.

INDUSTRY

3952   The dog that trots about finds a bone.

JUSTICE

3953   Justice is truth in action.—*Joubert*

3954   If all men were just, there would be no need of valor.—*Greek proverb*

KNOWLEDGE

3955   A man without knowledge is as one that is dead.

3956   Knowledge in youth is wisdom in age.

3957   The desire for knowledge increases with its acquisition.

3958   Those who really thirst for knowledge always get it.

LABOR

3959   To labor is to pray.—*Latin proverb*

3960   Life is in labor.—*Russian proverb*

LANGUAGE

3961   Speak that I may see thee.

LAUGH

3962

> And if I laugh at any mortal thing,
> 'Tis that I may not weep.
>
> —*Byron*

3963

> Our sincerest laughter
> With some pain is fraught.
>
> —*Shelley*

LAW

3964   Where is there any book of the law so clear to each man as that written in his heart?—*Tolstoi*

LAWYER

3965   A lawyer and a wagon wheel must be well greased.—*German proverb*

LEND

3966   He who lends to the poor gets his interest from God.—*German proverb*

LIBRARY

3967   A great library is the diary of the human race.

LIFE

3968   I wept when I was born, and every day shows why.

3969   The present hour alone is man's.

3970   A useless life is an early death.—*Goethe*

3971   There is more to life than increasing its speed.—*Gandhi*

LOSE

3972   Losers are always in the wrong.—*Spanish proverb*

3973   If you've nothing to lose, you can try everything.—*Yiddish proverb*

MAN

3974   Man is a machine into which we put food and produce thought.

3975

> Though every prospect pleases,
> And only man is vile.
>
> —*Heber*

MANNERS

3976   Good breeding consists in concealing how much we think of ourselves and how little we think of the other person.—*Mark Twain*

MARRIAGE

3977   Every woman should marry, and no man.—*Disraeli*

3978   Marriage halves our griefs, doubles our joys, and quadruples our expenses.

MISFORTUNE

3979   It is the nature of mortals to kick a man when he is down.—*Greek proverb*

3980   Misfortune is friendless.—*Greek proverb*

MONEY

3981   A golden key opens every lock.

3982   Money mars, and money makes.

3983   The love of money and the love of learning seldom meet.

MOTHER

3984   Simply having children does not make mothers.

MUSIC

3985   Music—the only universal tongue.

NATURE

3986   Nature pardons no mistake.

3987   Nature is the art of God.—*Latin proverb*

NECESSITY

3988   Necessity makes even the timid brave.—*Latin proverb*

OLD

3989   Old foxes want no tutors.

PARENT

3990   If parents want honest children, they should be honest themselves.

PATIENCE

3991   He preacheth patience that never knew pain.

3992   Patience is the art of hoping.—*French proverb*

PEACE

3993   When a man finds no peace within himself, it is useless to seek it elsewhere.—*French proverb*

PEOPLE

3994   The mob has many heads but no brains.

3995   No man who depends upon the caprice of the ignorant rabble can be accounted great.—*Cicero*

PHILANTHROPY

3996   The most acceptable service of God is doing good to man.—*Franklin*

3997   I am a man, and nothing human can be indifferent to me.—*Terence*

PLEASURE

3998   Pleasures are transient, honors are immortal.—*Greek proverb*

POOR

3999   Poor men seek meat for their stomachs; rich men stomach for their meat.

4000   Whoso stoppeth his ear at the cry of the poor shall cry himself and not be heard.—*Hebrew proverb*

4001   Not he who has little, but he who wishes for more, is poor.—*Latin proverb*

POVERTY

4002   Poverty is the mother of all the arts.

4003   Poverty—the mother of temperance.—*Greek proverb*

4004   No man should praise poverty but he who is poor.—*St. Bernard*

4005   There are many things which ragged men dare not say.—*Latin proverb*

4006   There are only two families in the world, the Haves and the Have-Nots.—*Cervantes*

PRAISE

4007   Self-praise is no recommendation.

PRAYER

4008

> And Satan trembles when he sees
> The weakest saint upon his knees.
>
> —*Cowper*

4009   God warms his hands at man's heart when he prays.—*Masefield*

4010   Who rises from prayer a better man, his prayer is answered.—
Meredith

4011   If you pray for another, you will be helped yourself.—*Yiddish
proverb*

PREJUDICE
4012   Prejudice is the child of ignorance.

PROSPERITY
4013   Prosperity is a great teacher; adversity, a greater.

4014   Prosperity makes friends, adversity tries them.—*Latin proverb*

4015   The prosperous man is never sure that he is loved for himself.—
Latin proverb

PRUDENCE
4016   That should be long considered which can be decided but once.—
Latin proverb

QUARREL
4017   When we quarrel, how we wish we had been blameless!

READING
4018   I love to lose myself in other men's minds.—*Lamb*

4019   The art of reading is to skip judiciously.

REPENTANCE
4020   He who repents his sins is almost innocent.—*Latin proverb*

RESPONSIBILITY
4021   No snowflake in an avalanche ever feels responsible.

REVENGE
4022   Living well is the best revenge.

4023   To forget a wrong is the best revenge.

RICH
4024   To gain wealth is easy; to keep it, hard.—*Chinese proverb*

4025   Better rich in God than rich in gold.

4026   At the door of the rich are many friends.—*Hebrew proverb*

SAINT

4027   The way of this world is to praise dead saints and persecute living ones.

SAVING

4028

For age and want save while you may:
No morning sun lasts a whole day.

SCANDAL

4029   There is nothing that can't be made worse by telling.—*Latin proverb*

SECRET

4030   If you wish another to keep your secret, first keep it yourself.—*Latin proverb*

SELF-LOVE

4031   Every living creature loves itself.—*Latin proverb*

4032   Self-love is the greatest of all flatterers.—*La Rochefoucauld*

SICKNESS

4033   The chamber of sickness is the chapel of devotion.

4034   In time of sickness the soul collects itself anew.—*Latin proverb*

4035   Sickness shows us what we are.—*Latin proverb*

SIMPLICITY

4036   The greatest truths are the simplest; and so are the greatest men.—*A. W. Hare*

SIN

4037   The cat shuts its eyes while it steals cream.

4038   Sin writes histories; goodness is silent.—*Goethe*

4039   There is a sin of omission as well as of commission.—*Greek proverb*

SOLITUDE

4040   Solitude is the best nurse of wisdom.

SORROW

4041   Earth has no sorrow that Heaven cannot heal.

4042   The longest sorrow finds at last relief.

SPEECH

4043   Little said is soonest mended.

4044   A man's character is revealed by his speech.—*Greek proverb*

SUCCESS

4045   Nothing is so impudent as success.

4046   Success makes a fool seem wise.

4047   Everything is subservient to success.

TALK

4048   He who talks much is sometimes right.—*Spanish proverb*

THOUGHT

4049

> I would that my tongue could utter
> The thoughts that arise in me.
>
> —*Tennyson*

4050   The profound thinker always suspects that he may be superficial.—*Disraeli*

TIME

4051   Nought treads so silent as the foot of time.

4052   All the treasures of earth cannot bring back one lost moment.—*French proverb*

TRAVEL

4053   A fool wanders; the wise man travels.

4054   See one mountain, one sea, one river—and see all.—*Greek proverb*

4055   To travel hopefully is a better thing than to arrive.—*Robert Louis Stevenson*

TRUTH

4056   When in doubt, tell the truth.—*Mark Twain*

4057   Individuals may perish; but truth is eternal.—*French proverb*

4058   Time discovers truth.—*Latin proverb*

UNIVERSITY

4059 A university is a place where pebbles are polished and diamonds are dimmed.—*Ingersoll*

UNLUCKY

4060 He falls on his back and breaks his nose.—*French proverb*

VICE

4061 Never open the door to a little voice lest a great one enter with it.

4062 The virtues of society are the vices of the saints.—*Emerson*

VIRTUE

4063 Virtue is always in a minority.—*French proverb*

4064 Virtue unites man with God.—*Latin proverb*

WAR

4065 Force and fraud are in war the two cardinal virtues.—*Hobbes*

4066 War never leaves where it found a nation.—*Burke*

WIFE

4067 A cheerful wife is the joy of life.

4068 An expensive wife makes a pensive husband.

4069 An obedient wife commands her husband.

4070 The wife that loves the looking-glass hates the saucepan.

WISDOM

4071 That man is wisest who realizes that his wisdom is worthless.—*Socrates*

4072 Wisdom comes by suffering.—*Greek proverb*

4073 There is often wisdom under a shabby cloak.—*Latin proverb*

WISE

4074 What's the good of being wise when foolishness serves?—*Yiddish proverb*

WIT

4075 Wit does not take the place of knowledge.

4076 Wit is the salt of conversation, not the food.

WOMAN

4077   We may live with, but cannot live without 'em.

4078   Kind words and few are a woman's ornament.—*Danish proverb*

4079   A woman can be anything the man who loves her would have her be.—*Barrie*

4080   A handsome woman is always right.—*German proverb*

4081   It is a sad house where the hen crows louder than the rooster.

WORK

4082   Blessed is he who has found his work; let him ask no other blessedness.—*Carlyle*

WRITING

4083   Either write things worth reading, or do things worth writing.—*Franklin*

4084   Look in thy heart and write.—*Sidney*

YOUTH

4085   Youth is the season of hope.

4086   The majority of men employ the first portion of their life in making the other portion miserable.—*LaBruyere*

ZEAL

4087   Zeal is fit only for wise men but is found mostly in fools.

4088   Zeal without knowledge is the sister of folly.

16
QUOTATIONS OF WISDOM AND HUMOR

4089 *Advertising Is Useful*
Advertising may be described as the science of arresting the human intelligence long enough to get money from it.—*Stephen Leacock*

4090 *Advertising Is Essential*
So far as advertising is concerned, I repeat that it must survive as a thriving dynamic force. Not only does it deserve to continue because of its contributions to our way of life but it has a job to do now.—*Leon Henderson*

4091 *The Flag*
The things that the flag stands for were created by the experience of a great people. Everything that it stands for was written by their lives. The flag is the embodiment, not of sentiment, but of history.—*Woodrow Wilson*

4092 *Vain*
To say that a man is vain means merely that he is pleased with the effect he produces on other people. A conceited man is satisfied with the effect he produces on himself.—*Max Beerbohm*

4093 *Expert*
What's an expert? I read somewhere that the more a man knows, the more he knows he doesn't know. So I suppose one definition of an expert would be someone who doesn't admit out loud that he knows enough about a subject to know he doesn't really know much.—*Malcolm S. Forbes*

4094 *Art*

For art, if it is to be reckoned with as one of the great values of life, must teach man humility, tolerance, wisdom and magnanimity. The value of art is not beauty, but right action.—*W. Somerset Maugham*

4095 *Life*

You can't tell how good it is to be alive, till you are facing death, because you don't live till then.—*John Galsworthy*

4096 *Tolerance*

Tolerance is the key to peace, for there can be no peace unless there is mutual tolerance between differing peoples and systems and cultures. —*Adlai E. Stevenson*

4097 *War*

There has never been a war yet which, if the facts had been put calmly before the ordinary folk, could not have been prevented. The common man is the greatest protection against war.—*Ernest Bevin*

4098 *New England*

The swaggering underemphasis of New England.—*Heywood Broun*

4099 *Civilizations*

So I should say that civilizations begin with religion and stoicism; they end with skepticism and unbelief, and the undisciplined pursuit of individual pleasure. A civilization is born stoic and dies epicurean.—*Will Durant*

4100 *Schoolteachers*

Emerson advised his fellow-townsmen to manufacture schoolteachers and make them the best in the world.—*Van Wyck Brooks*

4101 *Woman Suffrage*

Wouldn' th' way things are goin' these days make a fine argyment in favor of woman suffrage if we didn' already have it?—*Frank McKinney Hubbard*

4102 *Future*

Everyone is interested in the future, in what lies ahead, and particularly is this true in business. Peering into the crystal ball to discern the future can be interesting, frustrating, tedious, sometimes even humorous, but at all times it is an important phase of business leadership. Forecasting has been described as an educated guess.—*Wayne A. Johnston*

4103   *Cultured*

When you take a bath, you are civilized; when you don't take a bath, you are cultured.—*Lin Yutang*

4104   *Occupational Diseases*

Arrogance, pedantry, and dogmatism are the occupational diseases of those who spend their lives directing the intellects of the young.—*Henry S. Canby*

4105   *Trees*

I like trees because they seem more resigned to the way they have to live than other things do.—*Willa Cather*

4106   *Elegant Variation*

The very limitations of his field drive the sports writer to ingenious devices. . . . How many ways is it possible to say that one football team defeated another? As season follows season with annual and ruthless regularity, the sports writer is confronted with situations and subjects that he has faced not once or twice before, but many times. Almost inevitably, he becomes an expert in what Arthur Quiller-Couch long ago named "the trick of elegant variation, so rampant in the sporting press."—*Chicago Tribune*

4107   *Democracy*

My political ideal is democracy. Everyone should be respected as an individual, but no one idolized.—*Albert Einstein*

4108   *English*

By being so long in the lowest form (at Harrow) I gained an immense advantage over the cleverer boys. . . . I got into my bones the essential structure of the ordinary British sentence—which is a noble thing. Naturally I am biased in favor of boys learning English; and then I would let the clever ones learn Latin as an honor, and Greek as a treat.—*Sir Winston Churchill*

4109   *Discontent*

Restlessness is discontent—and discontent is the first necessity of progress. Show me a thoroughly satisifed man—and I will show you a failure.—*Thomas A. Edison*

4110   *Slogans*

Slogans are both exciting and comforting, but they are also powerful opiates for the conscience.—*James Bryant Conant*

4111   *Democracy's Conviction*

Democracy is based upon the conviction that there are extraordinary possibilities in ordinary people.—*Harry Emerson Fosdick*

4112   *War*

The greatest destroyer of democracy in the world is war itself.—*Harry Emerson Fosdick*

4113   *Education*

The most important function of education at any level is to develop the personality of the individual and the significance of his life to himself and to others. This is the basic architecture of a life; the rest is ornamentation and decoration of the structure. As such, it is desirable but only in a supplementary sense.—*Grayson Kirk*

4114   *American Education*

The primary concern of American education today is . . . to cultivate in the largest number of our future citizens an appreciation both of the responsibilities and the benefits which come to them because they are American and free.—*James Bryant Conant*

4115   *Humanity*

It is not tolerable, it is not possible, that from so much death, so much sacrifice and ruin, so much heroism, a greater and better humanity shall not emerge.—*Charles de Gaulle*

4116   *United States of Europe*

The conception of a United States of Europe is right. Every step to that end, which makes easier the traffic and reciprocal services of Europe, is good for all.—*Sir Winston Churchill*

4117   *New Thinker*

A "New Thinker" when studied closely, is merely a man who does not know what other people have thought.—*Frank Moore Colby*

4118   *Civilization in America*

New England is a finished place. Its destiny is that of Florence or Venice, not Milan, while the American empire careens onward toward its unpredicted end. . . . It is the first American section to be finished, to achieve stability in the conditions of its life. It is the first old civilization, the first permanent civilization in America.—*Bernard De Voto*

4119   *Human Personality*

Christian teaching alone, in its majestic integrity, can give full meaning and compelling motive to the demand for human rights and liberties, because it alone gives worth and dignity to human personality.—*Pope Pius XI*

4120   *Arrogance*

Early in life I had to choose between arrogance and hypocritical humility. I chose honest arrogance and have seen no occasion to change.—*Frank Lloyd Wright*

4121   *Private Wealth*

I like to walk about amidst the beautiful things that adorn the world; but private wealth I should decline, or any sort of personal possessions, because they would take away my liberty.—*George Santayana*

4122   *Success*

Success, which touches nothing that it does not vulgarize, should be its own reward. . . . The odium of success is hard enough to bear, without the added ignominy of popular applause.—*Robert Bontine Cunninghame Graham*

4123   *The Horse's Mouth*

We have a phrase in English "straight from the horse's mouth." I never knew why the particular animal chosen was a horse, especially as most horses are generally not very communicative.—*Joseph Clark Grew*

4124   *Architecture*

The only thing wrong with architecture is architects.—*Frank Lloyd Wright*

4125   *Underprivileged*

The war on privilege will never end. Its next great campaign will be against the special privileges of the underprivileged.—*Henry L. Mencken*

4126   *Undergraduates*

The most conservative persons I ever met are college undergraduates.—*Woodrow Wilson*

4127   *Biography*

Biography, like big game hunting, is one of the recognized forms of sport, and it is as unfair as only sport can be.—*Philip Guedalla*

4128   *Old Age*

Old age, believe me, is a good and pleasant time. It is true that you are gently shouldered off the stage, but then you are given such a comfortable front stall as spectator, and, if you have really played your part, you are more content to sit down and watch.—*Jane Ellen Harrison*

4129   *Attitude*

The important and decisive factor in life is not what happens to us, but the attitude we take toward what happens. The surest revelation of one's character is the way one bears one's suffering. Circumstances and situations may color life, but by the grace of God, we have been given the power to choose what that color shall be. The effect that misfortune, handicap, sickness, and sorrow have upon life is determined by the way in which we meet them.—*Charles R. Woodson*

4130   *Englishman*

An Englishman is a man who lives on an island in the North Sea governed by Scotsmen.—*Philip Guedalla*

4131   *Law*

The Law, wherein, as in a magic mirror we see reflected not only our own lives, but the lives of all men that have been! When I think on this majestic theme my eyes dazzle.—*Oliver Wendell Holmes, Jr.*

4132   *Brotherhood*

Human brotherhood is not just a goal. It is a condition on which our way of life depends. The question for our time is not whether all men are brothers. That question has been answered by God who placed us on this earth together. The question is whether we have the strength and the will to make the brotherhood of man the guiding principle of our daily lives.—*John F. Kennedy*

4133   *Understanding*

It is probably a pity that every citizen of each state cannot visit all the others, to see the differences, to learn what we have in common, and to come back with a richer, fuller understanding of America—in all its beauty, in all its dignity, in all its strength, in support of moral principle.—*Dwight D. Eisenhower*

4134   *Professional Work*

Whether four years of strenuous attention to football and fraternities is the best preparation for professional work has never been seriously investigated.—*Robert Maynard Hutchins*

4135   *Freedom of the Press*
Absolute freedom of the press to discuss public questions is a foundation stone of American liberty.—*Herbert Hoover*

4136   *Government*
For three long years I have been going up and down this country preaching that government ... costs too much. I shall not stop that preaching.—*Franklin D. Roosevelt*

4137   *Amusement*
In those days, the (Roman) government gave them bread and circuses. Today we give them bread and elections, but it is just a change in the style of a periodical amusement.—*Will Durant*

4138   *Committee*
If you want to kill any idea in the world today, get a committee working on it.—*C. F. Kettering*

4139   *Shoes*
I do wear a size 13, and I want you to know that size is hard, but not impossible, to get in your mouth.—*Former Secretary of Labor W. Willard Wirtz*

4140   *Taxes*
The men who collect taxes are working in one of the oldest professions known. Archaeological evidence dating from 1900 B.C. includes a clay tablet recording a tax for public works and a papyrus scroll which reveals that even 4,000 years ago, taxpayers had some complaints.—*Optimist Magazine*

4141   *Progress*
Unquestionably, there is progress. The average American now pays out twice as much in taxes as he formerly got in wages.—*Henry L. Mencken*

4142   *The Thing We Have to Fear*
The thing we have to fear in this country, to my way of thinking, is the influence of the organized minorities, because somehow or other the great majority does not seem to organize. They seem to feel that they are going to be effective because of their own strength, but they give no expression of it.—*Alfred E. Smith*

4143   *Educational Opportunities*
We do not know what education could do for us, because we have never tried it.—*Robert Maynard Hutchins*

4144   *Pity*

Pity is the feeling which arrests the mind in the presence of whatsoever is grave and constant in human sufferings and unites it with the human sufferer.—*James Joyce*

4145   *Ideas*

It is ideas, not vested interests, which are dangerous for good or evil.— *John Maynard Keynes*

4146   *Neckties*

> I like calm hats and I don't wear spats,
> But I want my neckties wild!
>
> > —*Stoddard King*

4147   *Enemies and Friends*

Very few established institutions, governments and constitutions . . . are ever destroyed by their enemies until they have been corrupted and weakened by their friends.—*Walter Lippmann*

4148   *History*

History repeats itself, that's one of the things that's wrong with history.—*Clarence Darrow*

4149   *Responsibility*

The nourishing of the American system requires a sense of responsibility, not only on the part of individual citizens, but especially on the part of America's leadership. I am not speaking alone of political leaders, but of the leaders of all phases of our society as well.

To the extent that they do not exercise their power and influence in the direction of the common good, they are undermining the very system that has given them that power and influence.—*Nelson A. Rockefeller*

4150   *Libraries*

A library is a landmark of civilization, a monument to the people's desire to learn. Whether the place looks monumental or not really doesn't matter. A library is a service organization, not a building. Whether it is a classic-pillared marble temple, a downtown store front or just a book-mobile is not nearly as important as what's inside and how it is used.—*Changing Times*

4151 *Young Writers*

A good many young writers make the mistake of enclosing a stamped, self-addressed envelope, big enough for the manuscript to come back in. This is too much of a temptation to the editor.—*Ring Lardner*

4152 *Ancestors*

... there is no point in our ancestors speaking to us unless we know how to listen.—*Mortimer J. Adler*

4153 *Historian*

Any event, once it has occurred, can be made to appear inevitable by a competent historian.—*Lee Simonson*

4154 *Emotion*

People don't ask for facts in making up their minds. They would rather have one good, soul-satisfying emotion than a dozen facts.—*Robert Keith Leavitt*

4155 *To Protect Liberty*

Experience should teach us to be most on our guard to protect liberty when the government's purposes are beneficent. Men born to freedom are naturally alert to repel invasion of their liberty by evil-minded rulers. The greatest dangers to liberty lurk in insidious encroachment by men of zeal, well-meaning, but without understanding.—*Louis D. Brandeis*

4156 *Contract*

A verbal contract isn't worth the paper it's written on.—*Samuel Goldwyn*

4157 *Law*

The law and the stage—both are a form of exhibition.—*Orson Welles*

4158 *Self-Educated*

Anyone who can read and who owns a dictionary can become an educated person. Hungry minds always become educated and sharpen their mental and emotional tools as they grow in life through experience.—*Dr. Galen Starr Ross*

4159 *The Moon*

Ten years ago the moon was an inspiration to poets and an opportunity for lovers. Ten years from now it will be just another airport.—*Emmanuel G. Mesthene*

4160   *Extraordinary*

It isn't the common man at all who is important; it's the uncommon man.—*Lady Nancy Astor*

4161   *Victim of Circumstance*

Men will often say that they have "found themselves" when they have really been worn down into a groove by the brutal and compulsive force of circumstance.—*Thomas Wolfe*

4162   *Liberty*

It is true that liberty is precious—so precious that it must be rationed.—*Nikolai Lenin*

4163   *Faults*

Nature didn't make us perfect so she did the next best thing. She made us blind to our faults.—*Grit*

4164   *American Professors*

To a true-blue professor of literature in an American university, literature is not something that a plain human being, living today, painfully sits down to produce. No; . . . it is something magically produced by super-human beings who must, if they are to be regarded as artists at all, have died at least one hundred years before the diabolical invention of the typewriter. . . .

Our American professors like their literature clear and cold and pure and very dead.—*From an address given by Sinclair Lewis on receiving the Nobel Prize for Literature, December 12, 1930*

4165   *World*

The world has different owners at sunrise. Fields belong to hired men opening gates for sows; meadows, to old women with carpetbags, collecting mushrooms. Even your own garden does not belong to you. Rabbits and blackbirds have the lawns; a tortoiseshell cat who never appears in daytime patrols the brick walls, and a golden-tailed pheasant glints his way through the iris spears.—*Anne Morrow Lindbergh*

4166   *Americanism*

Of "Americanism" of the right sort we cannot have too much. Mere vaporing and boasting become a nation as little as a man. But honest, outspoken pride and faith in our country are infinitely better and more to be respected than the cultivated reserve which sets it down as ill bred and in bad taste ever to refer to our country except by way of deprecation, criticism, or general negation.—*Henry Cabot Lodge*

4167 *Communism*

Communism is based on the belief that man is so weak and inadequate that he is unable to govern himself, and therefore requires the rule of strong masters.—*Harry S Truman*

4168 *Time*

Time has no divisions to mark its passage, there is never a thunderstorm or blare of trumpets to announce the beginning of a new month or year. Even when a new century begins it is only we mortals who ring bells and fire off pistols.—*Thomas Mann*

4169 *Advice*

Only when a man is safely ensconced under six feet of earth with several tons of enlauding granite upon his chest, is he in a position to give advice with any certainty, and then he is silent.—*A. Edward Newton*

4170 *Snowflakes*

Science informs us that no two snowflakes are alike, but along about this time of year I tend to feel that when you've seen one you've seen them all.—*Burton Hillis, in Better Homes & Gardens*

4171 *Youth*

A society that puts an exaggerated premium upon youth is gravely sick. Of course, any culture needs the leaven of youthful vigor, experiment, irreverence and drive; but it also needs mature judgment, understanding of and respect for its traditions, otherwise it will be all dazzle and no density.—*Stuart Holyroyd*

4172 *Family*

Woman knows what Man has too long forgotten, that the ultimate economic and spiritual unit of any civilization is still the family.—*Clare Boothe Luce*

4173 *Forgetting the Rugged Virtues*

A people bent on a soft security, surrendering their birthright of individual self-reliance for favors, voting themselves into Eden from a supposedly inexhaustible public purse, supporting everyone by soaking a fast-disappearing rich, scrambling for subsidy, learning the arts of political log-rolling and forgetting the rugged virtues of the pioneer, will not measure up to competition with a tough dictatorship.—*Vannevar Bush*

4174 *Winter*

The mountains in the Wintertime had a stern and demonic quality of savage joy that was, in its own way, as strangely, wildly haunting as all the magic and the gold of April.—*Thomas Wolfe*

4175 *How to Live*
I wish that some one would give a course in how to live. It can't be taught in the colleges; that's perfectly obvious, for college professors don't know any better than the rest of us.—*A. Edward Newton*

4176 *My Country*
I believe in the United States of America as a Government of the people, by the people, for the people; whose just powers are derived from the consent of the governed; a democracy in a republic, a sovereign Nation of many sovereign States; a perfect Union one and inseparable; established upon those principles of freedom, equality, justice and humanity for which American patriots sacrificed their lives and fortunes. I therefore believe it is my duty to my country to love it, to support its Constitution, to obey its laws, to respect its flag, and to defend it against all enemies.—*William Tyler Page*

4177 *Social Progress*
Social progress does not have to be bought at the price of individual freedom.—*John Foster Dulles*

4178 *American Heritage*
Our American heritage is threatened as much by our own indifference as by the most unscrupulous office or by the most powerful foreign threat. The future of this republic is in the hands of the American voter.—*Dwight D. Eisenhower*

4179 *Real Messages*
The real messages of hope in our generation are not those to be bounced from the moon, but those to be reflected from one human heart to another.—*Kenneth S. Wills*

4180 *Humility*
He is without humility who sees it within himself.—*William A. Ward, in Meadowbrook (Tex.) Herald*

4181 *Ignorance*
My father, a good man, told me, "Never lose your ignorance; you cannot replace it."—*Erich Maria Remarque*

4182 *Smile*
Her smile was not meant to be seen by anyone and served its whole purpose in being smiled.—*Rainer Maria Rilke*

4183   *Northwest Passage*

On every side of us are men who hunt perpetually for their personal Northwest Passage, too often sacrificing health, strength and life itself to the search; and who shall say they are not happier in their vain but hopeful quest than wiser, duller folks who sit at home, venturing nothing and, with sour laughs, deriding the seekers for that fabled thoroughfare?—*Kenneth Roberts*

4184   *Politics*

Politics has got so expensive that it takes lots of money to even get beat with.—*Will Rogers*

4185   *Reading*

I read for pleasure, mark you. In general I like wedding bells at the end of novels. "They married and lived happily ever after"—why not? It has been done.—*A. Edward Newton*

4186   *Rover*

For the fifth year in succession I have pored over the catalogue of dogs in the show at Madison Square Garden without finding a dog named Rover, Towser, Sport, Spot, or Fido.

Who is the man who can call from his back door at night: "Here, Champion Alexander of Clane o' Wind-Holme! Here, Champion Alexander of Clane o' Wind-Holme"?—*Westbrook Pegler*

4187   *Grief*

Happiness is beneficial for the body but it is grief that develops the powers of the mind.—*Marcel Proust*

4188   *Their Death*

I did not know the dignity of their birth, but I do know the glory of their death.—*Douglas MacArthur*

4189   *Speech*

Of course, sometimes it is not possible to prepare an address fully, but it is much better to do so even if you intend to speak extemporaneously.—*Robert A. Taft*

4190   *Army*

The army report confined itself to the single sentence: All quiet on the Western Front.—*Erich Maria Remarque*

4191   *Oratory*

Oratory: the art of making deep noises from the chest sound like important messages from the brain.—*H. I. Phillips*

4192 *Four Freedoms*

Four freedoms: The first is freedom of speech and expression—everywhere in the world. The second is freedom of every person to worship God in his own way, everywhere in the world. The third is freedom from want . . . everywhere in the world. The fourth is freedom from fear . . . anywhere in the world.—*Franklin D. Roosevelt*

4193 *Americans*

What they do, boys, is creep up on you, and I don't mean Indians. I mean Americans, over the radio, over the waves, from platform, pulpit, press and curb.—*William Saroyan*

4194 *Dress and Manners*

We don't bother much about dress and manners in England, because, as a nation we don't dress well and we've no manners.—*George Bernard Shaw*

4195 *Modern War*

They wrote in the old days that it is sweet and fitting to die for one's country. But in modern war there is nothing sweet nor fitting in your dying. You will die like a dog for no good reason.—*Ernest Hemingway*

4196 *Wars to End Wars*

Wars to end wars are an illusion. Wars, more than any other form of human activity, create the conditions which breed more war.—*John Foster Dulles*

4197 *War Is a Crime*

. . . never think that war, no matter how necessary, nor how justified, is not a crime. Ask the infantry and ask the dead.—*Ernest Hemingway*

4198 *Levity*

My method is to take the utmost trouble to find the right thing to say, and then to say it with the utmost levity.—*George Bernard Shaw*

4199 *The True Joy*

This is the true joy in life, the being used for a purpose recognized by yourself as a mighty one; the being thoroughly worn out before you are thrown on the scrap heap; the being a force of Nature instead of a feverish selfish little clod of ailments and grievances complaining that the world will not devote itself to making you happy.—*George Bernard Shaw*

4200   *A General's Map*

What do I care for the colored pins on a General's map. . . . It's not a fair bargain—this exchange of my life for a small part of a colored pin.—*Irwin Shaw*

4201   *Monotony*

Monotony is the law of nature. Look at the monotonous manner in which the sun rises. . . . The monotony of necessary occupations is exhilarating and life-giving.—*Mahatma Gandhi*

4202   *Knowledge*

Fullness of knowledge always and necessarily means some understanding of the depths of our ignorance, and that is always conducive to both humility and reverence.—*Robert A. Millikan*

4203   *Authors*

When audiences come to see us authors lecture, it is largely in the hope that we'll be funnier to look at than to read.—*Sinclair Lewis*

4204   *Beauty*

Beauty comes and passes, is lost the moment that we touch it, can no more be stayed or held than one can stay the flowing of a river.—*Thomas Wolfe*

4205   *Silence*

Silence is the most perfect expression of scorn.—*George Bernard Shaw*

4206   *Philosopher*

The greater philosopher a man is, the more difficult it is for him to answer the foolish questions of common people.—*Henryk Sienkiewicz*

4207   *Always the Same*

What a bore it is, waking up in the morning always the same person. I wish I were unflinching and emphatic, and had big, bushy eyebrows and a Message for the Age. I wish I were a deep Thinker, or a great Ventriloquist.—*Logan Pearsall Smith*

4208   *Life*

The significant questions of human destiny are not to be approached with a smile. God, misery, and salvation are no joke.—*Irwin Edman*

4209   *Possessions*

I don't want to own anything that won't fit into my coffin.—*Fred Allen*

4210 *Enjoyment*
Eat with the Rich, but go to the play with the Poor, who are capable of Joy.—*Logan Pearsall Smith*

4211 *The United States*
In the United States there is more space where nobody is than where anybody is.
    This is what makes America what it is.—*Gertrude Stein*

4212 *Man*
Man, unlike any other thing organic or inorganic in the universe, grows beyond his work, walks up the stairs of his concepts, emerges ahead of his accomplishments.—*John Steinbeck*

4213 *Democracy*
People who want to understand democracy should spend less time in the library with Aristotle and more time on the buses and in the subway.—*Simeon Strunsky*

4214 *Criminals*
The criminal is the product of spiritual starvation. Someone failed miserably to bring him to know God, love Him and serve Him.—*J. Edgar Hoover*

4215 *Listeners*
A good listener is not someone who has nothing to say. A good listener is a good talker with a sore throat.—*Katherine Whitehorn, in Daily Herald (London)*

4216 *Loneliness*
The whole conviction of my life now rests upon the belief that loneliness, far from being a rare and curious phenomenon, peculiar to myself and to a few other solitary men, is the central and inevitable fact of human existence.—*Thomas Wolfe*

4217 *Our Fears*
We are so largely the playthings of Fate in our fears. To one, fear of the dark, to another, of physical pain, to a third, of public ridicule, to a fourth of poverty, to a fifth of loneliness—for all of us our particular creature lurks in ambush.—*Hugh Walpole*

4218 *Dawn*
For what human ill does not dawn seem to be an alleviation?—*Thornton Wilder*

4219 *Freedom*

Freedom is an indivisible word. If we want to enjoy it, and fight for it, we must be prepared to extend it to everyone, whether they are rich or poor, whether they agree with us or not, no matter what their race or the color of their skin.—*Wendell L. Wilkie*

4220 *Alone*

Naked and alone we came into exile.... Which of us has known his brother? Which of us has looked into his father's heart? ... Which of us is not forever a stranger and alone?

4221 *Love*

... the unity that binds us all together, that makes this earth a family, and all men brothers and the sons of God, is love.—*Thomas Wolfe*

4222 *Confidence*

If Government is to retain the confidence of the people, it must not spend more than can be justified on grounds of national need or spent with maximum efficiency.—*John F. Kennedy*

4223 *Belief*

A belief is not merely an idea the mind possesses; it is an idea that possesses the mind.—*Robert Bolton*

4224 *Cooking Dinner*

There is no spectacle on earth more appealing than that of a beautiful woman in the act of cooking dinner for someone she loves.—*Thomas Wolfe*

4225 *Beauty of the World*

The beauty of the world has two edges, one of laughter, one of anguish, cutting the heart asunder.—*Virginia Woolf*

4226 *Play*

The play left a taste of lukewarm parsnip juice.—*Alexander Woollcott*

4227 *Discretion*

The things that a man does not say often reveal the understanding and penetration of his mind even more than the things he says.—*Robert A. Millikan*

4228 *Growing Old*

Growing old is no more than a bad habit which a busy man has no time to form.—*André Maurois*

4229   No Bigger

A man who is too big to study his job is as big as he will ever be.—*William E. North*

4230   Great Colleges

Great individuals, not great organization men, make a college or university great.—*Harold W. Dodds*

4231   Money

A man who has a million dollars is as well off as if he were rich.—*John Jacob Astor III*

4232   Brilliance

To give an accurate and exhaustive account of that period would need a far less brilliant pen than mine.—*Sir Thomas Beecham*

4233   Dozing

I had just dozed off into a stupor when I heard what I thought was myself talking to myself. I didn't pay much attention to it, as I knew practically everything I would have to say to myself, and wasn't particularly interested.—*Robert Benchley*

4234   Travel

I haven't been abroad in so long that I almost speak English without an accent.—*Robert Benchley*

4235   Speech

A wise man thinks once before he speaks twice.—*Robert Benchley*

4236   Middle of the Road

We know what happens to people who stay in the middle of the road. They get run over.—*Aneurin Bevan*

4237   Leader

I must follow them; I am their leader.—*Andrew Bonar Law*

4238   Actor

An actor's a guy who, if you ain't talking about him, ain't listening.—*Marlon Brando*

4239   Listening

I was never tired of listening to his wisdom or imparting my own.—*Sir Winston Churchill*

4240 *Illness*

I've just learnt about his illness; let's hope it's nothing trivial.—*Irvin S. Cobb*

4241 *No Difference*

Why should a worm turn? It's probably just the same on the other side.—*Irvin S. Cobb*

4242 *In the Long Run*

He (Maynard Keynes) was the first Englishman since Horace Walpole to tell The Long Run to go jump into a lake. "In the long run," said Maynard Keynes, ". . . we are all dead."—*Claud Cockburn*

4243 *An Editor*

An editor: A person who knows precisely what he wants—but isn't quite sure.—*Walter Davenport*

4244 *Ballet*

My own personal reaction is that most ballets would be quite delightful if it were not for the dancing.—*Evening Standard*

4245 *Family*

Our family is not yet so good as to be degenerating.—*Kurt Ewald*

4246 *Not All Bad*

Anybody who hates children and dogs can't be all bad.—*W. C. Fields*

4247 *No Time Left*

A big man has no time really to do anything but just sit and be big.—*F. Scott Fitzgerald*

4248 *What to Do*

"What'll we do with ourselves this afternoon?" cried Daisy, "and the day after that, and the next thirty years."—*F. Scott Fitzgerald*

4249 *Approved Religion*

Ronny approved of religion as long as it endorsed the National Anthem, but he objected when it attempted to influence his life.—*E. M. Forster*

4250 *People*

People are inexterminable—like flies and bed-bugs. There will always be some that survive in cracks and crevices—that's us.—*Robert Frost*

4251 *No Serious Hate*

I never hated a man enough to give his diamonds back.—*Zsa Zsa Gabor*

4252   *Wealth*

Wealth has never been a sufficient source of honor in itself. It must be advertised, and the normal medium is obtrusively expensive goods.—*J. K. Galbraith*

4253   *Modern Liberal*

The modern liberal rallies to protect the poor from the taxes which in the next generation, as the result of a higher investment for their children, would eliminate poverty.—*J. K. Galbraith*

4254   *Politicians*

I have come to the conclusion that politics are too serious a matter to be left to the politicians.—*Charles de Gaulle*

4255   *Snub*

I never snub anybody accidentally.—*Norman Ginsbury*

4256   *Goldwynisms*

I'll give you a definitive maybe.—*Samuel Goldwyn*

4257   It's more than magnificent — it's mediocre. — *Samuel Goldwyn*

4258   Why should people go out and pay money to see bad films when they can stay at home and see bad television for nothing?—*Samuel Goldwyn*

4259   I want a film that begins with an earthquake and works up to a climax.—*Samuel Goldwyn*

4260   *Burglar*

A burglar who respects his art always takes his time before taking anything else.—*O. Henry*

4261   *Transition*

When our first parents were driven out of Paradise, Adam is believed to have remarked to Eve: "My dear, we live in an age of transition."—*W. R. Inge, Dean of St. Paul's*

4262   *Appearance*

We tolerate shapes in human beings that would horrify us if we saw them in a horse.—*W. R. Inge, Dean of St. Paul's*

4263   *Religion*

Among all my patients in the second half of life—that is to say over thirty-five—there has not been one whose problem in the last resort was not that of finding a religious outlook on life.—*C. G. Jung*

4264 *Your Country*

Ask not what your country can do for you; ask what you can do for your country.—*John F. Kennedy*

4265 *Confusion*

I had nothing to offer anybody except my own confusion.—*Jack Kerouac*

4266 *Labor*

Workingmen are at the foundation of society. Show me that product of human endeavor in the making of which the workingman has had no share, and I will show you something that society can well dispense with.—*Samuel Gompers*

4267 *Kingfish*

I looked around at the little fishes present, and said, "I'm the Kingfish."—*Huey Long*

4268 *Popular*

In high school and college my sister Mary was very popular with the boys, but I had braces on my teeth and got high marks.—*Betty MacDonald*

4269 *Our Age*

If the nineteenth century was the age of the editorial chair, ours is the century of the psychiatrist's couch.—*Marshall McLuhan*

4270 *Poverty*

I've worked myself up from nothing to a state of extreme poverty.—*Groucho Marx*

4271 *Principle*

You can't learn too soon that the most useful thing about a principle is that it can always be sacrificed to expediency.—*W. Somerset Maugham*

4272 *My Greatest Friend*

My dear, she's been my greatest friend for fifteen years. I know her through and through, and I tell you that she hasn't got a single redeeming quality.—*W. Somerset Maugham*

4273 *A Precept He Followed*

I forget who it was that recommended men for their soul's good to do each day two things they disliked. . . . It is a precept that I have followed scrupulously; for every day I have got up and I have gone to bed.—*W. Somerset Maugham*

4274 *The Heart's Okay*
I'll give you my opinion of the human race in a nutshell.... Their heart's in the right place, but their head is a thoroughly inefficient organ.—W. Somerset Maugham

4275 *The Swiss*
The Swiss managed to build a lovely country around their hotels.—*George Mikes*

4276 *A Good Newspaper*
A good newspaper, I suppose, is a nation talking to itself.—*Arthur Miller*

4277 *Church*
There are many who stay away from church these days because you hardly ever mention God any more.—*Arthur Miller*

4278 *Thinking*
I wrote somewhere once that the third-rate mind was only happy when it was thinking with the majority, the second-rate mind was only happy when it was thinking with the minority, and the first-rate mind was only happy when it was thinking.—*A. A. Milne*

4279 *Prophets*
Prophets were twice stoned—first in anger; then, after their death, with a handsome slab in the graveyard.—*Christopher Morley*

4280 *Socialism*
To the ordinary working man, the sort you would meet in any pub on Saturday night, Socialism does not mean much more than better wages and shorter hours and nobody bossing you about.—*George Orwell*

4281 *Work*
Work expands so as to fill the time available for its completion. General recognition of this fact is shown in the proverbial phrase, "It is the busiest man who has time to spare."—*C. Northcote Parkinson*

4282 *Incompetence*
The Peter Principle: In a hierarchy every employee tends to rise to his level of incompetence.—*Lawrence J. Peter*

4283 *In Love with Himself*
He fell in love with himself at first sight and it is a passion to which he has always remained faithful. Self-love seems so often unrequited.—*Anthony Powell*

4284   *Money*

Money is good for bribing yourself through the inconveniences of life.—*Gottfried Reinhardt*

4285   *Thinking*

You can't think rationally on an empty stomach, and a whole lot of people can't do it on a full one either.—*Lord Reith*

4286   *Time*

Half our life is spent trying to find something to do with the time we have rushed through life trying to save.—*Will Rogers*

4287   *Party Politics*

The more you read about politics, you got to admit that each party is worse than the other.—*Will Rogers*

4288   *Ignorance*

Everybody is ignorant, only on different subjects.—*Will Rogers*

4289   *Ancestors*

My folks didn't come over on the Mayflower, but they were there to meet the boat.—*Will Rogers*

4290   *Cheaper*

Any time you see him he is generally by himself because being by himself is not apt to cost him anything.—*Damon Runyon*

4291   *Money*

My boy . . . always try to rub up against money, for if you rub up against money long enough, some of it may rub off on you.—*Damon Runyon*

4292   *Friends*

I step over to his table and give him a medium hello, and he looks up and gives me a medium hello right back, for, to tell the truth, Maury and I are never bosom friends.—*Damon Runyon*

4293   *Patriots*

Patriots always talk of dying for their country, and never of killing for their country.—*Bertrand Russell*

4294   *Agony*

They had a passion for getting something for nothing. Every blackberry in the hedgerow was an agony to Lavinia until she had bottled it.—*Victoria Sackville-West*

4295 *Income*

All decent people live beyond their incomes nowadays, and those who aren't respectable live beyond other people's. A few gifted individuals manage to do both.—*Saki (H. H. Munro)*

4296 *Young and Old*

The young have aspirations that never come to pass, the old have reminiscences of what never happened.—*Saki (H. H. Munro)*

4297 *Strictly Brought Up*

I think she must have been very strictly brought up, she's so desperately anxious to do the wrong thing correctly.—*Saki (H. H. Munro)*

4298 *Library*

A library is thought in cold storage.—*Herbert Samuel*

4299 *The Past*

Those who cannot remember the past are condemned to repeat it.—*George Santayana*

4300 *Time*

Three o'clock is always too late or too early for anything you want to do.—*Jean-Paul Sartre*

4301 *An Intellectual*

I too had thoughts once of being an intellectual, but I found it too difficult. (*To an African who refused to perform some humdrum duty on the grounds that he was an intellectual.*)—*Albert Schweitzer*

4302 *Titles*

Titles distinguish the mediocre, embarrass the superior, and are disgraced by the inferior.—*George Bernard Shaw*

4303 *Respectable*

The more things a man is ashamed of, the more respectable he is.—*George Bernard Shaw*

4304 *Carried Away*

Lying hardly describes it. I overdo it. I get carried away in an ecstasy of mendacity.—*George Bernard Shaw*

4305 *Education*

Education is what survives when what has been learnt has been forgotten.—*B. F. Skinner*

4306   *Prayers*

Prayers are like those appeals of ours. Either they don't get through or they're returned with "rejected" scrawled across 'em.—*A. Solzhenitsyn*

4307   *Finality*

Finality is death. Perfection is finality. Nothing is perfect. There are lumps in it.—*James Stephens*

4308   *Gains and Pains*

Let's talk sense to the American people. Let's tell them the truth, that there are no gains without pains.—*Adlai Stevenson*

4309   *Statesman*

A politician is a statesman who approaches every question with an open mouth.—*Adlai E. Stevenson*

4310   *Early to Rise*

Early to rise and early to bed makes a male healthy and wealthy and dead.—*James Thurber*

4311   *Sleep*

I haven't been to sleep for over a year. That's why I go to bed early. One needs more rest if one doesn't sleep.—*Evelyn Waugh*

4312   *Obsolescence*

Britain today is suffering from galloping obsolescence.—*Anthony Wedgewood Benn*

4313   *Cynicism*

Cynicism is humour in ill-health.—*H. G. Wells*

4314   *Christmas*

To perceive Christmas through its wrapping becomes more difficult every year.—*E. B. White*

4315   *Fools*

Ninety-nine percent of the people in the world are fools and the rest of us are in great danger of contagion.—*Thornton Wilder*

4316   *Marriage*

Marriage is a bribe to make a housekeeper think she's a householder.—*Thornton Wilder*

4317 *Business*

Business underlies everything in our national life, including our spiritual life. Witness the fact that in the Lord's Prayer the first petition is for daily bread. No one can worship God or love his neighbor on an empty stomach.—*Woodrow Wilson*

4318 *Cold Accusing Eyes*

It was one of those cold, clammy, accusing sort of eyes—the kind that makes you reach up to see if your tie is straight: and he looked at me as if I were some sort of unnecessary product which Cuthbert the Cat had brought in after a ramble among the local ash-cans.—*P. G. Wodehouse*

4319 *Feeling Poorly*

It must have been about one in the afternoon when I woke. I was feeling more or less like something the Pure Food Committee had rejected.—*P. G. Wodehouse*

4320 *Captain of Industry*

As a rule, from what I've observed, the American captain of industry doesn't do anything out of business hours. When he has put the cat out and locked up the office for the night, he just relapses into a state of coma from which he emerges only to start being a captain of industry again.—*P. G. Wodehouse*

4321 *Life*

I spent the afternoon musing on Life. If you come to think of it, what a queer thing Life is! So unlike anything else, don't you know, if you see what I mean.—*P. G. Wodehouse*

4322 *Secrets of the Past*

Each had his past shut in him like the leaves of a book known to him by heart; and his friends could only read the title.—*Virginia Woolf*

4323 *Design*

The chair ... was upholstered in one of those flagrant chintzes, designed, apparently, by the art editor of a seed catalog.—*Alexander Woollcott*

4324 *Contempt*

Ross, a man who knew nothing ... and had contempt for anything he didn't understand, which was practically everything.—*Alexander Woollcott*

4325   Architect

The physician can bury his mistakes, but the architect can only advise his client to plant vines.—*Frank Lloyd Wright*

4326   Music Teacher

The music teacher came twice each week to bridge the awful gap between Dorothy and Chopin.—*George Ade*

4327   Laughter Heals

Having entertained wounded GIs in three wars, I have seen the healing power of laughter. Now science has confirmed that having fun—just feeling happy or joyous—has a measurable effect on our health and well-being.—*Bob Hope*

4328   Church

He was of the faith chiefly in the sense that the church he currently did not attend was Catholic.—*Kingsley Amis*

4329   On Oath

(After describing himself in a court of law as the greatest living actor, excused his boastfulness with) You see, I am on oath.—*George Arliss*

4330   Success

Every man who is high up likes to feel that he has done it all himself; and the wife smiles, and lets it go at that. It's our only joke. Every woman knows that.—*James M. Barrie*

4331   Crowd Mind

You cannot make a man by standing a sheep on its hind legs. But by standing a flock of sheep in that position you can make a crowd of men.—*Max Beerbohm*

4332   Be Still

To my mind the most pregnant mystical exhortation ever written is "Be still and know that I am God."—*Anon.*

4333   Ostentation

I explained to him I had simple tastes and didn't want anything ostentatious, no matter what it cost me.—*Art Buchwald*

4334   An Artist

He is an artist, you know, and talks a great deal for his own pleasure.—*Joyce Cary*

4335   *Being President*
There is one thing about being President—nobody can tell you when to sit down.—*Dwight D. Eisenhower*

4336   *Intellectual*
An intellectual is a man who takes more words than necessary to tell more than he knows.—*Dwight D. Eisenhower*

4337   *Risk*
(*Asked if as a boy he had ever thought of the possibility he would grow up to be president*) Yes, but I just dismissed it as a normal risk that any red-blooded American boy has to take.—*Adlai E. Stevenson*

4338   *Redemption of Ignorance*
(*He once squelched a heckler with*) I believe in the forgiveness of sin and the redemption of ignorance.—*Adlai E. Stevenson*

4339   *Election*
To the victor belong the toils.—*Adlai E. Stevenson*

4340   *Politics*
Moderate progressivism: Don't just do something—stand there.—*Adlai E. Stevenson*

4341   *Similarity*
Churchill was always rewriting his speeches until he had to give them. But that's where my similarity to Churchill ends.—*Adlai E. Stevenson*

4342   *Free Society*
My definition of a free society is a society where it is safe to be unpopular.—*Adlai E. Stevenson*

4343   *Great Presidents*
Some of the Presidents were great and some of them weren't. I can say that, because I wasn't one of the great Presidents, but I had a good time trying to be one, I can tell you that.—*Harry S Truman*

4344   *Failure*
My father was not a failure. After all, he was the father of a President of the United States.—*Harry S Truman*

4345 *Peace*

Peace is the goal of my life. I'd rather have lasting peace in the world than be President. I wish for peace, I work for peace and I pray for peace continually.—*Harry S Truman*

4346 *Favorite Prayer*

O Almighty and Everlasting God, Creator of Heaven, Earth and the Universe:

Help me to be, to think, to act what is right, because it is right; make me truthful, honest and honorable in all things; make me intellectually honest for the sake of right and honor and without thought of reward to me. Give me the ability to be charitable, forgiving and patient with my fellow men—help me to understand their motives and their shortcomings—even as thou understandest mine! Amen, Amen, Amen.—*Harry S Truman*

4347 *Fund-raising*

I am deeply touched—not as deeply touched as you have been by coming to this dinner, but nevertheless, it is a sentimental occasion.—*John F. Kennedy*

4348 *Why He Was a War Hero*

It was absolutely involuntary. They sank my boat.—*John F. Kennedy*

4349 *Welcome*

There is no city in the United States in which I get a warmer welcome and less votes than Columbus, Ohio.—*John F. Kennedy*

4350 *Political Promotion*

Those of you who regard my profession of political life with some disdain should remember that it made it possible for me to move from being an obscure lieutenant in the United States Navy to Commander-in-Chief in fourteen years with very little technical competence.—*John F. Kennedy*

4351 *Learning*

You ain't learnin' nothin' when you're talkin'.—*Lyndon B. Johnson*

4352 *Honest*

At the card game one of the boys looked across the table and said: "Now, Reuben, play the cards fair. I know what I dealt you."—*Lyndon B. Johnson*

4353 *Golf*

I don't have any handicap. I am all handicap.—*Lyndon B. Johnson*

4354 *Taxation*

In 1790, the nation which had fought a revolution against taxation without representation discovered that some of its citizens weren't much happier about taxation with representation.—*Lyndon B. Johnson*

4355 *Security*

My White House job pays more than public school systems but the tenure is less certain.—*Lyndon B. Johnson*

4356 *Shortcomings*

An hour late and a dollar short, that's the way I've been all my life.—*Lyndon B. Johnson*

4357 *Indignation*

On a certain occasion in the House of Commons, Churchill said something which caused another Member to jump to his feet bursting so strongly with disagreement as to be almost unintelligible. "My right honourable friend," said Churchill, "should not develop more indignation than he can contain."

4358 *Political Life*

Politics are almost as exciting as war and quite as dangerous, although in war you can be killed only once, in politics many times.—*Sir Winston Churchill*

4359 *Communism*

Trying to maintain good relations with the Communists is like wooing a crocodile. You do not know whether to tickle it under the chin or beat it over the head. When it opens its mouth you cannot tell whether it is trying to smile or preparing to eat you up.—*Sir Winston Churchill*

4360 *Difficulties*

Don't argue about the difficulties. The difficulties will argue for themselves.—*Sir Winston Churchill*

4361 *Acuteness of Mind*

Neither of his colleagues can compare with him in that acuteness or energy of mind with which he devotes himself to so many topics injurious to the strength and welfare of the State (of Sir Stafford Cripps).—*Sir Winston Churchill*

4362 *Family*

Where does the family start? It starts with a young man falling in love with a girl. No superior alternative has yet been found.—*Sir Winston Churchill*

4363   *Intelligentsia*
The intelligent are to the intelligentsia what a gentleman is to a gent.—*Stanley Baldwin*

4364   *Well Spoken*
Herbert H. Asquith's lucidity of style is a positive disadvantage when he has nothing to say.—*Arthur Balfour*

4365   *Enthusiasm*
It is unfortunate, considering that enthusiasm moves the world, that so few enthusiasts can be trusted to speak the truth.—*Arthur Balfour*

4366   *Truth*
Nothing should impede the truth save a substantial sum of money.—*Hilaire Belloc*

4367   *Wealth*
Stand not too near the rich man lest he destroy thee—and not too far away lest he forget thee.—*Aneurin Bevan*

4368   *Don't Be Deterred*
Please don't be deterred in the fanatical application of your sterile logic.—*Aneurin Bevan*

4369   *Winston Churchill*
His ear is so sensitively attuned to the bugle note of history that he is often deaf to the more raucous clamour of contemporary life, a defect which his Conservative upbringing and background tend to reinforce. The seven-league-boots tempo of his imagination hastens him on to the "sunny uplands" of the future; he is apt to forget that the slow steps of humanity must travel every inch of the weary road that leads there.—*Aneurin Bevan*

4370   *Lord Attlee*
He seems determined to make a trumpet sound like a tin whistle. . . . He brings to the fierce struggle of politics the tepid enthusiasm of a lazy summer afternoon at a cricket match.—*Aneurin Bevan*

4371   *A Government Official*
A man walking backwards with his face to the future.—*Aneurin Bevan*

4372   *History*
That great dustheap called history.—*Augustine Birrell*

4373 Mind
Sir Stafford (Cripps) has a brilliant mind until it is made up.—*Lady Violet Bonham Carter*

4374 Income Tax
The one thing that hurts more than paying an income tax is not having to pay an income tax.—*Lord Dewar*

4375 Love
Love is an ocean of emotions, entirely surrounded by expenses.—*Lord Dewar*

4376 Criticism
To be criticised is not necessarily to be wrong.—*Sir Anthony Eden*

4377 Highbrow
A highbrow is the kind of person who looks at a sausage and thinks of Picasso.—*Sir Alan Herbert*

4378 Confidence
I do not object to Gladstone always having the ace of trumps up his sleeve but merely to his belief that God Almighty put it there.—*Henry Labouchere*

4379 Understanding
Poincaré knows everything and understands nothing—Briand understands everything and knows nothing.—*David Lloyd George*

4380 Criticism
I have never found, in a long experience of politics, that criticism is ever inhibited by ignorance.—*Harold Macmillan*

4381 No Greater Love
Greater love hath no man than this, that he lay down his friends for his life.—*Jeremy Thorpe*

4382 Editorial "We"
Only presidents, editors and people with tapeworm have the right to use the editorial "we."—*Mark Twain*

4383 Not Quite Impartial
It is well, when one is judging a friend, to remember that he is judging you with the same godlike and superior impartiality.—*Arnold Bennett*

4384   Charity Work
A congregation which can't afford to pay a clergyman enough want a missionary more than they do a clergyman.—*Josh Billings*

4385   That Dangerous Age
Middle age occurs when you are too young to take up golf and too old to rush up to the net.—*Franklin Pierce Adams*

4386   Good Advice
Nothing is often a good thing to do, and always a clever thing to say.—*Will Durant*

4387   Economic Forecast
Business will be either better or worse.—*Calvin Coolidge*

4388   A Good Source
The worst men often give the best advice.—*Philip James Bailey*

4389   Chief Regret
One of my chief regrets during my years in the theater was that I couldn't sit in the audience and watch me.—*John Barrymore*

4390   Luxury
My clothes are addressed to women who can afford to travel with forty suitcases.—*Yves Saint Laurent*

4391   Selfishness
Selfishness is that detestable vice which no one will forgive in others and no one is without in himself.—*Henry Ward Beecher*

4392   Editorial Advice
As to the Adjective; when in doubt, strike it out.—*Mark Twain*

4393   Campaign Tactics
He who slings mud generally loses ground.—*Adlai Stevenson*

4394   Jealousy
Many speak the truth when they say that they despise riches, but they mean the riches possessed by other men.—*Charles Caleb Colton*

4395   Work
Work is work if you're paid to do it, and it's pleasure if you pay to be allowed to do it.—*Finley Peter Dunne*

4396 *Speak Up*

If you wish in the world to advance; your merits you're bound to enhance. You must stir it and stump it—and blow your own trumpet—or trust me, you haven't a chance!—*W. S. Gilbert*

4397 *Double Trouble*

If a man could have half his wishes, he would double his troubles.—*Benjamin Franklin*

4398 *Enemies*

Love your enemies, for they tell you your faults.—*Benjamin Franklin*

4399 *Wishful Thinking*

A man will sometimes devote all his life to the development of one part of his body—the wishbone.—*Robert Frost*

4400 *Home*

A man's home may seem to be his castle on the outside; inside, it is more often his nursery.—*Clare Boothe Luce*

4401 *Idealism*

Idealism increases in direct proportion to one's distance from the problem.—*John Galsworthy*

4402 *Boredom*

Isn't your life extremely flat with nothing whatever to grumble at?—*William Schwenck Gilbert*

4403 *Gardening*

In order to live off a garden, you practically have to live in it.—*Frank McKinney Hubbard*

4404 *Hard to Tell*

It seems like one of the hardest lessons to be learned in this life is where your business ends and somebody else's begins.—*Frank McKinney Hubbard*

4405 *Great Manners*

The audience was swell. They were so polite they covered their mouths when they yawned.—*Bob Hope*

4406 *Encyclopedia*

To me the charm of an encyclopedia is that it knows—and I needn't.—*Francis Yeats-Brown*

4407 *Helpless*

No one can feel as helpless as the owner of a sick goldfish.—*Frank McKinney Hubbard*

4408 *Budget*

Let us all be happy and live within our means, even if we have to borrow the money to do it with.—*Artemus Ward*

4409 *Critic*

A critic is a man who expects miracles.—*James Gibbons Huneker*

4410 *Taxpayer*

I'm proud to be paying taxes in the United States. The only thing is—I could be just as proud for half the money.—*Arthur Godfrey*

4411 *Health Tip*

Whenever I feel like exercise, I lie down until the feeling passes.—*Robert Maynard Hutchins*

4412 *All Are at Risk*

If a little knowledge is dangerous, where is the man who has so much as to be out of danger?—*Thomas Henry Huxley*

4413 *Discussion or Argument?*

He is more apt to contribute heat than light to a discussion.—*Woodrow Wilson*

4414 *Fools*

There are two kinds of fools: one says, "This is old, therefore it is good"; the other says, "This is new, therefore it is better."—*Henrik Ibsen*

4415 *Secrets*

The reason we are so pleased to find out other people's secrets is that it distracts public attention from our own.—*Oscar Wilde*

4416 *Good Intentions*

Whenever a man does a thoroughly stupid thing, it is always from the noblest motives.—*Oscar Wilde*

4417 *Faults*

Misfortunes one can endure, they come from the outside; but to suffer for one's faults—ah! there is the sting of life.—*Oscar Wilde*

4418   *Don't Advise*
It is always a silly thing to give advice, but to give good advice is absolutely fatal.—*Oscar Wilde*

4419   *Reasonable*
Man is a rational animal who always loses his temper when he is called upon to act in accordance with the dictates of reason.—*Oscar Wilde*

4420   *I've Changed*
I beg your pardon, I didn't recognize you—I've changed a lot.—*Oscar Wilde*

4421   *Sympathy*
Anyone can sympathize with the sufferings of a friend, but it requires a very fine nature to sympathize with a friend's success.—*Oscar Wilde*

4422   *Sharing*
When I'm sad I sing, and then others can be sad with me.—*Mark Twain*

4423   *Foolish Man*
Man is the only animal that can be a fool.—*Holbrook Jackson*

4424   *Tell the Truth*
It is always the best policy to speak the truth, unless of course you are an exceptionally good liar.—*Jerome K. Jerome*

4425   *Patience*
In this world, truth can wait; she's used to it.—*Douglas Jerrold*

4426   *Hard Work*
Gardens are not made by singing "Oh how beautiful," and sitting in the shade.—*Rudyard Kipling*

4427   *Agriculture*
Blessed be agriculture—if one does not have too much of it.—*Charles Warner*

4428   *Good Boy*
One of the best things in the world to be is a boy; it requires no experience, but needs some practice to be a good one.—*Charles Warner*

4429   *Wit Speaks for Itself*
Conceit causes more conversation than wit.—*LaRochefoucauld*

4430 *Familiar Faults*
If we had no faults of our own, we should take less pleasure in noticing the faults of others.—*LaRochefoucauld*

4431 *Self-Satisfied*
A man who is always satisfied with himself is seldom satisfied with others.—*LaRochefoucauld*

4432 *Correct Opinions*
Our enemies come nearer the truth in their opinions of us than we do in our opinion of ourselves.—*LaRochefoucauld*

4433 *Blue Jay Grammar*
I've never heard a blue jay use bad grammar, but very seldom; and when they do, they are as ashamed as a human.—*Mark Twain*

4434 *Friendly*
He liked to like people, therefore people liked him.—*Mark Twain*

4435 *Vanity*
Vanity is the greatest of all flatterers.—*LaRochefoucauld*

4436 *Admiration*
We always like those who admire us but we do not always like those whom we admire.—*LaRochefoucauld*

4437 *The Fourth R*
We need to add to the three R's, namely Reading, 'Riting and 'Rithmetic, a fourth—Responsibility.—*Herbert Hoover*

4438 *Ideal Spouse*
An ideal wife is any woman who has an ideal husband.—*Booth Tarkington*

4439 *Opera*
Sleep is an excellent way of listening to an opera.—*James Stephens*

4440 *Flattery*
We sometimes imagine we hate flattery, but we only hate the way we are flattered.—*LaRochefoucauld*

4441 *Agreeable*
If you wish to appear agreeable in society you must consent to be taught many things which you already know.—*Johann Kaspar Lavater*

4442 *Political Economy*
It is called political economy because it has nothing to do with either politics or economy.—*Stephen Leacock*

4443 *Trust*
Men are able to trust one another, knowing the exact degree of dishonesty they are entitled to expect.—*Stephen Leacock*

4444 *Luck*
I am a great believer in luck, and I find the harder I work the more I have of it.—*Stephen Leacock*

4445 *Woman*
Once made equal to man, woman becomes his superior.—*Socrates*

4446 *Maladies*
I have gout, asthma, and seven other maladies, but am otherwise very well.—*Sydney Smith*

4447 *Reformers*
All reformers, however strict their conscience, live in houses just as big as they can pay for.—*Logan Smith*

4448 *Confusion*
One learns in life to keep silent and draw one's own confusions.—*Cornelia Otis Skinner*

4449 *Success*
Success covers a multitude of blunders.—*George Bernard Shaw*

4450 *Patriotism*
Patriotism is your conviction that this country is superior to all other countries because you were born in it.—*George Bernard Shaw*

4451 *Liar's Punishment*
The liar's punishment is not in the least that he is not believed, but that he cannot believe anyone else.—*George Bernard Shaw*

4452 *Learned*
A learned man is an idler who kills time by study.—*George Bernard Shaw*

4453 *Honest about Work*
My father taught me to work; he did not teach me to love it.—*Abraham Lincoln*

4454   *Memory*
No man has a good enough memory to make a successful liar.—*Abraham Lincoln*

4455   *The Most Flattered*
When I tell him he hates flatterers, he says he does, being then the most flattered.—*Shakespeare*

4456   *When Experts Agree*
Even when the experts all agree, they may well be mistaken.—*Bertrand Russell*

4457   *Universities*
Universities are full of knowledge; the freshmen bring a little in and the seniors take none away, and knowledge accumulates.—*Abbott Lawrence Lowell*

4458   *Rossini*
Give me a laundry list and I will set it to music.—*Gioacchino Antonio Rossini*

4459   *Prophesy*
Don't ever prophesy—unless you know.—*James Russell Lowell*

4460   *Punctuality*
I am a believer in punctuality though it makes me very lonely.—*Edward Verrall Lucas*

4461   *To Be Loved*
If you wish to be loved, show more of your faults than your virtues.—*Edward George Bulwer-Lytton*

4462   *Epigram*
A platitude with vine-leaves in its hair.—*H. L. Mencken*

4463   *Highbrow*
A highbrow is a person educated beyond his intelligence.—*Brander Matthews*

4464   *Head Problems*
A cold in the head causes less suffering than an idea.—*Jules Renard*

4465   *Necessity of Work*
I go on working for the same reason that a hen goes on laying eggs.—*H. L. Mencken*

4466 *Opera in English*
Opera, in English is, in the main, just about as sensible as baseball in Italian.—*H. L. Mencken*

4467 *Break Your Mirror*
If you wish to avoid seeking a fool you must first break your mirror.—*François Rabelais*

4468 *Blessed to Give*
'Tis more blessed to give than to receive; for example, wedding presents.—*H. L. Mencken*

4469 *Talk*
Wise men talk because they have something to say; fools, because they have to say something.—*Plato*

4470 *Drama Critic*
A drama critic is a person who surprises the playwright by informing him what he meant.—*Wilson Mizner*

4471 *No Lender*
The man who won't loan money isn't going to have many friends—or need them.—*Wilson Mizner*

4472 *Changeable Luck*
The only sure thing about luck is that it will change.—*Wilson Mizner*

4473 *Graciousness*
Be kind and considerate to others, depending somewhat upon who they are.—*Don Herold*

4474 *Mark Twain's Weather Report*
The weather reports these days remind us of Mark Twain's "136 varieties of New England weather." In that masterpiece he referred to the forecasters as not knowing what to predict, so their predictions went like this: "Probably northeast to southwest winds, varying to the southward and westward and eastward and points in between; high and low barometer sweeping around from place to place; probable areas of rain, snow, hail and drought succeeded or preceded by earthquakes, with thunder and lightning."

4475 *Easy Standard*
He who comes up to his own idea of greatness must always have had a very low standard of it in his mind.—*William Hazlitt*

4476   *Right Is Not Enough*

We are not satisfied to be right, unless we can prove others to be quite wrong.—*William Hazlitt*

4477   *Saving*

When one has had to work so hard to get money, why should he impose on himself the further hardship of trying to save it?—*Don Herold*

4478   *Good Sense*

There is nobody so irritating as somebody with less intelligence and more sense than we have.—*Don Herold*

4479   *First Century*

Life's a tough proposition, and the first hundred years are the hardest.—*Wilson Mizner*

4480   *Political War*

A political war is one in which everyone shoots from the lip.—*Raymond Moley*

4481   *Intellectual Stagnation*

At a certain age some people's minds close up; they live on their intellectual fat.—*William Lyon Phelps*

4482   *American Freedom*

There should be more in American liberty than the privilege we enjoy of insulting the President with impunity.—*Austin O'Malley*

4483   *Politicians*

At a Fourth of July celebration, it is wonderful how many great men there are and how they swarm on the speaker's platform.—*Edgar Wilson Nye*

4484   *Nonsense*

No one is exempt from talking nonsense; the mistake is to do it solemnly.—*Montaigne*

4485   *Men's Dress*

I hate to see men overdressed; a man ought to look like he's put together by accident, not added up on purpose.—*Christopher Morley*

4486   *George Bernard Shaw*

Bernard Shaw had discovered himself and gave ungrudgingly of his discovery to the world.—*Hector Hugh Munro*

4487   *Hyperactivity*
Work is a form of nervousness.—*Don Herold*

4488   *Book Reviews*
I never read a book before reviewing it. It prejudices me so.—*Sidney Smith*

4489   *The Proof*
It takes a lot of things to prove you are smart, but only one thing to prove you are ignorant.—*Don Herold*

4490   *Marriage*
When two people are under the influence of the most violent, most insane, most delusive, and most transient of passions, they are required to swear that they will remain in the excited, abnormal, and exhausting condition continuously until death do them part.—*George Bernard Shaw*

4491   *Apology*
Apology is only egotism wrong side out.—*Oliver Wendell Holmes*

4492   *Constructive Criticism*
If you want to get rid of somebody just tell 'em something for their own good.—*Frank McKinney Hubbard*

4493   *Mutual Admiration*
Marriage is a mutual admiration society in which one person is always right, and the other is always the husband.—*Mary Martin*

4494   *Economics*
There's no reason to be the richest man in the cemetery. You can't do any business from there.—*Colonel Sanders*

4495   *Hate*
Those who hate you don't win unless you hate them—and then you destroy yourself.—*Richard M. Nixon*

4496   *Tips*
The man who tips a shilling every time he stops for petrol is giving away annually the cost of lubricating his car.—*J. Paul Getty*

4497   *Groucho*
You're so beautiful and so rich, and so charming and so rich, and so intelligent and so rich.—*Groucho Marx to a wealthy widow*

4498 *Jimmy Hoffa*

I may have faults but being wrong ain't one of them.—*Jimmy Hoffa*

4499 *Agree to Disagree*

We agree completely on everything, including the fact that we don't see eye to eye.—*Henry Kissinger and Golda Meir*

4500 *Gossip*

She poured a little social sewage into his ears.—*George Meredith*

4501 *Election*

They pick a President and then for four years they pick on him.—*Adlai Stevenson*

4502 *Statistics*

I could prove God, statistically.—*George Gallup, Jr.*

4503 *American Habits*

Gora Morata, of Japan, on visiting the United States: "People showed me their modern kitchens, fancy new stoves, mixers, dish-washing machines. Then they would say, 'Let's all go out to dinner!' "

4504 *Doctor's Advice*

When his doctor told him to take a walk each day on an empty stomach, Sydney Smith inquired: "Whose?"

4505 *Dimples*

Many a man in love with a dimple makes the mistake of marrying the whole girl.—*Stephen Leacock*

4506 *Universal Acceptance*

When a lady told Thomas Carlyle that she accepted the universe, he said: "Madam, you'd better!"

4507 *Pleasant*

It seems so easy to be good-natured, I wonder anybody takes the trouble to be anything else.—*Douglas Jerrold*

17
QUOTATIONS AND ILLUSTRATIONS FOR SPECIAL DAYS

BIRTHDAY
4508

> My birthday! what a different sound
> That word had in my youthful ears;
> And how each time the day comes round,
> Less and less white its mark appears.
>
> *—Thomas Moore*

4509 You've heard of the three ages of man—youth, age, and "You are looking wonderful."—*Francis Cardinal Spellman*

4510 The older I grow the more I distrust the familiar doctrine that age brings wisdom.—*Henry L. Mencken*

4511 Of middle age the best that can be said is that a middle-aged person has likely learned how to have a little fun in spite of his troubles.—*Don Marquis*

4512 Old age isn't so bad when you consider the alternative.—*Maurice Chevalier*

4513 When a man has a birthday he takes a day off, but when a woman has a birthday she takes a year off.—*Anon.*

4514 At 19, everything is possible and tomorrow looks friendly.—*Jim Bishop*

CHRISTMAS
4515 Many Christmas customs are carryovers from pre-Christian celebrations. Hanging gifts on trees is supposed to stem from the tree

worship of the Druids, and the belief that the tree was the giver of all good things. The Druids are also partly responsible for the use of mistletoe at Christmastime. They regarded the mistletoe as sacred, made certain that it never touched the ground, and dedicated it to the Goddess of Love, which explains the kissing that goes on under it. Originally, when a boy kissed a girl, he plucked a berry from the cluster and presented it to her. When the berries were gone, so were the kisses.

4516   For many of us, sadly, the spirit of Christmas is "hurry." And yet, eventually, the hour comes when the rushing ends and the race against the calendar mercifully comes to a close. It is only now perhaps that we truly recognize the spirit of Christmas. It is not a matter of days or weeks, but of centuries—nearly twenty of them now since that holy night in Bethlehem. Regarded in this manner, the pre-Christmas rush may do us greater service than we realize. With all its temporal confusion, it may just help us to see that by contrast, Christmas itself is eternal.—*Burton Hillis*

4517

I heard the bells on Christmas Day
Their old, familiar carols play,
And wild and sweet the words repeat
Of peace on earth, good-will to men!

—*Longfellow*

4518   I will honor Christmas in my heart, and try to keep it all the year.—*Charles Dickens*

4519   No Santa Claus! Thank God, he lives, and he lives forever. A thousand years from now, Virginia, nay, ten times ten thousand years from now, he will continue to make glad the heart of childhood.—*Francis P. Church*

4520   A three-year-old gave this reaction to her Christmas dinner: "I don't like the turkey, but I like the bread he ate."

4521   Mother decided that ten-year-old Cathy should get something "practical" for Christmas. "Suppose we open a savings account for you?" mother suggested. Cathy was delighted.

"It's your account, darling," mother said as they arrived at the bank, "so you fill out the application."

Cathy was doing fine until she came to the space for "Name of your former bank." After a slight hesitation, she put down "Piggy."

4522   There was the little boy who approached Santa in a department store with a long list of requests. He wanted a bicycle and a sled, a chemical set, a cowboy suit, a set of trains, a baseball glove and roller skates.

"That's a pretty long list." Santa said sternly. "I'll have to check in my book and see if you were a good boy."

"No, no," the youngster said quickly. "Never mind checking. I'll just take the roller skates."

4523

'Twas the night before Christmas, when all through the house
Not a creature was stirring—not even a mouse:
The stockings were hung by the chimney with care
In hopes that St. Nicholas soon would be there.

—Clement C. Moore

4524   He who has no Christmas in his heart will never find Christmas under a tree.—*Sunshine Magazine*

4525

God rest you merry, gentlemen,
Let nothing you dismay,
For Jesus Christ, our Savior,
Was born upon this day.

—Anonymous, Old Carol

4526

'Most all the time, the whole year around, there ain't no flies on me,
But jest 'fore Christmas I'm as good as I kin be!

—Eugene Field

4527

Hark the herald angels sing,
Glory to the new-born king;
Peace on earth, and mercy mild,
God and sinners reconciled.

—Charles Wesley, Christmas Hymns

4528   The little child was to be an angel in the Christmas play and his one line was, "I bring you good tidings." He asked what tidings were and his mother said the word meant news.

On the night of the play, the child had stage fright and, after a long silence, blurted out, "Hey, have I got news for you."

4529   Santa enters through a hole in the chimney and leaves through a hole in your pocket.

4530   Christmas is the season when your neighbor's radio keeps you awake playing "Silent Night."

COLUMBUS DAY

4531   Every ship that comes to America got its chart from Columbus.—*Emerson*

4532   It was wonderful to find America, but it would have been more wonderful to miss it.—*Mark Twain*

EASTER

4533   Dating from Easter, life took on a newness which made it a different kind of life not known before—life that will not be content until all the world comes alive. Despair is death, and despair faded from the minds of men who believed. Fear is death, and fear no longer invaded the still hours. Cowardice ceased to be a part of those who knew Easter.—*Glenn H. Asquith*

4534

> Jesus Christ is risen today,
> Our triumphant holy day;
> Who did once upon the cross
> Suffer to redeem our loss.
> Hallelujah!
>
> —*From a Latin hymn of the*
> *fifteenth century*

4535   This is the promise that He hath promised us, even eternal life.—*I John 2:25*

4536   Easter so longed for is gone in a day.—*James Howell*

4537   The great Easter truth is not that we are to live newly after death—that is not the great thing—but that . . . we are to, and may, live nobly now because we are to live forever.—*Phillips Brooks*

ELECTION DAY

4538

> A weapon that comes down as still
> As snowflakes fall upon the sod,
> But executes a freeman's will
> As lightning does the will of God,
> And from its force nor doors nor locks
> Can shield you—'tis the ballot-box.
>
> —*John Pierpont*

4539 As long as I count the votes, what are you going to do about it?—*William M. Tweed*

4540 The one pervading evil of democracy is the tyranny of the majority, or rather of that party, not always the majority, that succeeds, by force or fraud, in carrying elections.—*Lord Acton*

4541 We will spend and spend, and tax and tax, and elect and elect.—*Harry L. Hopkins*

4542 Bad officials are elected by good citizens who do not vote.—*Unknown*

4543 Whatever government is not a government of laws is a despotism, let it be called what it may.—*Daniel Webster*

4544 All free governments are managed by the combined wisdom and folly of the people.—*Garfield*

4545 Democracy: in which you say what you like and do what you're told.—*Sir Gerald Barry*

4546 Though the people support the government, the government should not support the people.—*Grover Cleveland*

4547 The deterioration of a government begins almost always by the decay of its principles.—*Montesquieu*

FATHER'S DAY

4548 Fathers should be neither seen nor heard. That is the only proper basis for family life.—*Oscar Wilde*

4549 A father is a banker provided by nature.—*French proverb*

4550 What a father says to his children is not heard by the world, but it will be heard by posterity.—*Richter*

4551 Directly after God in Heaven comes Papa.—*Mozart as a boy*

4552 No man is responsible for his father. That is entirely his mother's affair.—*Margaret Trumbull*

4553 The child had every toy his father wanted.—*Robert C. Whitten*

FOURTH OF JULY—INDEPENDENCE DAY

4554 Yesterday the greatest question was decided which was ever debated in America; and a greater perhaps never was, nor will be, decided among men. A resolution was passed without one dissenting colony, that those United Colonies are, and of right ought to be, free and independent states.—*John Adams*

4555   The Fourth of July marks an epoch in the world's history. It marks the birth of a free nation, with all that implies—a nation in the existence of which the oppressed of all lands rejoice, and of which every true American is justly proud.—*Anon.*

4556   The United States is the only country with a known birthday.—*James G. Blaine*

4557   Although it is agreed by most historians that the momentous document, the Declaration of Independence, was adopted on July 4, 1776, there is doubt that it was actually signed on that date. However, it is agreed that John Hancock of Massachusetts, serving as President of the Continental Congress, was the first to affix his signature to the famous paper. Being a man of wit and humor, as well as patriotism, Hancock remarked as he wielded the pen, "I am signing my name so plain that even King George III can read it without his spectacles!" The signature of John Hancock has been a model of beautiful penmanship for two hundred years.

4558   The cause of Freedom is the cause of God.—*The Reverend W. L. Bowles*

4559   Eternal vigilance is the price of liberty.—*John Philpot Curran*

4560   God grants liberty only to those who love it, and are always ready to guard and defend it.—*Daniel Webster*

4561   To embody human liberty in workable government, America was born.—*Herbert Hoover*

4562   When in the course of human events, it becomes necessary for one people to dissolve the political bonds which have connected them with another, and to assume among the powers of the earth the separate and equal station to which the laws of nature and of nature's God entitle them, a decent respect for the opinion of mankind requires that they should declare the causes which impel them to the separation.—*Thomas Jefferson, Declaration of Independence*

4563   Sink or swim, live or die, survive or perish, I give my heart and hand to this vote.—*Daniel Webster (Speech supposed to have been made by John Adams)*

4564   At old-time Fourth of July celebrations the Declaration of Independence was always read. How about reviving this custom? If you stay at home, have someone read it aloud to the family. It's still great!—*Wheeler McMillen*

GOOD FRIDAY

4565   Good Friday . . . in a way . . . is not Good Friday at all. It is Black Friday—a very Black Friday. It is Good Friday only in the sense that we know Easter will follow.—*J. Edward Lantz*

4566   I find no fault in him.—*John 19:6*

4567   Then said Jesus, Father, forgive them; for they know not what they do.—*Luke 23:34*

4568

> At the cross her station keeping
> Stood the mournful mother weeping,
> Where He hung, the dying Lord.
>
> —*Anon.*

GRADUATION DAY

4569   A college education shows a man how little other people know.—*Sam Slick*

4570   It was a saying of his that education was an ornament in prosperity and a refuge in adversity.—*Diogenes*

4571   But it was in making education not only common to all, but in some sense compulsory on all, that the destiny of the free republic of America was practically settled.—*J. R. Lowell*

4572   The roots of education are bitter, but the fruit is sweet.—*Aristotle*

4573   A well-trained mind is made up, so to speak, of all the minds of past ages: only a single mind has been educated during all that time.—*Fontenelle*

4574   A university should be a place of light, of liberty, and of learning.—*Disraeli*

4575   To talk in public, to think in solitude, to read and to hear, to inquire and answer inquiries, is the business of a scholar.—*Samuel Johnson*

4576   Colleges hate geniuses, just as convents hate saints.—*Emerson*

4577   What sculpture is to a block of marble, education is to the soul.—*Addison*

4578   A scholar is the favorite of Heaven and earth, the excellency of his country, the happiest of men.—*Emerson*

4579   The foundation of every state is the education of its youth.—*Diogenes*

4580   There is nothing so stupid as an educated man, if you get off the thing that he was educated in.—*Will Rogers*

HIGH HOLYDAYS: ROSH HASHANAH AND YOM KIPPUR

4581   Every Autumn the Jewish people observe what are known as the High Holydays. This is a period of ten days beginning with Rosh Hashanah, which means New Year, and ending with Yom Kippur, the Day of Atonement. The term New Year is used by the Jews at this time to mean the new effort which they make to correct mistakes they have made in the past. It is a new year of conscience, not the calendar. The observance of Yom Kippur begins at sunset, with a worship service which includes the singing of the hymn "Kol Nidre," a plea for forgiveness for decisions made in haste and without regard for the feelings of others. This is Atonement Day, on which the worshiper tries to atone for his faults. Although the High Holydays are the most important religious occasion for the Jewish people, there is nothing about them which does not apply to all people.

LABOR DAY

4582 He who prays and labors lifts his heart to God with his hands.—*St. Bernard*

4583 A truly American sentiment recognizes the dignity of labor and the fact that honor lies in honest toil.—*Grover Cleveland*

4584 Labor conquers all things.—*Homer*

4585 Labor, if it were not necessary for the existence, would be indispensable for the happiness of man.—*Samuel Johnson*

4586 Life gives nothing to man without labor.—*Horace*

4587 Labor was the first price, the original purchase money that was paid for all things.—*Adam Smith*

4588 To labor is to pray.—*Motto of the Benedictines*

4589 God sells us all things at the price of labor.—*Leonardo da Vinci*

LINCOLN'S BIRTHDAY
4590

Honesty rare as a man without self-pity,
Kindness as large and plain as a prairie wind.

—*Stephen Vincent Benet*

4591

His heart was as great as the world
but there was no room in it to hold
the memory of wrong.

—*Emerson*

4592 Now he belongs to the ages.—*Edwin M. Stanton*

4593

Here was a man to hold against the world,
A man to match the mountains and the sea.

—Edwin Markham

MEMORIAL DAY—DECORATION DAY

4594 There is a shrine in the temple of ages, where lie forever embalmed the memories of such as have deserved well of their country and their race.*—John Mason Brown*

4595 Here sleeps heroic dust! It is meet that a redeemed nation should come, to pay it homage at such tombs, wreathing the memory of its patriot dead in the emblems of grateful affection. These grass-grown mounds, these flower-decked graves, awake the memories of the past, and the history of our nation's perils and its triumphs come crowding on us here.*—American Wesleyan*

4596 Here rests in honored glory an American soldier known but to God.*—Inscription on the Tomb of the Unknown Soldier, Arlington National Cemetery*

4597 The little green tents where the soldiers sleep and the sunbeams play and the women weep, are covered with flowers today.*—Walt Mason*

4598 The brave men, living and dead, who struggled here, have consecrated it far above our poor power to add or detract. The world will little note, nor long remember, what we say here, but it can never forget what they did here.*—Abraham Lincoln*

4599 Memorial Day is a good time to remember our wonderful heritage, and some of the blessings we so take for granted. We often treat with indifference the sound foundations of our nation's life that were laid by consecrated and industrious hands. We should be grateful for our Constitution, which has safeguarded our liberty and protected its destruction by malicious minds or by blinded political prejudice. Every day is not too often to remember those men and women of vision and valor who bought our liberty, and particularly should they be remembered on Memorial Day.*—Sir Oracle*

MOTHER'S DAY

4600

A mother is a mother still,
The holiest thing alive.

—Coleridge

4601

Over my slumbers your loving watch keep;
Rock me to sleep, mother; rock me to sleep.

—Elizabeth Chase

4602

The hand that rocks the cradle
Is the hand that rules the world.

—W. R. Wallace

4603 Her children arise up, and call her blessed.—*Proverbs 31:28*

4604 Mother is the name for God in the lips and hearts of little children.—*William M. Thackeray*

4605 The mother's heart is the child's schoolroom.—*H. W. Beecher*

4606 What are Raphael's madonnas but the shadow of a mother's love, fixed in permanent outline forever?—*T. W. Higginson*

NEW YEAR'S

4607

If I were asked to form a perfect prayer,
No fluent phrases would my lips employ.
No flourishes of speech would I prepare
For only those of learning to enjoy.
With simple verbal drapery I'd make
A prayer that everyone could understand.
Were I to make a perfect prayer designed
To rid the world of selfishness and greed,
With books of lore I would not tax my mind,
For these two simple lines would fill my need—
"Renew, O God, within the hearts of men
The Golden Rule, and give it life again."

—Anon.

4608 In the New Year I resolve to do just about what I did last year.

4609 New Year's Day is every man's birthday.—*Charles Lamb*

PASSOVER

4610 This day (Passover) shall be unto you for a memorial; and ye shall keep it a feast to the Lord throughout your generations.—*Exodus 12:14*

4611 Ye shall observe the feast of unleavened bread.—*Exodus 12:17*

4612 It is the sacrifice of the Lord's passover, who passed over the houses of the children of Israel in Egypt, when he smote the Egyptians, and delivered our houses.—*Exodus 12:27*

4613 The feast of unleavened bread drew nigh, which is called the Passover.—*Luke 22:1*

4614 Passover affirms the great truth that liberty is the inalienable right of every human being.—*M. Joseph*

4615 The Seder nights ... tie me with the centuries before me.— *L. Frank*

ST. PATRICK'S DAY

4616 It is somewhat suggestive that the apostle of Ireland was himself a foreign-born citizen. He acquired a better right to speak for Ireland than any man that was ever born in it, before or since. And that should be a lesson to moderate certain Irish patriots who would have it that there is nothing good that does not come from Ireland. There are good things, always have been and always will be, out of Ireland, as well as every country, as well as in it, and while it is permissible for us on this one day of the year to blow our own horn a little, it is well for us to be modest enough to acknowledge and to be thankful for the apostle who was not an Irishman and yet was the best Irishman that ever lived.—*Dr. Edward McGlynn*

ST. VALENTINE'S DAY

4617

> Oh, if it be to choose and call thee mine,
> Love, thou art every day my Valentine!
>
> *—Thomas Hood*

4618

> I claim there ain't another Saint
> As great as Valentine.
>
> *—Ogden Nash*

4619 A lovely heart-shaped box of chocolates was received on Valentine's Day by a coed from her newest date. On the enclosed card was the inscription, "To Helen—with all my allowance."

4620

> Love me little, love me long,
> Is the burden of my song.
>
> *—Old ballad*

4621

And on her lover's arm she leant,
And round her waist she felt it fold,
And far across the hills they went
In that new world which is the old.

—*Tennyson*

SPRING

4622

Came the Spring with all its splendor,
All its birds and all its blossoms,
All its flowers, and leaves, and grasses.

—*Longfellow*

SUNDAY

4623

Of all the days that's in the week
I dearly love but one day—
And that's the day that comes betwixt
A Saturday and Monday.

—*Henry Carey*

4624   One very optimistic minister had the habit in his opening prayer each Sunday of thanking God for the weather. On a particularly cold, icy, windy, slushy Sunday morning, the few people who had ventured out wondered how the minister could possibly refer to the weather in his morning prayer with any sense of gratitude. To their surprise, he said in the beginning of his prayer, "Dear God, we thank Thee that Thou dost send us so few Sundays like today."

THANKSGIVING

4625   Thanksgiving Day is one of the most remarkable days of the year. Decreed by a layman, the President of the United States, by authorization of Congress, it is obeyed by Catholic, Jew, and Protestant, and by many who have no church affiliation. The response of more than 200 million people to this call is one of the most encouraging events in our national life. Thankfulness blesses and enriches our daily life. Not only is it deserving of a special day; it merits everyday observance.—*Sunshine Magazine*

4626   Thanksgiving Day comes, by statute, once a year; to the honest man it comes as frequently as the heart of gratitude will allow, which may mean every day, or at least once in seven days.—*Edward Sandford Martin*

4627   Let the people praise thee, O God; let all the people praise thee.—*Psalms 67:3*

4628   Let us come before his presence with thanksgiving.—*Psalms 95:2*

4629   No duty is more urgent than that of returning thanks.—*St. Ambrose*

4630   A thankful heart is not only the greatest virtue, but the parent of all the other virtues.—*Cicero*

4631

Heap high the board with plenteous cheer, and gather to the feast,
And toast the sturdy Pilgrim band whose courage never ceased.

—*Alice W. Brotherton, The First Thanksgiving Day*

4632   A French proverb tells us: "Gratitude is the heart's memory." And so it is. For when we are thankful, we are thinking not only of blessings of the immediate present, but also of good things received in the past. Especially is this so at Thanksgiving.—*Esther Burkholder*

4633   Beggar that I am, I am even poor in thanks.—*Shakespeare*

4634   It is a good thing to give thanks unto the Lord.—*Old Testament: Psalms*

4635   The first Thanksgiving Proclamation was made by Governor Bradford three years after the Pilgrims settled at Plymouth:
"To all ye Pilgrims:
"Inasmuch as the great Father has given us this year an abundant harvest of Indian corn, wheat, peas, beans, squashes, and garden vegetables, and has made the forests to abound with game and the sea with fish and clams, and inasmuch as he has protected us from the ravages of the savages, has spared us from pestilence and disease, has granted us freedom to worship God according to the dictates of our own conscience; now I, your magistrate, do proclaim that all ye Pilgrims, with your wives and ye little ones, do gather at ye meeting house, on ye hill, between the hours of 9 and 12 in the day time, on Thursday, November ye 29th, of the year of our Lord one thousand six hundred and twenty-three, and the third year since ye Pilgrims landed on ye Pilgrim Rock, there to listen to ye pastor and render thanksgiving to ye Almighty God for all his blessings. William Bradford, Ye Governor of Ye Colony."

4636   Here are a few first-grader's views of the first Thanksgiving:
"Thanksgiving isn't all day. It comes suddenly at night for dinner. The

Pilgrims ate for a living. They used turkey feathers to stuff pillows. I think they wore old-fashioned clothes." "The Pilgrims started it. I never met a Pilgrim. They swam across the ocean with three boats, I think. You give thanks to God on Thanksgiving and you stuff yourself, too." "I knew about the Pilgrims a long time ago—when I was five. They sailed in the Mayflower. The boat got its name because it was finished in May. Its last name was Flower."—*Food for Thot*

4637 "Now children," said the teacher just before Thanksgiving, "tell me something you're thankful for."

"I'm thankful," said one small boy, "that I'm not a turkey."

4638 'Tis the season for kindling the fire of hospitality in the hall, the genial fire of charity in the heart.—*Washington Irving*

VACATION

4639 Between the spring and the autumn, when the sun in its zenith doth climb, comes a pause in the year's occupations that is known as vacation time.

VETERANS DAY—ARMISTICE DAY

4640 The Federal government should treat with the utmost consideration every disabled soldier, sailor and marine of the World War, whether his disability be due to wounds received in line of action or to health impaired in service; and for the dependents of the brave men who died in the line of duty the government's tenderest concern and richest bounty should be their requital.—*Democratic National Platform 1920*

4641 Closer to the truth than he meant to be was the schoolboy who wrote on an exam paper: "The Armistice was signed on the 11th of November in 1918, and since then every year there have been two minutes of peace."

4642

> Soldier, rest! thy warfare o'er,
> Sleep the sleep that knows not breaking;
> Dream of battled fields no more,
> Days of danger, nights of waking.
>
> —*Scott*

4643 The nation which forgets its defenders will be itself forgotten.—*Calvin Coolidge*

4644 Veterans Day, originally called Armistice Day, continues the tradition of honoring the unknown soldier buried in Arlington National Cemetery on the eleventh hour of the eleventh day of the eleventh month of the year. From 1971 to 1977, Veterans Day was observed on the fourth Monday in October in compliance with a 1968 law which changed some national holidays to Mondays. Believing that the November 11 date held great significance for this country, Congress passed a law in 1975 returning the official observance to November 11. The law became effective in 1978, the sixtieth anniversary of the armistice ending World War I.

WASHINGTON'S BIRTHDAY

4645   Washington is the mightiest name on earth—long since mightiest in the course of civil liberty; still mightiest in moral reformation. On that name an eulogy is expected. Let none attempt it. In solemn awe pronounce the name and in its naked, deathless splendor leave it shining on.—*Lincoln*

4646   A gentleman of one of the first fortunes upon the continent . . . sacrificing his ease, and hazarding all in the cause of his country.—*John Adams*

4647   His memory will be adored while liberty shall have votaries, his name will triumph over time and will in future ages assume its just station among the most celebrated worthies of the world.—*Jefferson*

4648   When Washington declined a military escort on the occasion of his inauguration (1789), he said, "I require no guard but the affections of the people."—*Dr. Edward Everett*

4649   'Tis substantially true that virtue or morality is a necessary spring of popular government.—*George Washington*

4650   Washington—a fixed star in the firmament of great names, shining without twinkling or obscuration, with clear, beneficent light.—*Daniel Webster, Eulogy*

4651   A citizen, first in war, first in peace, and first in the hearts of his countrymen.—*Col. Henry Lee, Resolution in Congress, about George Washington*

4652   General George Washington resigned his command before Congress at Annapolis. (It is interesting to note that Washington bade farewell to his officers in New York City on December 4 and left at once for Annapolis. What is now a brief journey required at that early date more than two and one-half weeks.)

4653

TEACHER: What was George Washington noted for?

STUDENT: His memory.

TEACHER: What makes you think his memory was so great?

STUDENT: They erected a monument to it.

WEATHER

4654   Sunshine is delicious, rain is refreshing, wind braces up, snow is exhilarating; there is really no such thing as bad weather, only different kinds of good weather.—*Ruskin*

WEDDING DAY

4655   What woman, however old, has not the bridal-favors and raiment stowed away, and packed in lavender, in the inmost cupboards of her heart?—*William M. Thackeray*

4656   The smallest piece of silver which can qualify as a wedding gift is a marmalade spoon.—*Charles W. Morton*

4657   To have and to hold from this day forward, for better for worse, for richer for poorer, in sickness and in health, to love and to cherish, till death us do part.—*Book of Common Prayer*

4658   There is something about a wedding-gown prettier than any other gown in the world.—*Douglas Jerrold*

4659

The kindest and the happiest pair
Will find occasion to forbear,
And something every day they live
To pity, and perhaps forgive.

—Cowper

WINTER

4660   For, lo, the winter is past, the rain is over and gone; the flowers appear on the earth; the time of the singing of birds is come, and the voice of the turtle is heard in our land.—*Old Testament, Song of Solomon 2:11,12*

4661   About as active as a leftover fly in January.

4662   Adroit as a rhinoceros.—*Franklin P. Adams*

4663   Ambition is like a treadmill; it knows no limits; you no sooner get to the end of it than you begin again.—*Josh Billings*

4664   Hard as a pawnbroker's smile.—*Herbert V. Prochnow*

4665   He had crumbled like an old ruin.

4666   Bashful as a ten-year-old girl.

4667   Beautiful as a drug store blonde.

4668   Beautiful as a rustic bridge over a mountain stream.

4669   Black as a coal shaft.

4670   He went through things like a customs inspector.

4671   Quiet as a monastery.

4672   As inert as an oyster on the beach in August.

4673   A man of oak and rock.

4674   He is as cosmopolitan as a comet.

4675   He was a man with a mind like an accounting ledger.

4676   He had all the qualities of a fireplace poker except its occasional warmth.

4677   He talks like a man who is unable to keep up with his thoughts no matter how rapidly he speaks.

4678 You will find angling to be like the virtue of humility, which has a calmness of spirit and a world of other blessings attending upon it.— *Izaak Walton*

4679 He is a steamroller in a pair of pants.

4680 Coolidge's perpetual expression was of smelling something burning on the kitchen stove.—*Sherwin L. Cook*

4681 A rude man of the open.—*Lynn H. Hough*

4682 A face with lines as fine as old parchment.

4683 Government by stampede.

4684 Her face was as white and colorless as an icicle.

4685 As uncompromising as a policeman's club.

4686 As companionable as a cat and a goldfish.

4687 An unambitious snore, like a slow leak in an old tire.

4688 As never ending as a brook.

4689 He was as welcome as a monthly bill.

4690 As cynical as Diogenes.

4691 As desolate as a cemetery.

4692 Avarice is like a pig, which seeks its food in the mud, without caring where it comes from.—*Jean B. M. Vianney*

4693 Absence, like death, sets a seal on the image of those we have loved.—*Goldsmith*

4694 Could tell the hour by his movements as accurately as by a sundial.—*Washington Irving*

4695 Advancing like the shadow of death.—*Ruskin*

4696

Sweet are the uses of adversity,
Which, like the toad, ugly and venomous,
Wears yet a precious jewel in his head.

—*Shakespeare*

4697

Aimless as an autumn leaf
Borne in November's idle winds afar.

—*P. H. Hayne*

4698 Ambition is like hunger; it obeys no law but its appetite.—*Josh Billings*

4699 Ancient as the stars.—*Voltaire*

4700 An army, like a serpent, goes upon its belly.—*Frederick the Great*

4701 Attracted about as much attention in the artistic world as the advent of another fly in a slaughter house.—*James L. Ford*

4702 Blighted and forlorn, like Autumn waiting for the snow.—*Whittier*

4703 Bright as mountain snow.—*Southey*

4704

Calm as a child to slumber soothed,
As if an Angel's hand had smoothed
The still, white features into rest.

—Whittier

4705 Changeless as heaven.—*Whittier*

4706 Clear as a bell.—*Chaucer*

4707 Her faded beauty was like summer twilight.—*Henry James*

4708 Beautiful as a flower in a seed catalogue.—*Robert H. Davis*

4709 Contagious, like the gladness of a happy child.—*Bulwer-Lytton*

4710 Cool as a snow bank.—*Louisa M. Alcott*

4711 Countless as the desert sands.—*Bayard Taylor*

4712 Crisp as new banknotes.—*Dickens*

4713 A critic is a legless man who teaches running.—*Channing Pollock*

4714 Critics are like brushers of noblemen's clothes.—*Sir Henry Wotton*

4715 Cry of anguish, like the last dying wail of some dumb, hunted creature.—*Adelaide A. Procter*

4716 Cunning as Satan.—*Philip Freneau*

4717 Dark as the grave.—*Cowley*

4718 Dead as a herring.—*Samuel Butler*

4719 She was delicate and fair as moonlight.—*Hans Christian Andersen*

4720 His speech was like a tangled chain; nothing impaired, but all disordered.—*Shakespeare*

4721   Driven . . . like leaves before the autumnal wind.—*Southey*

4722   Blind as ignorance.—*Beaumont and Fletcher*

4723

> The slow mists of the evening dropped,
> Dropped as a cloth upon a dead man's face.
>
> —*Kipling*

4724   As modest as a violet.

4725   It is as dignified and beautiful as a Beethoven Sonata.—*Israel Zangwill*

4726   Eyes, brilliant and humid like the reflection of stars in a well.—*Edmondo de Amicis*

4727   These lovely lamps, these windows of the soul.—*Du Bartas*

4728   As hollow as a villain's laugh.—*Herbert V. Prochnow*

4729   Her eyes are blue and dewey as the glimmery Summer-dawn.—*James Whitcomb Riley*

4730

> In her hazel eyes her thoughts lay clear
> As pebbles in a brook.
>
> —*Alexander Smith*

4731   He was oilier than a kerosene lamp.

4732   He had a face like a benediction.—*Cervantes*

4733   His face looked like a face that had refused to jell and was about to run down on his clothes.—*Irvin S. Cobb*

4734   'Tis not that she paints so ill but, when she has finished her face, she joins so badly to her neck, that she looks like a mended statue, in which the connoisseur may see at once that the head is modern, though the trunk's antique.—*Richard B. Sheridan*

4735   His face had as many wrinkles as an old parchment.—*Herbert V. Prochnow*

4736   Faded like a dream of youth.—*O. W. Holmes*

4737   Faint as a glimmering taper's wasted light.—*Sir William Jones*

4738   As futile as a clock in an empty house.—*James Thurber*

4739   A room without books is like a body without a soul.—*Cicero*

4740   As fair a thing as e'er was form'd of clay.—*Byron*

4741   A face as fair as the summer dawn.—*James Whitcomb Riley*

4742   Fall off, like the leaves from a withered tree.—*Voltaire*

4743   It is with feelings as with waters: the shallow murmur, but the deep are dumb.—*Sir Walter Raleigh*

4744   His face fell like a cookbook cake.—*Joseph C. Lincoln*

4745   My head rang like a fire station gong.

4746   Like the mower's grass at the close of day.—*Byron*

4747   Fits as a shell fits a crab.—*Sir A. Conan Doyle*

4748   As flabby as a sponge.—*Guy de Maupassant*

4749   Flexible as figures in the hands of the statistician.—*Israel Zangwill*

4750   Follow, as the night the day.—*Shakespeare*

4751   Folds up like a crush hat or a concertina.—*Irvin S. Cobb*

4752   Shall fold their tents like the Arabs and as silently steal away.—*Longfellow*

4753   A forehead more pure than the Parian stone.—*Whittier*

4754   Poor and forgotten like a clod upon the field.—*Victor Hugo*

4755   Good fortune, like ripe fruit, ought to be enjoyed while it is present.—*Epictetus*

4756   Rattled like window shutters in a cyclone.

4757   As deceptive as the new paint on a secondhand car.—*Herbert V. Prochnow*

4758   The fragrance of her rich and delightful character still lingered about the place where she had lived, as a dried rosebud scents the drawer where it has withered and perished.—*Hawthorne*

4759   Free as mountain winds.—*Shakespeare*

4760   The feeling of friendship is like that of being comfortably filled with roast beef.—*Dr. Johnson*

4761   As frightened as Macbeth before the ghost of Banquo.—*Louis Veuillot*

4762   Fruitless as the celebrated bee who wanted to swarm alone.—*G. K. Chesterton*

4763   Futile as a tenor in a boiler shop.—*Henry Irving Dodge*

4764   She had more ornaments than a circus bandwagon.—*Herbert V. Prochnow*

4765   Genius, like a torch, shines less in the broad daylight of the present than in the night of the past.—*J. Petit Senn*

4766   Ghastly as a laugh in hell.—*Thomas Hardy*

4767   As regular as the roll of an army drum.

4768   Gleamed upon the water like a bride at her looking-glass.—*R. D. Blackmore*

4769   His eyes dilated and glistened like the last flame that shoots up from an expiring fire.—*Guy de Maupassant*

4770   Glitter . . . like the bayonets of a regiment on parade.—*John C. Van Dyke*

4771   Going as if he had trod upon eggs.—*Robert Burton*

4772   Gossip, like ennui, is born of idleness.—*Ninon de Lenclos*

4773   As busy as a Swiss admiral.

4774   Graceful as a faun.—*Samuel Rogers*

4775   Her eyes are grey like morning dew.—*W. B. Yeats*

4776   Genuine grief is like penitence, not clamorous, but subdued.—*Josh Billings*

4777   Gush like a fountain at its source.—*Donald G. Mitchell*

4778   His speech came in gusts, like linnets in the pauses of the wind.—*William De Morgan*

4779   He returned as often as the postman.

4780   Hairless as an egg.—*Robert Herrick*

4781   He had a hand like a bunch of bananas.—*R. F. Outcault*

4782   Happy as birds in the spring.—*William Blake*

4783   Fingers, hard as lobster's claws.—*Guy de Maupassant*

4784   Hard as a pine-knot.—*James K. Paulding*

4785   As hard as for an empty sack to stand upright.—*Benjamin Franklin*

4786   The head of a woman is like a weather cock on the top of a house, which turns with the slightest wind.—*Molière*

4787 The head, like the stomach, is most easily infected with poison when it is empty.—*Richter*

4788 Calm as an iceberg.—*Gelett Burgess*

4789 As shallow as a pie pan.

4790 A noble heart, like the sun, showeth its great countenance in its lowest estate.—*Sir Philip Sidney*

4791

> Heaves . . .
> Like a mighty ship in pain,
> Facing the tempest with struggle and strain.
>
> —*Elizabeth Barrett Browning*

4792 Lies heavy . . . like murder on a guilty soul.—*Schiller*

4793 The sea hissed like twenty thousand kettles!—*Joseph Conrad*

4794 Hissing like a snake.—*Victor Hugo*

4795 He stuck to it about as long as a drugstore cowboy on a bronco.

4796 Holds . . . together as the shell does the egg.—*John C. Van Dyke*

4797 As much at home . . . as a fish in water.—*Balzac*

4798 Our hopes, like withered leaves, fall fast.—*Longfellow*

4799 Hopeful as the break of day.—*T. B. Aldrich*

4800 Hot as Hell-fire.—*Dryden*

4801 Hover—like a moth intoxicated with light.—*John Galsworthy*

4802 Howlings, like a herd of ravenous wolves disappointed of their prey.—*William H. Prescott*

4803 Huddled like beasts beneath the drovers' whips.—*John Masefield*

4804 Humility like darkness reveals the heavenly lights.—*Henry D. Thoreau*

4805 Hungry as the chap that said a turkey was too much for one, not enough for two.—*O. W. Holmes*

4806 Hungry as a wolf.—*John Palgrave*

4807 A true Christian is like the ripening corn; the riper he grows the more lowly he bends his head.

4808

> The nations narrow and expand,
> As tides that ebb, or tides that flow.
>
> —*Lord de Tabley*

4809 As hopeful as a spring morning.

4810 Natural to die as to be born.—*Bacon*

4811 Neglected, as the moon by day.—*Swift*

4812 Obstinate as death.—*Dryden*

4813 Opportunitays, like eggs, don't kum but one at a time.—*Josh Billings*

4814 No more conscience than a fox in a poultry farm.—*George Bernard Shaw*

4815 Pains like a horrible vulgarism.—*Lafcadio Hearn*

4816 He was as polished, and as hard, as the brass plate upon which his name was etched.—*Herbert V. Prochnow, Jr.*

4817 God pardons like a mother who kisses away the repentant tears of her child.—*H. W. Beecher*

4818 Pathetic as an autumn leaf.—*George Moore*

4819 Patiently as the spider weaves the broken web.—*Bulwer-Lytton*

4820 As innocent as a child.

4821 Pleading like a frightened child.—*Robert Louis Stevenson*

4822 Pliable as wax.—*James Shirley*

4823 She was as pretty as the springtime.—*Balzac*

4824 Poignant and silent like the terrible questioning of one's conscience.—*Joseph Conrad*

4825 I was not accustomed to flattery. I was rather like the Hoosier with the gingerbread—who reckoned he loved it better than any man, and got less of it.—*Abraham Lincoln*

4826 Prim as a Quaker.—*G. P. Morris*

4827 Kings will lose their privilege, as stars which have completed their time lose their splendor.—*Dumas, Père*

4828 Puffed himself up like a ship in full sail.—*Hans Christian Andersen*

4829   As soft as a Southern wind.

4830   Punctual—like morning.—*James Whitcomb Riley*

4831   Conversation should be like a salad, composed of various ingredients, and well stirred with salt, oil, and vinegar.—*Joquin Setanti*

4832   She is as pure, as good, and as beautiful as an angel.—*Guy de Maupassant*

4833   Receded, as mists fade before a morning sun.—*Barrett Wendell*

4834   Red as the Baldinsville skool-house.—*Artemus Ward*

4835   Ruddy and fresh as the waking morn.—*Eugene Field*

4836   Fell slowly into ruin, like all dwellings to which the presence of man no longer communicates life.—*Victor Hugo*

4837   As illusive as a dream.

4838   Sad as twilight.—*George Eliot*

4839   Saunters . . . like an idle river very leisurely strolling down a flat country to the sea.—*Dickens*

4840   In scandal, as in robbery, the receiver is always as bad as the thief.—*Lord Chesterfield*

4841   Sealed as the voice of a frost-bound stream.—*Swinburne*

4842   Serene as night.—*Byron*

4843   Set, as a piece of sculpture.—*Dickens*

4844   It stuck tighter than bark on a tree.

4845   Shone like the evening star.—*O. W. Holmes*

4846   Shrink as though Death were passing in his shroud.—*John Masefield*

4847   Shun him like the plague.—*Robert Browning*

4848   Delicate as the play of moonbeams on a field of snow.—*Robert P. Downs*

4849   Sifted like great snowdrifts o'er the landscape.—*Longfellow*

4850   Sighed with such a sigh as drops from agony to exhaustion.—*Elizabeth Barrett Browning*

4851   Sighs as men sigh relieved from care.—*J. R. Lowell*

4852   Men, like peaches and pears, grow sweet a little while before they begin to decay.—*O. W. Holmes*

4853 Great men are like meteors; they glitter and are consumed to enlighten the world.—*Napoleon*

4854 Marriage is not like the hill of Olympus, wholly clear, without clouds.—*Thomas Fuller*

4855 As restless as the wind.

4856 Melancholy sound . . . like the weeping of a solitary, deserted human heart.—*Guy de Maupassant*

4857 Swell menacingly like the first whisper of a rising wind.—*Joseph Conrad*

4858 Merciless as ambition.—*Joubert*

4859 As freely as the firmament embraces the world, so mercy must encircle friend and foe.—*Schiller*

4860 As expressionless as a row of empty mailboxes.—*Herbert V. Prochnow*

4861 Monotonous as mutton.—*Richard Le Gallienne*

4862 Motionless as a king's mummy in a catacomb.—*Flaubert*

4863 A voice as mournful as the dying light in the west—for a vague reminder of Death is divinely set in the heavens, and the sun above gives the same warning that is given here on earth by the flowers and the bright insects of the day.—*Balzac*

4864 Moved one like the finest eloquence.—*Alexander Smith*

4865 Multitudinous tongues, like the whispering leaves of a windstirred oak.—*Hawthorne*

4866 Murmurs . . . like a bell that calls to prayer.—*Ruskin*

4867 Muscular as dogmeat.—*Rex Beach*

4868 As mute as the tomb.—*Dumas, Père*

4869 As mute as Pygmalion.—*James Smith*

4870 Hysterical as a tree full of chickens.—*Irvin S. Cobb*

4871 As frivolous as April.—*Herbert V. Prochnow, Jr.*

4872 As idle as a painted ship upon a painted ocean.—*Coleridge*

4873 He makes his ignorance pass for reserve, and, like a hunting-nag, leaps over what he cannot get through.—*Samuel Butler*

4874 Immortal as the stars.—*Mathilde Blind*

4875 Impersonal as the justice of God.—*Victor Hugo*

4876   Imposing as a set of solid gold teeth.—*Rex Beach*

4877   Indolent as an old bachelor.—*Goethe*

4878   The highest intellects, like the tops of mountains, are the first to catch and reflect the dawn.—*Macaulay*

4879   Irrevocable as death.—*Charlotte Bronte*

4880   Ended abruptly like a rabbit's tail.

4881   As languid as a lilied pond.—*Norman Gale*

4882   Life is like a tale ended ere 'tis told.—*T. B. Aldrich*

4883   A lie is like a snowball; the longer it is rolled, the larger it is.— *Luther*

4884   Lifeless as a string of dead fish.—*G. K. Chesterton*

4885   Comfortable as a toothache.—*Mark Twain*

4886   Light and feathery as a squirrel's tail.—*John Muir*

4887   A face as wrinkled as a dried plum.

4888   Lingering like an unloved guest.—*Shelley*

4889

> I wandered lonely as a cloud
> That floats on high o'er vales and hills.
>
> —*Wordsworth*

4890   He looked like a composite picture of five thousand orphans too late to catch a picnic steamboat.—*O. Henry*

4891   He was as wise as Solomon, but as humble as Uriah Heep.— *Herbert V. Prochnow*

4892   Majestic in its movements as a sonnet of Milton.—*Israel Zangwill*

4893   Silent as a country churchyard.—*Macaulay*

4894   Silent as the grave.—*Schiller*

4895   As greedy as the jaws of hell.

4896   Sobbing, as if the body and soul were torn.—*Bulwer-Lytton*

4897   Society, like the Roman youth at the circus, never shows mercy to the fallen gladiator.—*Balzac*

4898   Soft as the falling thistle downe.—*Joseph Hall*

4899   Soft and still, like birds half hidden in a nest.—*Longfellow*

4900 Walked as softly as the ghost in Hamlet.—*Dickens*

4901 As hardboiled as an Easter egg.

4902 Sparkle like brooks in the morning sun.—*William Cullen Bryant*

4903 Stood spellbound, like a child to whom his nurse is telling some wonderful story.—*Balzac*

4904 As shriveled as an old prune.

4905 Melancholy as a defeated politician.—*Herbert V. Prochnow*

4906 He stood . . . stiff as a marble statue.—*Goethe*

4907 Staggered away as a defeated man staggers away from the field of battle.—*Conrad*

4908 Stealthily like rocks that tear a ship's life out under the smooth sea.—*Conrad*

4909 As harmless as a meadowlark.

4910 Struggling like a man led towards death and crucifixion.—*Carlyle*

4911 Swayed like a bird on a twig.—*Arnold Bennett*

4912 Hesitating like an animal at bay.

4913 Talent, like gout, sometimes skips two generations.—*Balzac*

4914

Tenderly, as round the sleeping infant's feet
We softly fold the cradle-sheet.

—*William Cullen Bryant*

4915 Terrifying as the monologue of a storm.—*Victor Hugo*

4916 He was as short and stubby as a hedge fence.

4917 Human thought is like a monstrous pendulum: It keeps swinging from one extreme to the other.—*Eugene Field*

4918 Tossed . . . like a cork on the waves.—*Thomas Hardy*

4919 As frank as a mirror.

4920 Turned like a weathercock with every wind.—*Guy de Maupassant*

4921 As inflexible as a marble pillar.

4922 Unconquerable as chewing gum.—*Arnold Bennett*

4923 Demoralizing as a holiday.—*Abe Martin*

4924 Stand unmoved, like a rock 'mid raging seas.—*Calderon*

4925   As inseparable as a baseball fan and a bag of peanuts.

4926   Upright as a wooden sentinel at the door of a puppet-show.—*Sir Walter Scott*

4927   Vagrant as the wind.—*John Ford*

4928   Pranced around like a colt in a pasture.

4929   Vanished altogether, like the last spark on a burnt piece of paper. —*Hans Christian Andersen*

4930   Vanished like the furrow cut by a ship's keel in the sea.—*Balzac*

4931   Vices, like beasts, are fond of none but those that feed them.— *Samuel Butler*

4932   Lies like a man with a secondhand car to sell.

4933   Virtue is like the polar star, which keeps its place, and all stars turn towards it.—*Confucius*

4934   Void of sense as the movement of the trees and the sound of the winds.—*Victor Hugo*

4935   A wail, as of a babe new-born.—*George Meredith*

4936   She walked with a proud, defiant step, like a martyr to the Coliseum.—*Balzac*

4937   Elusive as a wet fish.

4938   Wandered up and down there like an early Christian refugee in the catacombs.—*Conrad*

4939   Wandered about at random, like dogs that have lost the scent.— *Voltaire*

4940   His purse was as full as his head was empty.

4941   Warm as a sunned cat.—*Thomas Hardy*

4942   Watchful as a spider sits in his web.—*Bulwer-Lytton*

4943   As faultless as a spring flower.

4944   Withered and pale as an old pauper.—*Dickens*

4945   His words, like so many nimble and airy servitors, trip about him at command.—*Milton*

4946   The world is like a great staircase, some go up and others go down.—*Hipponax*

4947   He floundered around like a fish on the beach.

4948   Yawns like a grave in a cemetery.—*Victor Hugo*

4949 Zeal without knowledge is like expedition to a man in the dark.—*Newton*

4950 As fresh as the dawn.

4951 Adroit as a dinosaur.

4952 His cheek was like a rose in the snow.—*O. W. Holmes*

4953 A face that looks as if it had worn out four bodies.

4954 His head was as empty as a politician's speech.

4955 He stood as erect as a Grecian pillar.

4956 Desolate looking as a summer resort in midwinter.—*Richard Harding Davis*

4957 Her eyes looked like two rainy autumn moons.—*Henry James*

4958 He felt like the symptoms on a medicine bottle.—*George Ade*

4959 He was as exacting as a top sergeant.

4960 Freckles, like rust spots.—*Willa Cather*

4961 The human mind should be like a good hotel—open the year around.—*William Lyon Phelps*

4962 His face was as expressionless as a smoked herring.

4963 A white mustache, cut short like a worn-out brush.—*Henry James*

4964 Unremembered as an old rain.—*Edna St. Vincent Millay*

4965 As changeable as a woman's mood.

4966 Vanish as raindrops which fall in the sea.—*Susan Coolidge*

4967 I could see the man's very soul writhing in his body like an impaled worm.—*Conrad*

4968 His joints creaked like those of an old weatherbeaten wooden farm gate.—*Herbert V. Prochnow, Jr.*

4969 As unemotional as a baseball umpire.

4970 As unsatisfied as a boy's appetite.

4971 He was as patient as a cigar store Indian.

4972 Gentle as the falling tear.—*Thomas Chatterton*

4973 Hollow as the ghastly amiabilities of a college reunion.—*Raymond M. Weaver*

4974 Intolerant as a sinner newly turned saint.

4975 Marriage is like a department store. It is all over when you buy.

4976 Marriage is like twirling a baton, turning handsprings, or eating with chopsticks; it looks so easy till you try it.—*Helen Rowland*

4977 The heart of man is like a creeping plant, which withers unless it has something around which it can entwine.—*Charles James Apperley*

4978 An irritable man is like a hedgehog rolled up the wrong way, tormenting himself with his own prickles.—*Thomas Hood*

4979 Money is in some respects like fire; it is a very excellent servant, but a terrible master.—*P. T. Barnum*

19
COLORFUL PHRASES FOR SPARKLING SPEECH

4980 *Abraham's bosom*—A figure of speech from the Bible. To rest in Abraham's bosom. A place of reward after death for the blessed and righteous. There was an old custom of allowing a good friend to recline at dinner on one's bosom. John reclined on the bosom of Jesus. The beggar died and was taken by the angels into Abraham's bosom.

4981 *Au fait*—To be a thorough master of; skillful. One may be *au fait* in certain matters.

4982 *Achilles' heel*—A vulnerable spot. Achilles' mother, to makè him invulnerable, dipped him into the River Styx. She failed to immerse the heel by which she held him. Paris wounded him mortally by striking him in the heel with an arrow. Everyone may be said to have his Achilles' heel—his weakness.

4983 *A sulking Achilles*—One who withdraws from a part in an important enterprise or undertaking because he holds a personal grievance. In mythology it is said that Achilles sulked in his tent because of an argument with Agamemnon and declined for some time to take part in the battle of the Greeks against the Trojans.

4984 *An Adonis*—An exceptionally handsome man. In mythology he was a handsome young man loved by Venus.

4985 *After me, the deluge*—Means that "I shall keep on doing what pleases me regardless of what happens and even if I am overcome; after me, the deluge." The origin of the phrase is uncertain. Madame Pompadour, a favorite of Louis XV, was one among several who were credited with having used this phrase. She was extravagant and refused to listen to her counselors, who said she would ruin the country. She made light of their warnings, saying in French, "After us, the flood."

4986   *All my swans are geese*—To have your plans fail you. To be disappointed. If one says, "All her swans are turned to geese," it means her plans or boasts have failed her. The swan is beautiful; the goose far less attractive.

4987   *Alpha and omega*—The beginning and the end of anything. In the Greek alphabet, *alpha* is the first letter, and *omega* the last. In the Bible the Lord said: "I am Alpha and Omega, the beginning and the ending."

4988   *He cannot bend Ulysses' bow*—The person is not equal to the task. Ulysses had a bow so great ordinary men could not bend it.

4989   *An odyssey*—The story of great adventure. An epic attributed to Homer describing the ten years' wanderings of Ulysses in returning home after the siege of Troy.

4990   *An Amazon*—A woman of unusual physical strength. Sometimes also used to describe a woman of masculine boldness. The Amazons in mythology were a nation of fighting women.

4991   *Greek gifts or a case of the Greeks bearing gifts*—This means a fatal gift which is presented under friendly guise. In Virgil's *Aeneid* there is a line which says, "I fear the Greeks even when they bear gifts." This refers to the well-known "gift" of the wooden horse which the Trojans offered to the gods. The Greeks had left it outside of the city of Troy and apparently had departed. The Trojans took it within the city's walls. At night Greek soldiers hidden within the horse came out, and captured the city by morning.

4992   *To feed on ambrosia and nectar*—To have excellent food and drink. To the ancient Greeks, "ambrosia" meant the food which the gods ate. Now it means anything delicious to taste or fragrant in perfume. "Nectar" is the drink of the gods.

4993   *To make the amende honorable*—This means a formal and humble recognition of offense, and an apology in payment or reparation for another's injured honor. The punishment was used under the Roman, Dutch, French, and other legal systems. An apology in church or court might require the person to appear with bare feet and head, dressed in white, and carrying a torch.

4994   *A Ulysses*—A person who is clever in developing schemes. Ulysses was one of the Greek heroes in the Trojan War, famous for his craft, intelligence, and eloquence.

4995   *To work or fight like a Trojan*—To fight with great courage or to work with exceptional energy. The ancient Trojans were noted for endurance and pluck.

4996   *A Cassandra utterance*—A prophecy foretelling evil which is not heeded. Cassandra, a daughter of King Priam, was given the power to prophesy by Apollo, according to Greek mythology. Becoming displeased with her, Apollo changed the power Cassandra had to prophesy so she could still prophesy truly, only to be laughed at by those who heard her.

4997 *To hector someone*—To annoy a person. Hector was greatly concerned over the shame brought upon his family and city by his brother, Paris, according to Greek legend, and consequently found fault with him.

4998 *An apple of discord*—A reason for dispute. According to mythology, Discord threw a golden apple on the table "for the most beautiful." Juno, Minerva, and Venus claimed it. Paris awarded it to Venus, thus bringing upon him the vengeance of Juno and Minerva which helped to cause the Trojan War.

4999 *Argonaut*—One of those who sailed with Jason, in the ship Argo, to Colchis to search for the Golden Fleece, according to Greek mythology. An adventurer who seeks fame or fortune in unexplored lands.

5000 *Argus-eyed*—Extraordinarily watchful. An Argus-eyed committee may watch the counting of the money or the ballots. Argus, a monster in Greek mythology, had one hundred eyes, only two of which were said to sleep at once. "Argus-eyed" means to see a great deal.

5001 *Halcyon days*—Days of peace and happiness. Greek legends tell of a girl named Halcyone whose husband perished. Juno, a goddess, did everything in her power to lessen Halcyone's grief and give her serenity of mind and happiness.

5002 *Ark of the covenant*—According to Jewish history, the chest in the most sacred place in the temple in which were placed the two tablets of stone with the Ten Commandments written upon them. Anything which is exceptionally sacred. The Constitution of the United States and the Declaration of Independence might each be spoken of as an American ark of the covenant.

5003 *Armageddon*—The place where a titanic battle will be fought on "the great day of God," between the powers of good and evil, according to the Bible. Any great battle, political contest, or climactic conflict.

5004 *To work the oracle*—To attempt to influence some powerful agency so it will bestow a favor upon you.

5005 *Janus-headed*—An early Italian god, Janus, had two faces—one in front and one behind. Presumably he could see backward and forward at the same time. One may say of a committee with two heads that it is Janus-headed.

5006 *Janus-faced*—Means two-faced or deceptive.

5007   *A saturnine smile*—A smile which is not cheerful, perhaps because the idea of gloominess is connected with the planet Saturn.

5008   *A mercurial temperament*—The Greek god Mercury was light-hearted, clever, changeable, and even a little deceptive; so a mercurial temperament would be of that character.

5009   *Apollo*—In Greek mythology, the god of manly beauty and youth. An unusually handsome man.

5010   *Palladium of our liberty*—A safeguard. The safety of the ancient city of Troy was supposed to depend upon the preservation of a certain wooden statue of Pallas Athena. Our constitution is the Palladium of our liberty.

5011   *Extending the olive branch of peace*—The goddess Minerva was closely connected with the olive tree, having given it to Greece as a gift. She ruled over the arts of peace. An olive branch policy is a policy of peace.

5012   *A Bacchanalian revel*—Bacchus was the god of wine. Bacchanalian means riotous merriment resulting from the use of too much liquor. A wild orgy. Frenzied dancing, singing, and revelry.

5013   *A mere bagatelle*—The word *bagatelle* comes from the French who took it from the Italian *bagattella,* meaning a trifle. A man may spend his money on bagatelles.

5014   *Mounting Pegasus*—Describes the efforts of a person who hopes or attempts to write poetry or deliver orations. Pegasus was the winged horse of the Muses that sprang from Mount Helicon. Therefore, poetic inspiration. Sometimes the airplane is called a modern Pegasus.

5015   *Is there no balm in Gilead?*—This means "Is there no remedy or consolation, even in religion, for our troubles?" In the Book of Jeremiah in the Bible, the prophet, sorrowing over the sins and troubles of his people asked: "Is there no balm in Gilead; is there no physician there? Why then is not the health of the daughter of my people recovered?"

5016   *Stygian darkness*—Gloomy darkness or deep night. It may also mean infernal darkness. The Styx in mythology was the river of the dark underworld. It flowed seven times around Hades.

5017   *Barkis is willin'*—When an individual especially desires to do something, we may say of him, "Barkis is willin'." In the story *David Copperfield,* by Charles Dickens, Barkis loved Clara Peggotty. He asked young David to tell Clara Peggotty, after David had said she had no sweethearts, that "Barkis is willin'."

5018   *An Elysium*—In classical mythology, the place where the good dwelt after death. A state of delight and happiness.

5019 *A task of Sisyphus*—A task that is never completed. In Greek mythology, Sisyphus was a crafty king who was condemned in Hades to roll up a hill a huge stone, which constantly rolled back.

5020 *Beggar on horseback*—A person who has risen to wealth and position, forgets his previous poverty, and lords it over his poorer friends.

5021 *The waters of Lethe*—Implies forgetfulness. An experience that makes one forget care. In mythology, a river of Hades whose waters when drunk caused forgetfulness of the past.

5022 *To beg the question*—To assume the truth of something in question. To assume as true something you are supposed to prove, and to argue from that point. Aristotle first used the phrase.

5023 *A Danaiden task*—An impossible task. King Danaus had fifty daughters (the Danaides), of whom forty-nine slew their husbands at their father's request. The forty-nine were doomed forever to draw water with a sieve in Hades, according to mythology.

5024 *A Pandora's box*—Surprises which are generally unpleasant and in the form of trouble, but sometimes are pleasant. A legislative act may turn out to be a Pandora's box of surprises, unpleasant and pleasant. In Greek mythology, Pandora was a woman sent by Zeus as punishment for the human race because Prometheus had stolen fire from heaven. Zeus gave her a box in which were all human ills; they escaped when she opened the box. In the box also was hope, which remained.

5025 *Belling the cat*—To take it upon one's self to undertake a great risk for friends and associates. The expression comes from the old story in which a mouse suggested that someone should hang a bell on the cat so the mice would know when she was coming. The only problem was "who is to bell the cat?"

5026 *Belshazzar's feast*—When one takes part in a "feast of Belshazzar," he does so in the spirit of "eat, drink, and be merry, for tomorrow we die." The feast of Belshazzar is described in the fifth chapter of the Book of Daniel in the Bible. "In that night was Belshazzar the king of the Chaldeans slain." At that feast Belshazzar saw the fateful "handwritting on the wall" which told him that the days of his kingdom were numbered, that he had been found wanting, and that his kingdom would be divided and assigned to others.

5027 *To yearn for the fleshpots*—Means to long for the material things of life. In the Book of Exodus in the Bible, it is related how the children of Israel regretted their deliverance from Egypt and the hardships of the wilderness. They wished they could have died in Egypt when they "sat by the fleshpots" and "did eat bread to the full."

5028   *A Cadmean victory*—A victory which involves the victor in even greater danger than that from which he escaped. In Greek mythology, Cadmus slew a dragon, and sowed its teeth, but armed warriors sprang from the teeth and attacked him.

5029   *To sow dragon's teeth*—To do things out of which troubles are certain to spring. Cadmus sowed dragon's teeth and warriors sprang up threatening trouble for him. People may do things out of which troubles for themselves will almost certainly spring.

5030   *A bonanza*—Anything yielding a large return in money. There were several Americans in our earlier history who made great fortunes from the gold and silver mines of the West. They were the original "Bonanza Kings."

5031   *A Herculean task*—A task which only Hercules could accomplish. We sometimes speak also of a Herculean feat, or Herculean labors; these are extraordinary exertions. Hercules was a Greek hero noted for unusual strength and for achieving twelve great tasks or "labors" imposed on him as the result of the hatred of Juno.

5032   *Hydra-headed difficulties or evils*—A hydra-headed evil is one which, if it is overcome in one case, breaks out in several places. An evil having many sources, which cannot be overcome by a single effort. In Greek mythology, Hydra was a nine-headed monster slain by Hercules. When any one of its nine heads was cut off, it was succeeded by two others, unless the wound was cauterized.

5033   *Born to the purple*—To be born to a position of great wealth or to an exalted station. In Cicero's time, wool dyed purple was very expensive because the dye came in small quantities from a Mediterranean fish. Purple was, therefore, a highly sought after color and symbolized royal power. Today purple dye has become inexpensive, but the phrase is still used.

5034   *Buncombe*—Anything said or written for mere show; hence, nonsense. "Bunk" is an abbreviation. In the early days of this country there was a member of Congress from the part of North Carolina including Buncombe County. The representatives were anxious to vote on an issue, but the member from Buncombe insisted on speaking. He refused to stop speaking when urged by members of Congress and said he was "bound to talk for Buncombe."

5035   *An Augean task*—A seemingly impossible task. An enormous job. In Greek mythology, King Augeas was said to have had an enormous stable containing many oxen. The stable had not been cleaned for years. Hercules cleaned it by diverting two rivers through it.

5036 *One cannot seize the club of Hercules*—It is impossible to steal the power and ability of one who is great. Hercules was noted for his strength.

5037 *Byzantine luxury*—A lavish and almost barbaric display of wealth and riches. Pertains to the Byzantine empire, Byzantium being the former name of Constantinople, now Istanbul. The Byzantine empire was rich and powerful.

5038 *To wear the cap and bells*—To play the part of a jester. Many years ago the court jesters wore bells attached to their caps.

5039 *A shirt of Nessus*—A gift which is harmful or causes trouble. According to mythology, Dejanira sent her husband, Hercules, a garment dipped in blood which had been given to her in a bottle by a centaur named Nessus. The garment poisoned Hercules.

5040 *Caviar to the general*—"General" means the "common run" of human beings. "Caviar to the general" means anything above the taste or appreciation of "ordinary" people. Caviar is roe of the sturgeon and other fish. It is a delicacy, an expensive appetizer, desired by those who acquire a taste for it. Shakespeare says in Hamlet: "The play, I remember, pleased not the million; 'twas caviar to the general." One could say also, "It was caviar to the masses."

5041 *Cheating the devil*—To believe that you can follow evil methods, particularly in making money unscrupulously, and then compromise with your conscience by giving part of your monetary gain to charity, the church, or some other worthy objective. That is an attempt to "cheat the devil."

5042 *A Cincinnatus*—One who puts aside his regular work to serve his country. Indicates unselfish patriotism. Cincinnatus was a Roman who was called from the field he was plowing to lead the Roman army. After the enemy was overcome, he put aside any personal ambition and returned to the plow. George Washington might be called an American Cincinnatus.

5043 *Hoc opus, hic labor est (Latin)*—This is the real difficulty; this is the task; there's the rub.

5044 *A Minotaur*—One who will sacrifice youths for his personal ambition. A ruler who will lead young men to death to satisfy his own ambition. In mythology, the Minotaur was a monster that devoured young men and women.

5045 *A Circe*—A beautiful woman whose charms are so great they cannot be resisted. In the *Odyssey*, Circe was a sorceress who turned her victims by magic into beasts, but she was thwarted by Odysseus with the herb moly given to him by Hermes.

5046   *A stentorian voice*—A very loud voice. Stentor was a herald in the *Iliad* with a very loud voice.

5047   *A Helen or a Helen of Troy*—A woman of extraordinary beauty. In mythology, Helen was the beautiful daughter of Jupiter and Leda.

5048   *Cordelia's gift*—A soft voice. Cordelia was the youngest of King Lear's three daughters in Shakespeare's play *King Lear*. Shakespeare says in that play, "Her voice was ever soft, gentle and low; an excellent thing in woman."

5049   *Cornelia's jewels*—Children. Cornelia was the mother of the famous Gracchi. An old Roman story relates that a woman was displaying her jewels to Cornelia and asked to see the latter's jewels. Cornelia called her two sons and said, "These are my jewels, in which alone I delight."

5050   *A lotus eater*—A person who lives a life without ambition or effort and in ease and idleness. In the *Odyssey,* one of a people who subsisted on the lotus and lived in the dreamy indolence it induced.

5051   *To give a sop to Cerberus*—To give a gift to some person who might make trouble, in order to keep him quiet. In mythology, Cerberus was a three-headed dog that guarded the entrance to Hades.

5052   *Rich as Croesus*—A very rich person. Croesus was a king of Lydia in the sixth century B.C., and had vast wealth.

5053   *Under the aegis of*—To have the power or authority of some strong person or institution back of one. In Greek mythology, Jupiter was said to have permitted Minerva to wear his terrible aegis, a covering for the breast with the head of Medusa in the center, which was so awful to behold that even the strong were terrified upon seeing it.

5054   *Between Scylla and Charybdis*—When a person must choose between two great dangers. Scylla is a rock on the Italian coast opposite the whirlpool Charybdis off the Sicilian coast. In early legends, Scylla and Charybdis were monsters who lived in caves in the strait between Italy and Sicily. They preyed upon passing vessels and wrecked them.

5055   *A protean artist*—One who can take various roles successfully. In mythology, Proteus was a sea god who could assume various shapes.

5056   *A Penelope*—A wife who remains faithful to her husband. Penelope was the wife of Ulysses. During his absence she was importuned by suitors, but postponed her decision until she had finished weaving a funeral pall for her father-in-law. Every night she unraveled what she had woven by day, and so deferred making any choice until Ulysses returned, when the unwelcome suitors were sent away.

5057 *An Icarian adventure*—A bold adventure which comes to a fatal end. In Greek mythology, Icarus fell into the sea when he attempted to escape from the Cretan Labyrinth by means of wings made from feathers. He flew too near the sun, the wax of his wings melted, and he fell into the sea.

5058 *To cut up didoes*—To make mischief; to cut up; to play tricks. Dido was a queen of Carthage. When Dido was obtaining land for her city, she was told she could have as much land as an ox hide would cover. She cut the hide into pieces so it would cover more ground.

5059 *Suffering the punishment of Tantalus*—To come close to attaining one's objectives and yet never reach them. According to mythology, Tantalus was punished in Hades by the sight of food and water which he could never quite reach.

5060 *To look to one's laurels*—To be careful that one's position or rank be not lost. The ancient Greeks used the foliage of the laurel to crown victors in the Pythian games and as a mark of distinction for certain offices. Later a crown of laurels was used for academic honors.

5061 *To win laurels*—To secure fame as a result of some significant accomplishment.

5062 *Coup de grace*—In French, a blow of mercy. The death blow by which the executioner ended the suffering of the condemned. A decisive, finishing stroke which mercifully puts an end to the sufferings of a victim.

5063 *A siren*—A fascinating woman who entices one to destruction. In mythology, the Sirens were beautiful women who lured mariners to their destruction by singing.

5064 *A Triton among minnows*—One who excels his competitors. The Tritons, in mythology, were sea gods.

5065 *A fidus Achates*—A faithful friend. Achates was a faithful companion of Aeneas in Virgil's *Aeneid*.

5066 *Coup d'état*—A sudden decisive use of force by which an existing government is subverted. Power is seized and an existing government is overthrown. Napoleon III in 1851 dissolved the French Assembly by force and seized the supreme rule over France, becoming emperor; that was a coup d'état.

5067 *A Ganymede*—A handsome boy. In mythology, Ganymede was a beautiful Trojan boy who took the place of Hebe as a cupbearer of the gods.

5068 *Crossing the Rubicon*—to take an important or decisive step. At the beginning of the civil war with Pompey, Caesar crossed a river called the Rubicon, and exclaimed: "the die is cast." By crossing this river contrary to government orders, Caesar precipitated the war.

5069 *Apollo serving Admetus*—A person of special ability who is compelled by necessity to do a menial task. Admetus was a king in Thessaly whom Apollo at one time served as a shepherd.

5070 *To feel the sword of Damocles hanging over one's head*—A sense of impending disaster. Damocles was a flatterer at the court of Dionysius of Syracuse. Damocles constantly called attention to the happiness of kings, so Dionysius invited him to a banquet, seating him under a sword hung by a single hair to show what dangers were present in the fancied happiness of kings. It showed how foolish it was to long for happiness which might end so soon.

5071 *To drink from the fountain of Hippocrene*—To obtain inspiration for a literary work. Hippocrene was a fountain in Mount Helicon in Boeotia whose water was said in Greek mythology to impart poetic inspiration.

5072 *A titanic effort*—An exceptional effort. The Titans in mythology were deities of enormous strength.

5073 *The Dark Ages*—One may say that a terrible war will drive civilization back into the Dark Ages. The Dark Ages represent a period in the history of the world characterized by the decline or eclipse of the arts, letters, and sciences. The Dark Ages are considered the period between ancient and modern times, between the fall of the Roman Empire and the revival of letters; the period from about A.D. 400 to 1400.

5074 *Olympian anger*—Anger such as the gods might display. In Greek mythology, the gods were supposed to dwell upon a mountain called Olympus; Olympian implies something that is godlike.

5075 *A harpy*—A very greedy person who will do anything to obtain wealth. In Greek mythology, a Harpy was one of a group of foul creatures, part woman, part bird, that snatched away the souls of the dead or seized or defiled the food of their victims.

5076 *In the doldrums*—State of listlessness, boredom, or indifference. The doldrums are a part of the ocean near the equator, abounding in calms, squalls, and baffling winds, making it difficult for a sailing vessel to make progress. A person may be "in the doldrums"—bored and listless, uninterested in progress.

5077 *As riotous as Donnybrook Fair*—A riotous disorder or occasion. Donnybrook Fair was an annual fair, noted for fighting and disorder, formerly held in Donnybrook, Ireland.

5078 *To dragoon someone*—To compel one, or try to force one, to follow a certain course by harsh means. To harass by, or as if by, dragoons. A dragoon was formerly a mounted infantryman heavily armed; and the name dragoon came from the dragoons, or short muskets, which were said to spout fire like dragons.

5079   *To draw a red herring across the track*—To draw attention from the principal question to some secondary matter. To divert attention. The phrase is said to have arisen two or three centuries ago when a red herring or a dead cat or animal was drawn across the track to train dogs in hunting.

5080   *To play ducks and drakes*—To throw away heedlessly or squander foolishly. May be used in connection with money; for example, to show how an unworthy heir squanders his estate. Ducks and drakes refers to the sport of throwing flat stones or shells so that they will skim or bound along the water.

5081   *A Dulcinea*—A sweetheart. Dulcinea was one of the most famous sweethearts in all literature, being Don Quixote's lady love in Cervantes' novel of that name.

5082   *A Xanthippe*—Xanthippe was Socrates' wife. Her peevish scolding and quarrelsome temper have become proverbial. A woman with these characteristics is a Xanthippe.

5083   *Utopia*—Any place of ideal perfection. In a book written in 1516, Sir Thomas More described an imaginary ideal commonwealth, enjoying perfection in politics, law, and in every way. The word "Utopia" comes from two Greek words meaning "no place." Utopian schemes are impractical and impossible of realization.

5084   *To cut the Gordian knot*—To solve a problem or to get rid of a difficulty in a fearless, determined manner. Gordius, the king of Phrygia, tied a knot no one could loosen. An oracle declared that whoever untied the knot would be master of Asia. Alexander the Great cut it with his sword.

5085   *To eat crow*—To be forced to eat one's own words; to confess one was wrong; to accept what one has fought against. The crow is not considered fit for human food; one would only eat it against one's will.

5086   *An El Dorado*—A place of fabulous richness. El Dorado refers to a legendary rich king of a South American tribe or his imaginary kingdom.

5087   *To tilt at windmills*—To fight against imaginary wrongs, evils, or opponents. The phrase comes from *Don Quixote* by Cervantes. Don Quixote declared thirty or forty windmills were giants and, riding his horse, he drove at one of the windmills with his lance.

5088   *On tenterhooks*—In suspense, or under a distressing strain. Cloth may be stretched or tenterhooked, a tenterhook being a sharp, hooked nail used for fastening cloth on a tenter. A tenter is a frame for stretching cloth.

5089   *A stormy petrel*—A harbinger of trouble. One who may cause trouble. The petrel is a bird which it is believed is active before a storm at sea and so foretells the storm.

5090   *She is stately as Juno*—A complimentary remark to a woman. Juno in mythology was the wife of Jupiter and the queen of heaven.

5091   *Eureka*—An expression of triumph over a discovery. To cry out "Eureka" means one has found something after much effort, or that is greatly desired. "I have found it" is the exclamation attributed to Archimedes upon discovering a method of determining the purity of gold.

5092   *To speak or write ex cathedra*—To speak from the chair—the chair of power and knowledge; to speak with authority. Sometimes used to comment sarcastically on the remarks of a dogmatic writer or speaker, as "Mr. Jones certainly spoke in an ex cathedra manner on a subject about which he was little informed." In the Roman Catholic Church, the pope may speak ex cathedra in his pontifical character—from his throne as the representative of Saint Peter.

5093   *To cudgel one's brains*—To make a painful effort to remember or understand something.

5094   *Star Chamber proceedings*—A secret or irresponsible tribunal. In early English history, the Star Chamber was a high court exercising wide civil and criminal jurisdiction; it could proceed on mere rumor and could apply torture. One might say, "The committee applied Star Chamber methods in its examination of witnesses."

5095   *Neither fish, flesh, nor good red herring*—Means not one thing or another—no particular thing—nothing at all. Many years ago, "not fish" meant not food for monks; "not flesh" meant not food for people; "not good red herring" meant not food for the poor. So anything that did not fit one of these groups was nothing.

5096   *He can hear the pipes of Pan*—He is sensitive to the wind, the waves, and nature. He is at one with nature. In mythology, Pan was the god of pastures, forests and their wild life, and patron of shepherds and hunters.

5097   *A stalking horse*—A mask or pretense. Something put forward as the apparent reason of a person or group, whereas the real purpose remains hidden, temporarily at least. In politics, a candidate put forward to divide the opposition or to conceal someone's real candidacy.

5098   *Sons of Belial*—Wicked, evil, immoral, or corrupt persons. In the New Testament the name "Belial" became identified with Satan; in Milton's *Paradise Lost,* one of the fallen angels.

5099   *In the Slough of Despond*—In the depths of despair or discouragement. In *Pilgrim's Progress,* the Slough of Despond was a deep quagmire which Christian, the pilgrim, had to cross.

5100   *A fool's paradise*—A condition of illusive happiness. A person who indulges in vain hopes lives in a fool's paradise.

5101   *A fool's errand*—A ridiculous, profitless undertaking.

5102   *The fourth estate*—Newspapers; the public press. It has been said that Burke originated the term when he spoke of three estates in Parliament and then added that the reporters' gallery was the fourth estate, the most important of all. Macaulay used it also. The first three estates were the lords spiritual, the lords temporal, and the commons.

5103   *An Iliad of ills or an Iliad of woes*—A long series of evils or woes. Many evils experienced at the same time. The *Iliad* is a Greek epic poem ascribed to Homer. It narrates events of the last year of the Trojan War, and is filled with many tragic experiences.

5104   *A Frankenstein's monster*—A work or agency that ultimately destroys its originator. Frankenstein was a student of physiology in Mrs. Shelley's romance of the same name. He constructed a monster and gave it a kind of life. The monster inflicted the most terrible retribution upon his creator. The name now is used to indicate someone destroyed by his own works.

5105   *A gay Lothario*—A man who trifles with women's affections. In Rowe's drama *The Fair Penitent,* Lothario was a gay and unscrupulous seducer. The name is also found in stories by Cervantes and Goethe.

5106   *At sixes and sevens*—A condition when affairs, matters, or things are in disorder and confusion. The origin of the phrase is not certain, but Shakespeare and other writers have used it.

5107   *Simon-pure*—Genuine; authentic. In the comedy *Bold Stroke for a Wife* (1718) by Mrs. S. Centlivre, a Colonel Feignwell poses as Simon Pure, a Pennsylvania Quaker. He wins the heart of Miss Lovely, and when Simon Pure himself arrives, he is at first treated as an imposter until he identifies himself as the true Simon Pure.

5108   *A Scrooge or an Ebenezer Scrooge*—A hard, greedy person. In *A Christmas Carol* by Dickens, Ebenezer Scrooge was an avaricious man visited by spirits on Christmas Eve and made kindly when they showed him the meaning of consideration and generosity to others.

5109   *To find a Golconda*—To discover a source of great wealth. Golconda is the name of a city in India which was famous for its great riches.

5110   *A Sinon*—A skillful liar. Sinon was a Greek through whose lies the Trojans were led to take the wooden horse, in which were concealed Greek warriors, into the city of Troy.

5111   *A Golgotha*—A place of torment or martyrdom; a cemetery. In the New Testament, the place where Christ was crucified.

5112   *A saturnalia of crime*—An unusually large number of crimes. Saturnalia was the old Roman festival beginning December 17 in honor of the god Saturn. It was a time of much rejoicing, but was also marked by excesses and periods of general license.

5113   *A round robin*—A written petition or protest with the signatures in a circle so as not to indicate who signed first. The origin of the phrase is not certain, but some believe it came from the French.

5114   *A Rosetta stone*—A key by which a mystery or difficult problem may be solved. The Rosetta stone was found in 1799 near the Rosetta mouth of the Nile. It contains an inscription in hieroglyphic characters which gave the first clue for deciphering the Egyptian hieroglyphics.

5115   *To commit political harakiri*—To commit political suicide. *Harakiri* was formerly a Japanese method of suicide practiced in cases of disgrace or by government order.

5116   *Hobson's choice*—A choice in which one has no alternative; one must take the things offered or nothing. Thomas Hobson was an Englishman (1631) who let out horses in Cambridge; he had many horses, but every customer had to take the horse nearest the door.

5117   *Wealthy as a nabob*—To have great riches. A *nabob* is a native deputy or viceroy in India, or a Mogul provincial governor. These men have great wealth.

5118   *To be proud as Lucifer*—To be proud or rebellious in spirit even in the face of power that may not be challenged. Lucifer is the name sometimes used for Satan as the rebel archangel before his fall.

5119   *Homeric laughter*—Loud and uncontrolled laughter. The Greek epic poet Homer is said to have written the famous *Iliad,* and this phrase refers to a passage in that poem.

5120   *On the hustings*—Any place where political speeches are being made. The Hustings is the platform from which candidates for Parliament were formerly nominated.

5121 *On the horns of a dilemma*—A dilemma is an argument which gives an antagonist two or more alternatives (or horns), but equally against him. One has a choice between equally undesirable and unsatisfactory alternatives. The horns probably refer to a bull, which may toss an object from one horn to the other.

5122 *Pons asinorum*—A Latin phrase meaning an asses' bridge. The phrase is used to mean some obstacle to be overcome which is difficult for beginners to comprehend. The asses' bridge is a proposition from geometry which it is not always easy for beginners to understand. To illustrate the phrase: The *pons asinorum* that worried the sidewalk on-lookers was how engineers could build a subway under streets over which heavy traffic was moving.

5123 *A jackanapes*—A conceited or impertinent person. The word is said to have come from a *jack* (monkey or ape) from *napes* (Naples in Italy).

5124 *The Pierian spring*—A source of knowledge. The poet Pope wrote: "A little learning is a dangerous thing; drink deep, or taste not the Pierian spring." To drink from the Pierian spring, according to Greek legend, was to obtain knowledge. The spring was in Pieria, a region of ancient Macedonia, one of the earliest seats of the worship of the Muses, who were the goddesses of the arts, history, and music.

5125 *From Dan to Beersheba*—From limit to limit. From one end of the land to the other. A candidate for office might carry the election from Dan to Beersheba, that is, from one end of the state or nation to the other. Dan and Beersheba were formerly the northern and southern limits of Palestine.

5126 *A Jason's quest*—A difficult search. According to Greek mythology, Jason was sent by Pelias in search of the Golden Fleece. Jason met very difficult conditions, but obtained the fleece. To be asked to find a Shakespeare among today's playwrights might be said to be a Jason's quest. When one goes in search of the Golden Fleece, it may also mean to try to find one's fortune.

5127 *Quid pro quo*—A Latin phrase meaning something for something or an equal exchange or substitution.

5128 *Job's comforter*—One who maliciously injures with words which supposedly are meant to comfort. A person who pretends he feels sorry for you and sympathizes with you, but who blames you for your troubles. The phrase comes from the experience Job had, as related in the Bible, with his friends when he was in great trouble.

5129 *Robbing Peter to pay Paul*—To pay one person with something to which another person has a prior right. To satisfy one obligation by leaving another unsatisfied. The expression is said to have originated as follows: About 300 years ago the Abbey Church of St. Peter, Westminster, London, was made a cathedral; a decade later it became a part of the diocese of London and a large part of its property was taken over by St. Paul's Cathedral. Someone writing at the time implied it was not right to rob St. Peter's altar to build one for St. Paul's Cathedral.

5130   *Namby-pamby*—Weakly sentimental; insipid. One may speak, for example, of namby-pamby writing or talk. Ambrose Phillips was an English poet whose verses for children were ridiculed. *Namby* came from a baby way of pronouncing Ambrose and *pamby* merely rhymed with namby.

5131   *Peripatetic*—The word comes from the Greek and means to walk about. Aristotle and his followers were called peripatetics because they taught or discussed matters while walking or moving about.

5132   *Knight-errant*—One who travels about looking for opportunities to exhibit skill, prowess, and generosity. May also be used to indicate one who goes about attempting to correct conditions or actions he believes are wrong. In ancient legends the knights-errant went about seeking to set free imprisoned kings, right wrongs, and aid the oppressed. They are mentioned in *Don Quixote*. A tourist from this country in a Central American country might be considered a knight-errant if he expressed his opinion about correcting what he thought was wrong in the social life and customs of the people of the foreign country.

5133   *Pickwickian*—An adjective relating to characteristics of Mr. Pickwick of Dickens' *Pickwick Papers*. Mr. Pickwick was simple and goodhearted.

5134   *A jingo*—One who is in favor of a belligerent or warlike policy in foreign affairs. A chauvinist. The phrase was used in England about 1877 when some people wanted England to assist Turkey against Russia. A popular song at that time said:

"We don't want to fight; but by jingo, if we do,
"We've got the ships, we've got the men, and got the money too."

5135   *A patriarch*—A father, leader, chief. A venerable old man. In biblical history, the father and ruler of a family or tribe. A person regarded as the father or founder, as of a race, science, religion. Adam Smith might be called the patriarch of political economy. The monarch oak might be called the patriarch of the trees.

5136   *Pecksniffian*—To resemble the hypocrisy or suave insincerity of Pecksniff, who was a canting rascal in Dickens' story *Martin Chuzzlewit*.

5137 *To hunt with the lantern of Diogenes*—Diogenes was a Greek Cynic philosopher who was said to have gone about the streets of Corinth in broad daylight with a lighted lantern looking for an honest man. To illustrate the expression: It would take a Diogenes hunting with a lantern to find an honest man in a graft-ridden municipal government.

5138 *A Macedonian cry*—A call for help or assistance. The expression is of biblical origin. In Chapter 16 of the Book of Acts, verses 9 and 10, it is recorded that a vision appeared to Paul by night, the vision of a Macedonian standing and appealing to him with the words, "Cross over to Macedonia and help us," from which it was inferred that "God had called us to preach the gospel to them." As soon as Paul saw the vision, "we made efforts to start for Macedonia."

5139 *Patient as Griselda*—A very patient woman. In romantic stories of medieval days, Griselda was a lady who was proverbial for virtue and patience. Her husband put her to severe trials, and she became a model of patience.

5140 *Out-Herod Herod*—To surpass in violent treatment or in wickedness. Shakespeare uses the expression in *Hamlet*. Herod was the king of Judea (37 B.C.) who destroyed the infants of Bethlehem.

5141 *Machiavellian*—Political cunning or bad faith; unscrupulous. Machiavelli was a Florentine statesman (1469–1527) who believed that any means, however unscrupulous, may be properly employed by a ruler in order to maintain a strong central government.

5142 *A Mugwump*—An independent in politics; one who reserves the right to bolt the candidate or platform of his party. The term was originally used to describe a bolter from the Republican party in the presidential campaign of 1884.

5143 *A Mississippi bubble*—A visionary and fantastic financial scheme in which many people are financially interested and which later collapses. The reference is to a scheme a Scotsman, John Law, had for colonizing along the Mississippi River. Law lived in Paris. Ridiculous stories of gold mines were circulated. The mint of France was even involved in Law's schemes. The shares of his company increased greatly, but eventually the whole financial structure crashed.

5144 *To pile Ossa upon Pelion*—To pile one problem or difficulty upon another. In Greek mythology, the giants, striving to attack the Olympians, piled Pelion, a high wooded mountain, on Mount Olympus and Ossa, a steep mountain, on Pelion.

5145 *A Munchausen*—One who tells fantastic and impossible stories; a liar. Baron Munchausen was the pretended author of a book of travels (by Rudolph Eric Raspe, 1785) filled with extravagant fictions.

5146 *A Mrs. Malaprop*—One who makes blunders in the use of words. "Malapropism" means the ridiculous misuse of a word. Mrs. Malaprop was a character in Sheridan's *The Rivals,* noted for her blunders in the use of words.

5147 *Aliquando bonus dormitat Homerus (Latin)*—Sometimes even the good Homer nods—that is, the greatest are sometimes caught napping. Homer, the Greek poet, was said to be the author of the famous *Iliad.*

5148 *A mare's nest*—Something that is believed to be wonderful but it turns out to be a hoax or fraud. To find a mare's nest is to make what you think is an important discovery, but which actually turns out to be a hoax.

5149 *A mess of pottage*—A mess is an amount of food for a meal, course or dish. A pottage is a thick soup or a dish of vegetables, sometimes including meat. The reference is to the book of Genesis in the Bible where it is related that Esau sold his birthright to Jacob for bread and pottage. To sell something of value for a mess of pottage would obviously be very unwise. A mess of pottage would be something of little value.

5150 *The mills of God*—In literature the idea has often been conveyed of God ruling over a great mill which grinds out the destinies of men. One finds the expression, "The mills of God grind slowly, yet they grind exceeding small." One may escape punishment for a time for wrongdoing, but eventually it comes. Justice may be a long time coming, but its coming is inevitable.

5151 *Bourgeois (French)*—Middle class; ordinary; humdrum.

5152 *Cliché (French)*—Stereotyped expression; hackneyed phrase.

5153 *Commencement de la fin (French)*—Beginning of the end.

5154 *Caveat emptor (Latin)*—Let the purchaser beware. The buyer should keep his eyes open.

INDEX

All numbers in this index refer to numbers placed in numerical order at the left-hand margins of the pages. The 5,154 items of source material are completely indexed so that it is possible quickly to find all the items throughout the book which relate to a particular idea. To illustrate, under the classification "Marriage" in the index, one can immediately locate the numbers of all quotations, epigrams, humorous stories, definitions and other items relating to this subject. In addition, almost every one of the 5,154 items has been classified in the index under several headings so the reader who is seeking a quotation, epigram, or humorous story to illustrate even a particular word or a relatively restricted idea may find it by using the index.